RAT CATCHER

VERTIGO CRIME

WRITER
ANDY DIGGLE

ART
VICTOR IBAÑEZ

LETTERS
JARED K. FLETCHER

RAT CATCHER

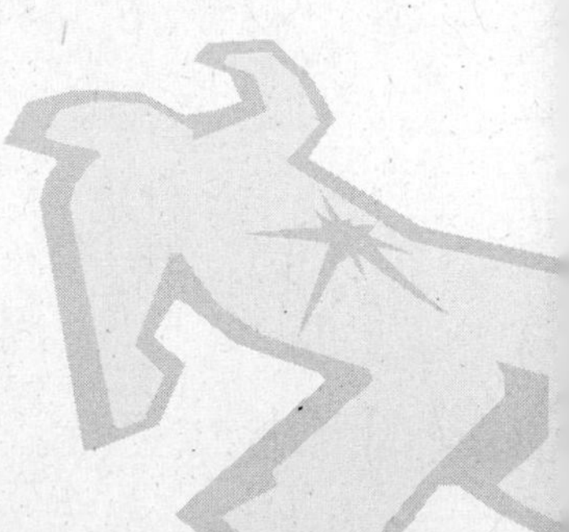

Karen Berger SVP – Executive Editor
Pornsak Pichetshote Editor
Robbin Brosterman Design Director – Books
Louis Prandi Art Director

DC COMICS
Diane Nelson President
Dan DiDio and Jim Lee Co-Publishers
Geoff Johns Chief Creative Officer
Patrick Caldon EVP – Finance and Administration
John Rood EVP – Sales, Marketing and Business Development
Amy Genkins SVP – Business and Legal Affairs
Steve Rotterdam SVP – Sales and Marketing
John Cunningham VP – Marketing
Terri Cunningham VP – Managing Editor
Alison Gill VP – Manufacturing
David Hyde VP – Publicity
Sue Pohja VP – Book Trade Sales
Alysse Soll VP – Advertising and Custom Publishing
Bob Wayne VP – Sales
Mark Chiarello Art Director

RAT CATCHER
VERTIGO CRIME

Published by DC Comics, 1700 Broadway, New York, NY 10019. Copyright © 2010
by Andy Diggle and Victor Ibanez Ramirez. All rights reserved. All characters, the
distinctive likenesses thereof and all related elements are trademarks of Andy Diggle
and Victor Ibanez Ramirez. VERTIGO and VERTIGO CRIME are trademarks of
DC COMICS. The stories, characters and incidents mentioned in this book are entirely
fictional. DC Comics does not read or accept unsolicited submissions of ideas, stories or
artwork. Printed in USA . First Printing. DC Comics, a Warner Bros. Entertainment
Company. HC ISBN: 978-1-4012-1158-5   SC ISBN: 978-1-4012-3063-0

Certified Chain of Custody
80% Certified Fiber Sourcing and
40% Post-Consumer Recycled
www.sfiprogram.org

NSF-SFICOC-C0001B01

This label applies to the text stock.

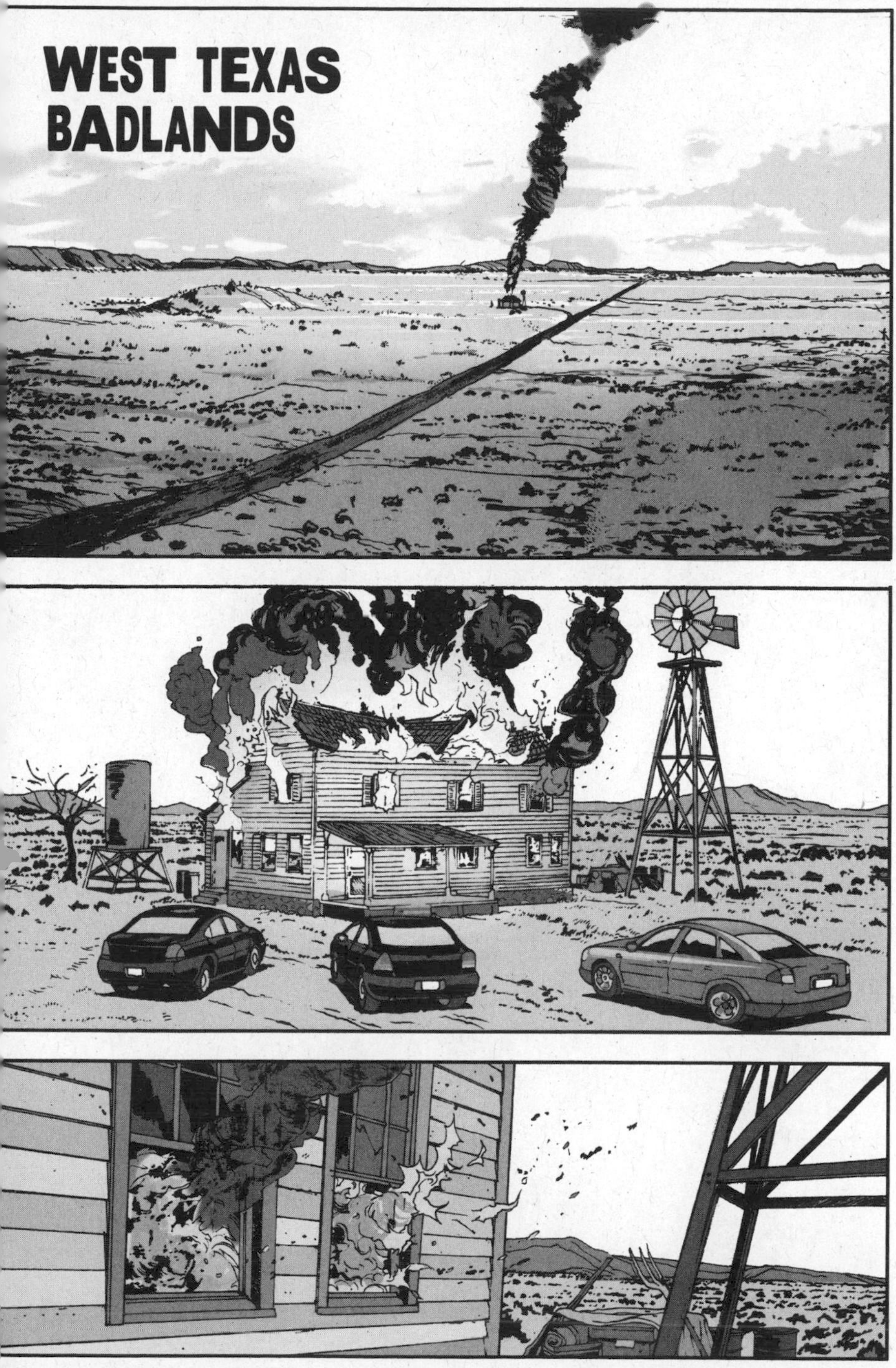
WEST TEXAS
BADLANDS

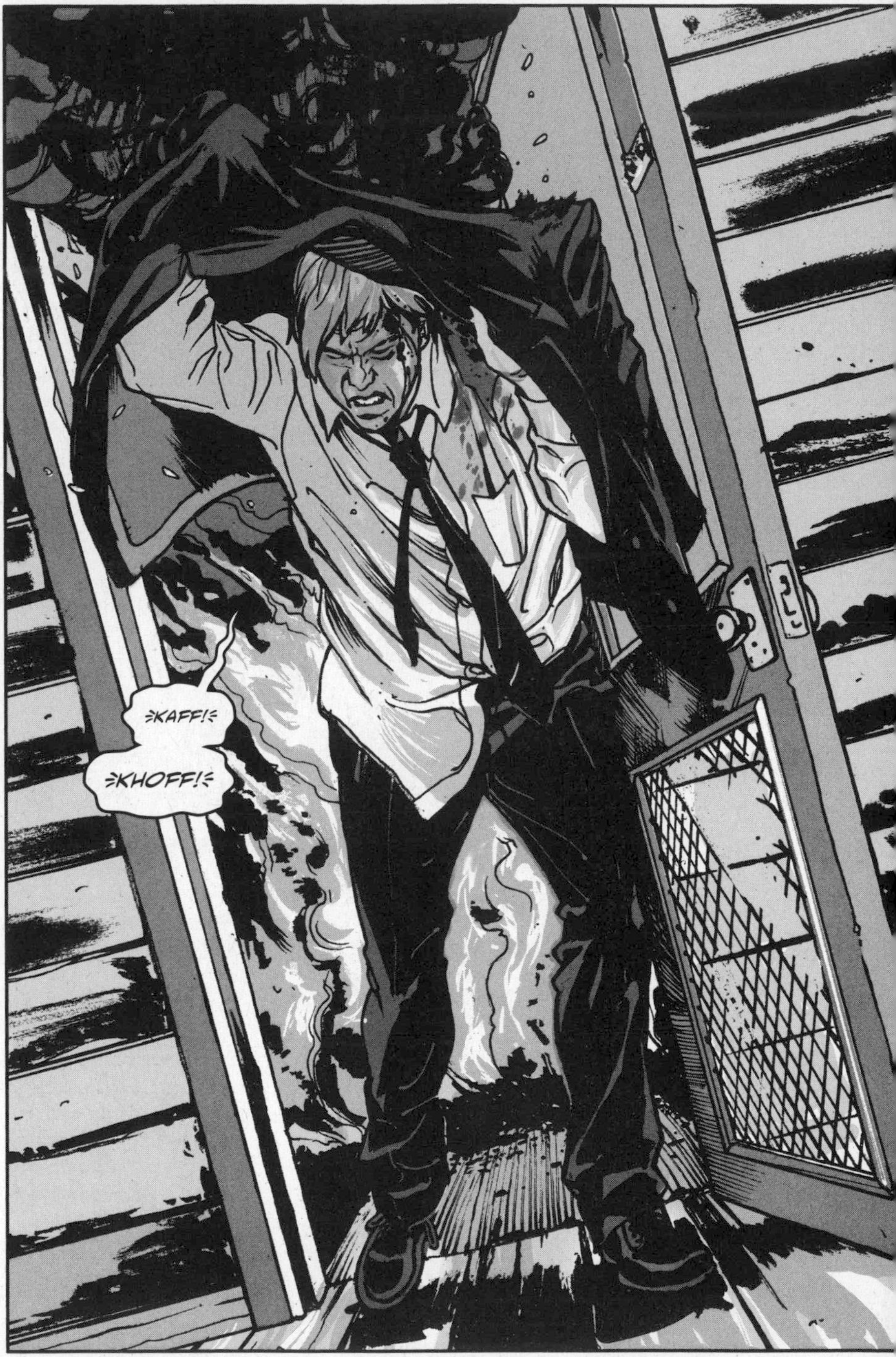
KAFF!
KHOFF!

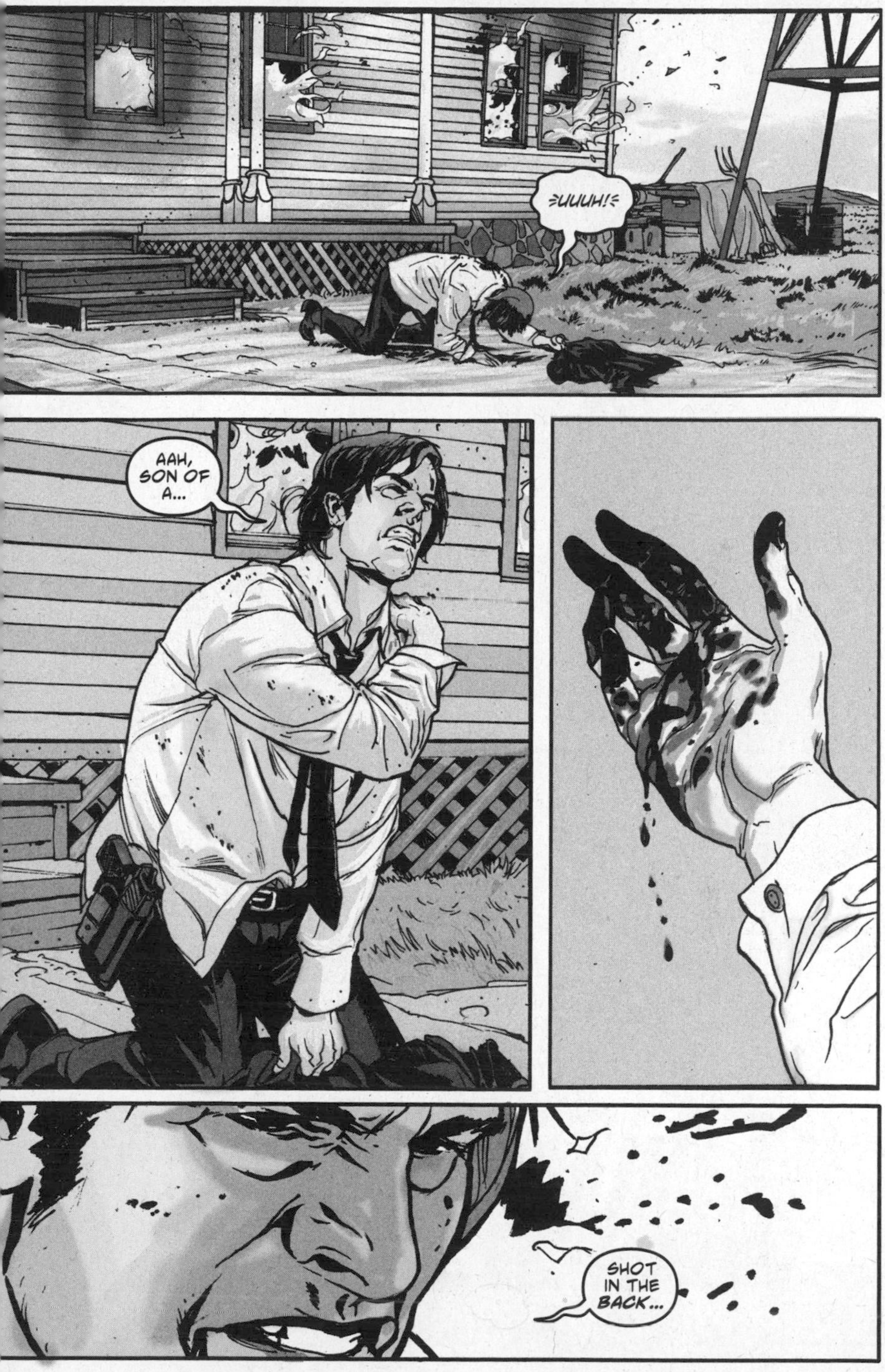
UUUH!
AAH, SON OF A...
SHOT IN THE BACK...

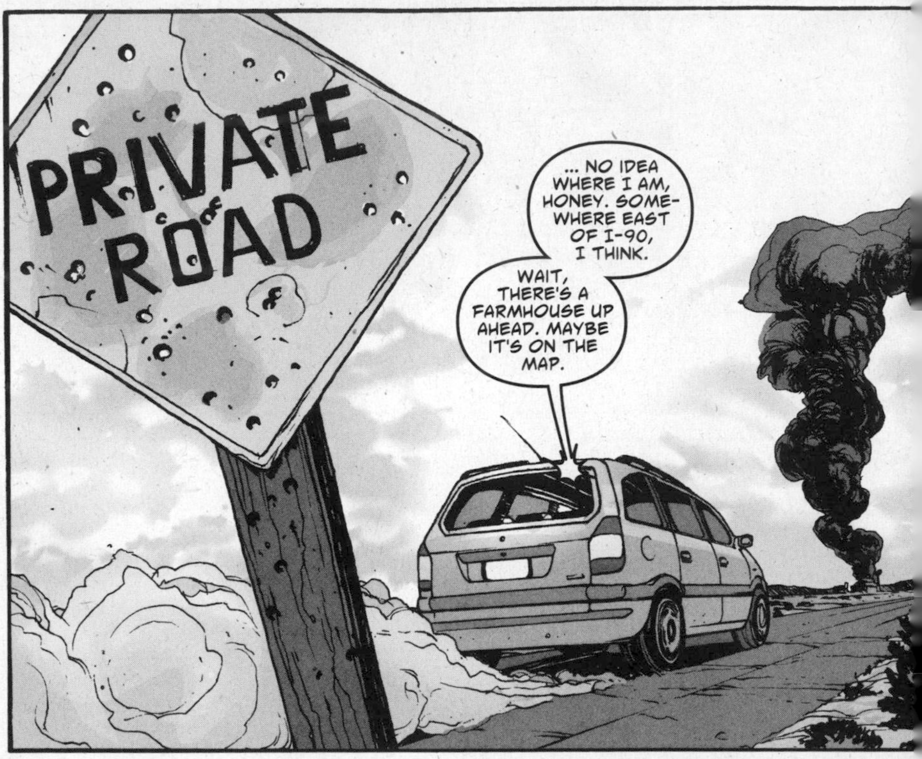
PRIVATE ROAD
... NO IDEA WHERE I AM, HONEY. SOME-WHERE EAST OF I-90, I THINK.
WAIT, THERE'S A FARMHOUSE UP AHEAD. MAYBE IT'S ON THE MAP.

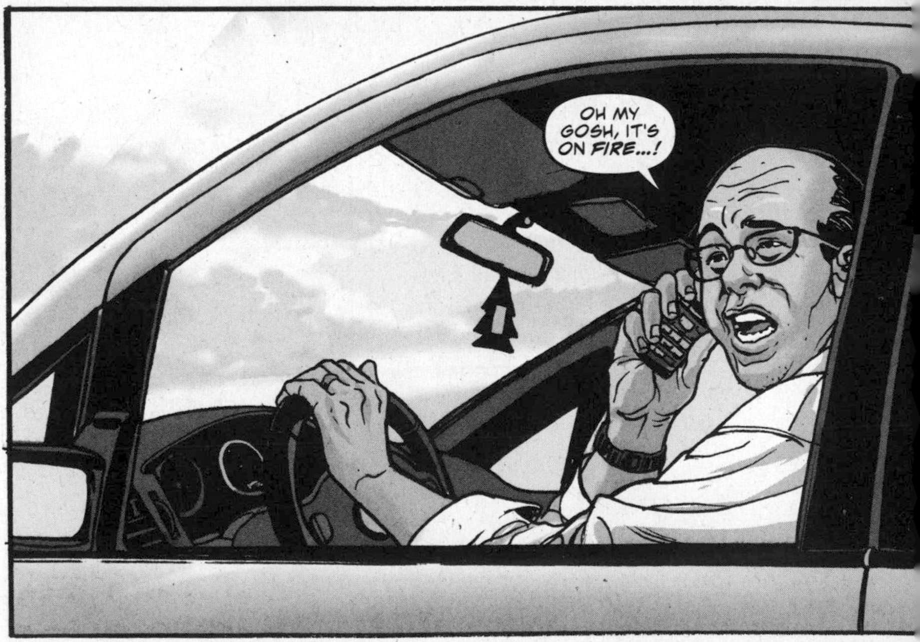
OH MY GOSH, IT'S ON *FIRE*...!

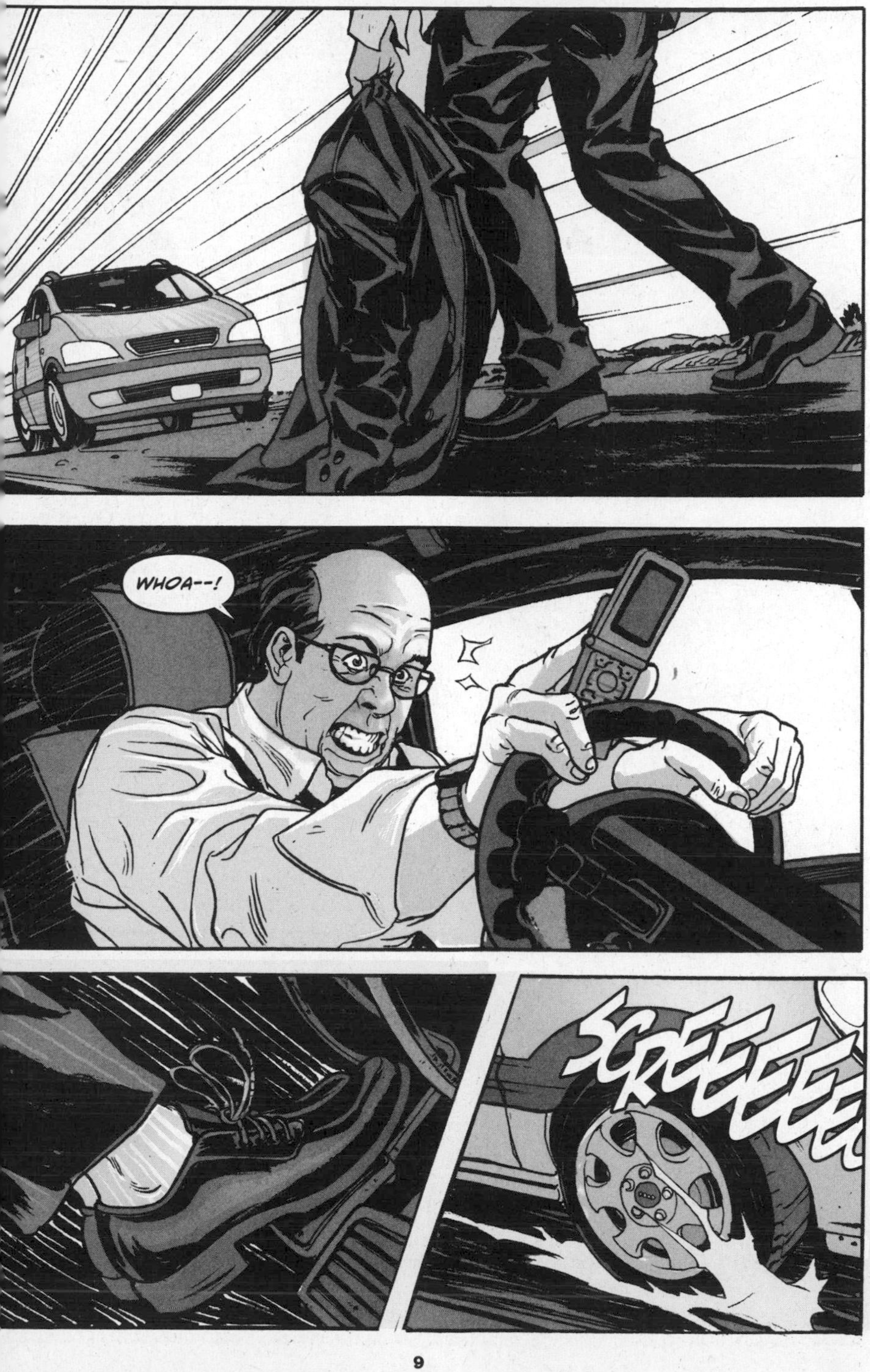
WHOA--!
SCREEEEEE

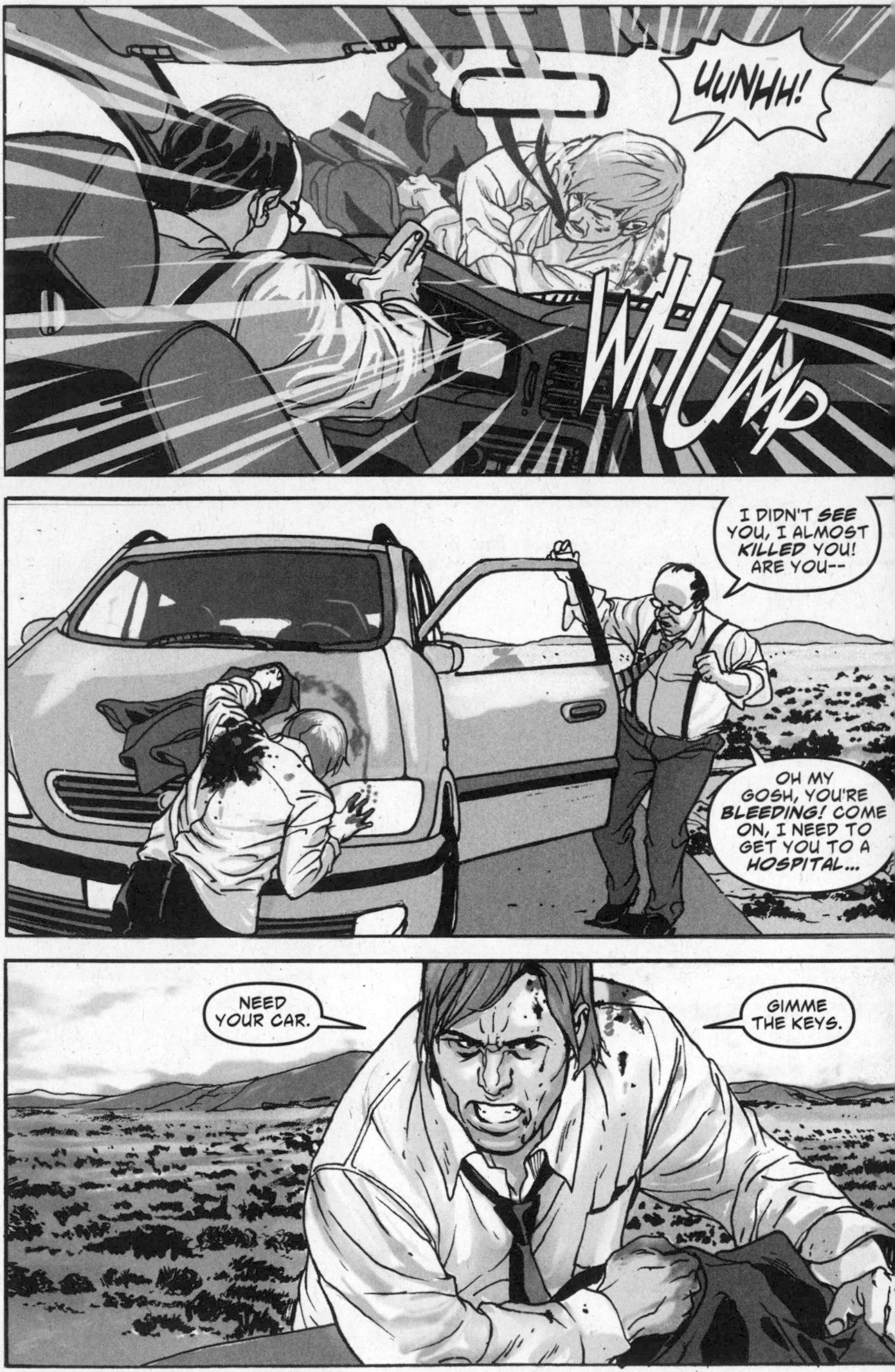
UUNHH!
WHUMP
I DIDN'T SEE YOU, I ALMOST KILLED YOU! ARE YOU--
OH MY GOSH, YOU'RE BLEEDING! COME ON, I NEED TO GET YOU TO A HOSPITAL...
NEED YOUR CAR.
GIMME THE KEYS.

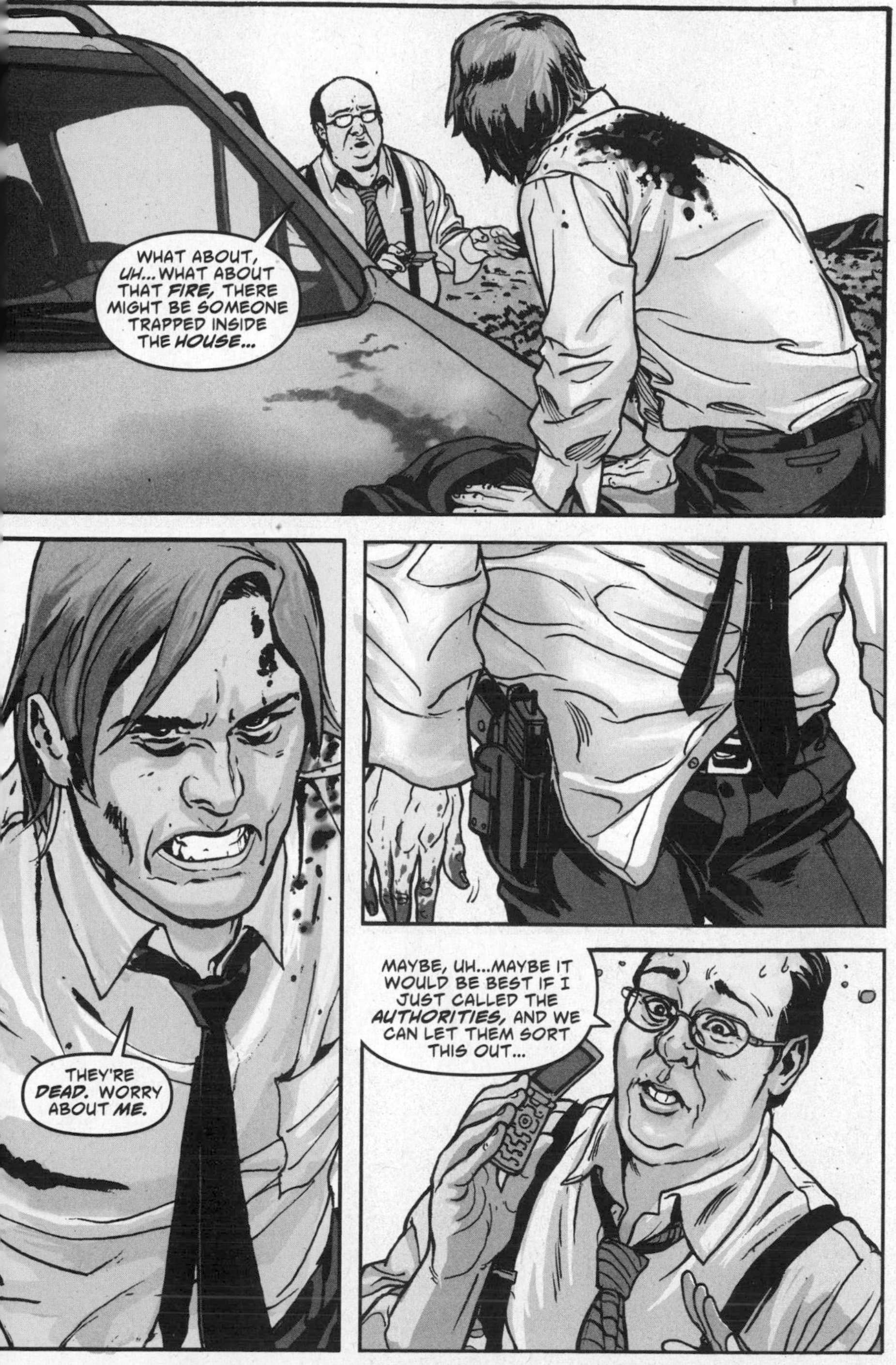
WHAT ABOUT, UH... WHAT ABOUT THAT FIRE, THERE MIGHT BE SOMEONE TRAPPED INSIDE THE HOUSE...
THEY'RE DEAD. WORRY ABOUT ME.
MAYBE, UH...MAYBE IT WOULD BE BEST IF I JUST CALLED THE AUTHORITIES, AND WE CAN LET THEM SORT THIS OUT...

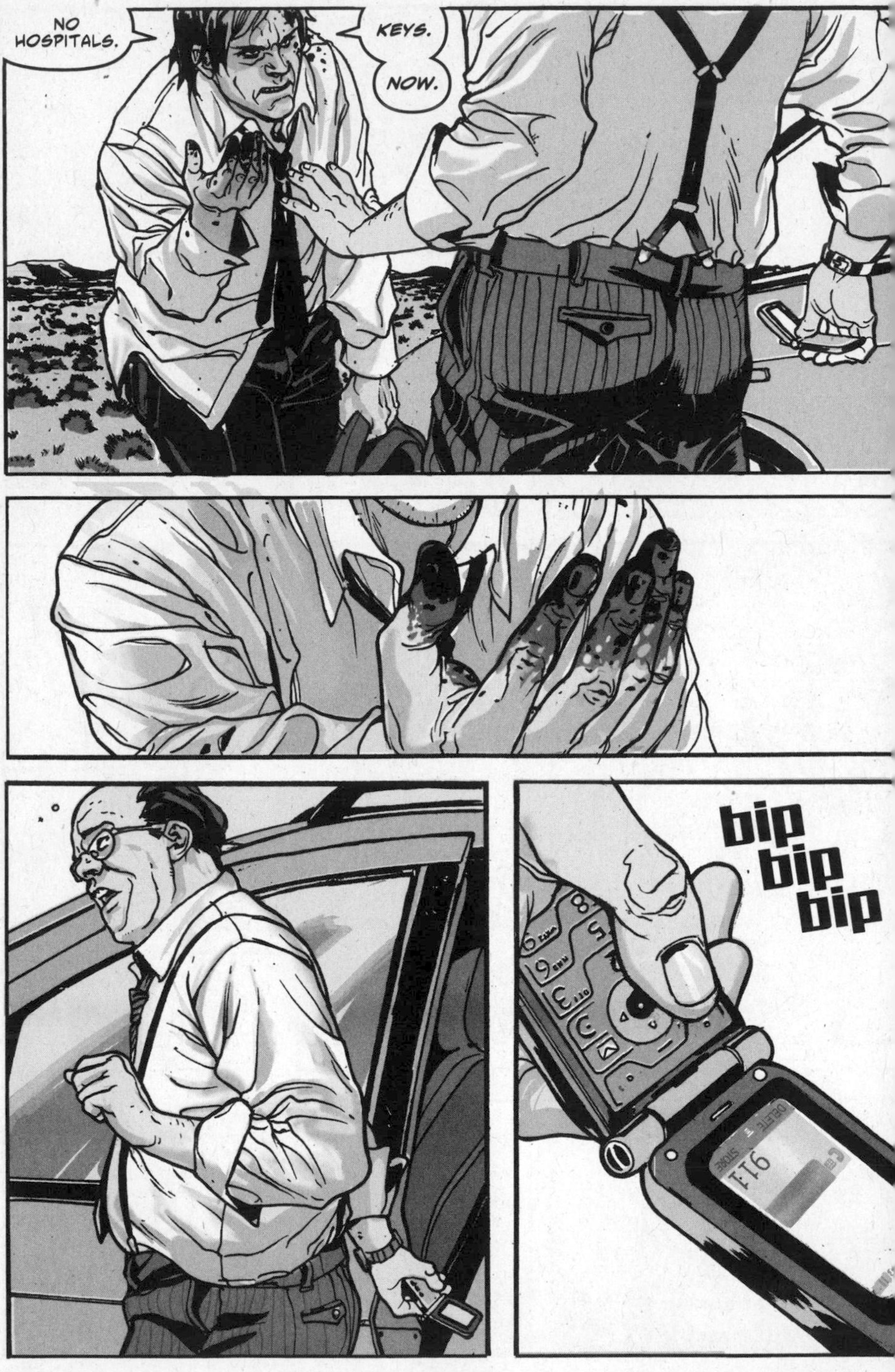
NO HOSPITALS.
KEYS.
NOW.
bip bip bip
DELETE
STORE
911

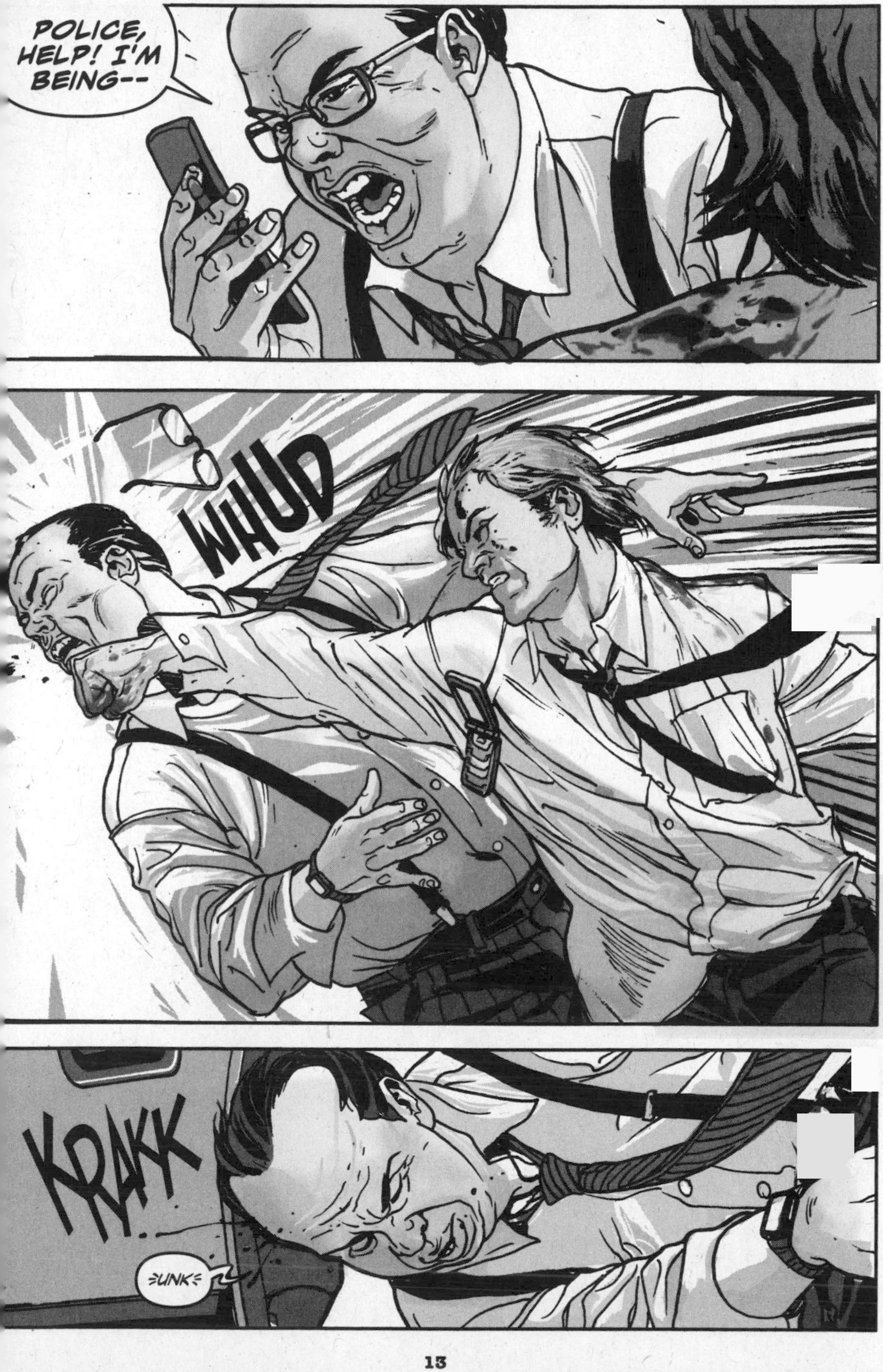
POLICE, HELP! I'M BEING--
WHUD
KRAKK
UNK

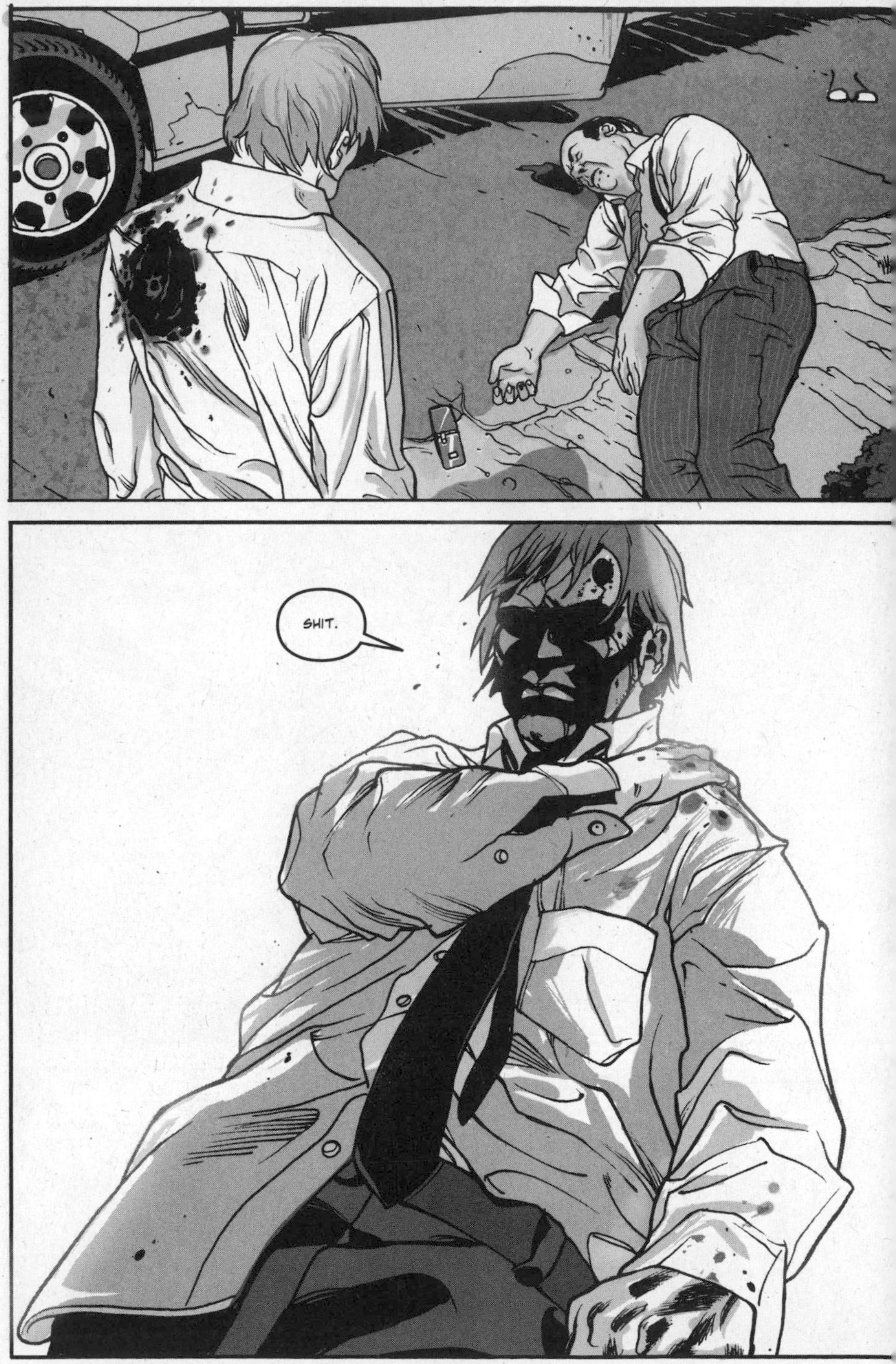
SHIT.

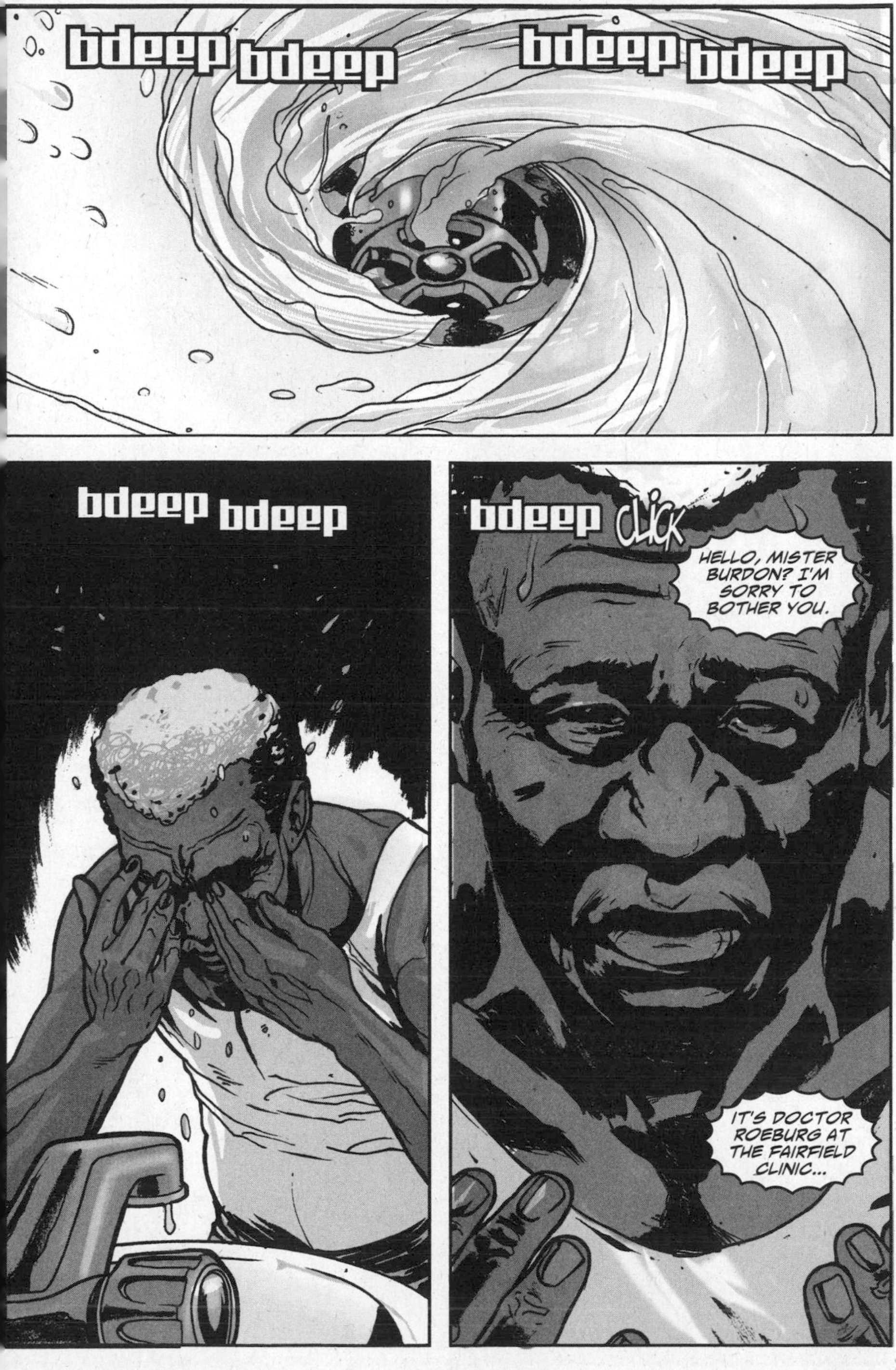
bdeep bdeep
bdeep bdeep
bdeep bdeep
bdeep
CLICK
HELLO, MISTER BURDON? I'M SORRY TO BOTHER YOU.
IT'S DOCTOR ROEBURG AT THE FAIRFIELD CLINIC...

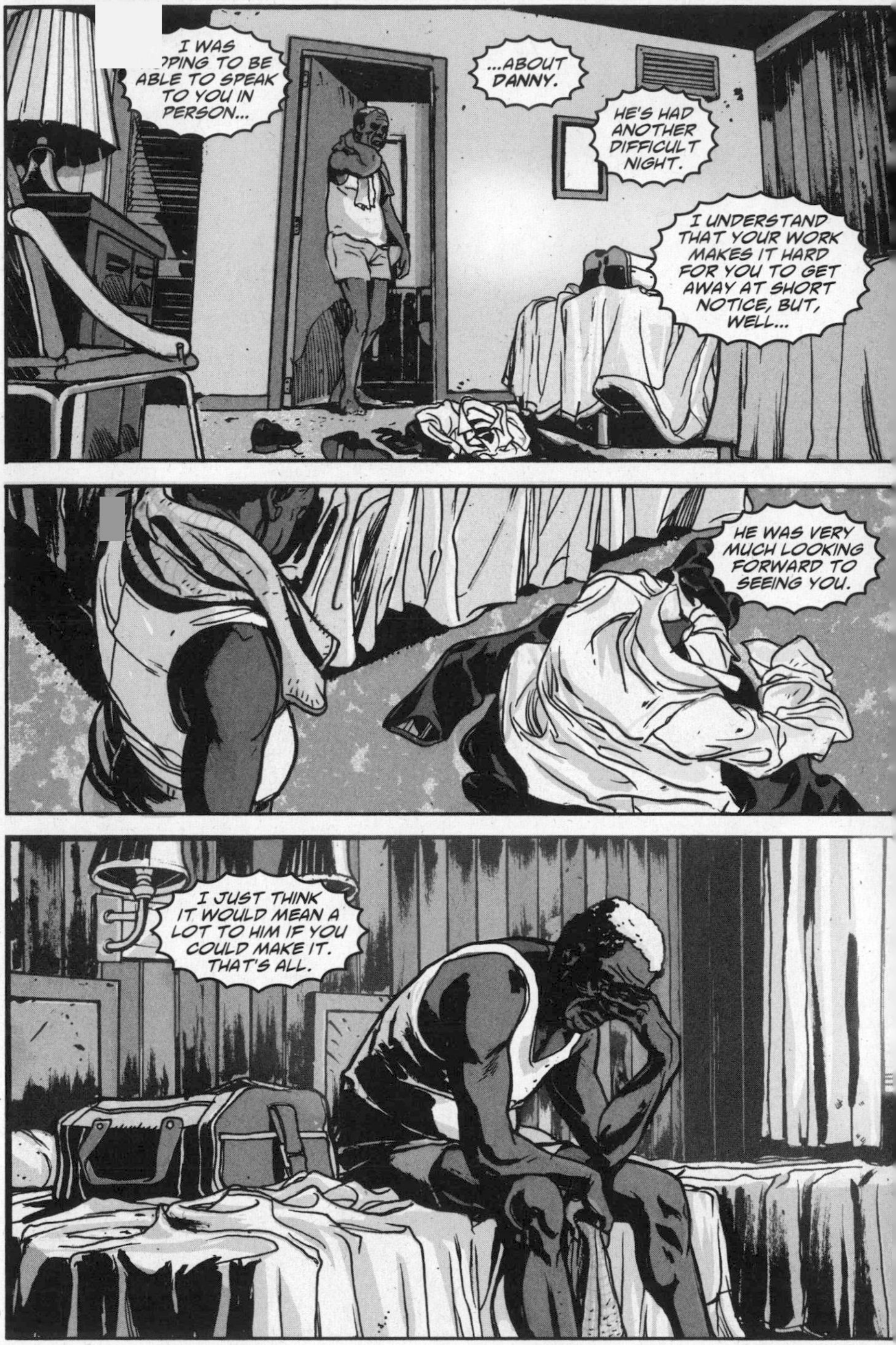
I WAS OPING TO BE ABLE TO SPEAK TO YOU IN PERSON...
...ABOUT DANNY.
HE'S HAD ANOTHER DIFFICULT NIGHT.
I UNDERSTAND THAT YOUR WORK MAKES IT HARD FOR YOU TO GET AWAY AT SHORT NOTICE, BUT, WELL...
HE WAS VERY MUCH LOOKING FORWARD TO SEEING YOU.
I JUST THINK IT WOULD MEAN A LOT TO HIM IF YOU COULD MAKE IT. THAT'S ALL.

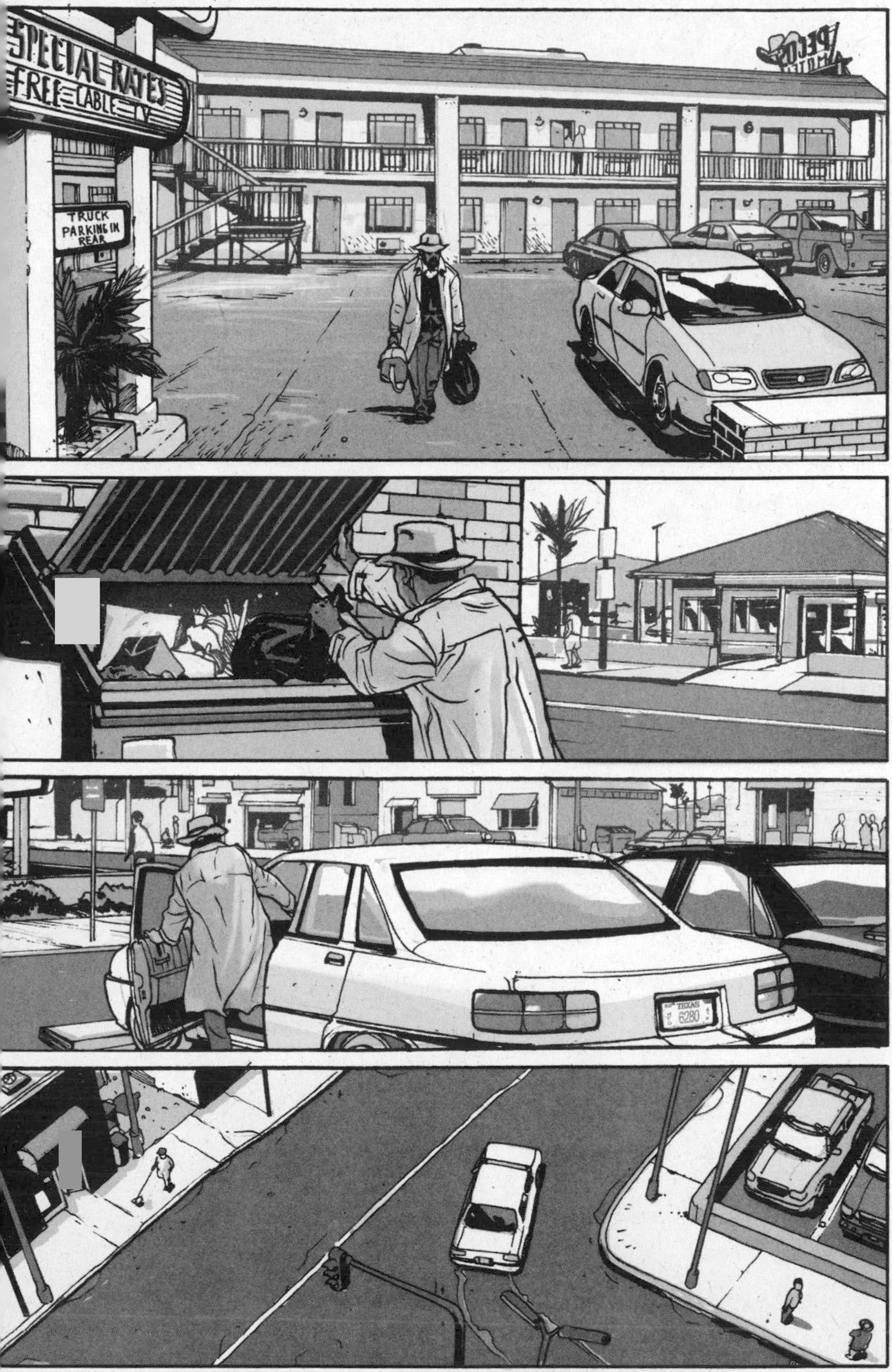
SPECIAL RATES
FREE CABLE TV
TRUCK PARKING IN REAR
TEXAS
6280

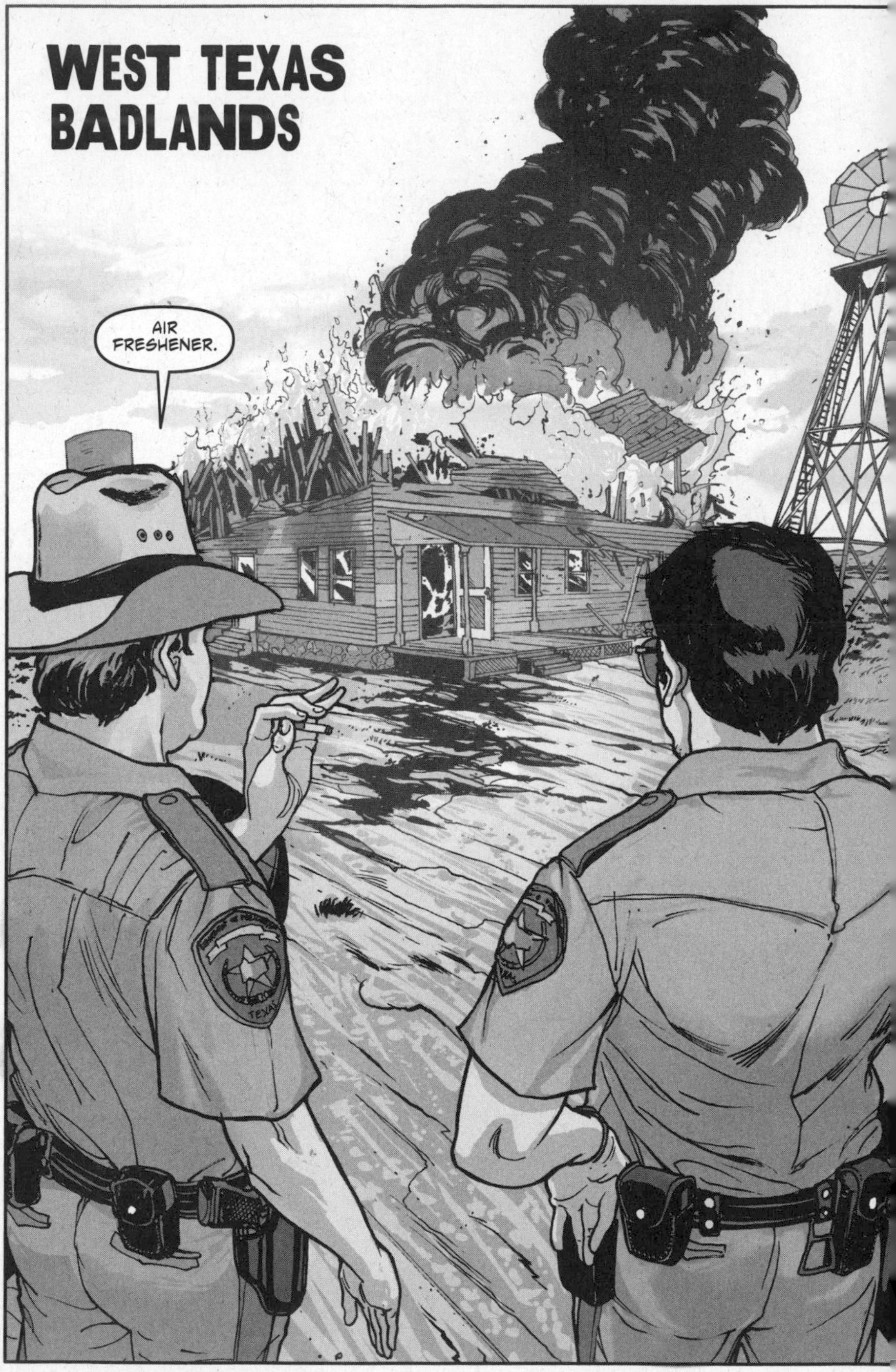
WEST TEXAS BADLANDS
AIR FRESHENER.

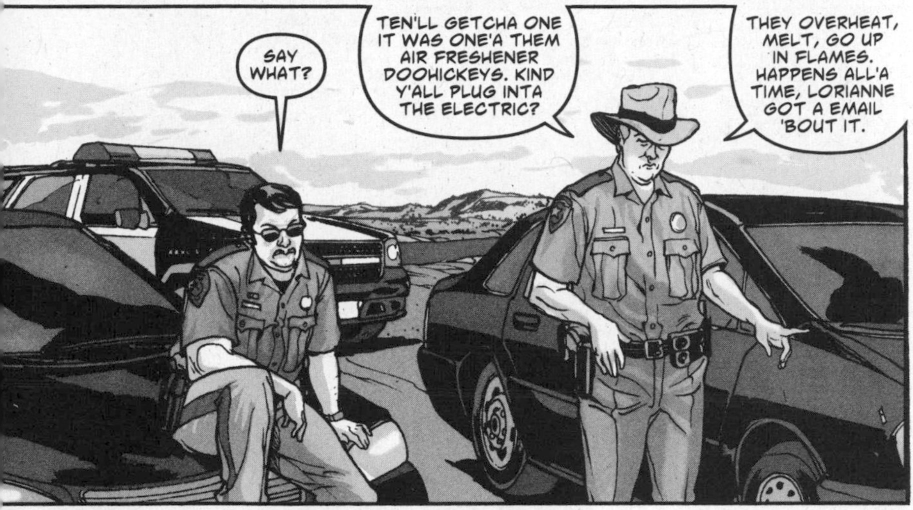
SAY WHAT?
TEN'LL GETCHA ONE IT WAS ONE'A THEM AIR FRESHENER DOOHICKEYS. KIND Y'ALL PLUG INTA THE ELECTRIC?
THEY OVERHEAT, MELT, GO UP IN FLAMES. HAPPENS ALL'A TIME, LORIANNE GOT A EMAIL 'BOUT IT.

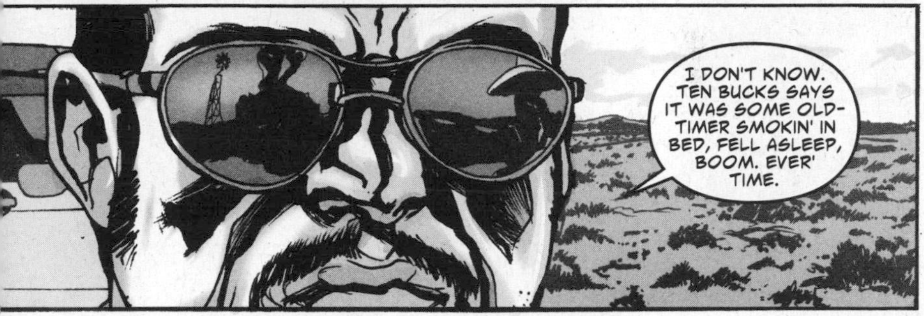
I DON'T KNOW. TEN BUCKS SAYS IT WAS SOME OLD-TIMER SMOKIN' IN BED, FELL ASLEEP, BOOM. EVER' TIME.

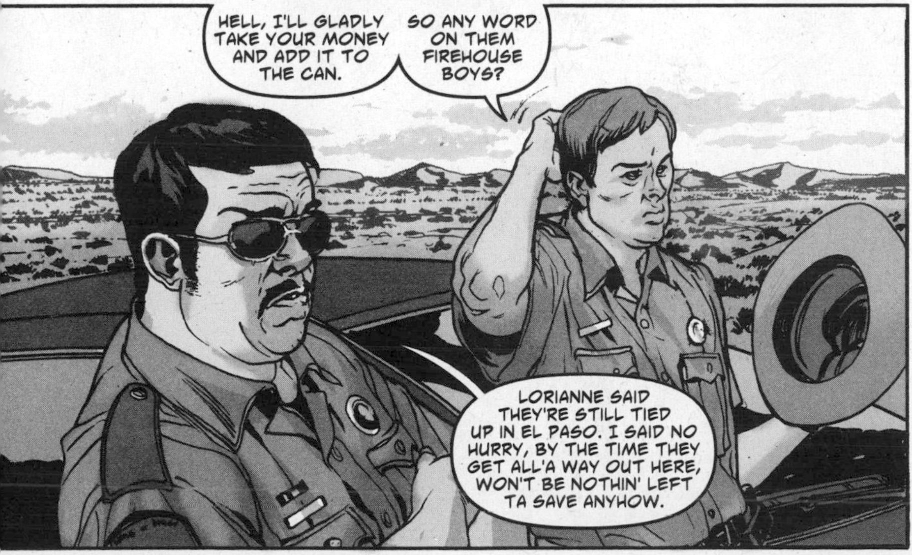
HELL, I'LL GLADLY TAKE YOUR MONEY AND ADD IT TO THE CAN.
SO ANY WORD ON THEM FIREHOUSE BOYS?
LORIANNE SAID THEY'RE STILL TIED UP IN EL PASO. I SAID NO HURRY, BY THE TIME THEY GET ALL'A WAY OUT HERE, WON'T BE NOTHIN' LEFT TA SAVE ANYHOW.

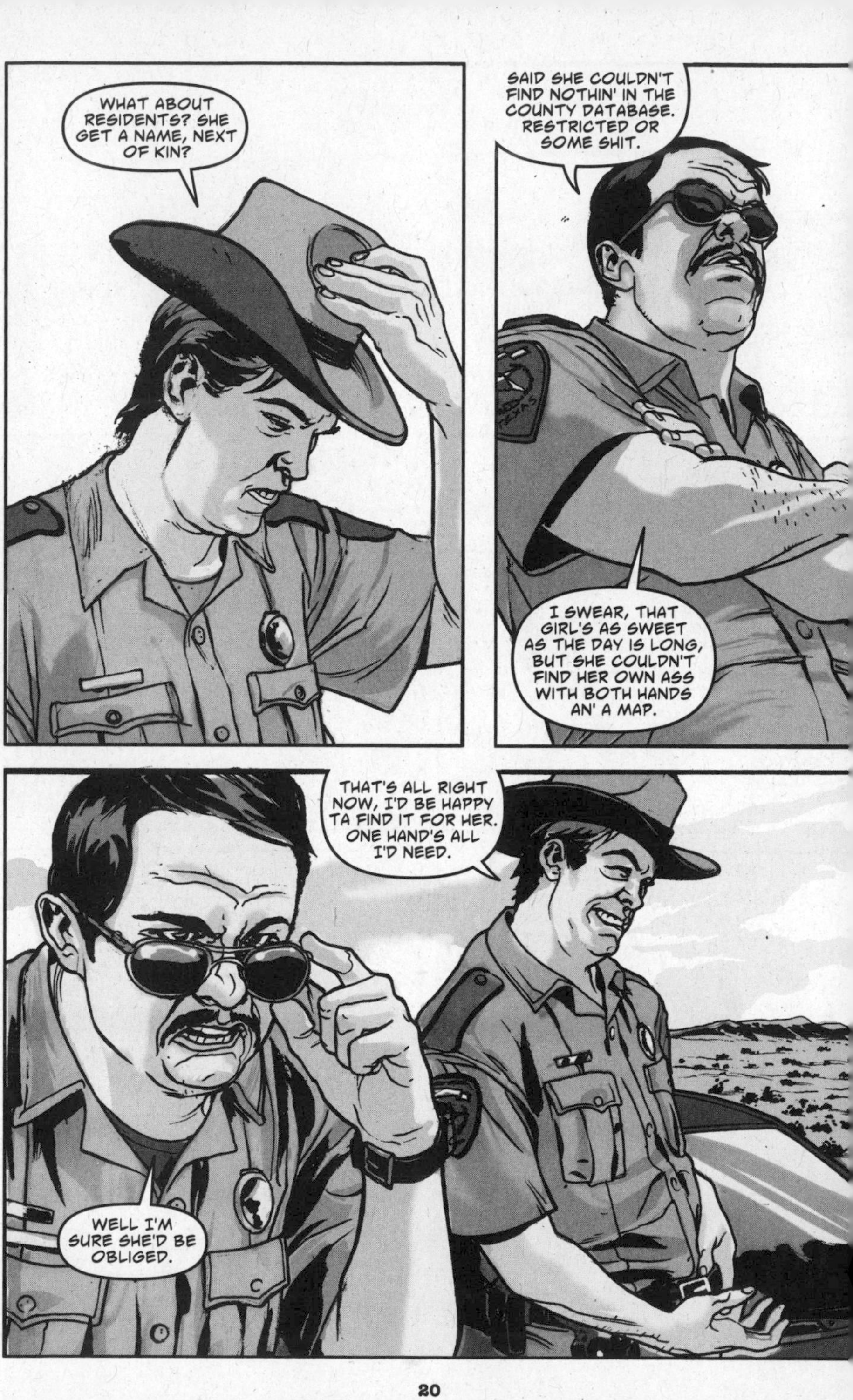
WHAT ABOUT RESIDENTS? SHE GET A NAME, NEXT OF KIN?
SAID SHE COULDN'T FIND NOTHIN' IN THE COUNTY DATABASE. RESTRICTED OR SOME SHIT.
I SWEAR, THAT GIRL'S AS SWEET AS THE DAY IS LONG, BUT SHE COULDN'T FIND HER OWN ASS WITH BOTH HANDS AN' A MAP.
THAT'S ALL RIGHT NOW, I'D BE HAPPY TA FIND IT FOR HER. ONE HAND'S ALL I'D NEED.
WELL I'M SURE SHE'D BE OBLIGED.

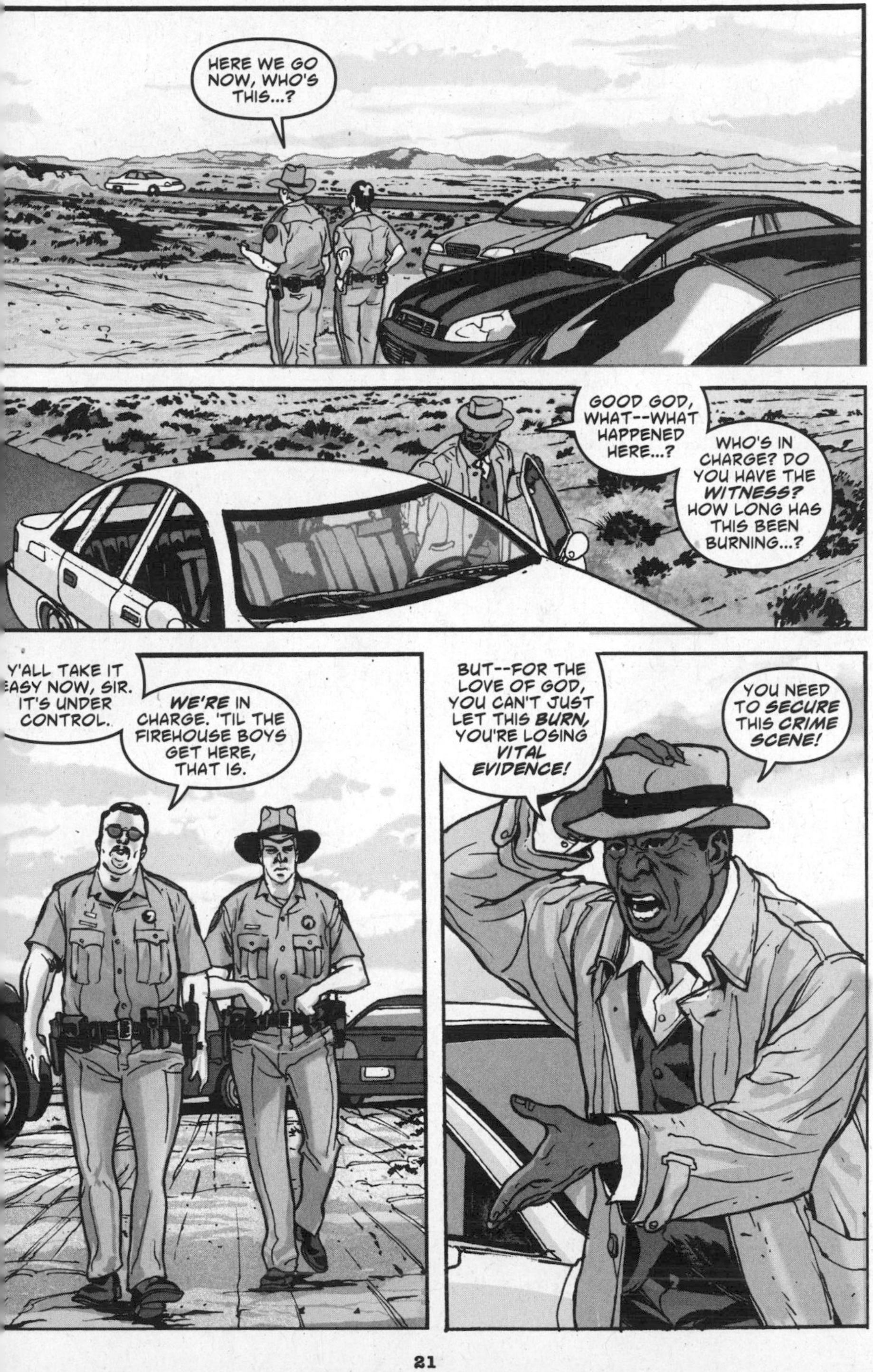
HERE WE GO NOW, WHO'S THIS...?
GOOD GOD, WHAT--WHAT HAPPENED HERE...?
WHO'S IN CHARGE? DO YOU HAVE THE *WITNESS?* HOW LONG HAS THIS BEEN BURNING...?
Y'ALL TAKE IT EASY NOW, SIR. IT'S UNDER CONTROL.
WE'RE IN CHARGE. 'TIL THE FIREHOUSE BOYS GET HERE, THAT IS.
BUT--FOR THE LOVE OF GOD, YOU CAN'T JUST LET THIS *BURN,* YOU'RE LOSING *VITAL EVIDENCE!*
YOU NEED TO *SECURE* THIS *CRIME SCENE!*

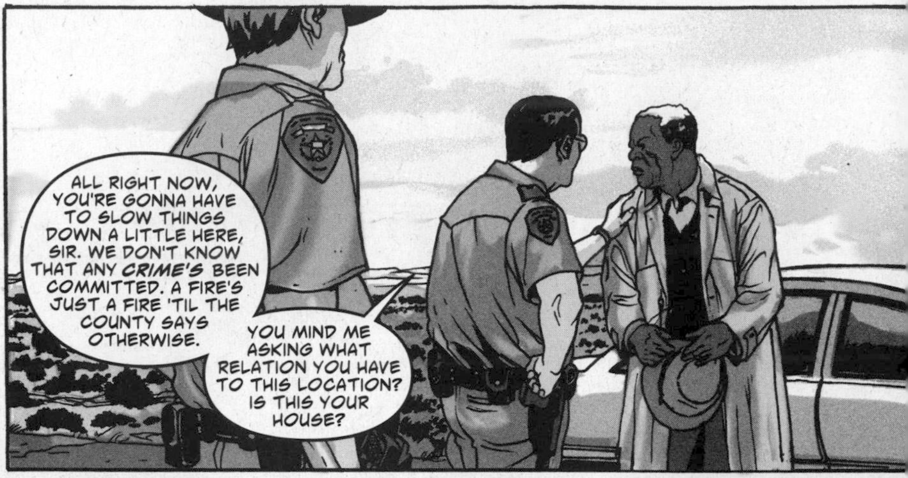
ALL RIGHT NOW, YOU'RE GONNA HAVE TO SLOW THINGS DOWN A LITTLE HERE, SIR. WE DON'T KNOW THAT ANY CRIME'S BEEN COMMITTED. A FIRE'S JUST A FIRE 'TIL THE COUNTY SAYS OTHERWISE.
YOU MIND ME ASKING WHAT RELATION YOU HAVE TO THIS LOCATION? IS THIS YOUR HOUSE?

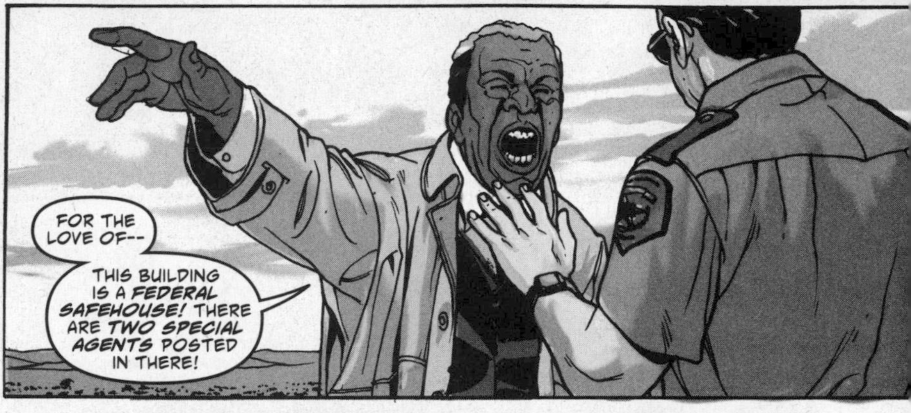
FOR THE LOVE OF--
THIS BUILDING IS A FEDERAL SAFEHOUSE! THERE ARE TWO SPECIAL AGENTS POSTED IN THERE!

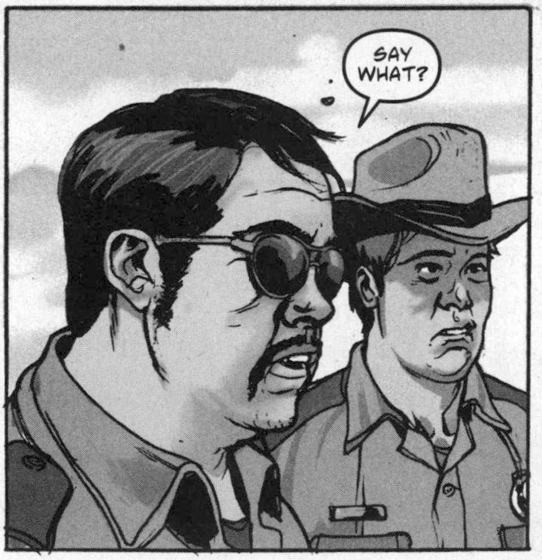
SAY WHAT?

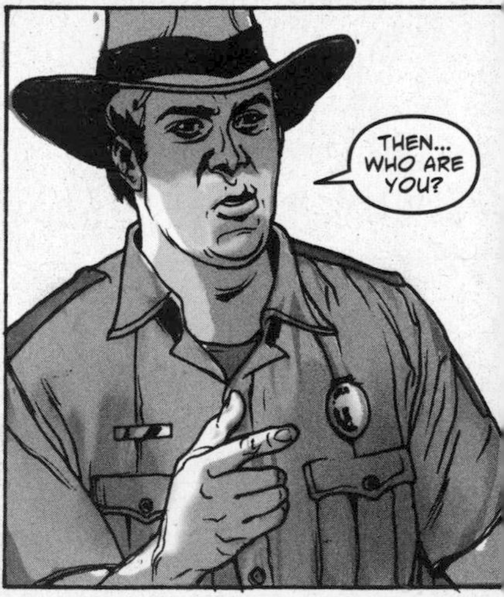
THEN... WHO ARE YOU?

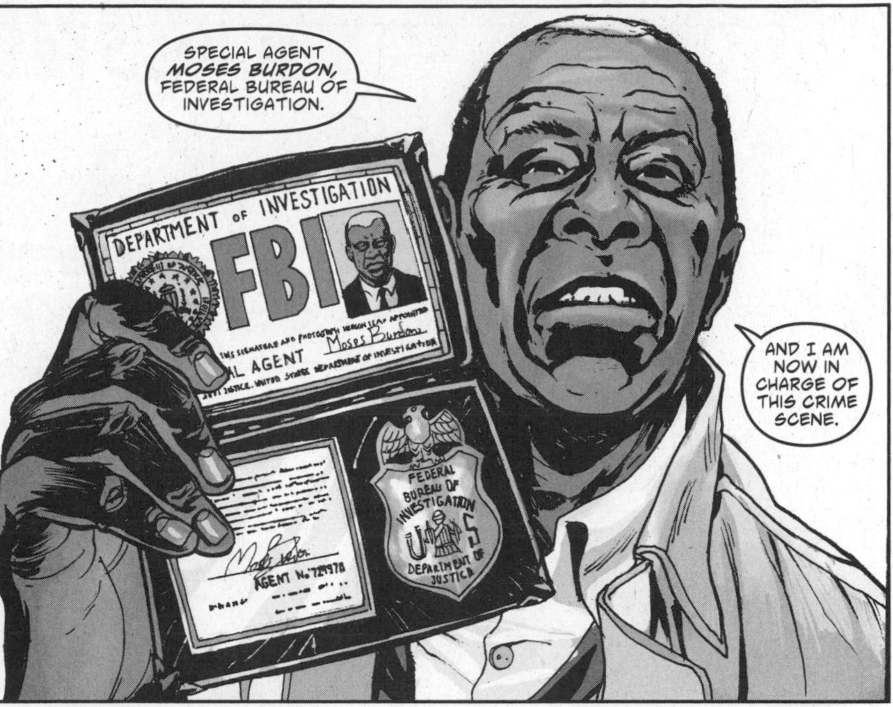
SPECIAL AGENT
MOSES BURDON,
FEDERAL BUREAU OF
INVESTIGATION.
DEPARTMENT of INVESTIGATION
FBI
FEDERAL
BUREAU OF
INVESTIGATION
DEPARTMENT OF
JUSTICE
AND I AM NOW IN CHARGE OF THIS CRIME SCENE.

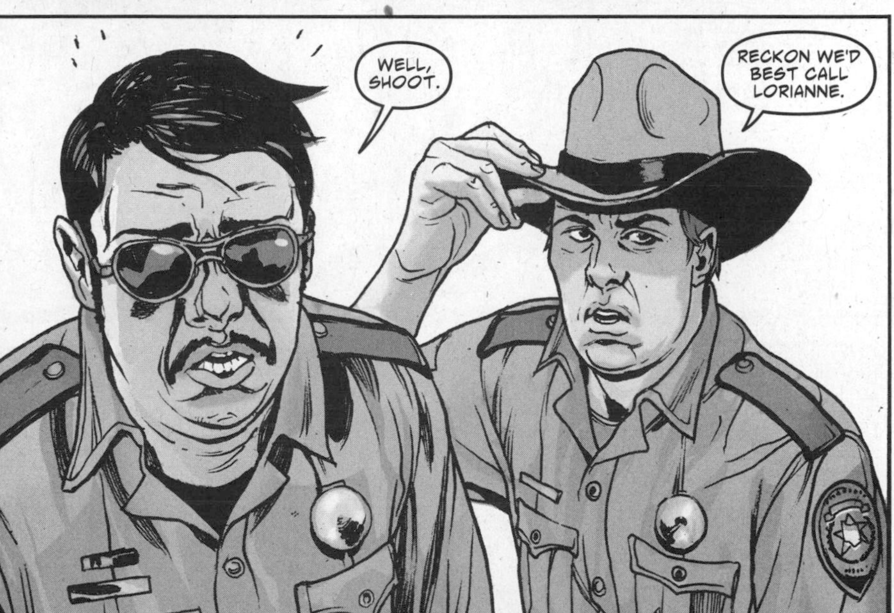
WELL, SHOOT.
RECKON WE'D BEST CALL LORIANNE.

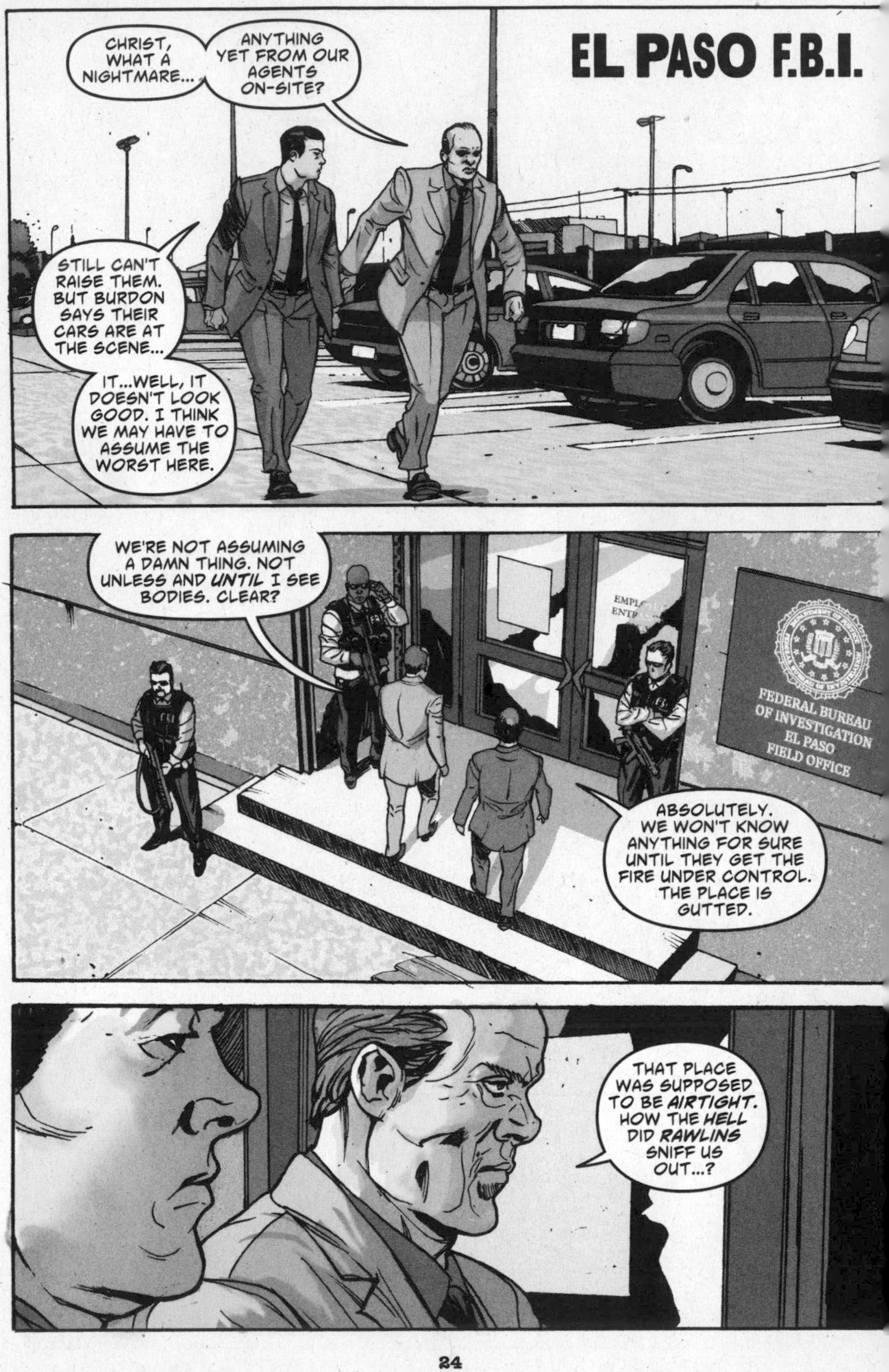
EL PASO F.B.I.
CHRIST, WHAT A NIGHTMARE...
ANYTHING YET FROM OUR AGENTS ON-SITE?
STILL CAN'T RAISE THEM. BUT BURDON SAYS THEIR CARS ARE AT THE SCENE...
IT...WELL, IT DOESN'T LOOK GOOD. I THINK WE MAY HAVE TO ASSUME THE WORST HERE.
WE'RE NOT ASSUMING A DAMN THING. NOT UNLESS AND UNTIL I SEE BODIES. CLEAR?
FEDERAL BUREAU OF INVESTIGATION EL PASO FIELD OFFICE
ABSOLUTELY. WE WON'T KNOW ANYTHING FOR SURE UNTIL THEY GET THE FIRE UNDER CONTROL. THE PLACE IS GUTTED.
THAT PLACE WAS SUPPOSED TO BE AIRTIGHT. HOW THE HELL DID RAWLINS SNIFF US OUT...?

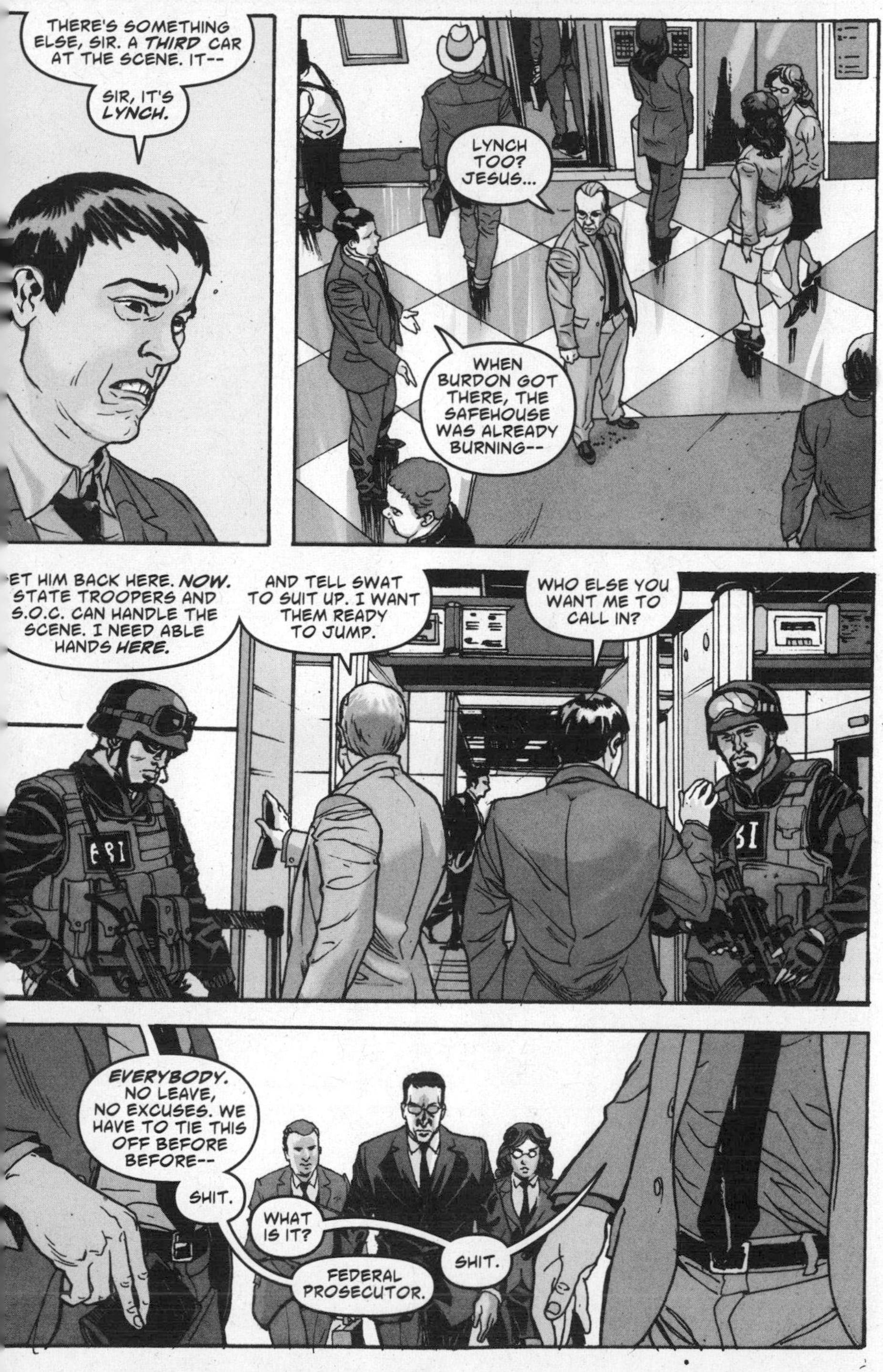
THERE'S SOMETHING ELSE, SIR. A *THIRD* CAR AT THE SCENE. IT--
SIR, IT'S *LYNCH.*
LYNCH TOO? JESUS...
WHEN BURDON GOT THERE, THE SAFEHOUSE WAS ALREADY BURNING--
ET HIM BACK HERE. *NOW.* STATE TROOPERS AND S.O.C. CAN HANDLE THE SCENE. I NEED ABLE HANDS *HERE.*
AND TELL SWAT TO SUIT UP. I WANT THEM READY TO JUMP.
WHO ELSE YOU WANT ME TO CALL IN?
EVERYBODY. NO LEAVE, NO EXCUSES. WE HAVE TO TIE THIS OFF BEFORE BEFORE--
SHIT.
WHAT IS IT?
SHIT.
FEDERAL PROSECUTOR.

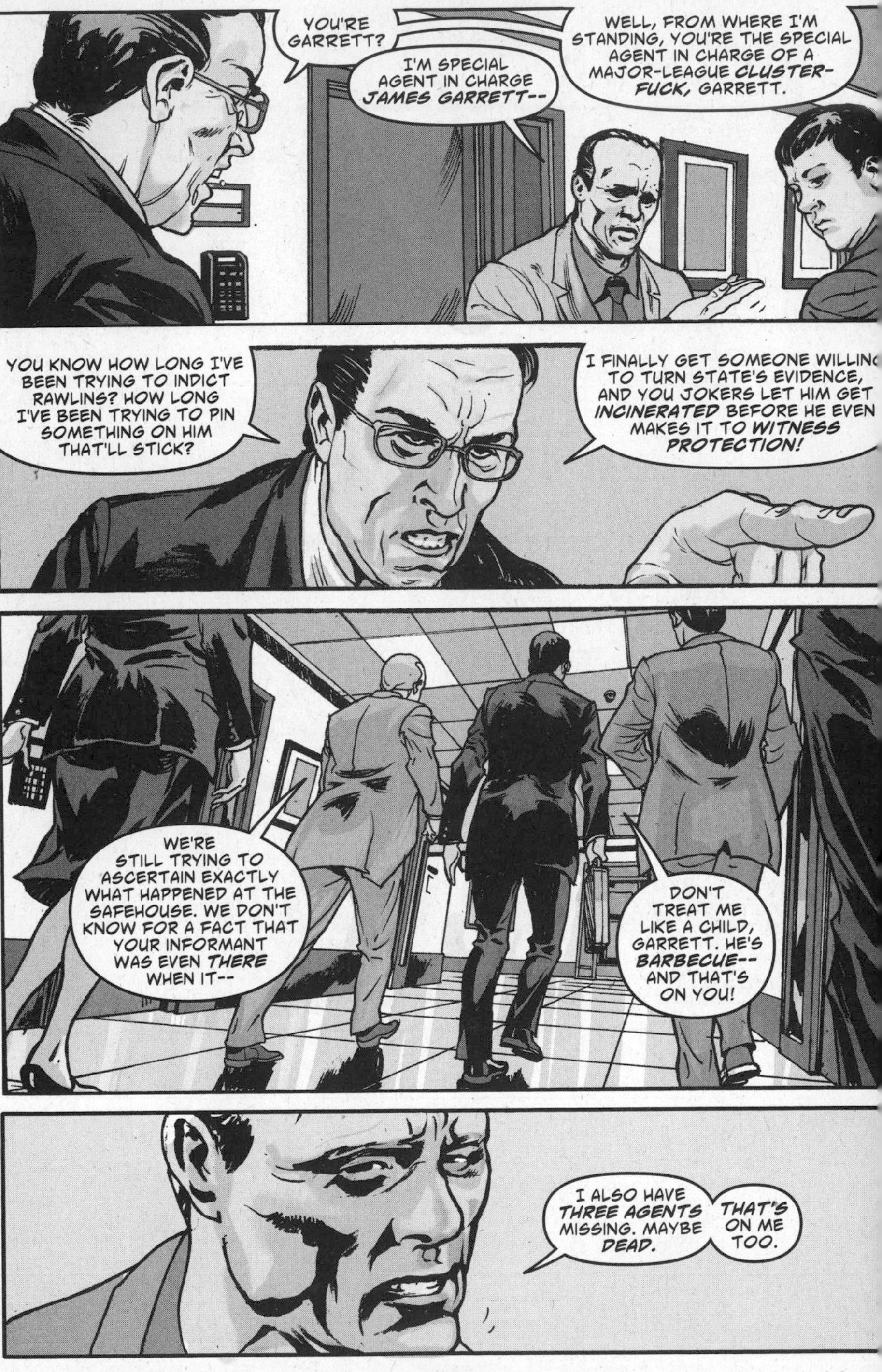
YOU'RE GARRETT?
I'M SPECIAL AGENT IN CHARGE JAMES GARRETT--
WELL, FROM WHERE I'M STANDING, YOU'RE THE SPECIAL AGENT IN CHARGE OF A MAJOR-LEAGUE CLUSTER-FUCK, GARRETT.
YOU KNOW HOW LONG I'VE BEEN TRYING TO INDICT RAWLINS? HOW LONG I'VE BEEN TRYING TO PIN SOMETHING ON HIM THAT'LL STICK?
I FINALLY GET SOMEONE WILLING TO TURN STATE'S EVIDENCE, AND YOU JOKERS LET HIM GET INCINERATED BEFORE HE EVEN MAKES IT TO WITNESS PROTECTION!
WE'RE STILL TRYING TO ASCERTAIN EXACTLY WHAT HAPPENED AT THE SAFEHOUSE. WE DON'T KNOW FOR A FACT THAT YOUR INFORMANT WAS EVEN THERE WHEN IT--
DON'T TREAT ME LIKE A CHILD, GARRETT. HE'S BARBECUE-- AND THAT'S ON YOU!
I ALSO HAVE THREE AGENTS MISSING. MAYBE DEAD.
THAT'S ON ME TOO.

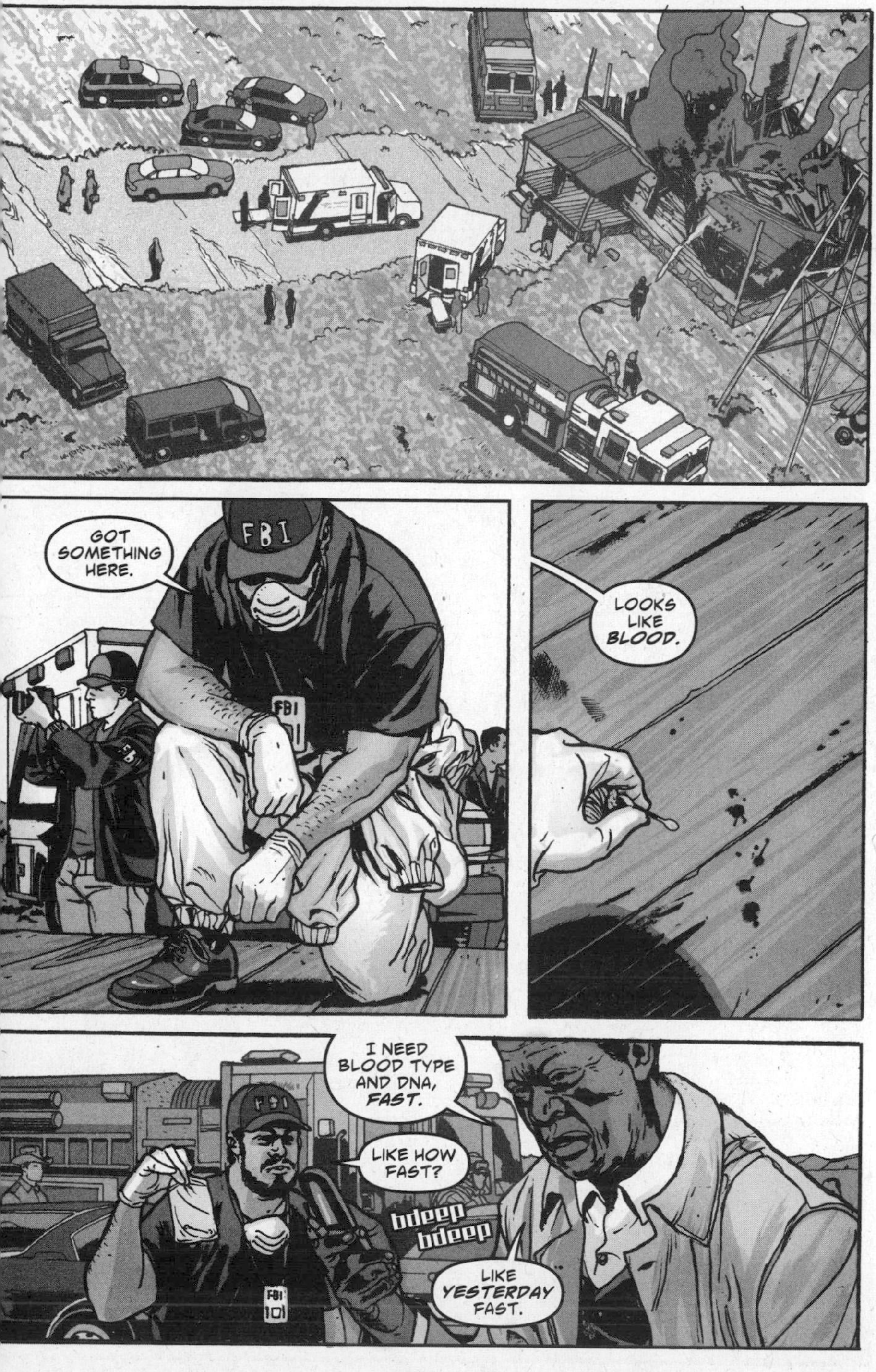
GOT SOMETHING HERE.
LOOKS LIKE BLOOD.
I NEED BLOOD TYPE AND DNA, FAST.
LIKE HOW FAST?
bdeep bdeep
LIKE YESTERDAY FAST.

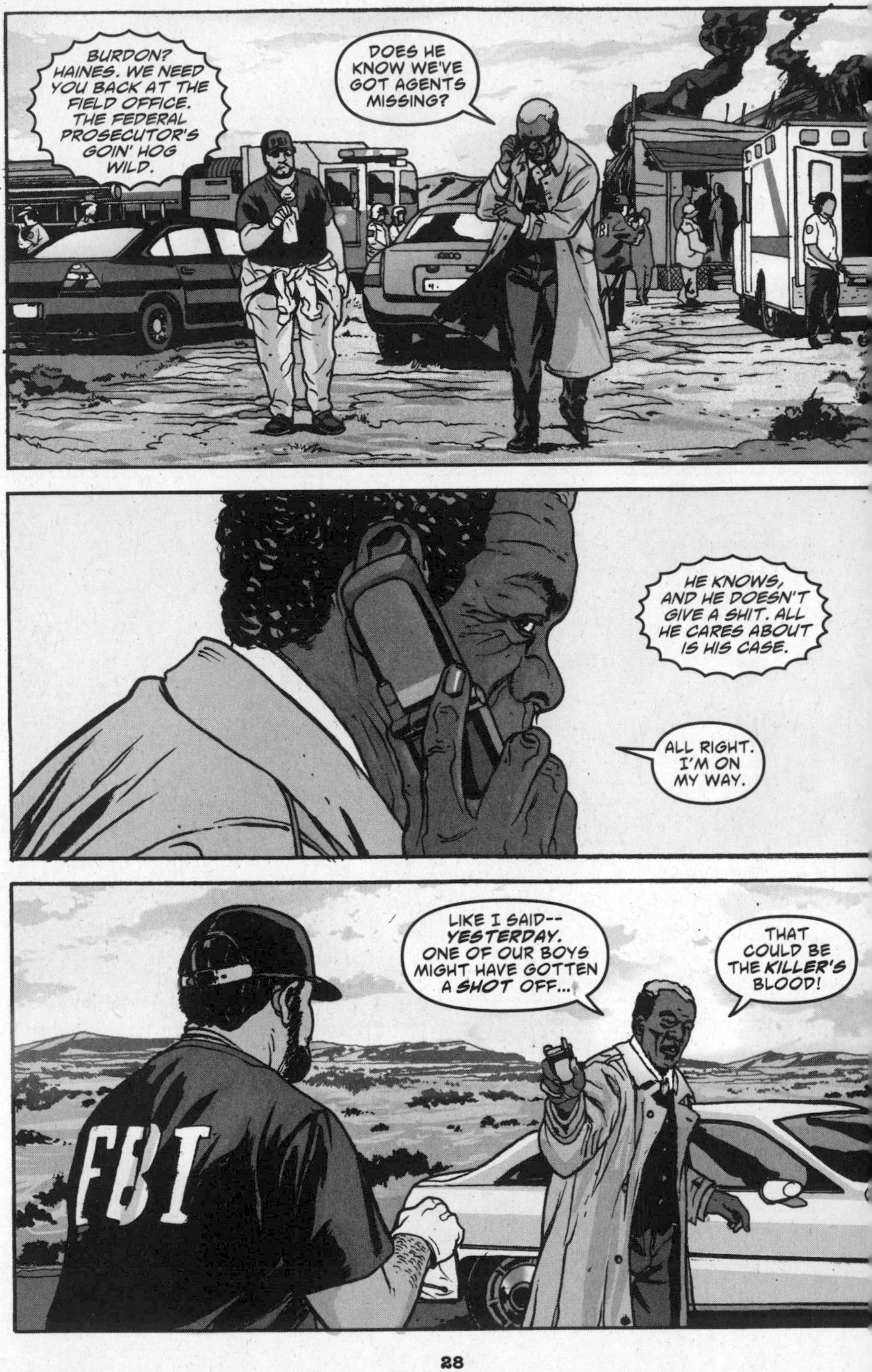
BURDON? HAINES. WE NEED YOU BACK AT THE FIELD OFFICE. THE FEDERAL PROSECUTOR'S GOIN' HOG WILD.
DOES HE KNOW WE'VE GOT AGENTS MISSING?
HE KNOWS, AND HE DOESN'T GIVE A SHIT. ALL HE CARES ABOUT IS HIS CASE.
ALL RIGHT. I'M ON MY WAY.
LIKE I SAID-- YESTERDAY. ONE OF OUR BOYS MIGHT HAVE GOTTEN A SHOT OFF...
THAT COULD BE THE KILLER'S BLOOD!
FBI

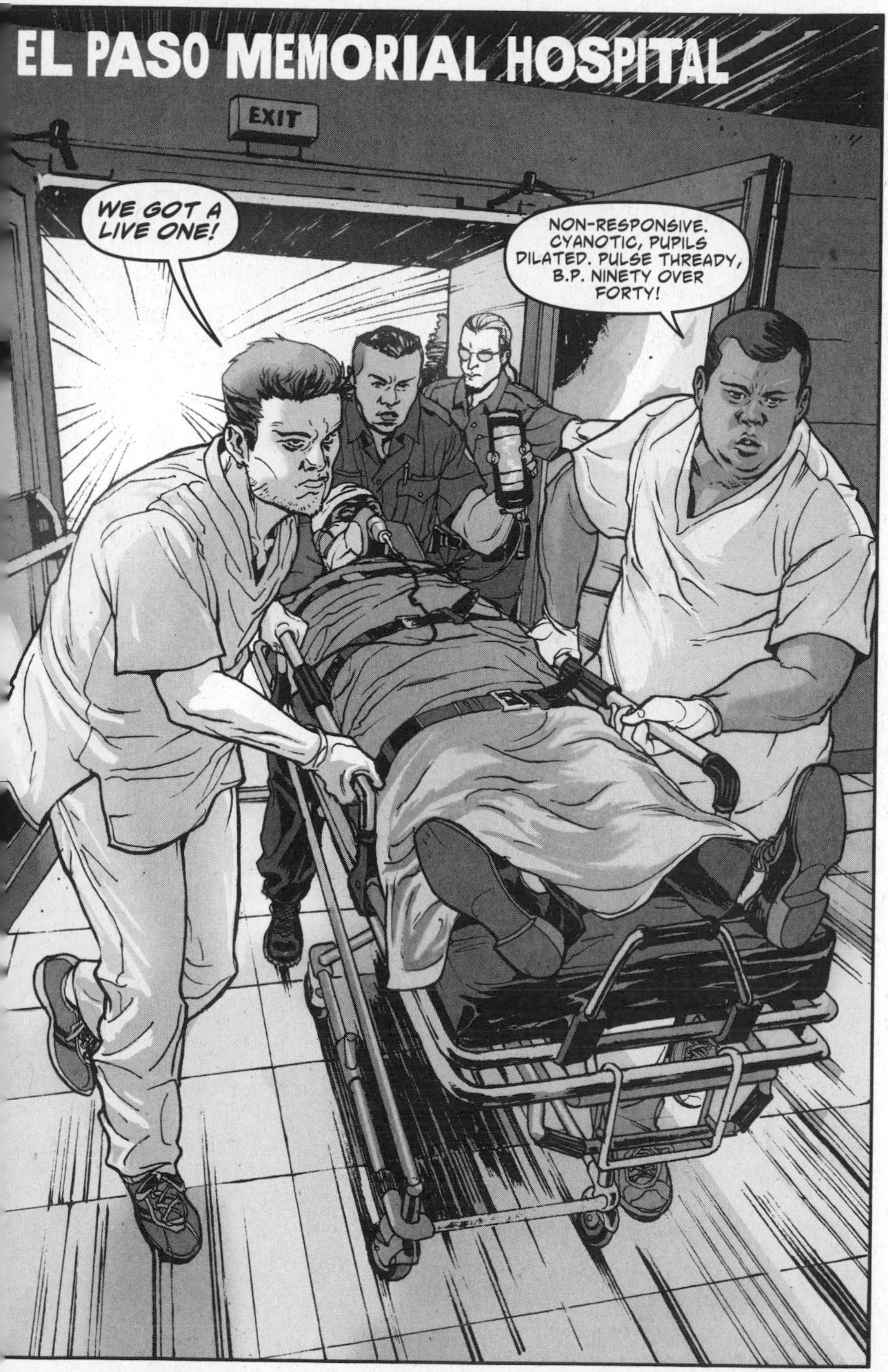
EL PASO MEMORIAL HOSPITAL
EXIT
WE GOT A LIVE ONE!
NON-RESPONSIVE. CYANOTIC, PUPILS DILATED. PULSE THREADY, B.P. NINETY OVER FORTY!

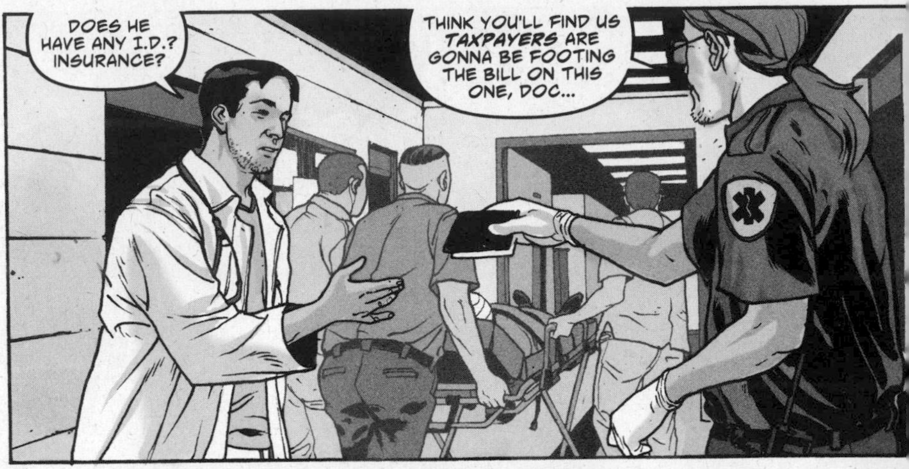
DOES HE HAVE ANY I.D.? INSURANCE?
THINK YOU'LL FIND US *TAXPAYERS* ARE GONNA BE FOOTING THE BILL ON THIS ONE, DOC...

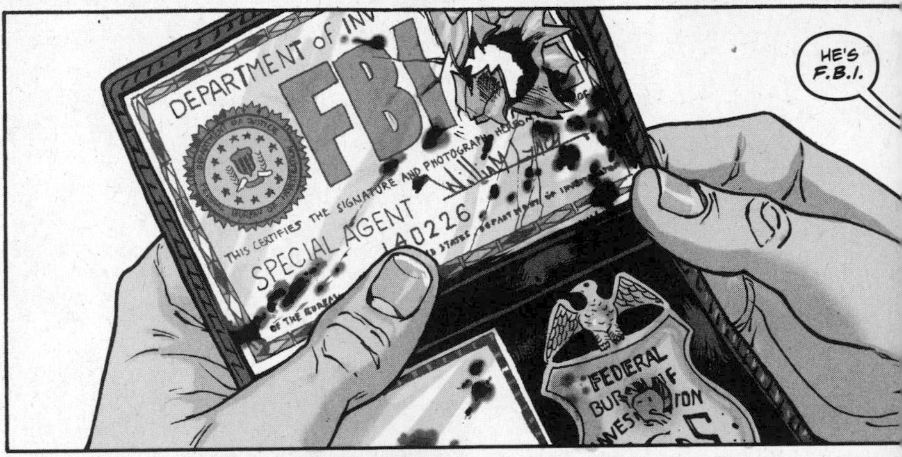
HE'S F.B.I.
DEPARTMENT OF INV
FBI
THIS CERTIFIES THE SIGNATURE AND PHOTOGRAPH
SPECIAL AGENT
LA0226
FEDERAL

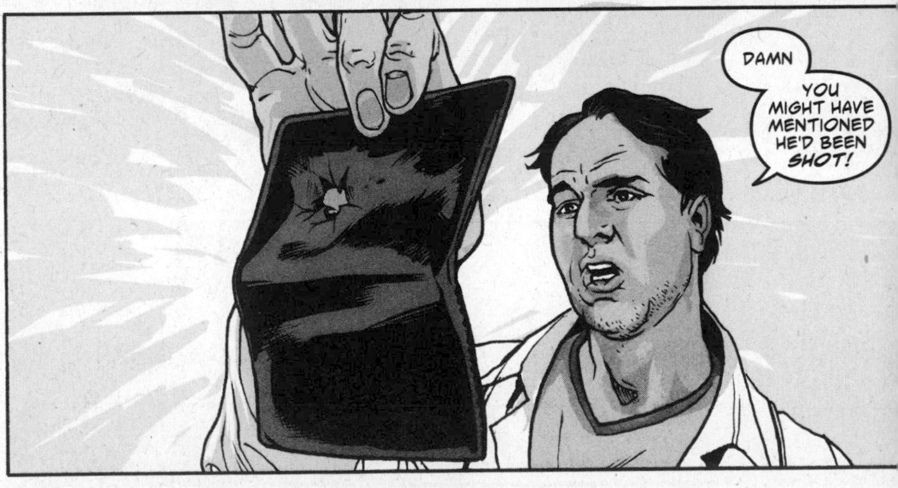
DAMN
YOU MIGHT HAVE MENTIONED HE'D BEEN *SHOT!*

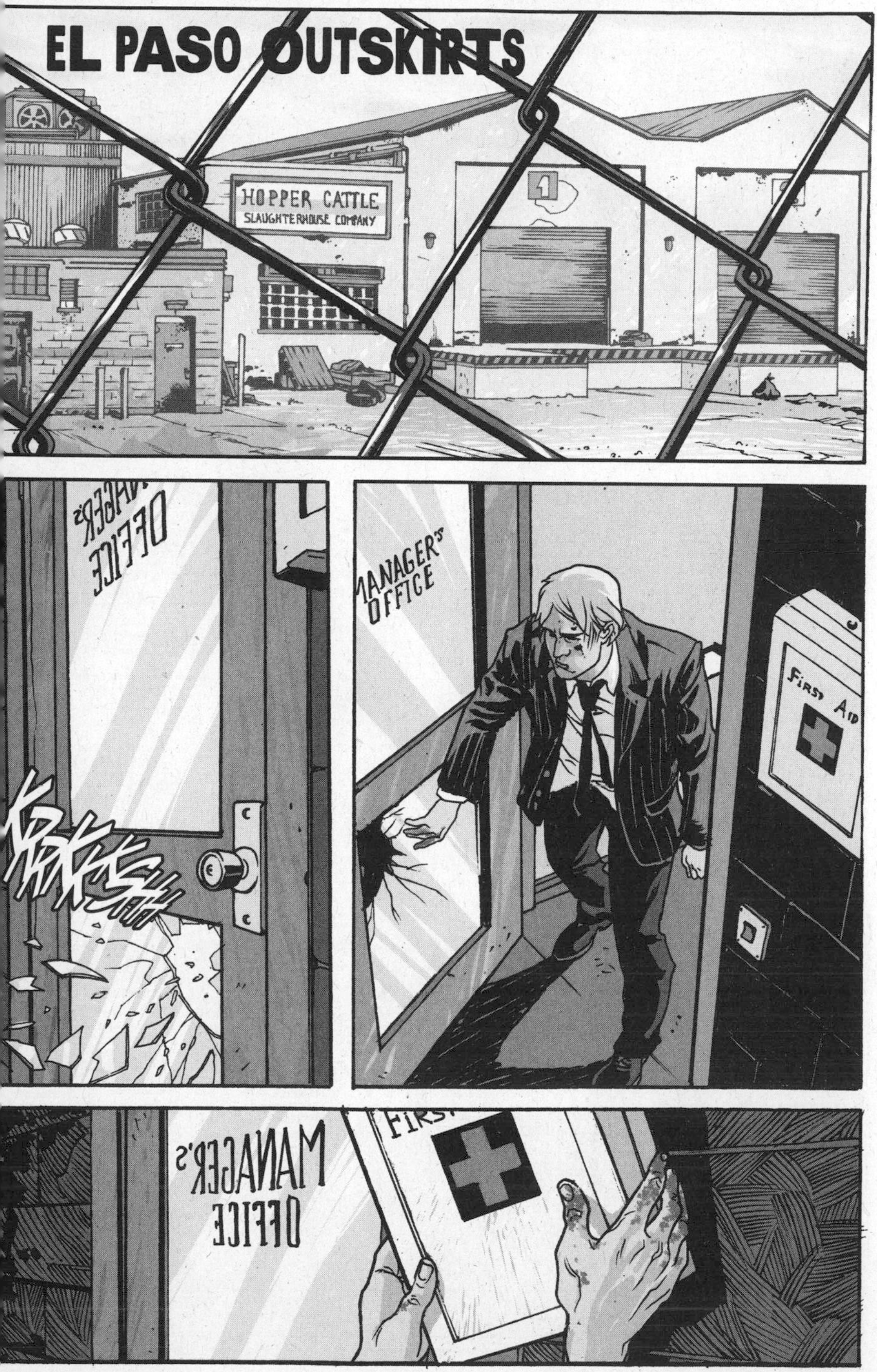
EL PASO OUTSKIRTS
HOPPER CATTLE
SLAUGHTERHOUSE COMPANY
MANAGER'S OFFICE
KRKKSHH
MANAGER'S OFFICE
FIRST AID
MANAGER'S OFFICE

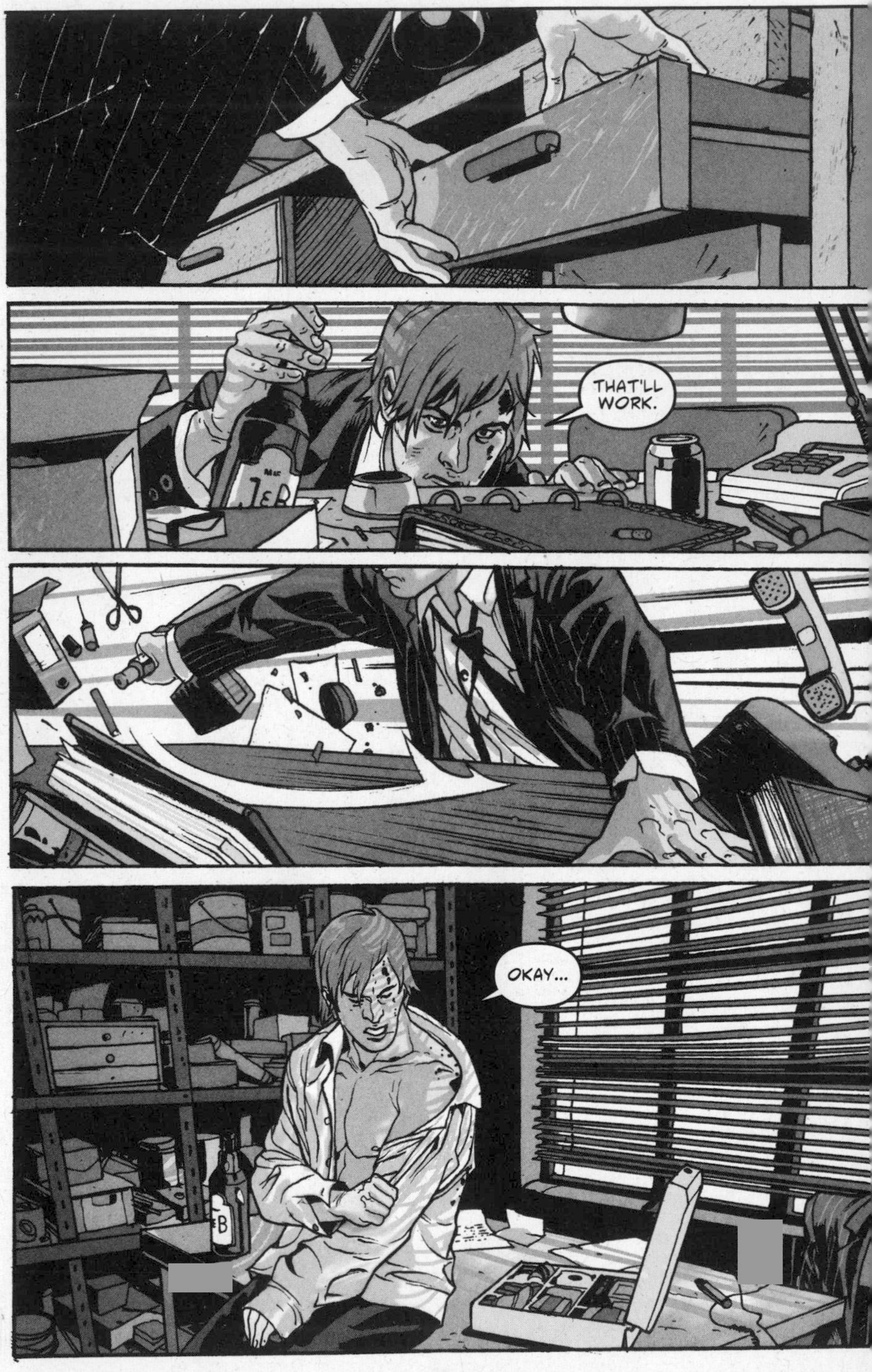
THAT'LL WORK.
OKAY...

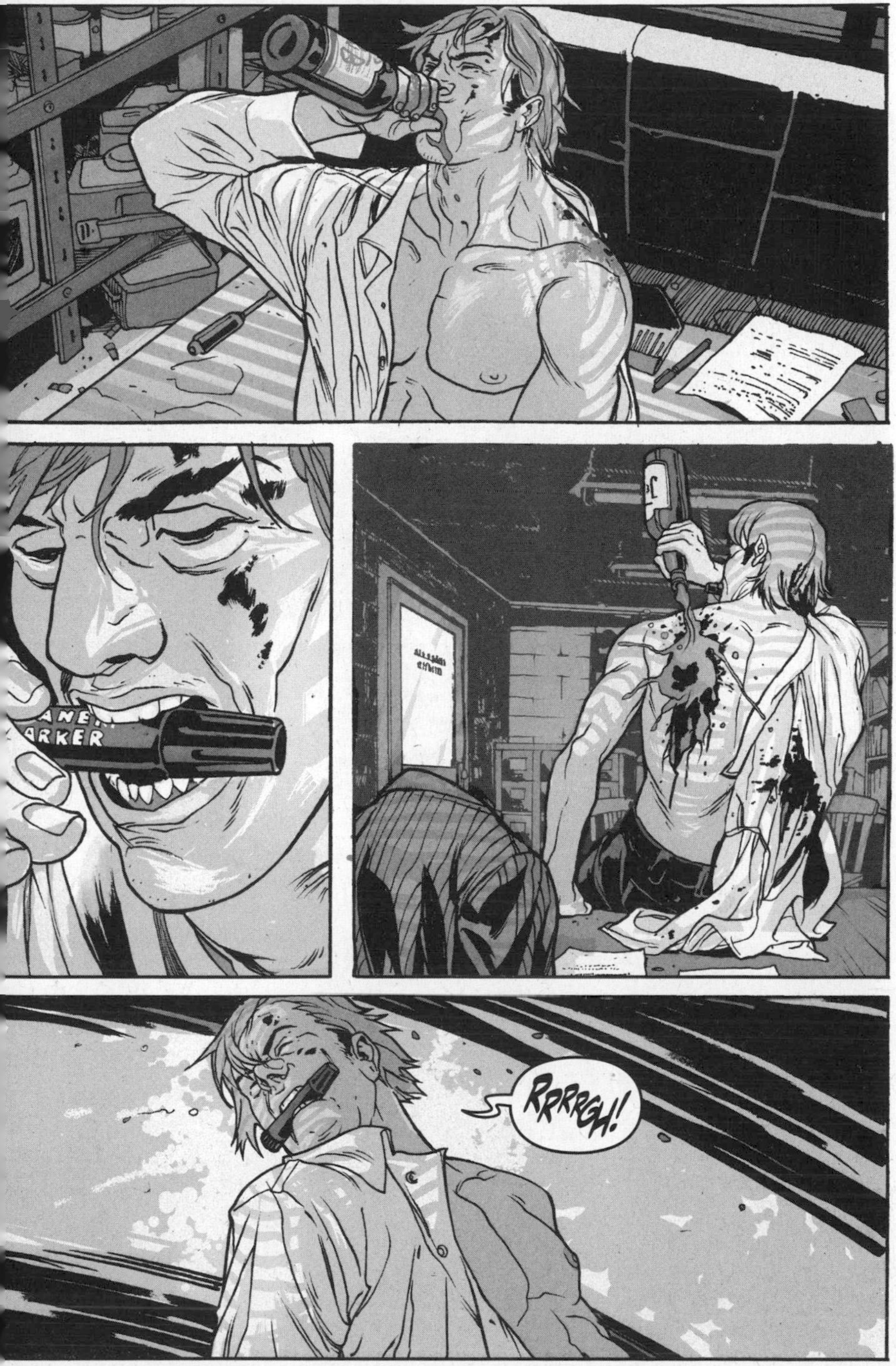
RRRRGH!

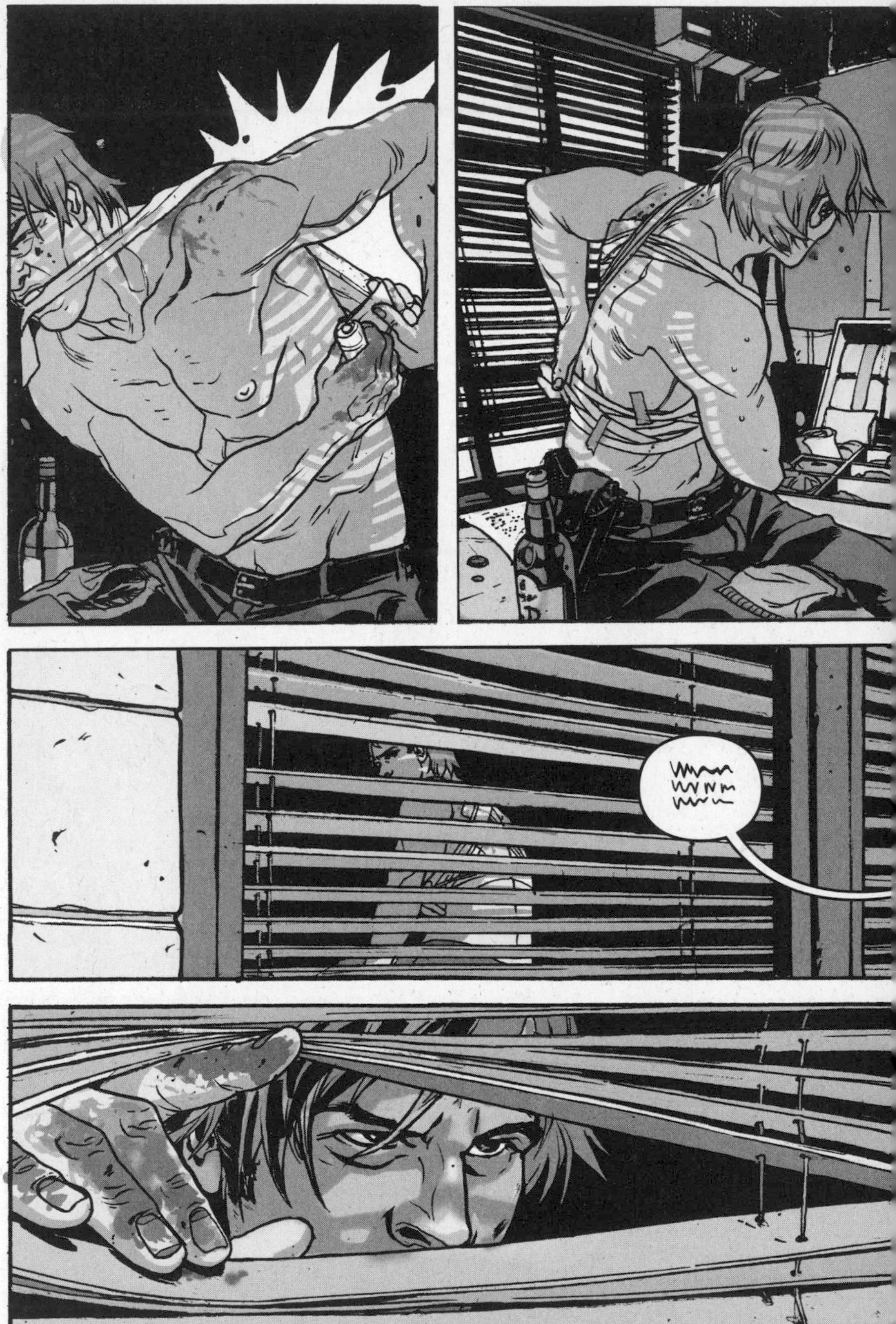

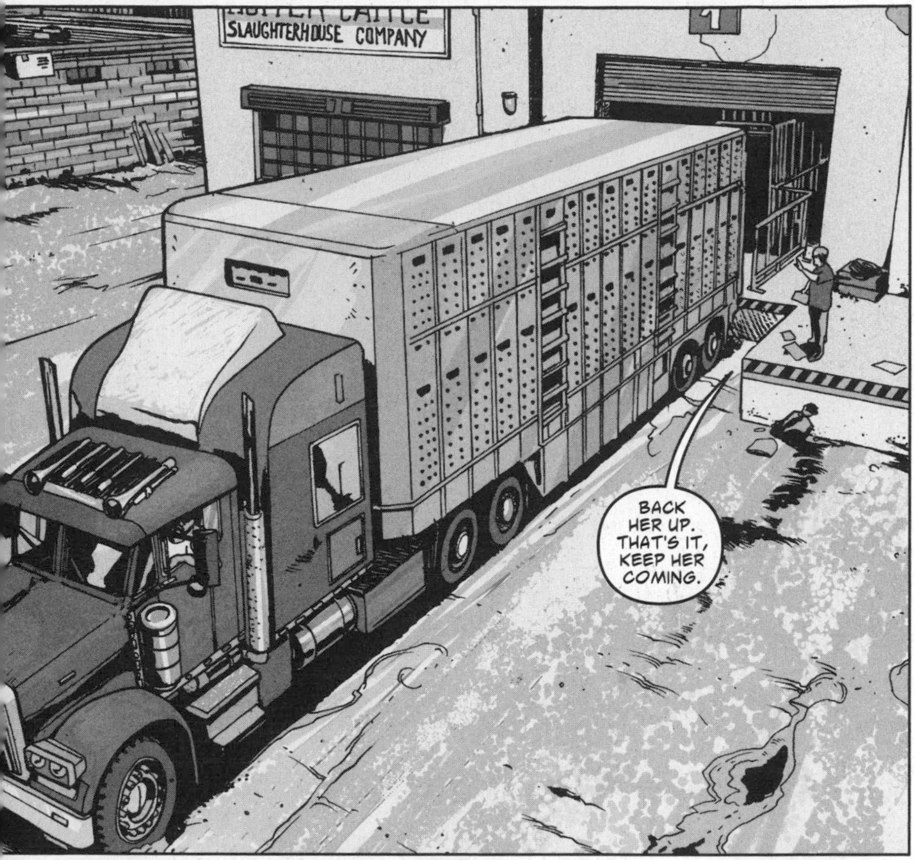
SLAUGHTERHOUSE COMPANY
BACK HER UP. THAT'S IT, KEEP HER COMING.

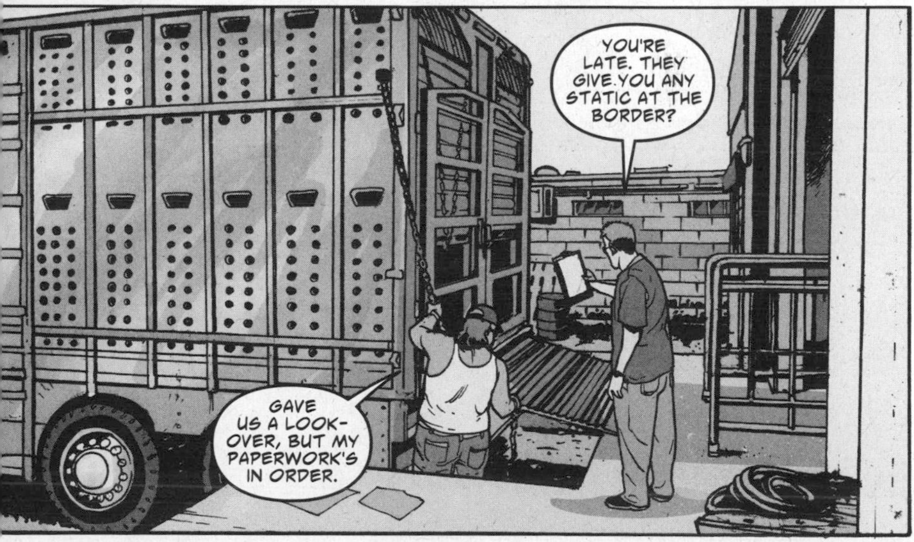
YOU'RE LATE. THEY GIVE YOU ANY STATIC AT THE BORDER?
GAVE US A LOOK-OVER, BUT MY PAPERWORK'S IN ORDER.

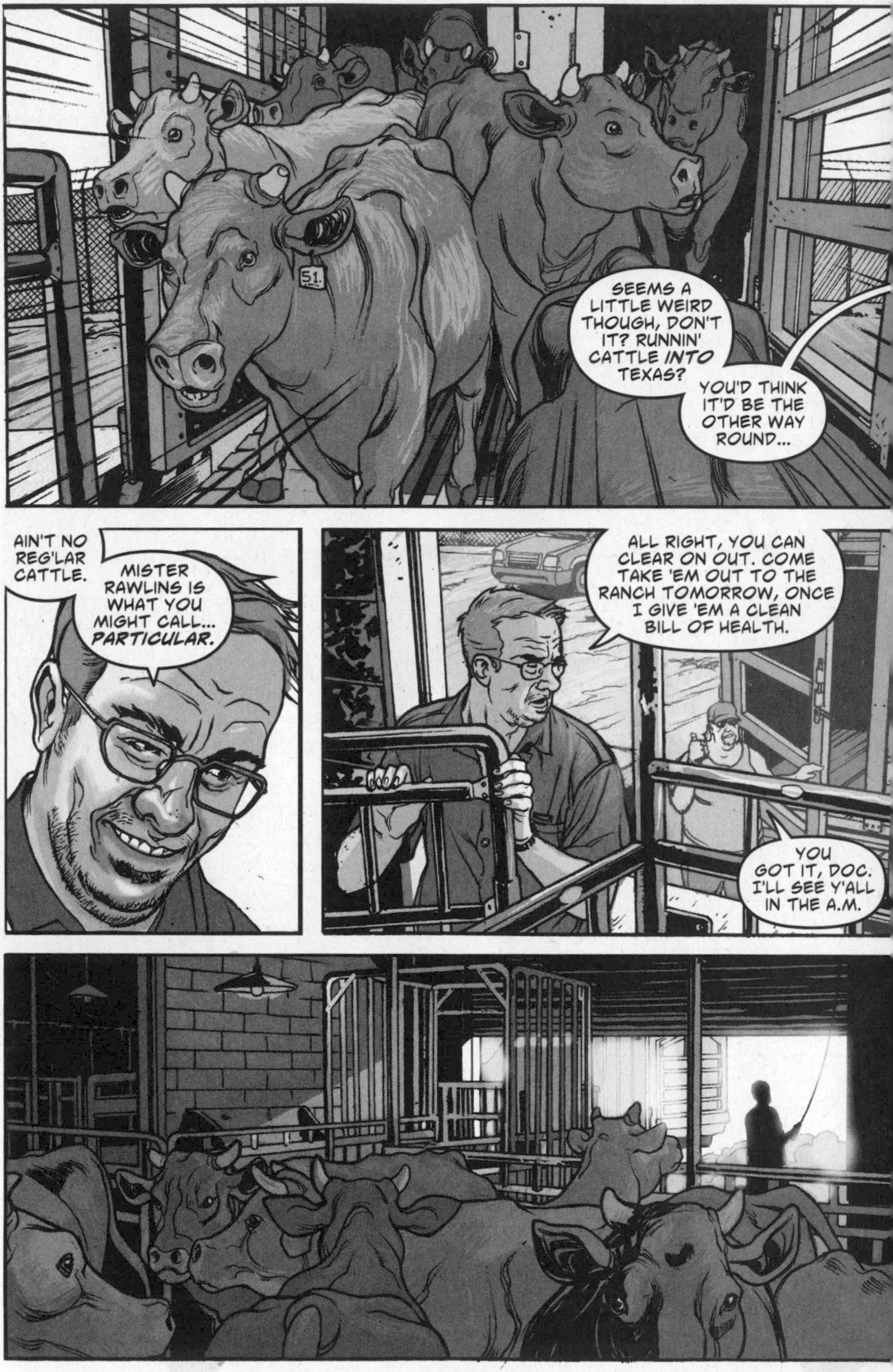
SEEMS A LITTLE WEIRD THOUGH, DON'T IT? RUNNIN' CATTLE *INTO* TEXAS?
YOU'D THINK IT'D BE THE OTHER WAY ROUND...
AIN'T NO REG'LAR CATTLE.
MISTER RAWLINS IS WHAT YOU MIGHT CALL... ***PARTICULAR.***
ALL RIGHT, YOU CAN CLEAR ON OUT. COME TAKE 'EM OUT TO THE RANCH TOMORROW, ONCE I GIVE 'EM A CLEAN BILL OF HEALTH.
YOU GOT IT, DOC. I'LL SEE Y'ALL IN THE A.M.

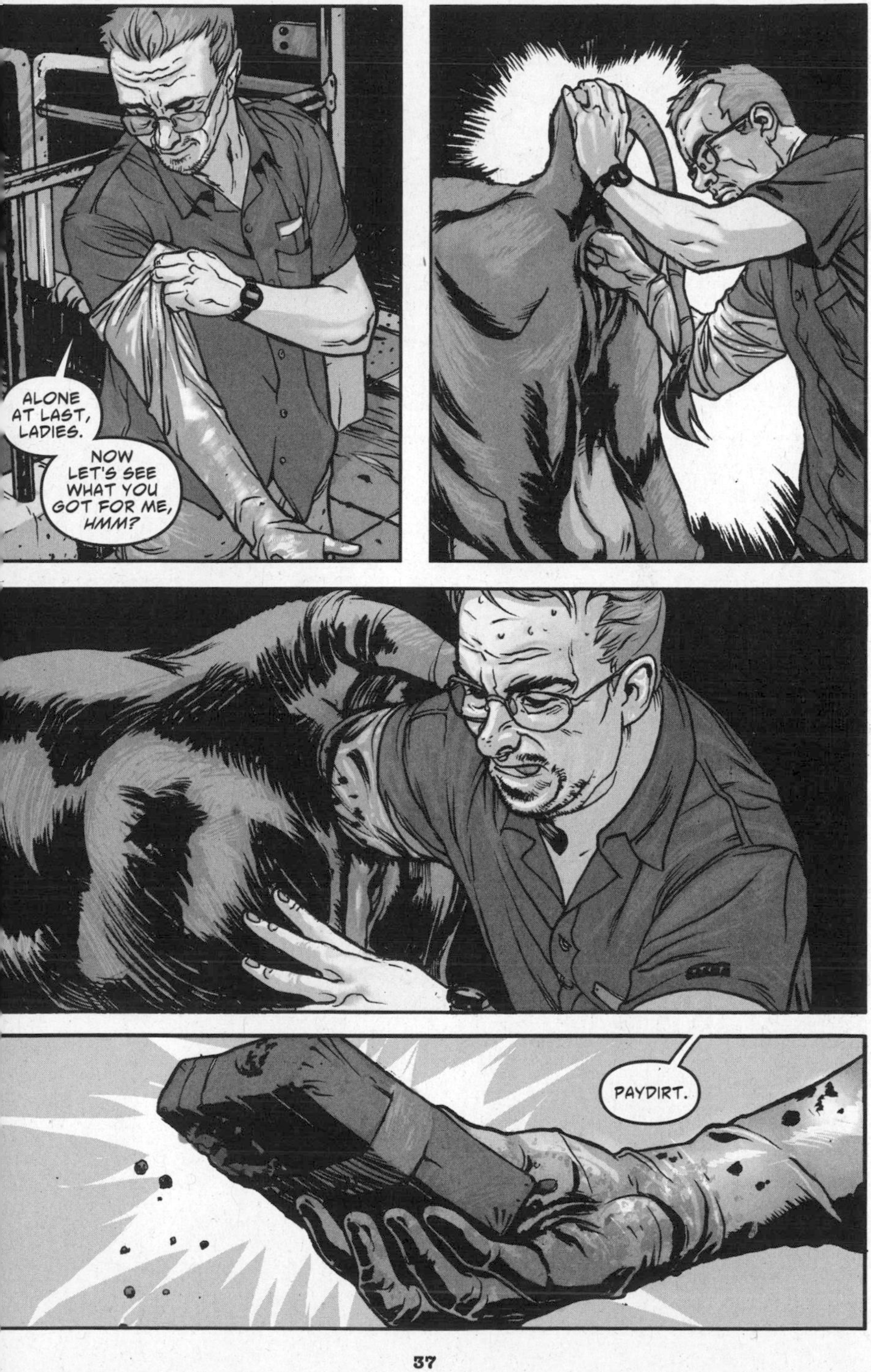
ALONE AT LAST, LADIES.
NOW LET'S SEE WHAT YOU GOT FOR ME, HMM?
PAYDIRT.

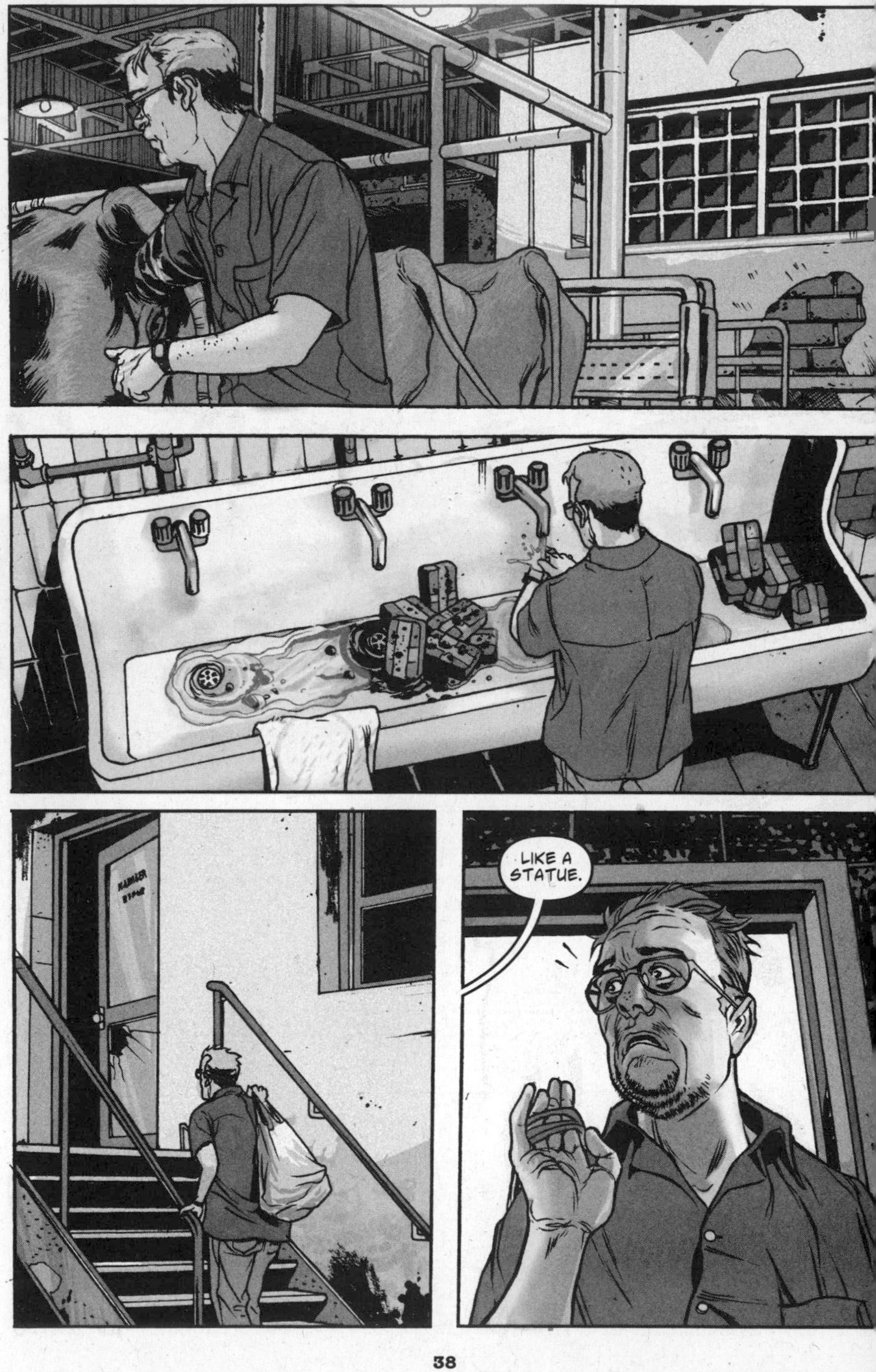
LIKE A STATUE.

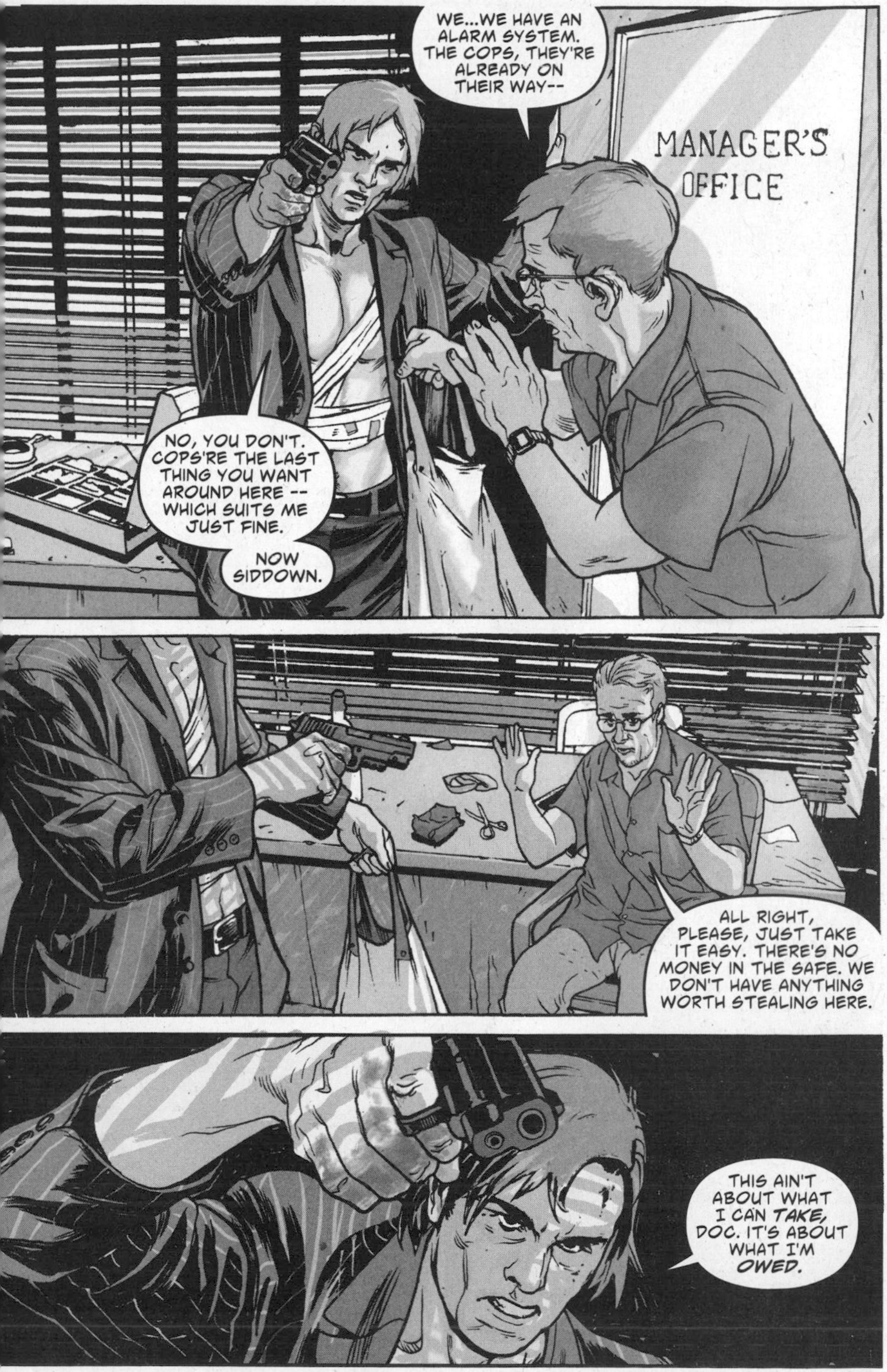
WE...WE HAVE AN ALARM SYSTEM. THE COPS, THEY'RE ALREADY ON THEIR WAY--
MANAGER'S OFFICE
NO, YOU DON'T. COPS'RE THE LAST THING YOU WANT AROUND HERE -- WHICH SUITS ME JUST FINE.
NOW SIDDOWN.
ALL RIGHT, PLEASE, JUST TAKE IT EASY. THERE'S NO MONEY IN THE SAFE. WE DON'T HAVE ANYTHING WORTH STEALING HERE.
THIS AIN'T ABOUT WHAT I CAN *TAKE*, DOC. IT'S ABOUT WHAT I'M *OWED*.

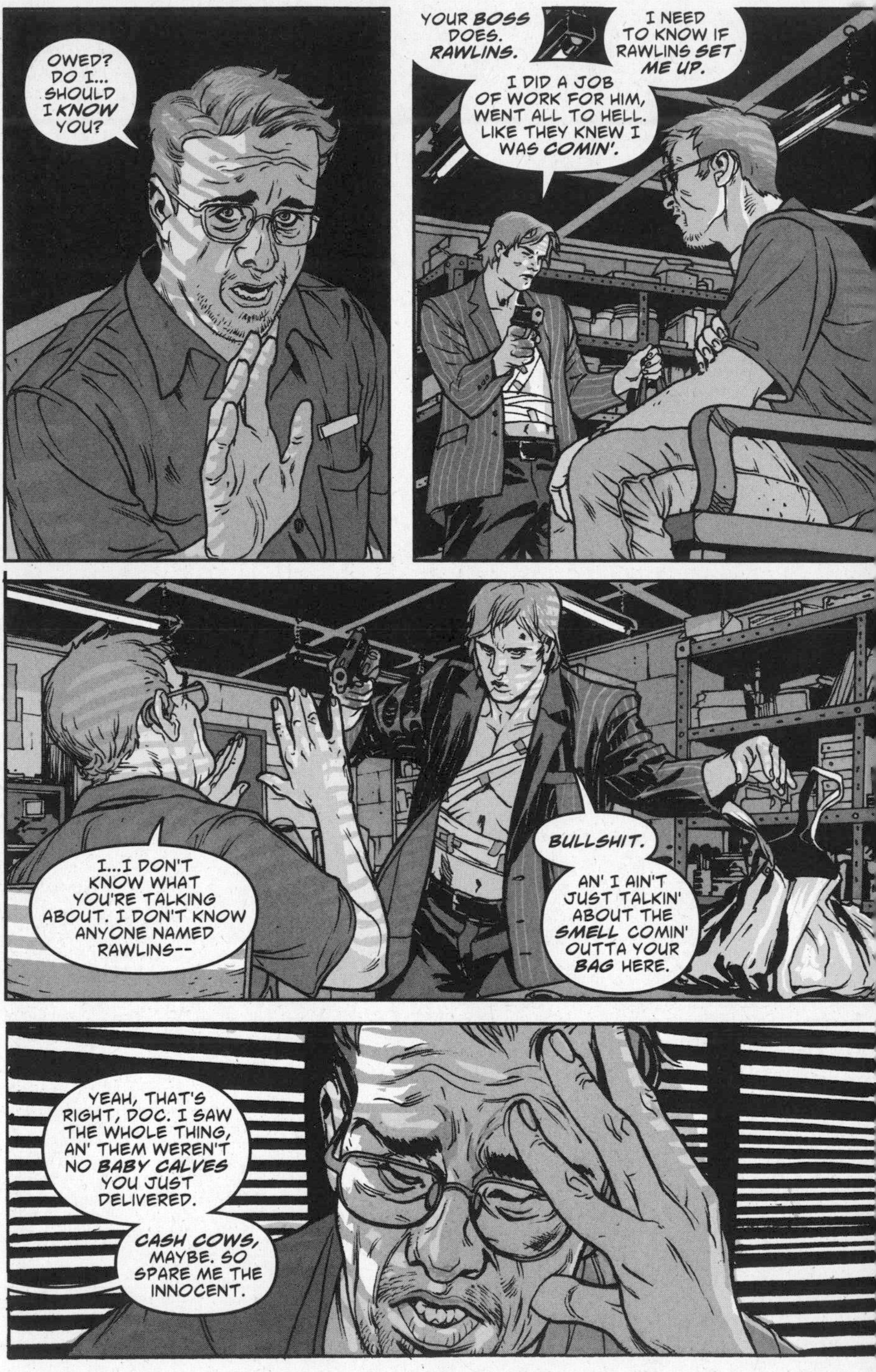
OWED? DO I... SHOULD I KNOW YOU?
YOUR BOSS DOES. RAWLINS.
I NEED TO KNOW IF RAWLINS SET ME UP.
I DID A JOB OF WORK FOR HIM, WENT ALL TO HELL. LIKE THEY KNEW I WAS COMIN'.
I...I DON'T KNOW WHAT YOU'RE TALKING ABOUT. I DON'T KNOW ANYONE NAMED RAWLINS--
BULLSHIT.
AN' I AIN'T JUST TALKIN' ABOUT THE SMELL COMIN' OUTTA YOUR BAG HERE.
YEAH, THAT'S RIGHT, DOC. I SAW THE WHOLE THING, AN' THEM WEREN'T NO BABY CALVES YOU JUST DELIVERED.
CASH COWS, MAYBE. SO SPARE ME THE INNOCENT.

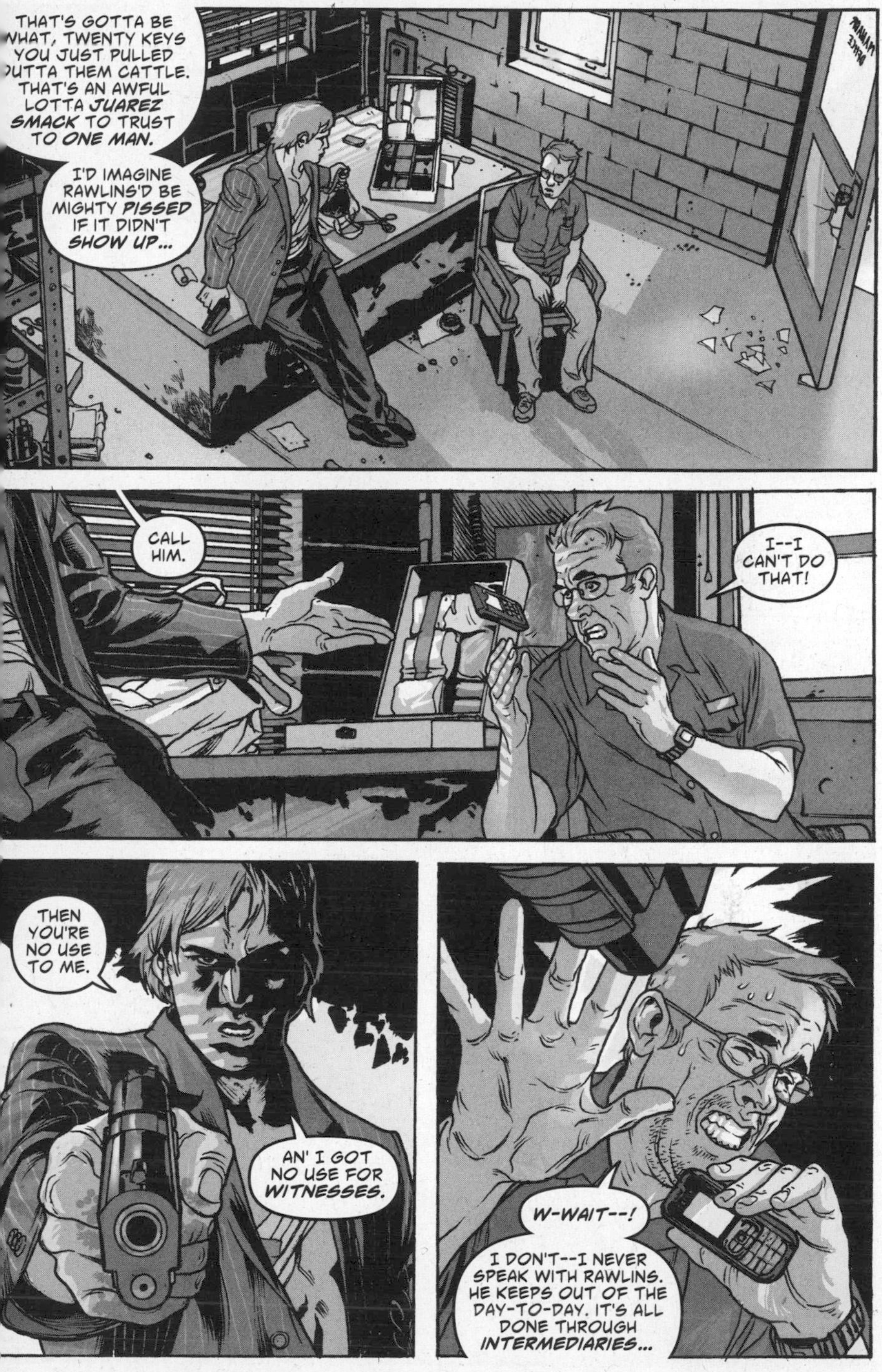
THAT'S GOTTA BE WHAT, TWENTY KEYS YOU JUST PULLED OUTTA THEM CATTLE. THAT'S AN AWFUL LOTTA JUAREZ SMACK TO TRUST TO ONE MAN.
I'D IMAGINE RAWLINS'D BE MIGHTY PISSED IF IT DIDN'T SHOW UP...
CALL HIM.
I--I CAN'T DO THAT!
THEN YOU'RE NO USE TO ME.
AN' I GOT NO USE FOR WITNESSES.
W-WAIT--!
I DON'T--I NEVER SPEAK WITH RAWLINS. HE KEEPS OUT OF THE DAY-TO-DAY. IT'S ALL DONE THROUGH INTERMEDIARIES...

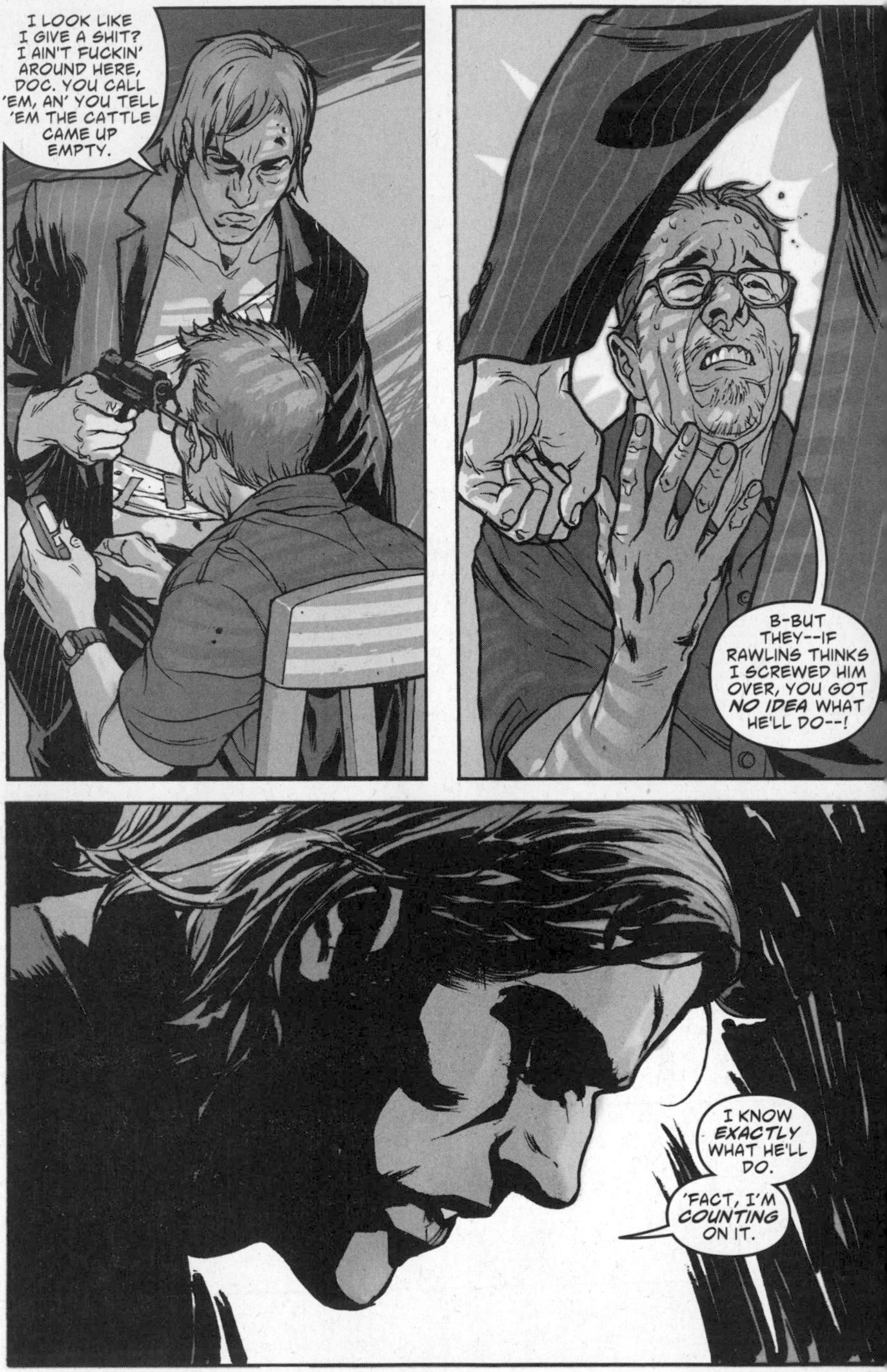
I LOOK LIKE I GIVE A SHIT? I AIN'T FUCKIN' AROUND HERE, DOC. YOU CALL 'EM, AN' YOU TELL 'EM THE CATTLE CAME UP EMPTY.
B-BUT THEY--IF RAWLINS THINKS I SCREWED HIM OVER, YOU GOT NO IDEA WHAT HE'LL DO--!
I KNOW EXACTLY WHAT HE'LL DO.
'FACT, I'M COUNTING ON IT.

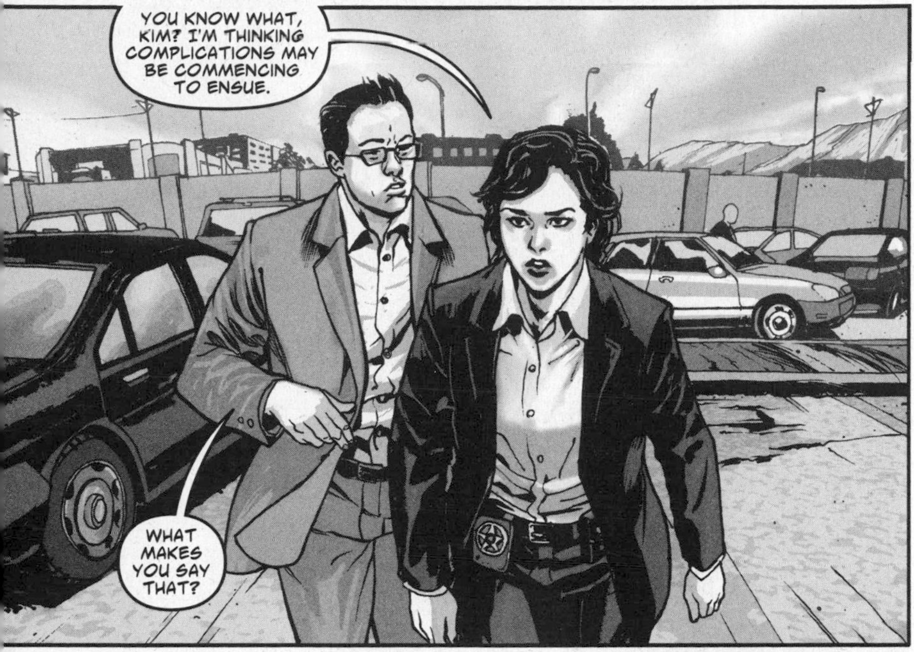
YOU KNOW WHAT, KIM? I'M THINKING COMPLICATIONS MAY BE COMMENCING TO ENSUE.
WHAT MAKES YOU SAY THAT?

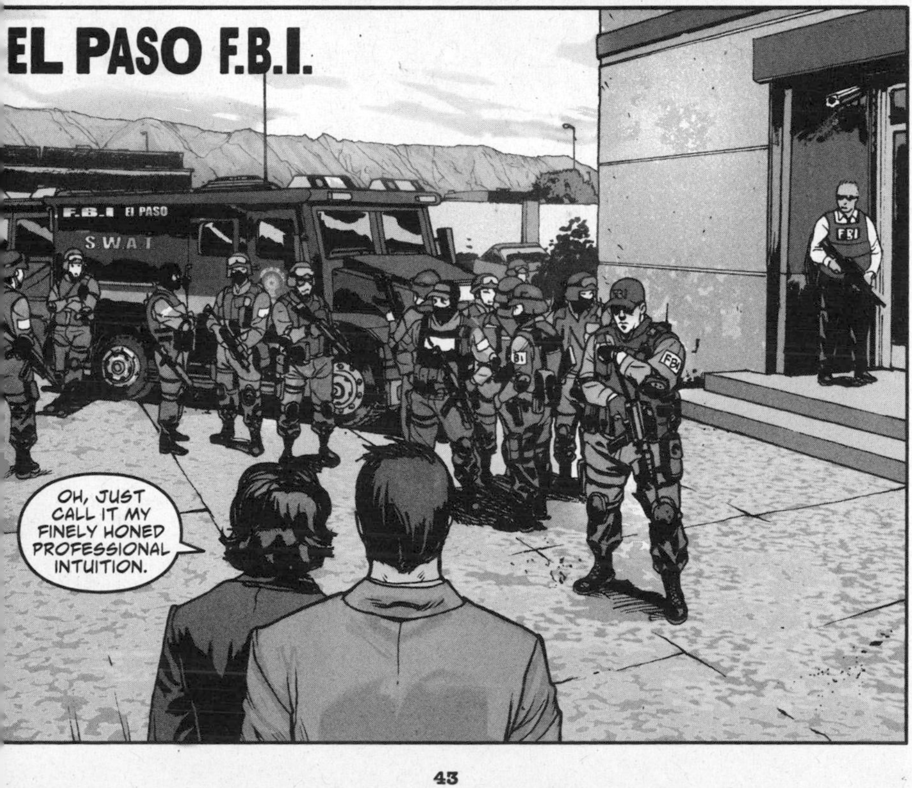
EL PASO F.B.I.
F.B.I EL PASO
S.W.A.T
FBI
OH, JUST CALL IT MY FINELY HONED PROFESSIONAL INTUITION.

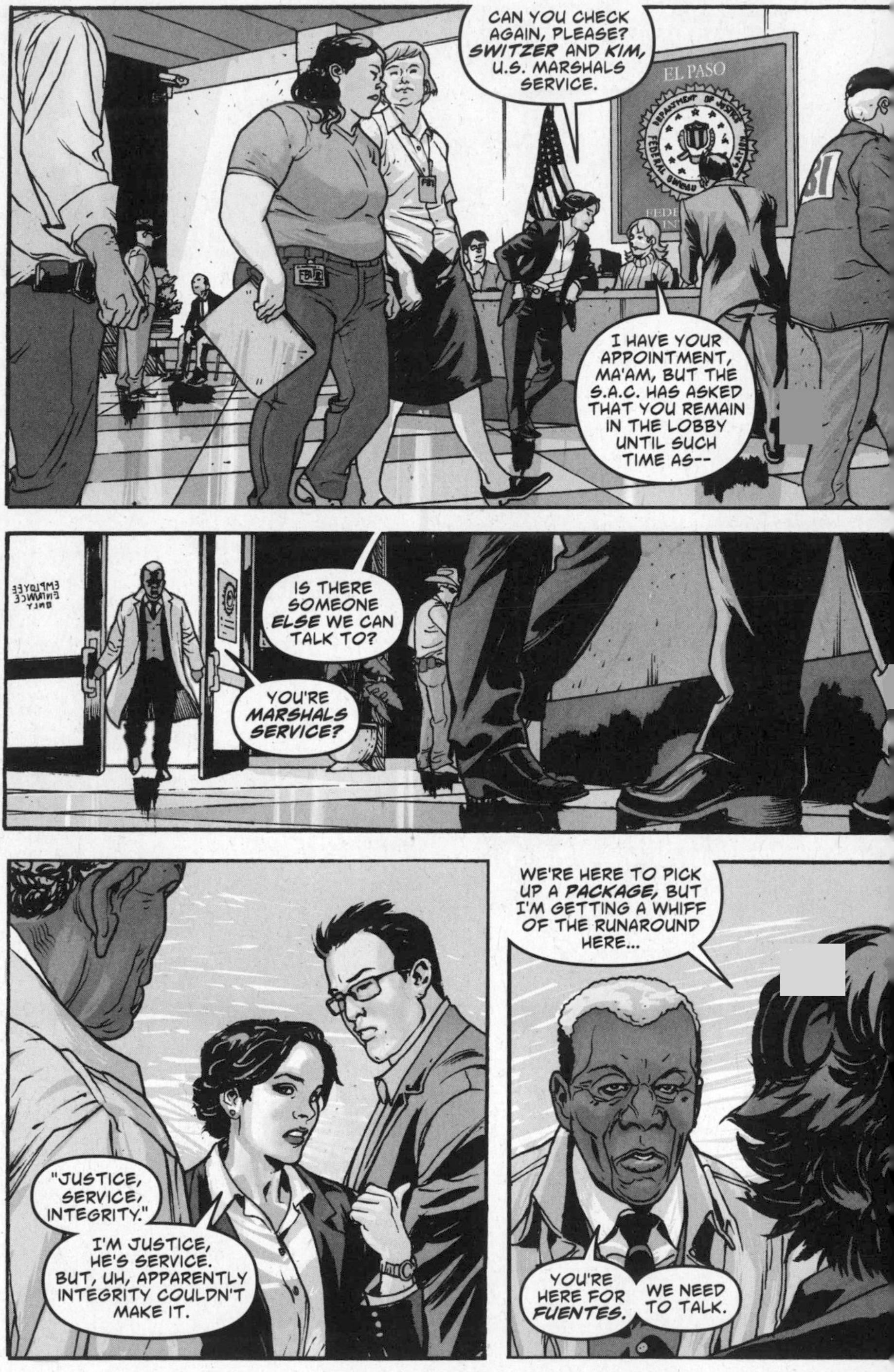
CAN YOU CHECK AGAIN, PLEASE? SWITZER AND KIM, U.S. MARSHALS SERVICE.
EL PASO
I HAVE YOUR APPOINTMENT, MA'AM, BUT THE S.A.C. HAS ASKED THAT YOU REMAIN IN THE LOBBY UNTIL SUCH TIME AS--
IS THERE SOMEONE ELSE WE CAN TALK TO?
YOU'RE MARSHALS SERVICE?
"JUSTICE, SERVICE, INTEGRITY."
I'M JUSTICE, HE'S SERVICE. BUT, UH, APPARENTLY INTEGRITY COULDN'T MAKE IT.
WE'RE HERE TO PICK UP A PACKAGE, BUT I'M GETTING A WHIFF OF THE RUNAROUND HERE...
YOU'RE HERE FOR FUENTES.
WE NEED TO TALK.

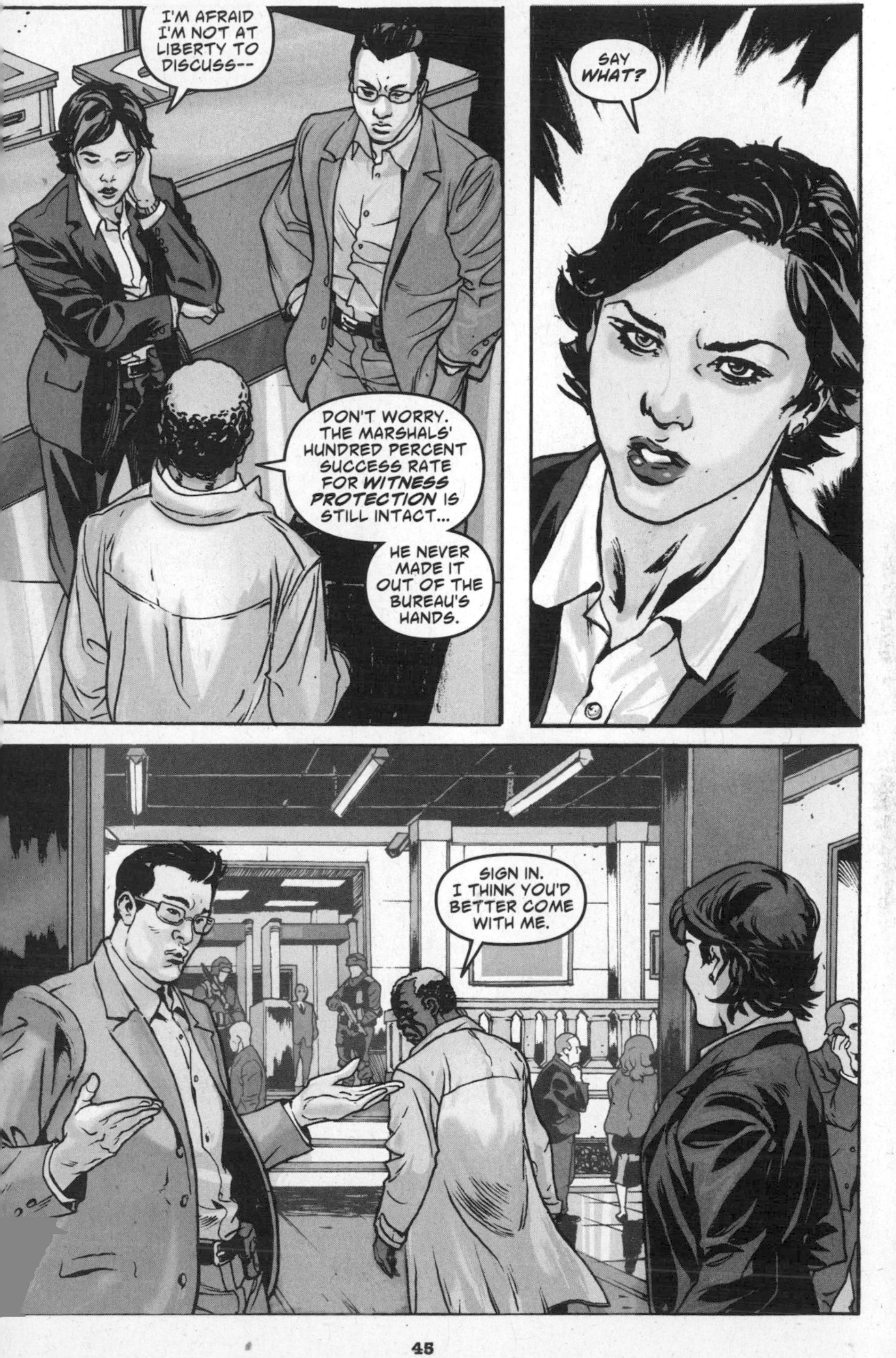
I'M AFRAID I'M NOT AT LIBERTY TO DISCUSS--
SAY WHAT?
DON'T WORRY. THE MARSHALS' HUNDRED PERCENT SUCCESS RATE FOR WITNESS PROTECTION IS STILL INTACT...
HE NEVER MADE IT OUT OF THE BUREAU'S HANDS.
SIGN IN. I THINK YOU'D BETTER COME WITH ME.

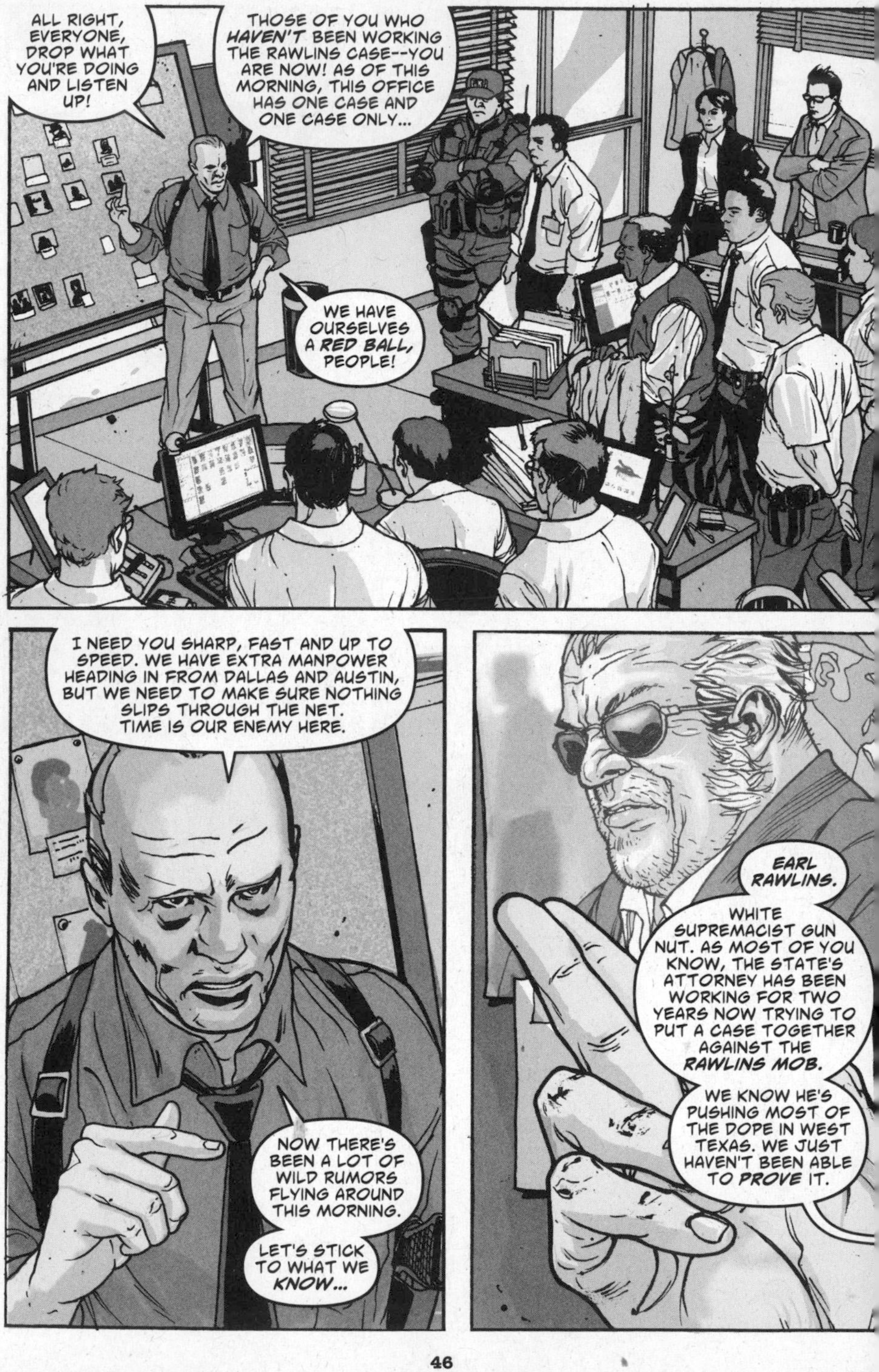
ALL RIGHT, EVERYONE, DROP WHAT YOU'RE DOING AND LISTEN UP!
THOSE OF YOU WHO *HAVEN'T* BEEN WORKING THE RAWLINS CASE--YOU ARE NOW! AS OF THIS MORNING, THIS OFFICE HAS ONE CASE AND ONE CASE ONLY...
WE HAVE OURSELVES A ***RED BALL,*** PEOPLE!
I NEED YOU SHARP, FAST AND UP TO SPEED. WE HAVE EXTRA MANPOWER HEADING IN FROM DALLAS AND AUSTIN, BUT WE NEED TO MAKE SURE NOTHING SLIPS THROUGH THE NET. TIME IS OUR ENEMY HERE.
NOW THERE'S BEEN A LOT OF WILD RUMORS FLYING AROUND THIS MORNING.
LET'S STICK TO WHAT WE ***KNOW...***
EARL RAWLINS.
WHITE SUPREMACIST GUN NUT. AS MOST OF YOU KNOW, THE STATE'S ATTORNEY HAS BEEN WORKING FOR TWO YEARS NOW TRYING TO PUT A CASE TOGETHER AGAINST THE ***RAWLINS MOB.***
WE KNOW HE'S PUSHING MOST OF THE DOPE IN WEST TEXAS. WE JUST HAVEN'T BEEN ABLE TO ***PROVE*** IT.

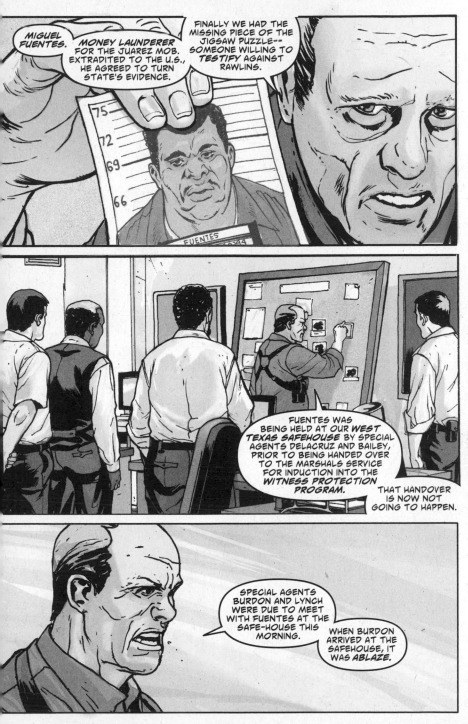

MIGUEL FUENTES. MONEY LAUNDERER FOR THE JUAREZ MOB. EXTRADITED TO THE U.S., HE AGREED TO TURN STATE'S EVIDENCE.

FINALLY WE HAD THE MISSING PIECE OF THE JIGSAW PUZZLE-- SOMEONE WILLING TO *TESTIFY* AGAINST RAWLINS.

FUENTES WAS BEING HELD AT OUR *WEST TEXAS SAFEHOUSE* BY SPECIAL AGENTS DELACRUZ AND BAILEY, PRIOR TO BEING HANDED OVER TO THE MARSHALS SERVICE FOR INDUCTION INTO THE *WITNESS PROTECTION PROGRAM.*

THAT HANDOVER IS NOW NOT GOING TO HAPPEN.

SPECIAL AGENTS BURDON AND LYNCH WERE DUE TO MEET WITH FUENTES AT THE SAFE-HOUSE THIS MORNING.

WHEN BURDON ARRIVED AT THE SAFEHOUSE, IT WAS *ABLAZE.*

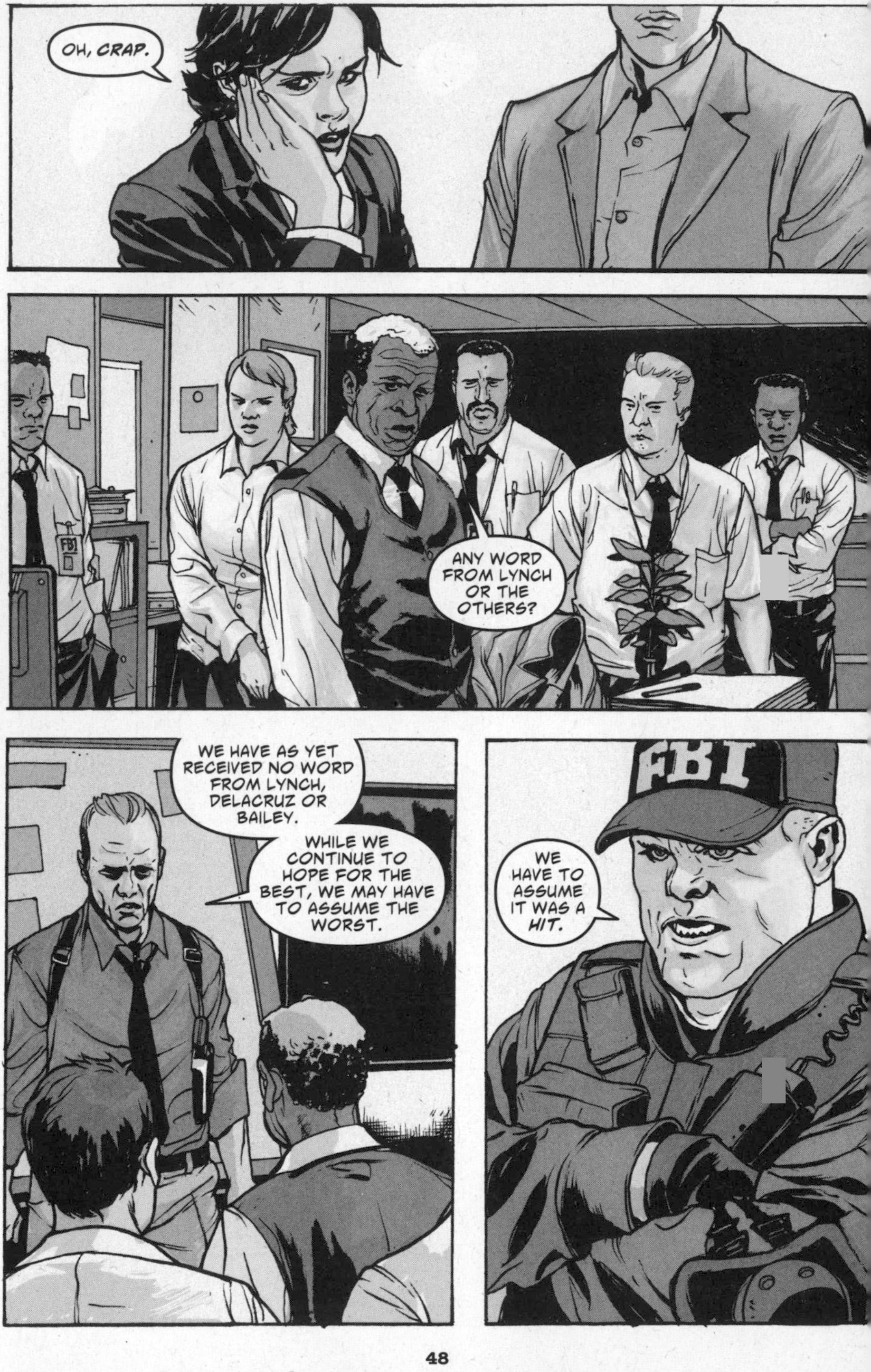
OH, CRAP.
ANY WORD FROM LYNCH OR THE OTHERS?
WE HAVE AS YET RECEIVED NO WORD FROM LYNCH, DELACRUZ OR BAILEY.
WHILE WE CONTINUE TO HOPE FOR THE BEST, WE MAY HAVE TO ASSUME THE WORST.
FBI
WE HAVE TO ASSUME IT WAS A *HIT*.

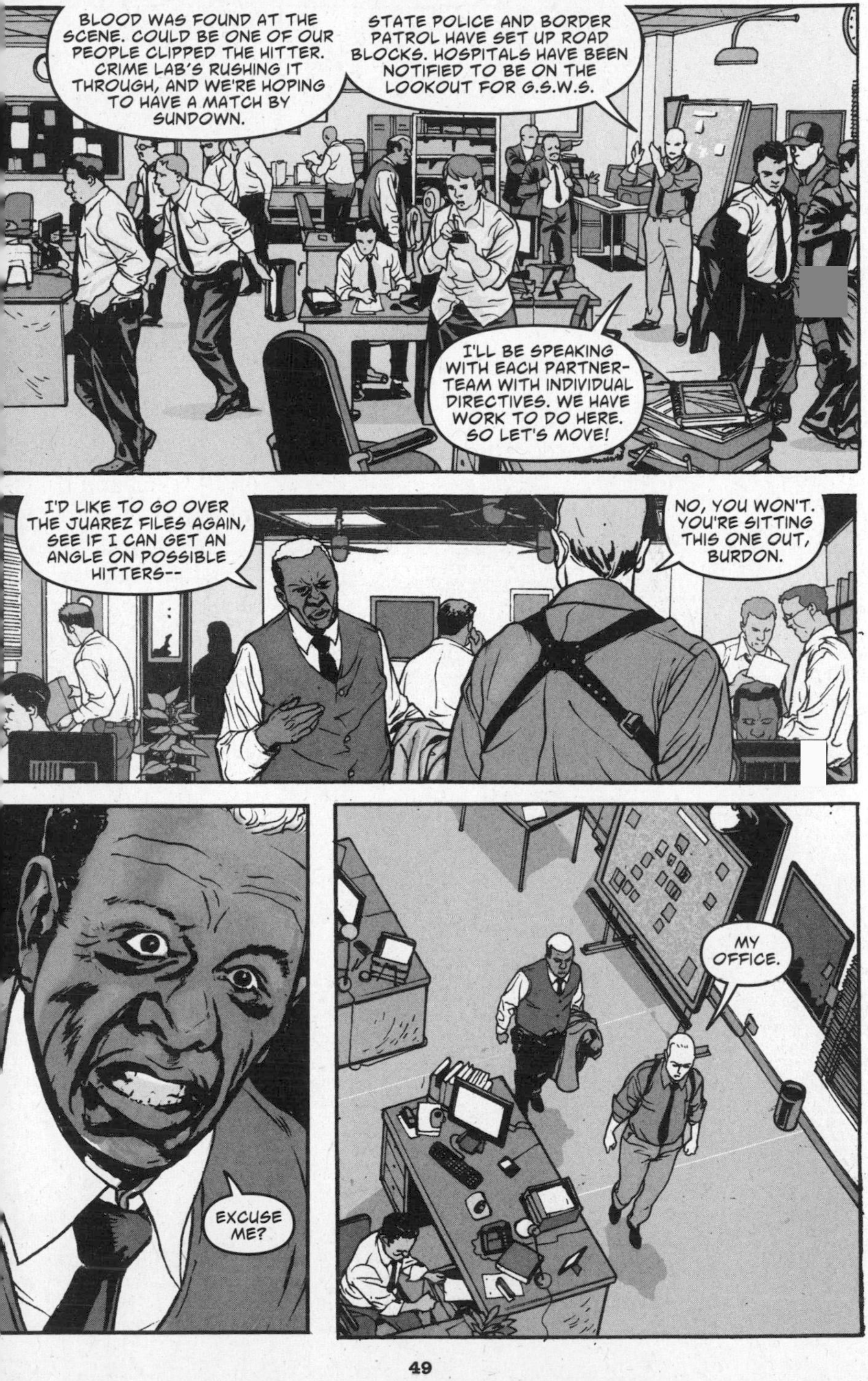
BLOOD WAS FOUND AT THE SCENE. COULD BE ONE OF OUR PEOPLE CLIPPED THE HITTER. CRIME LAB'S RUSHING IT THROUGH, AND WE'RE HOPING TO HAVE A MATCH BY SUNDOWN.
STATE POLICE AND BORDER PATROL HAVE SET UP ROAD BLOCKS. HOSPITALS HAVE BEEN NOTIFIED TO BE ON THE LOOKOUT FOR G.S.W.S.
I'LL BE SPEAKING WITH EACH PARTNER-TEAM WITH INDIVIDUAL DIRECTIVES. WE HAVE WORK TO DO HERE. SO LET'S MOVE!
I'D LIKE TO GO OVER THE JUAREZ FILES AGAIN, SEE IF I CAN GET AN ANGLE ON POSSIBLE HITTERS--
NO, YOU WON'T. YOU'RE SITTING THIS ONE OUT, BURDON.
EXCUSE ME?
MY OFFICE.

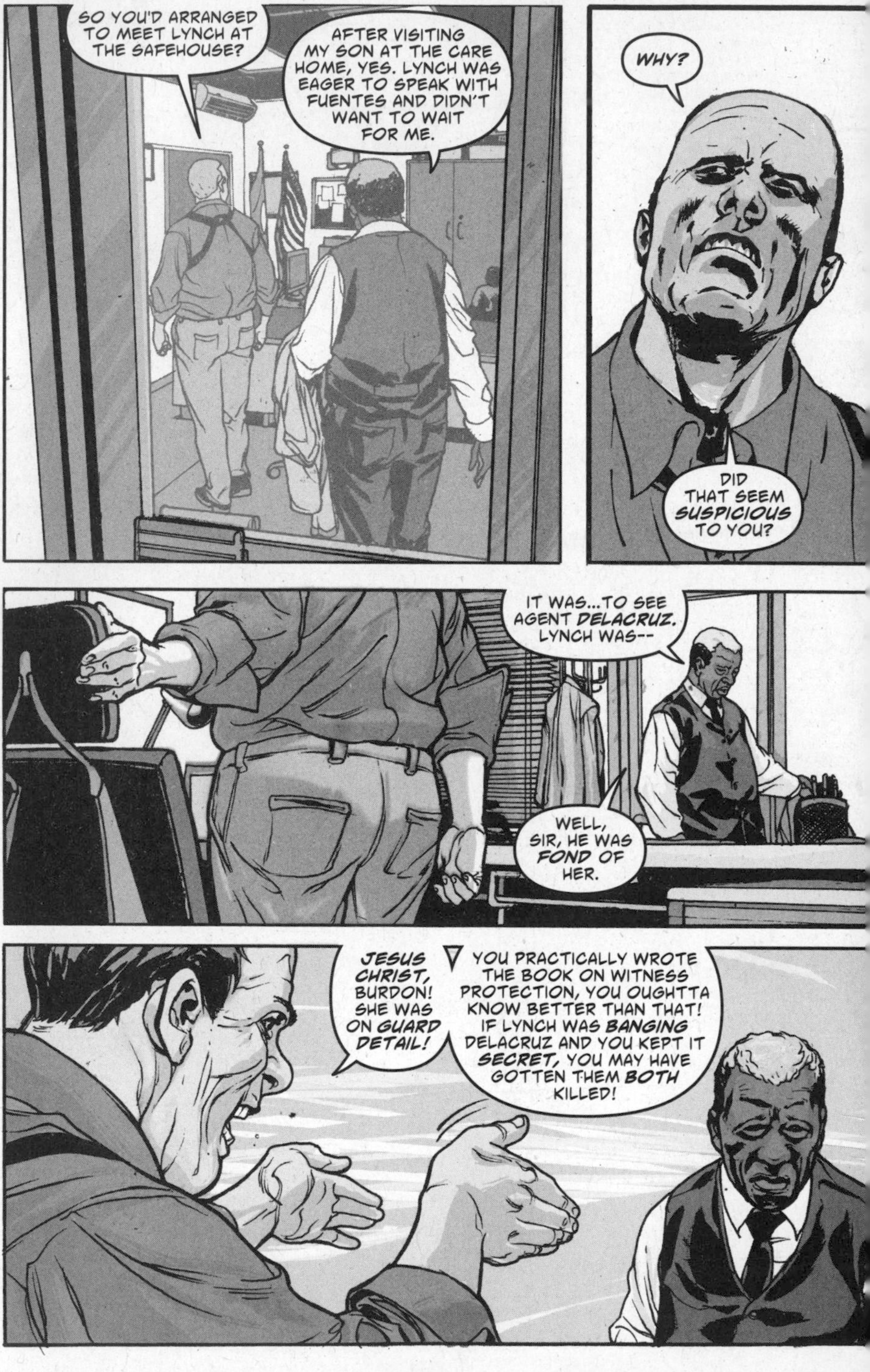
SO YOU'D ARRANGED TO MEET LYNCH AT THE SAFEHOUSE?
AFTER VISITING MY SON AT THE CARE HOME, YES. LYNCH WAS EAGER TO SPEAK WITH FUENTES AND DIDN'T WANT TO WAIT FOR ME.
WHY?
DID THAT SEEM SUSPICIOUS TO YOU?
IT WAS...TO SEE AGENT DELACRUZ. LYNCH WAS--
WELL, SIR, HE WAS FOND OF HER.
JESUS CHRIST, BURDON! SHE WAS ON GUARD DETAIL!
YOU PRACTICALLY WROTE THE BOOK ON WITNESS PROTECTION, YOU OUGHTTA KNOW BETTER THAN THAT! IF LYNCH WAS BANGING DELACRUZ AND YOU KEPT IT SECRET, YOU MAY HAVE GOTTEN THEM BOTH KILLED!

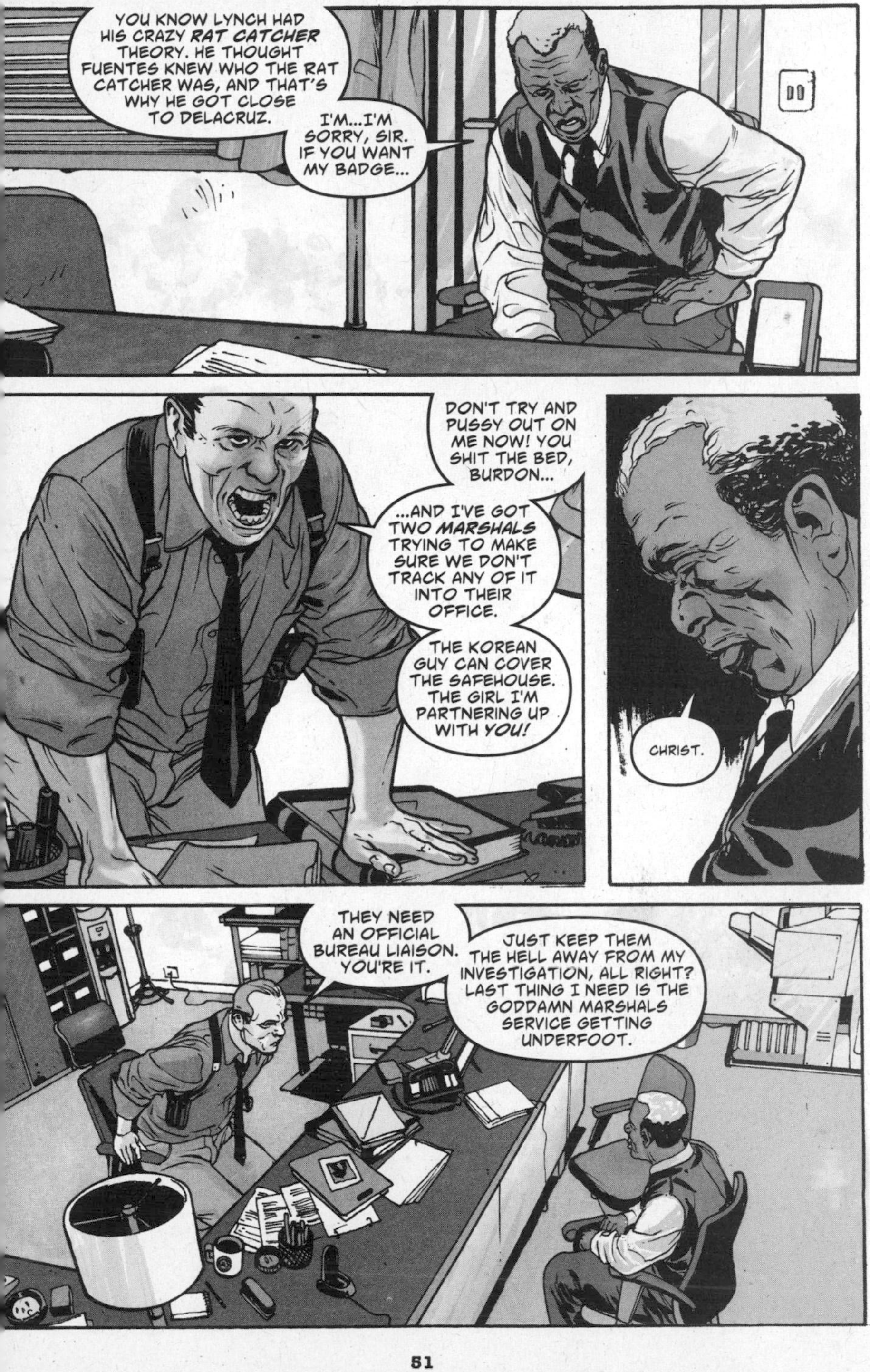
YOU KNOW LYNCH HAD HIS CRAZY RAT CATCHER THEORY. HE THOUGHT FUENTES KNEW WHO THE RAT CATCHER WAS, AND THAT'S WHY HE GOT CLOSE TO DELACRUZ.
I'M...I'M SORRY, SIR. IF YOU WANT MY BADGE...
DON'T TRY AND PUSSY OUT ON ME NOW! YOU SHIT THE BED, BURDON...
...AND I'VE GOT TWO MARSHALS TRYING TO MAKE SURE WE DON'T TRACK ANY OF IT INTO THEIR OFFICE.
THE KOREAN GUY CAN COVER THE SAFEHOUSE. THE GIRL I'M PARTNERING UP WITH YOU!
CHRIST.
THEY NEED AN OFFICIAL BUREAU LIAISON. YOU'RE IT.
JUST KEEP THEM THE HELL AWAY FROM MY INVESTIGATION, ALL RIGHT? LAST THING I NEED IS THE GODDAMN MARSHALS SERVICE GETTING UNDERFOOT.

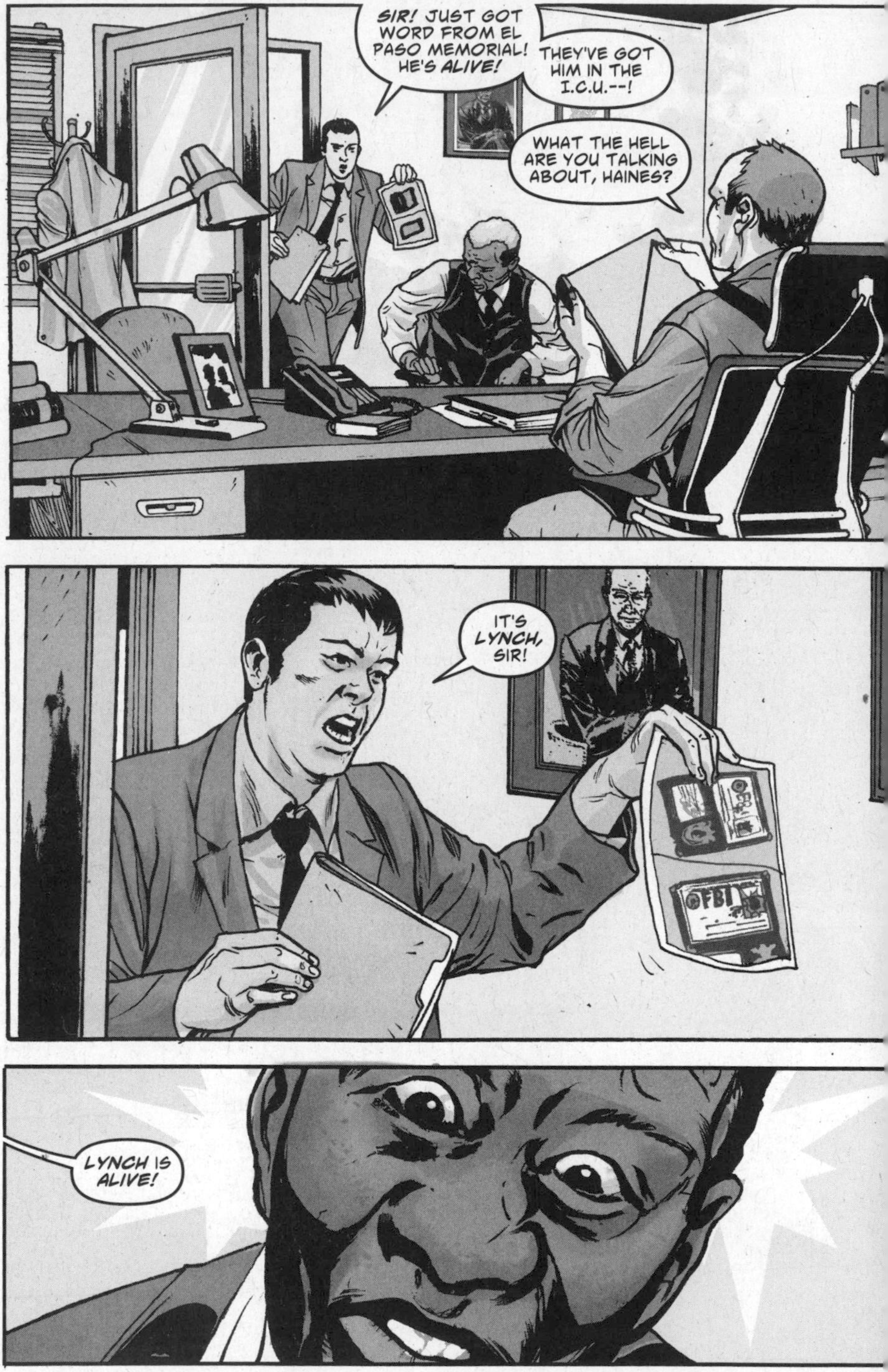
SIR! JUST GOT WORD FROM EL PASO MEMORIAL! HE'S ALIVE!
THEY'VE GOT HIM IN THE I.C.U.--!
WHAT THE HELL ARE YOU TALKING ABOUT, HAINES?
IT'S LYNCH, SIR!
FBI
LYNCH IS ALIVE!

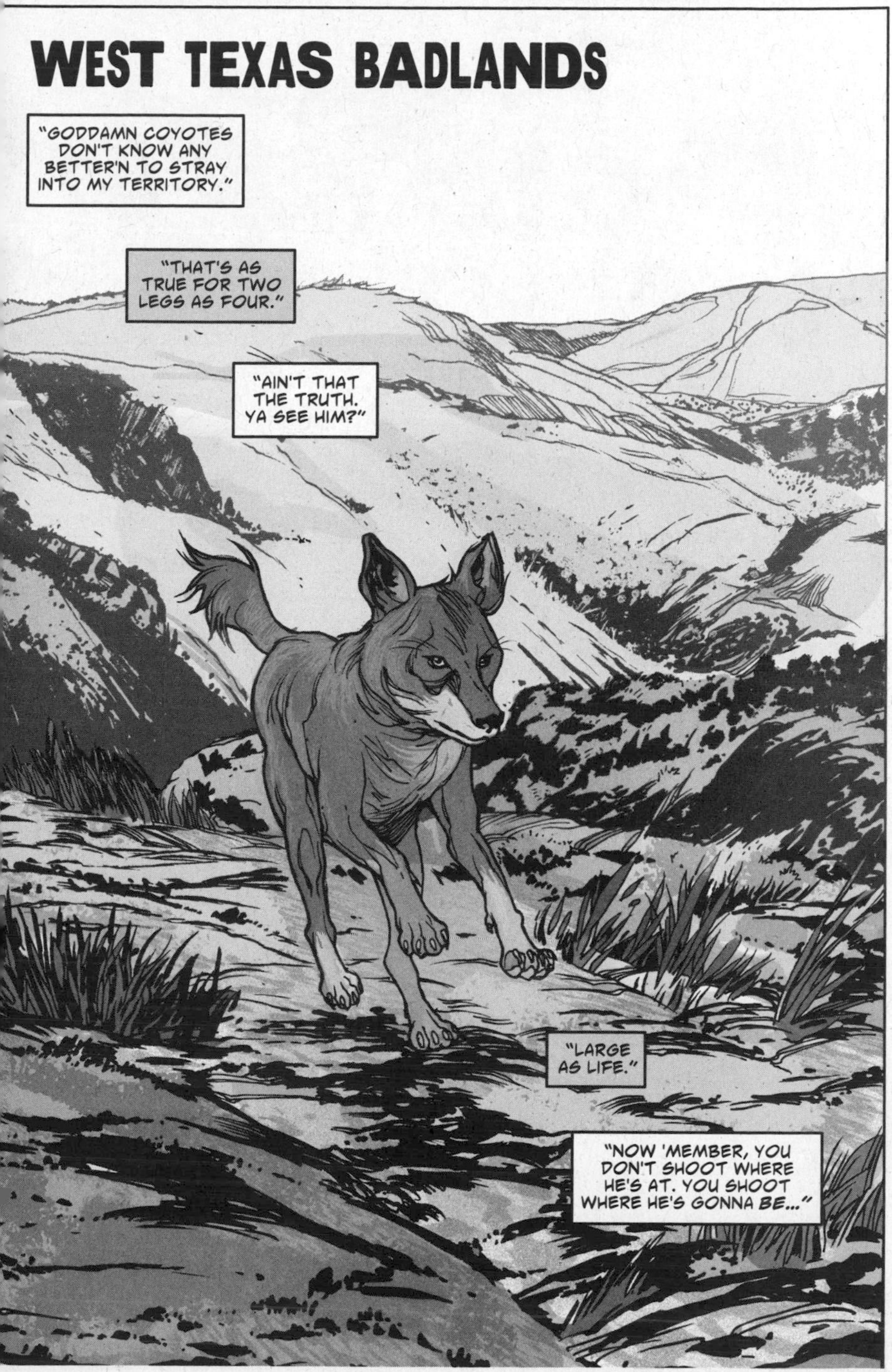
WEST TEXAS BADLANDS
"GODDAMN COYOTES DON'T KNOW ANY BETTER'N TO STRAY INTO MY TERRITORY."
"THAT'S AS TRUE FOR TWO LEGS AS FOUR."
"AIN'T THAT THE TRUTH. YA SEE HIM?"
"LARGE AS LIFE."
"NOW 'MEMBER, YOU DON'T SHOOT WHERE HE'S AT. YOU SHOOT WHERE HE'S GONNA BE..."

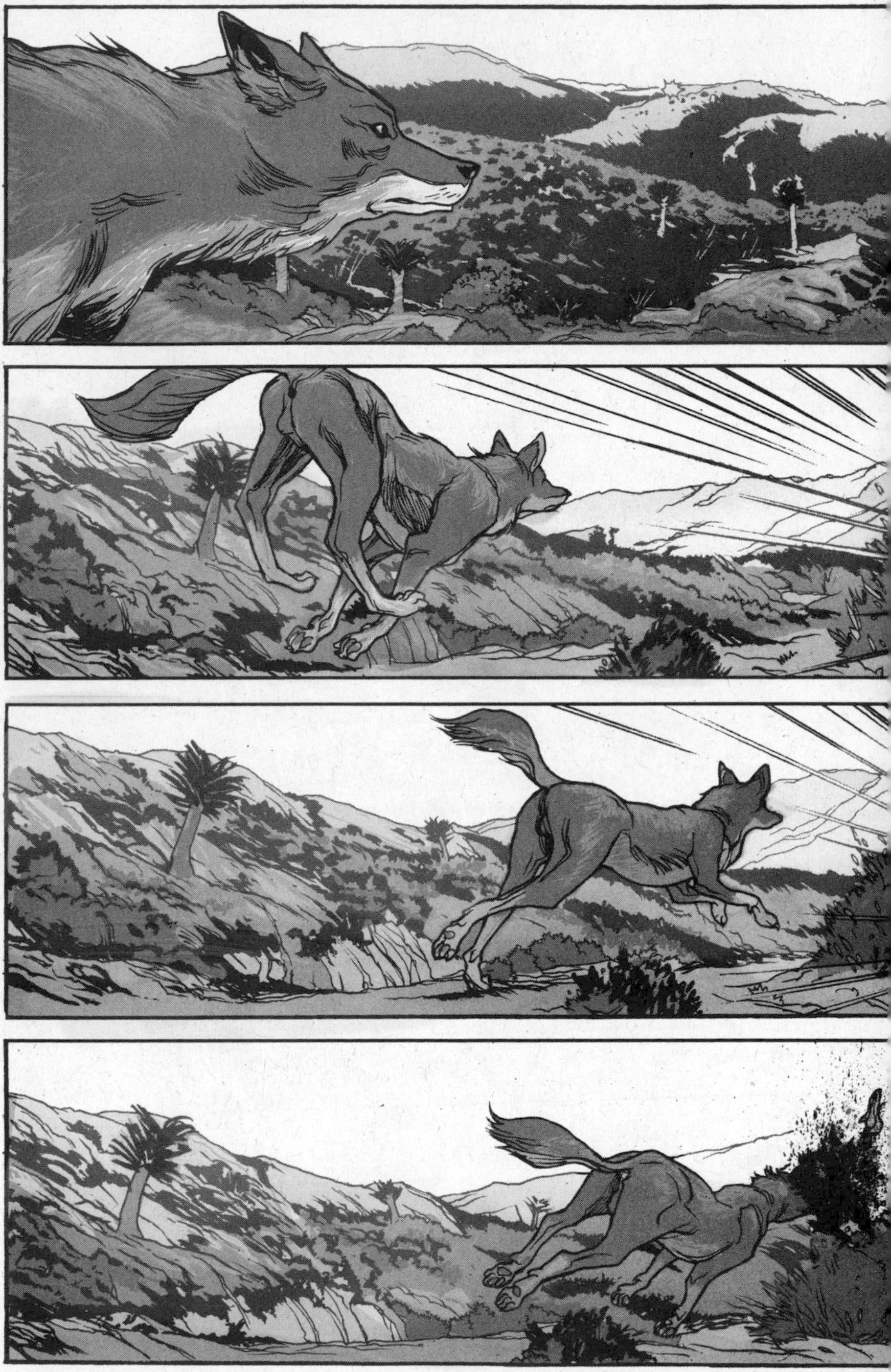

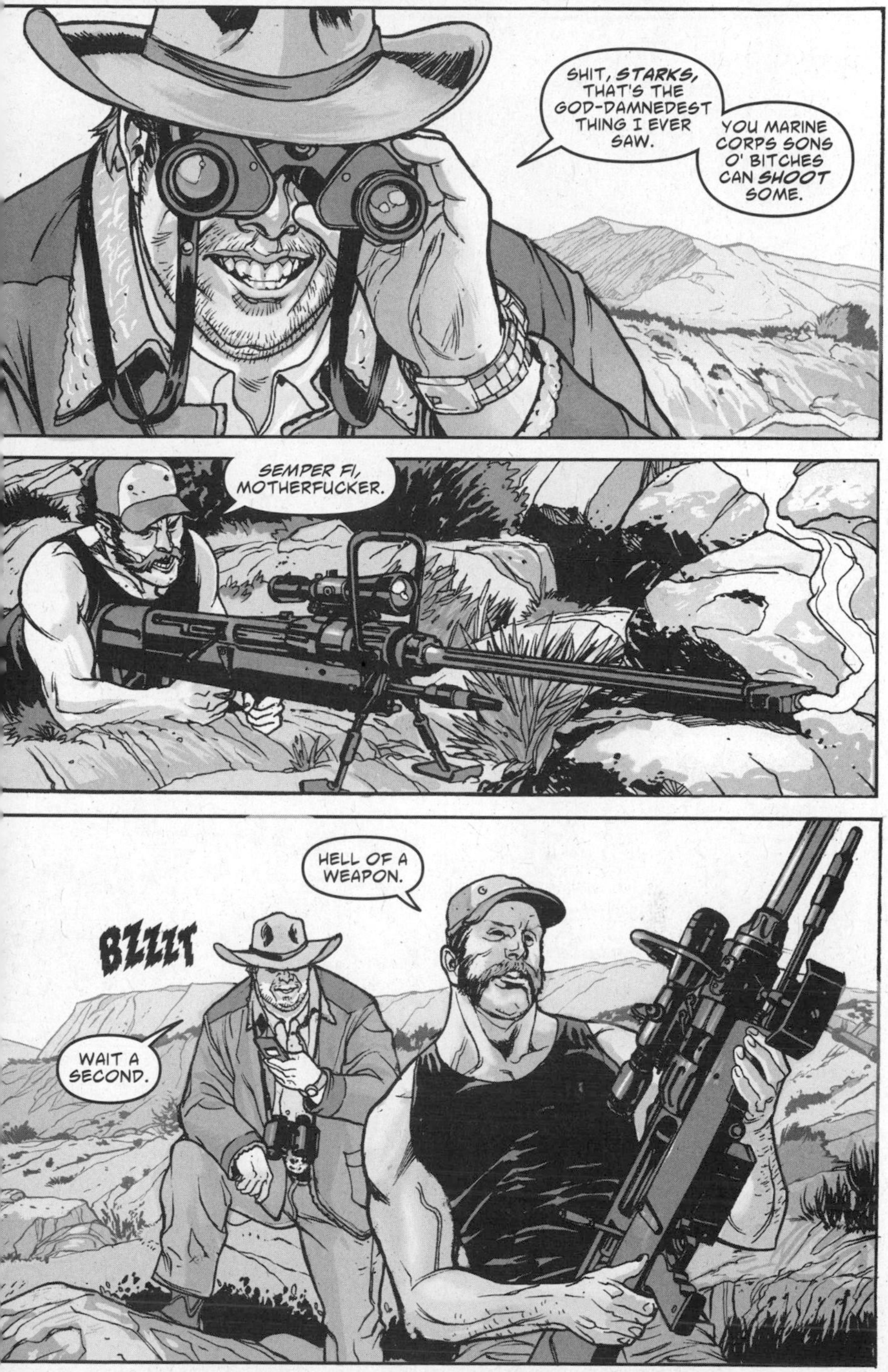
SHIT, STARKS, THAT'S THE GOD-DAMNEDEST THING I EVER SAW.
YOU MARINE CORPS SONS O' BITCHES CAN SHOOT SOME.
SEMPER FI, MOTHERFUCKER.
HELL OF A WEAPON.
BZZZT
WAIT A SECOND.

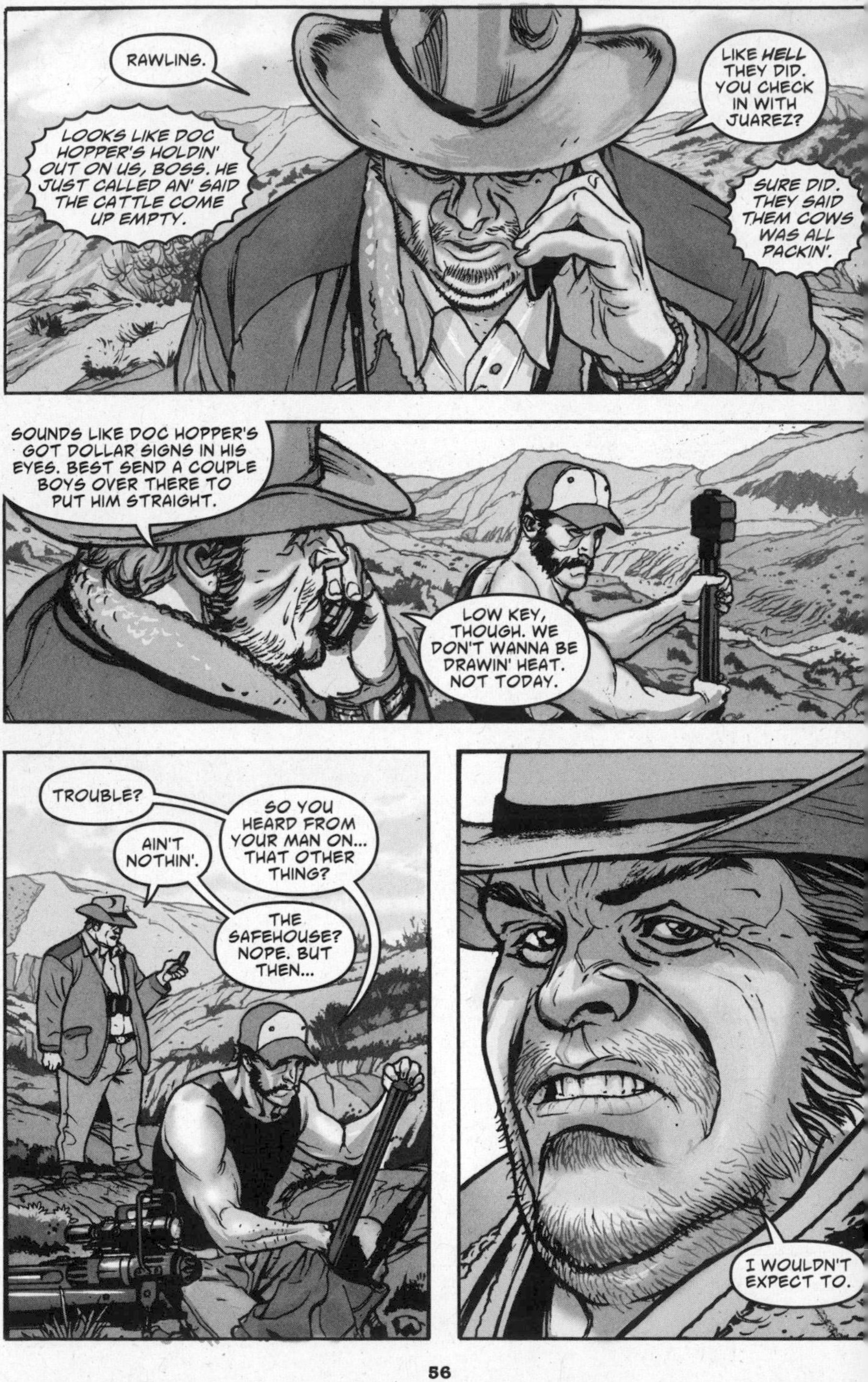
RAWLINS.
LOOKS LIKE DOC HOPPER'S HOLDIN' OUT ON US, BOSS. HE JUST CALLED AN' SAID THE CATTLE COME UP EMPTY.
LIKE HELL THEY DID. YOU CHECK IN WITH JUAREZ?
SURE DID. THEY SAID THEM COWS WAS ALL PACKIN'.
SOUNDS LIKE DOC HOPPER'S GOT DOLLAR SIGNS IN HIS EYES. BEST SEND A COUPLE BOYS OVER THERE TO PUT HIM STRAIGHT.
LOW KEY, THOUGH. WE DON'T WANNA BE DRAWIN' HEAT. NOT TODAY.
TROUBLE?
AIN'T NOTHIN'.
SO YOU HEARD FROM YOUR MAN ON... THAT OTHER THING?
THE SAFEHOUSE? NOPE. BUT THEN...
I WOULDN'T EXPECT TO.

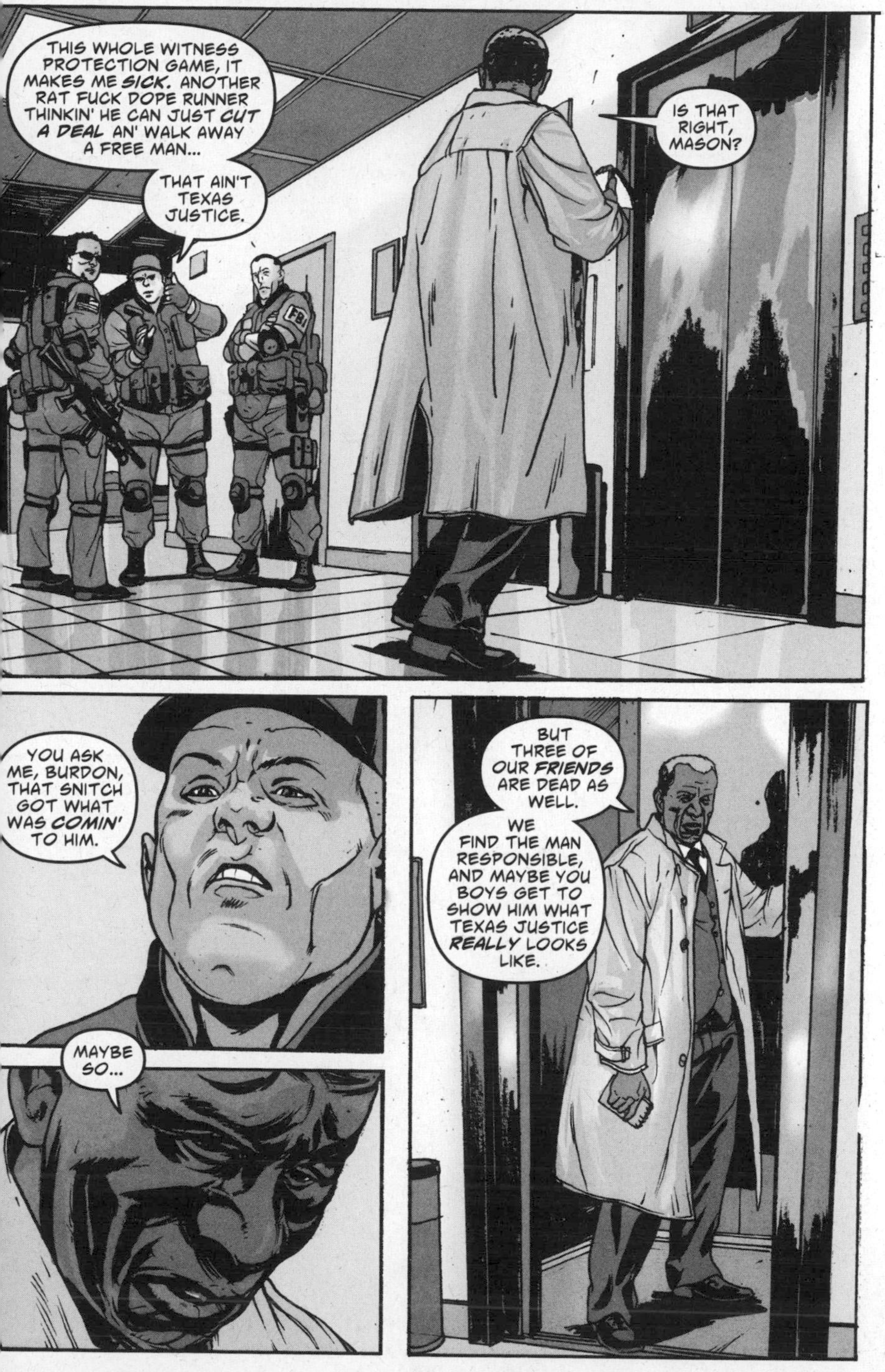
THIS WHOLE WITNESS PROTECTION GAME, IT MAKES ME SICK. ANOTHER RAT FUCK DOPE RUNNER THINKIN' HE CAN JUST CUT A DEAL AN' WALK AWAY A FREE MAN...
THAT AIN'T TEXAS JUSTICE.
IS THAT RIGHT, MASON?
YOU ASK ME, BURDON, THAT SNITCH GOT WHAT WAS COMIN' TO HIM.
MAYBE SO...
BUT THREE OF OUR FRIENDS ARE DEAD AS WELL.
WE FIND THE MAN RESPONSIBLE, AND MAYBE YOU BOYS GET TO SHOW HIM WHAT TEXAS JUSTICE REALLY LOOKS LIKE.

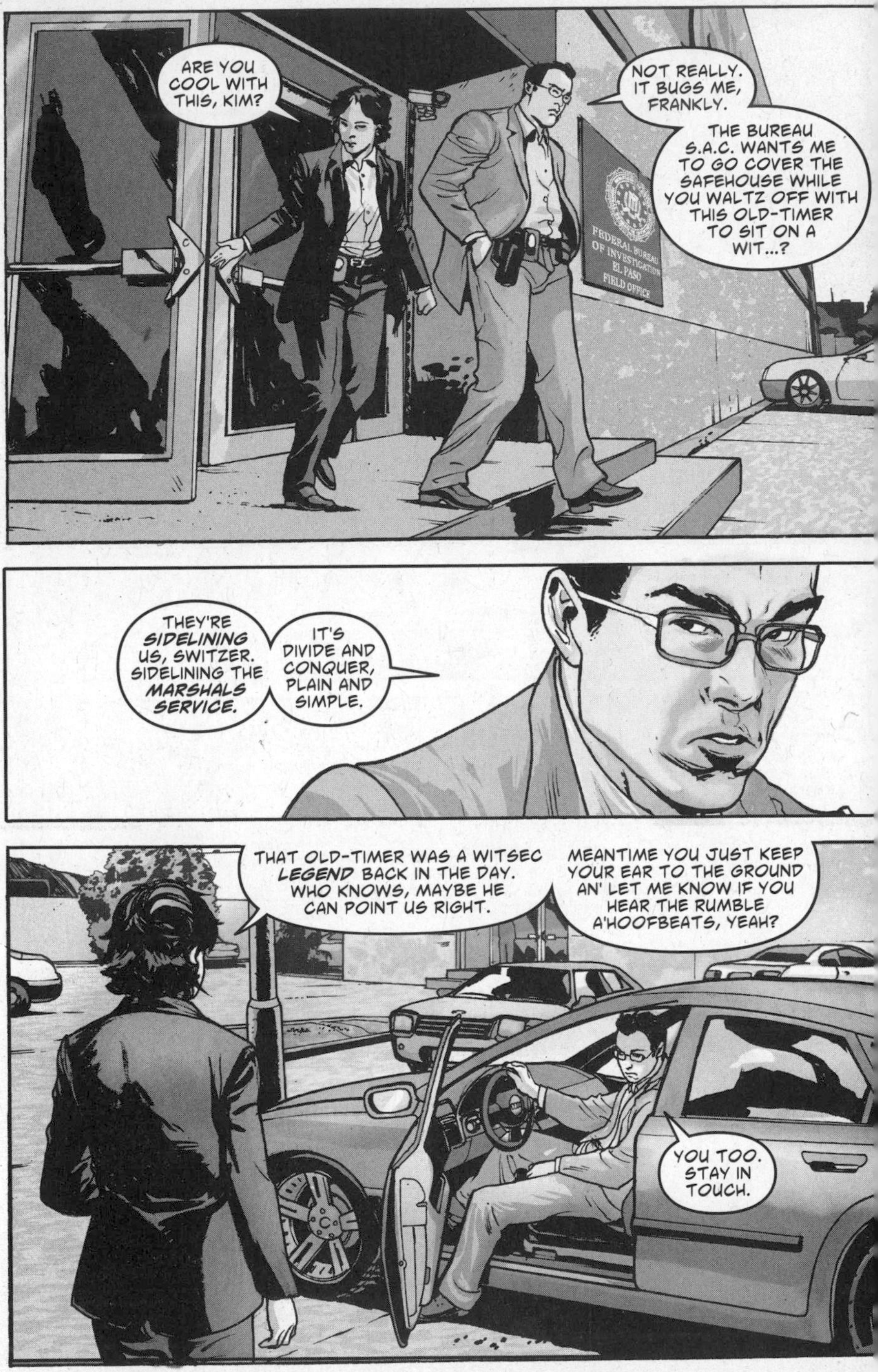
ARE YOU COOL WITH THIS, KIM?
NOT REALLY. IT BUGS ME, FRANKLY.
THE BUREAU S.A.C. WANTS ME TO GO COVER THE SAFEHOUSE WHILE YOU WALTZ OFF WITH THIS OLD-TIMER TO SIT ON A WIT...?
FEDERAL BUREAU OF INVESTIGATION EL PASO FIELD OFFICE
THEY'RE *SIDELINING* US, SWITZER. SIDELINING THE *MARSHALS SERVICE.*
IT'S DIVIDE AND CONQUER, PLAIN AND SIMPLE.
THAT OLD-TIMER WAS A WITSEC *LEGEND* BACK IN THE DAY. WHO KNOWS, MAYBE HE CAN POINT US RIGHT.
MEANTIME YOU JUST KEEP YOUR EAR TO THE GROUND AN' LET ME KNOW IF YOU HEAR THE RUMBLE A'HOOFBEATS, YEAH?
YOU TOO. STAY IN TOUCH.

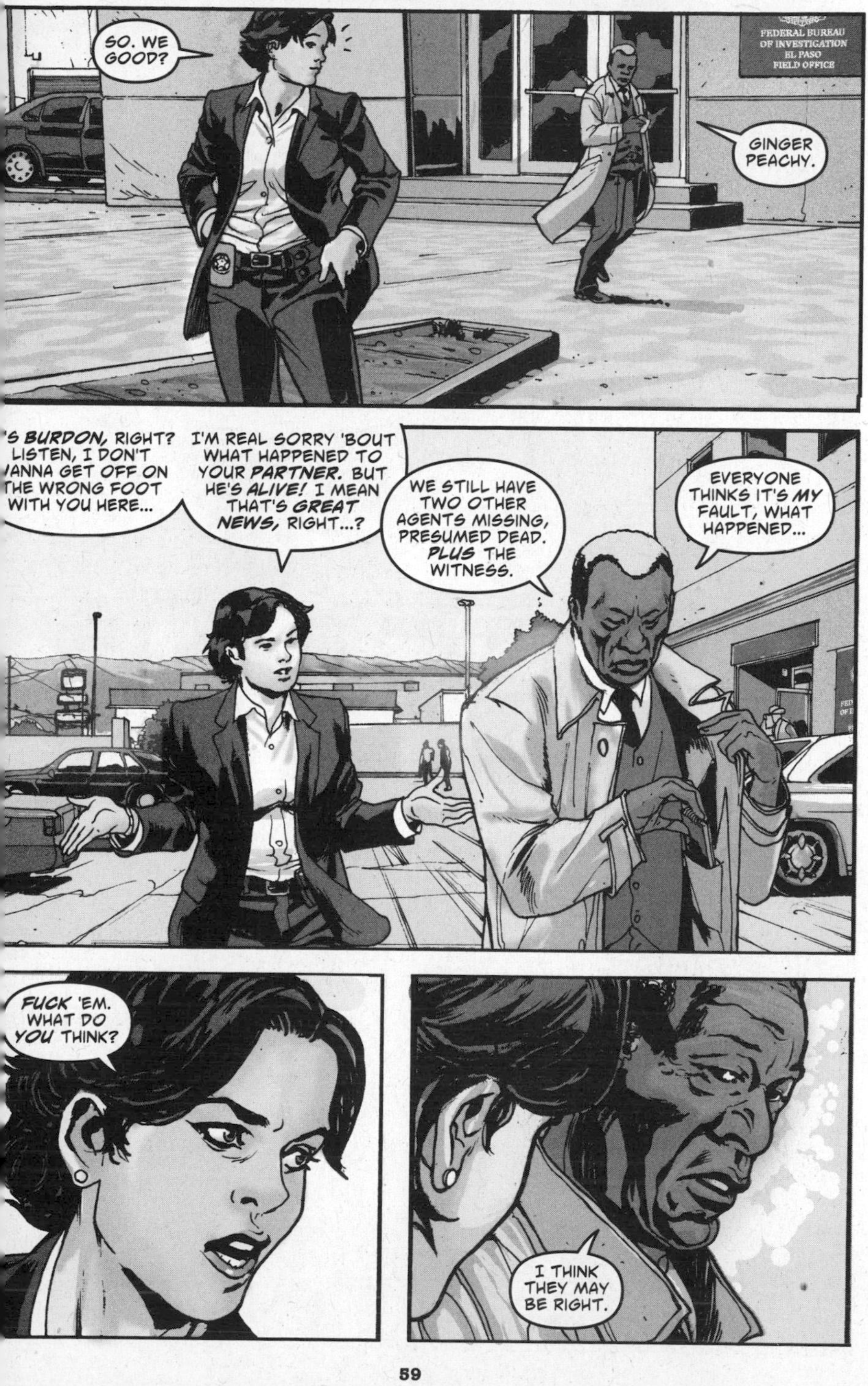
SO. WE GOOD?
FEDERAL BUREAU OF INVESTIGATION EL PASO FIELD OFFICE
GINGER PEACHY.
'S BURDON, RIGHT? LISTEN, I DON'T WANNA GET OFF ON THE WRONG FOOT WITH YOU HERE...
I'M REAL SORRY 'BOUT WHAT HAPPENED TO YOUR PARTNER. BUT HE'S ALIVE! I MEAN THAT'S GREAT NEWS, RIGHT...?
WE STILL HAVE TWO OTHER AGENTS MISSING, PRESUMED DEAD. PLUS THE WITNESS.
EVERYONE THINKS IT'S MY FAULT, WHAT HAPPENED...
FUCK 'EM. WHAT DO YOU THINK?
I THINK THEY MAY BE RIGHT.

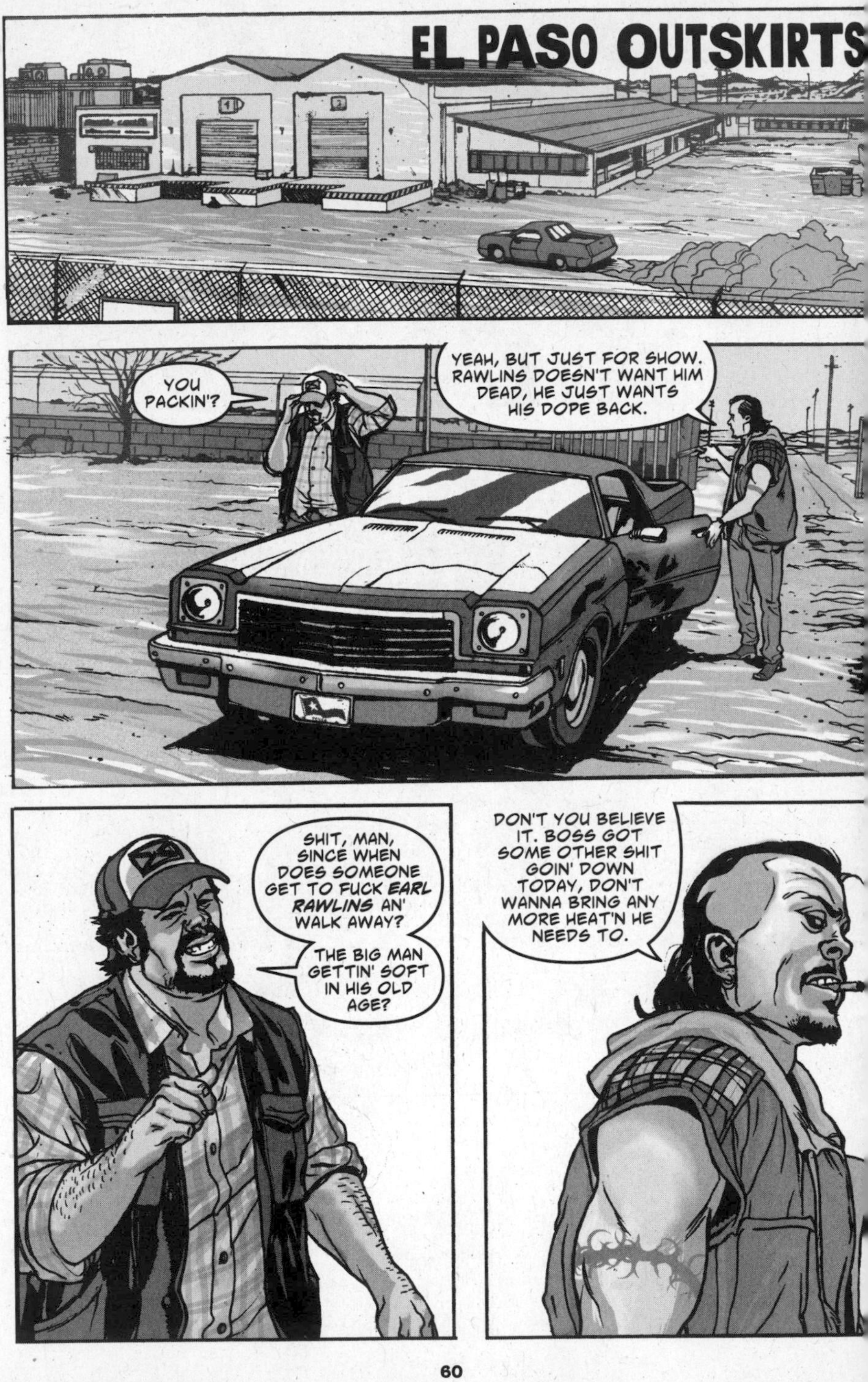
EL PASO OUTSKIRTS
YOU PACKIN'?
YEAH, BUT JUST FOR SHOW. RAWLINS DOESN'T WANT HIM DEAD, HE JUST WANTS HIS DOPE BACK.
SHIT, MAN, SINCE WHEN DOES SOMEONE GET TO FUCK EARL RAWLINS AN' WALK AWAY?
THE BIG MAN GETTIN' SOFT IN HIS OLD AGE?
DON'T YOU BELIEVE IT. BOSS GOT SOME OTHER SHIT GOIN' DOWN TODAY, DON'T WANNA BRING ANY MORE HEAT'N HE NEEDS TO.

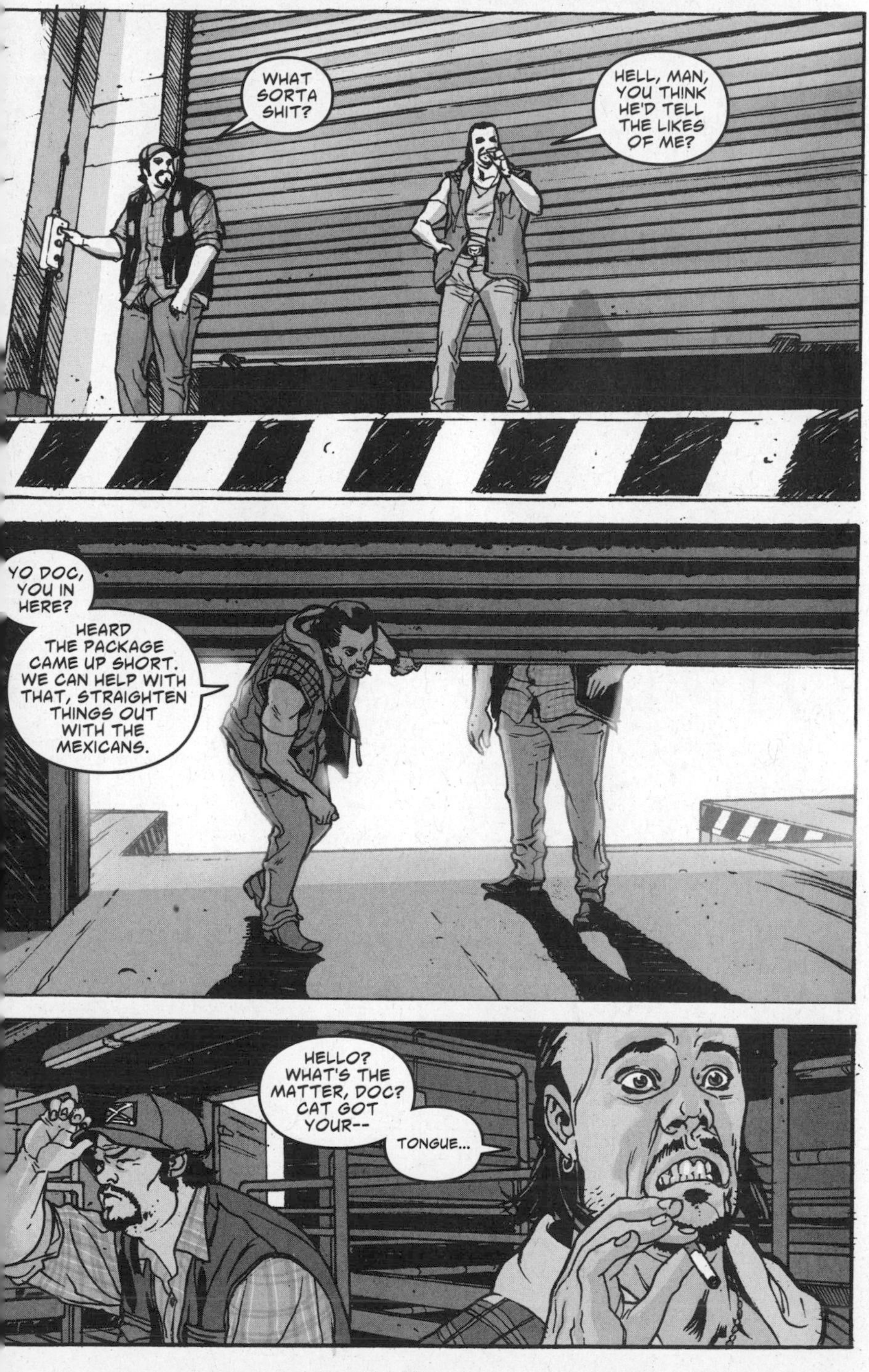
WHAT SORTA SHIT?
HELL, MAN, YOU THINK HE'D TELL THE LIKES OF ME?
YO DOC, YOU IN HERE?
HEARD THE PACKAGE CAME UP SHORT. WE CAN HELP WITH THAT, STRAIGHTEN THINGS OUT WITH THE MEXICANS.
HELLO? WHAT'S THE MATTER, DOC? CAT GOT YOUR--
TONGUE...

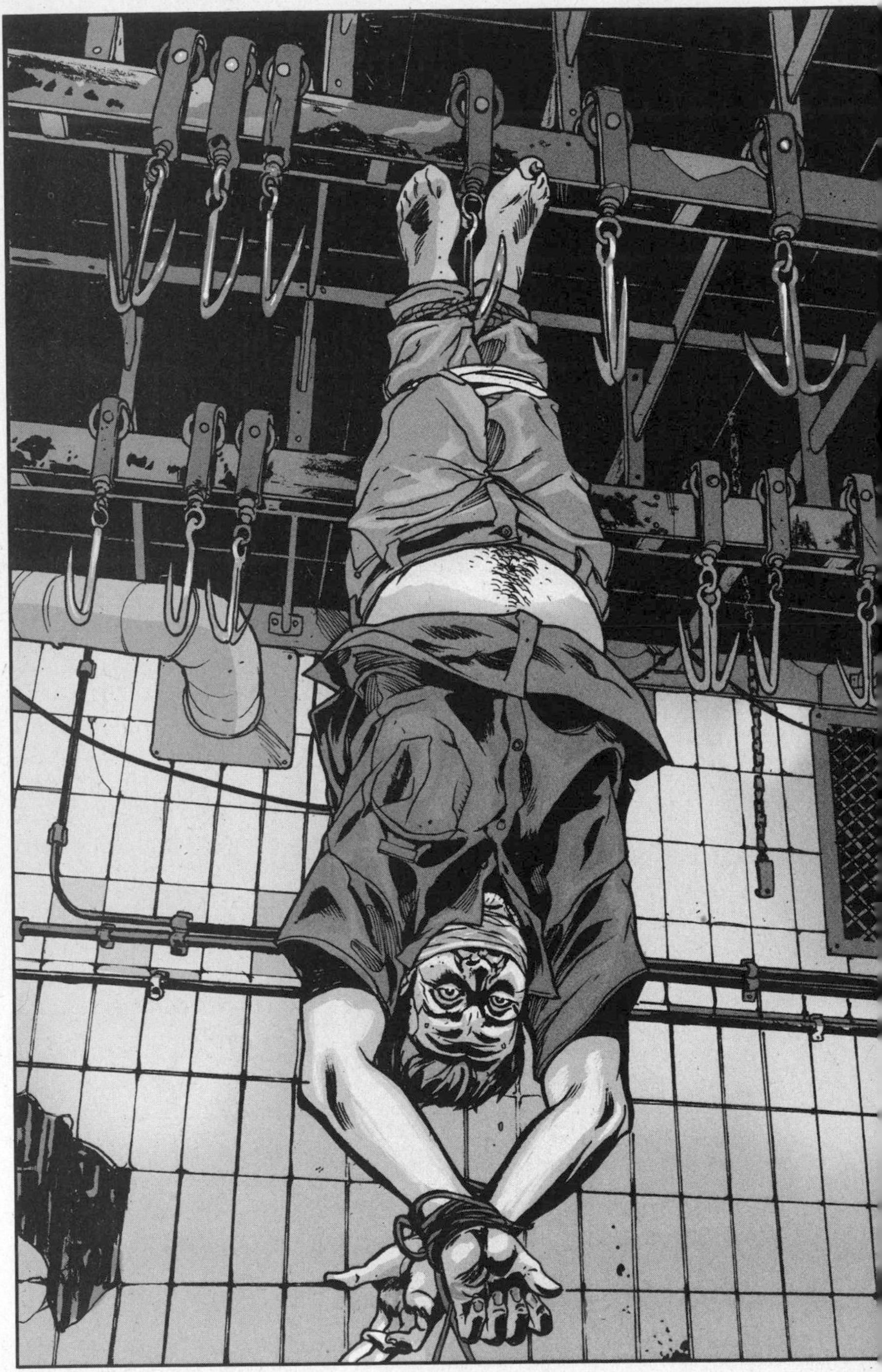

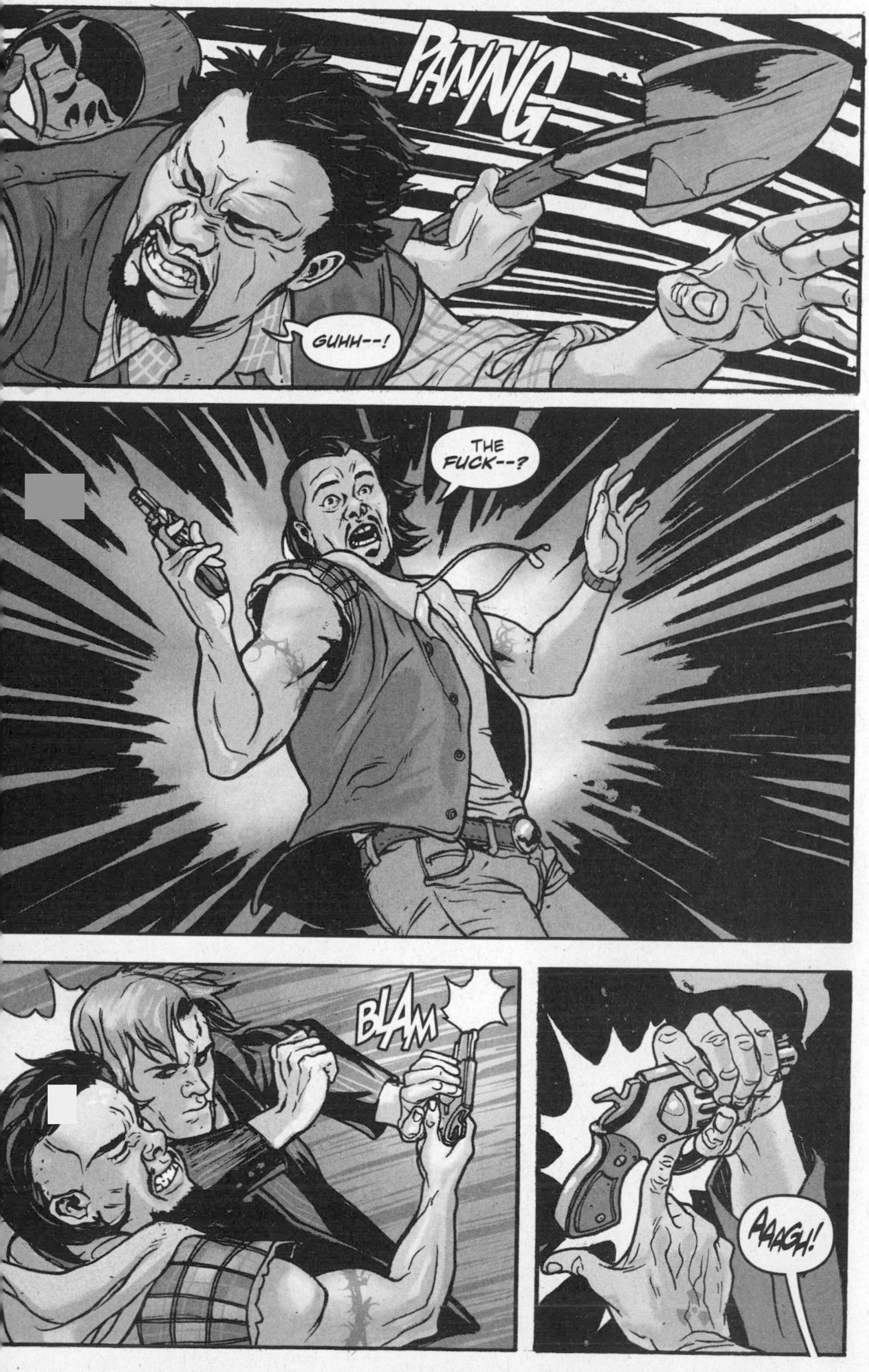
PANNG
GUHH--!
THE FUCK--?
BLAM
AAAGH!

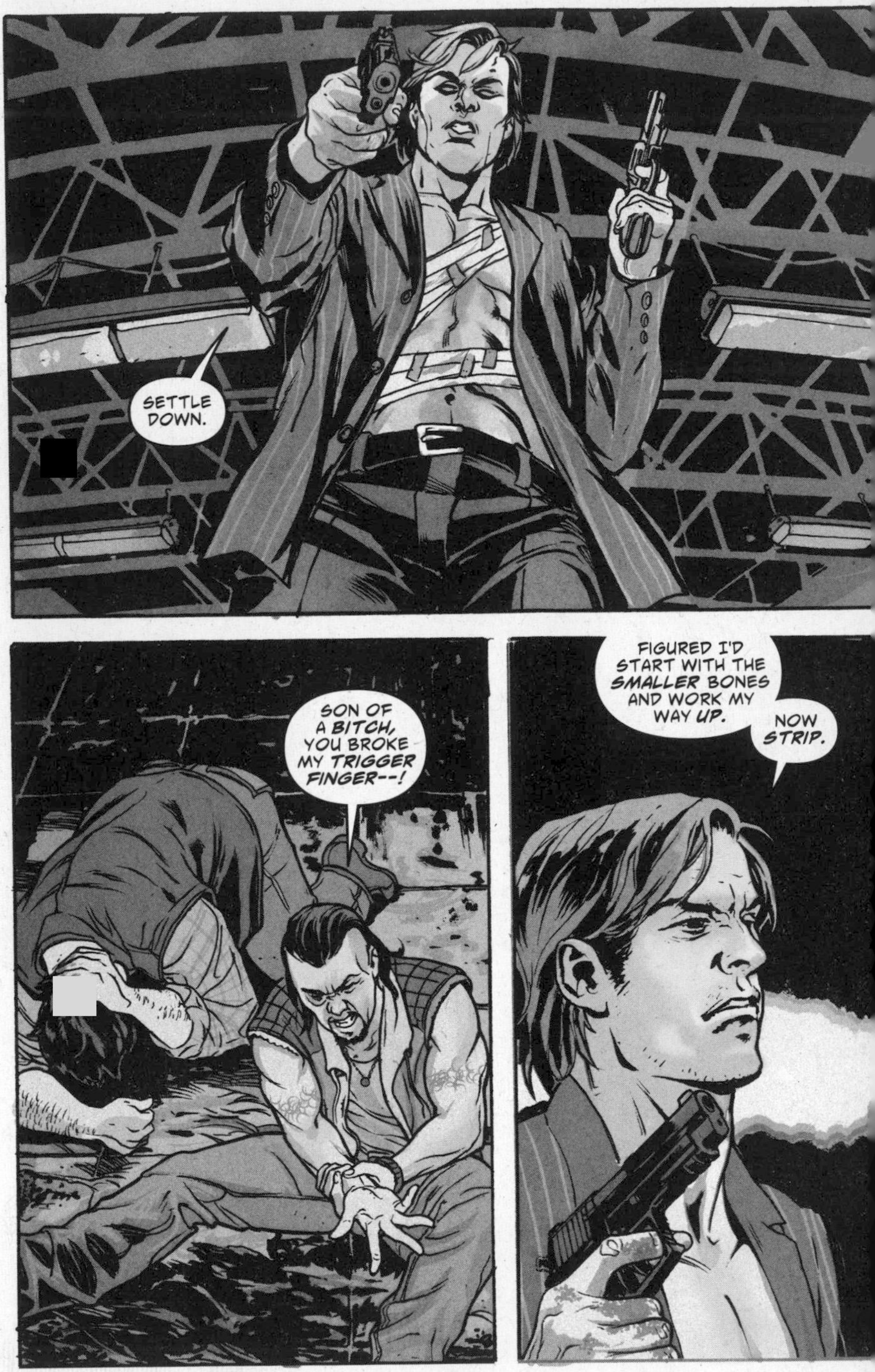
SETTLE DOWN.
SON OF A BITCH, YOU BROKE MY TRIGGER FINGER--!
FIGURED I'D START WITH THE SMALLER BONES AND WORK MY WAY UP.
NOW STRIP.

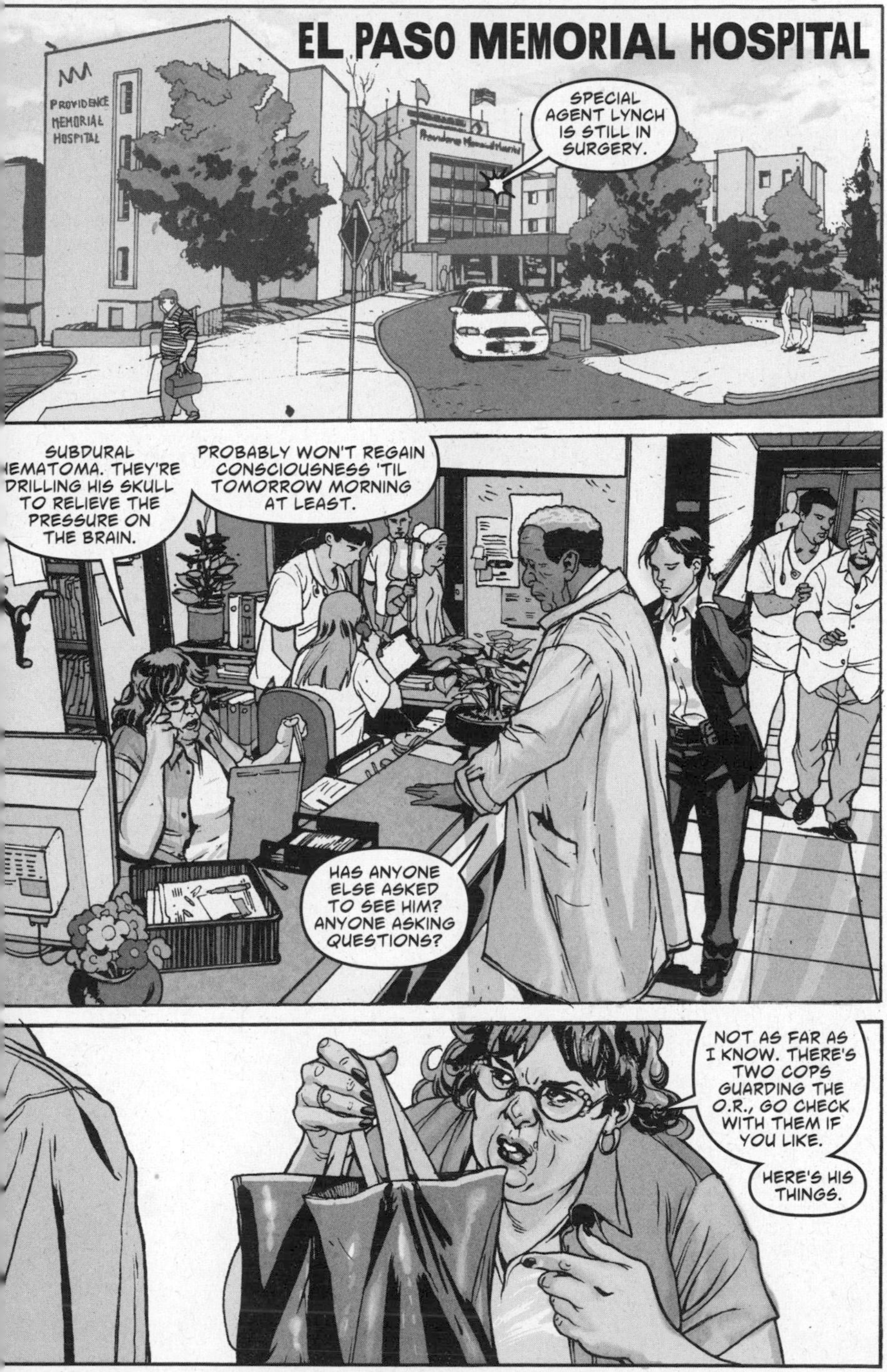
EL PASO MEMORIAL HOSPITAL
PROVIDENCE MEMORIAL HOSPITAL
SPECIAL AGENT LYNCH IS STILL IN SURGERY.
SUBDURAL HEMATOMA. THEY'RE DRILLING HIS SKULL TO RELIEVE THE PRESSURE ON THE BRAIN.
PROBABLY WON'T REGAIN CONSCIOUSNESS 'TIL TOMORROW MORNING AT LEAST.
HAS ANYONE ELSE ASKED TO SEE HIM? ANYONE ASKING QUESTIONS?
NOT AS FAR AS I KNOW. THERE'S TWO COPS GUARDING THE O.R., GO CHECK WITH THEM IF YOU LIKE.
HERE'S HIS THINGS.

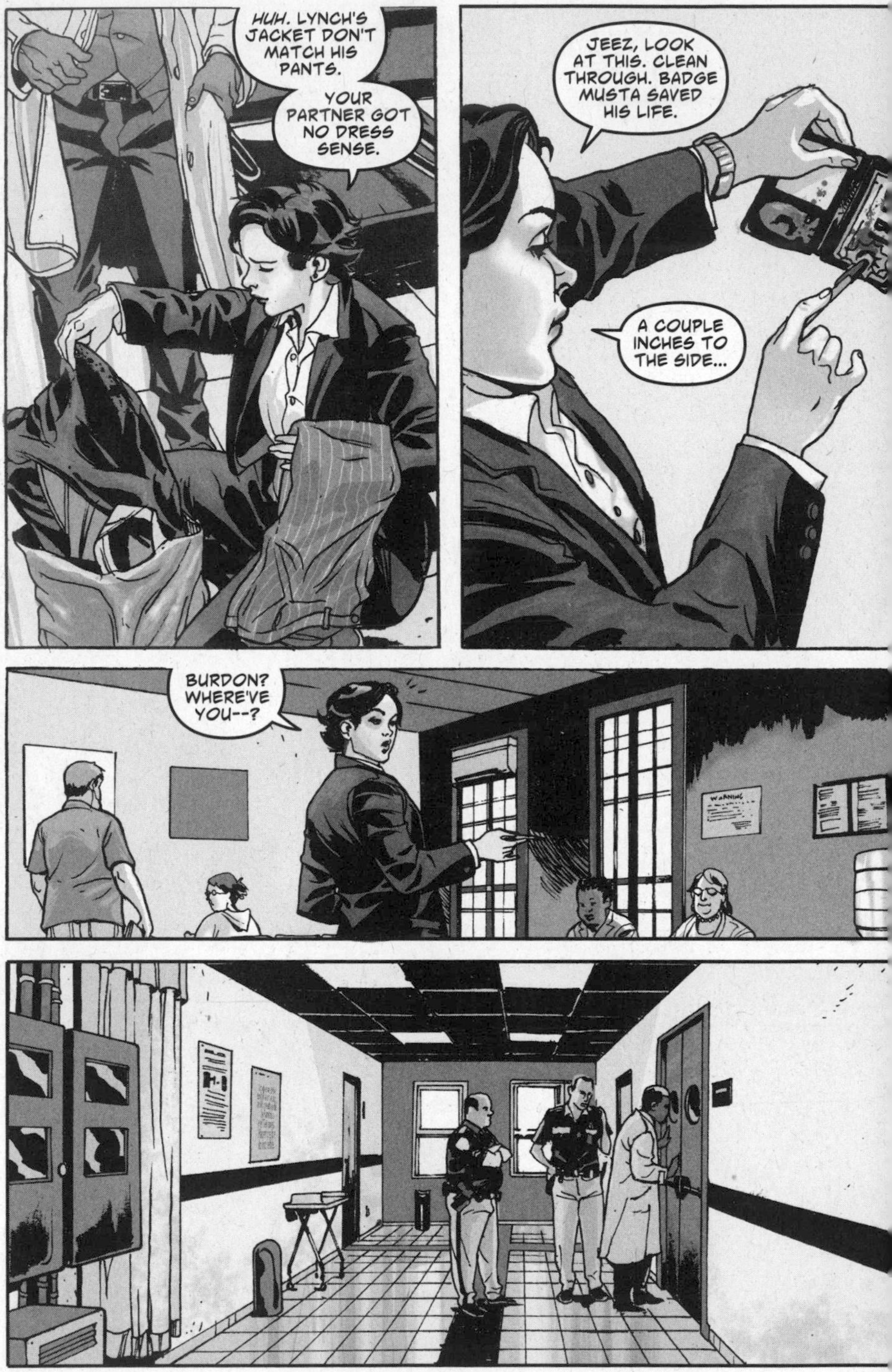
HUH. LYNCH'S JACKET DON'T MATCH HIS PANTS.
YOUR PARTNER GOT NO DRESS SENSE.
JEEZ, LOOK AT THIS. CLEAN THROUGH. BADGE MUSTA SAVED HIS LIFE.
A COUPLE INCHES TO THE SIDE...
BURDON? WHERE'VE YOU--?
WARNING

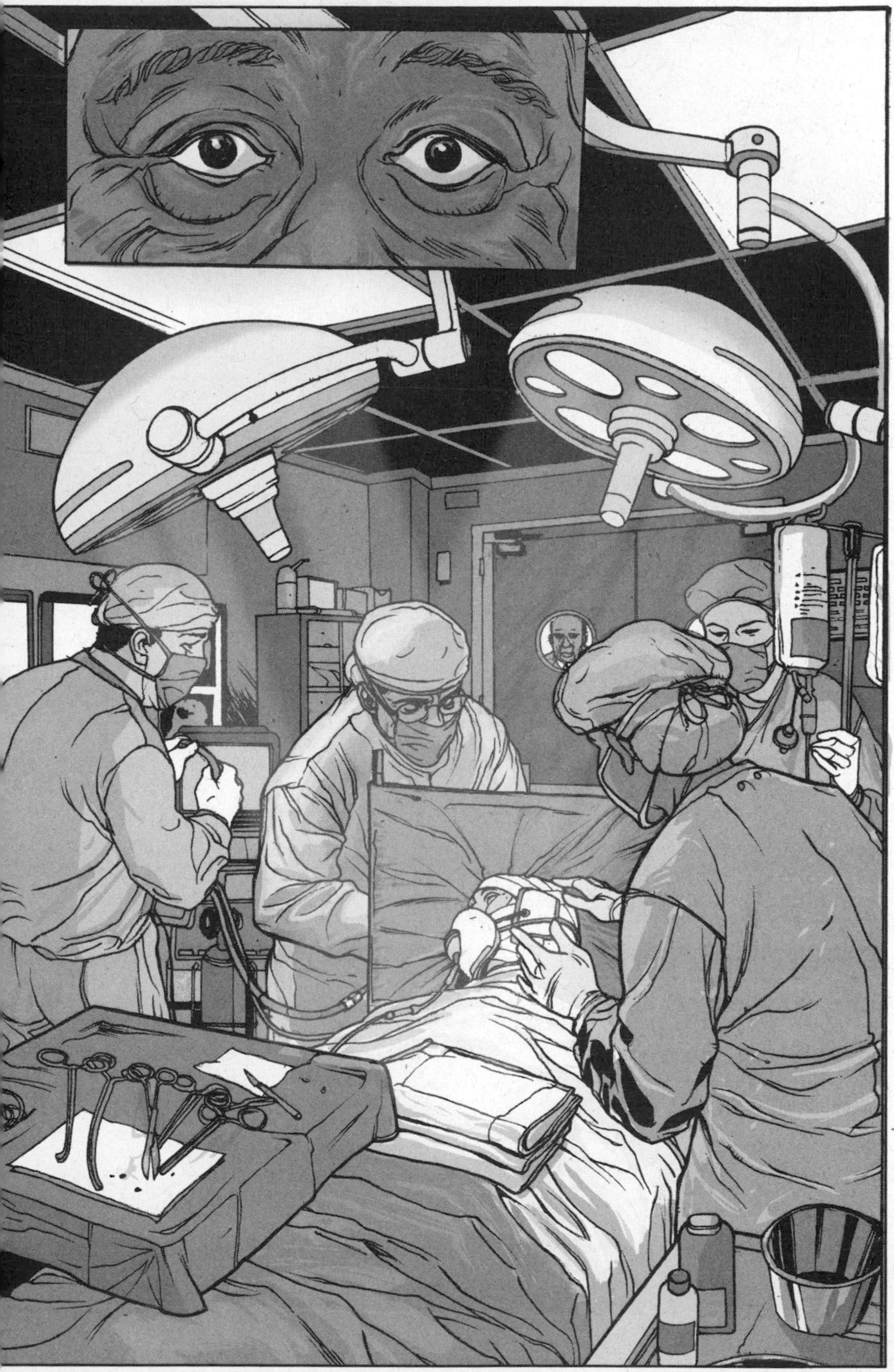

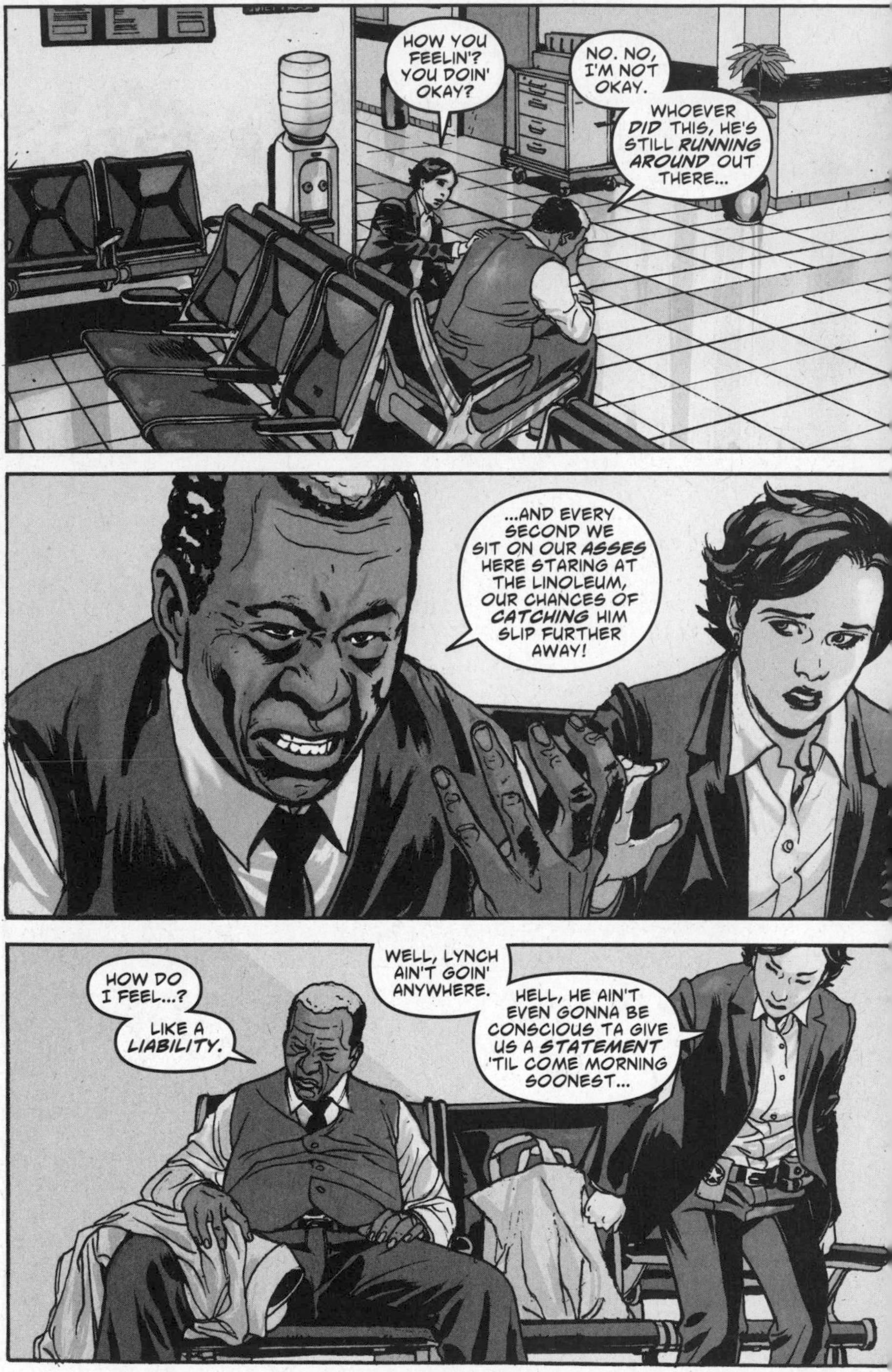
HOW YOU FEELIN'? YOU DOIN' OKAY?
NO. NO, I'M NOT OKAY.
WHOEVER DID THIS, HE'S STILL RUNNING AROUND OUT THERE...
...AND EVERY SECOND WE SIT ON OUR ASSES HERE STARING AT THE LINOLEUM, OUR CHANCES OF CATCHING HIM SLIP FURTHER AWAY!
HOW DO I FEEL...?
LIKE A LIABILITY.
WELL, LYNCH AIN'T GOIN' ANYWHERE.
HELL, HE AIN'T EVEN GONNA BE CONSCIOUS TA GIVE US A STATEMENT 'TIL COME MORNING SOONEST...

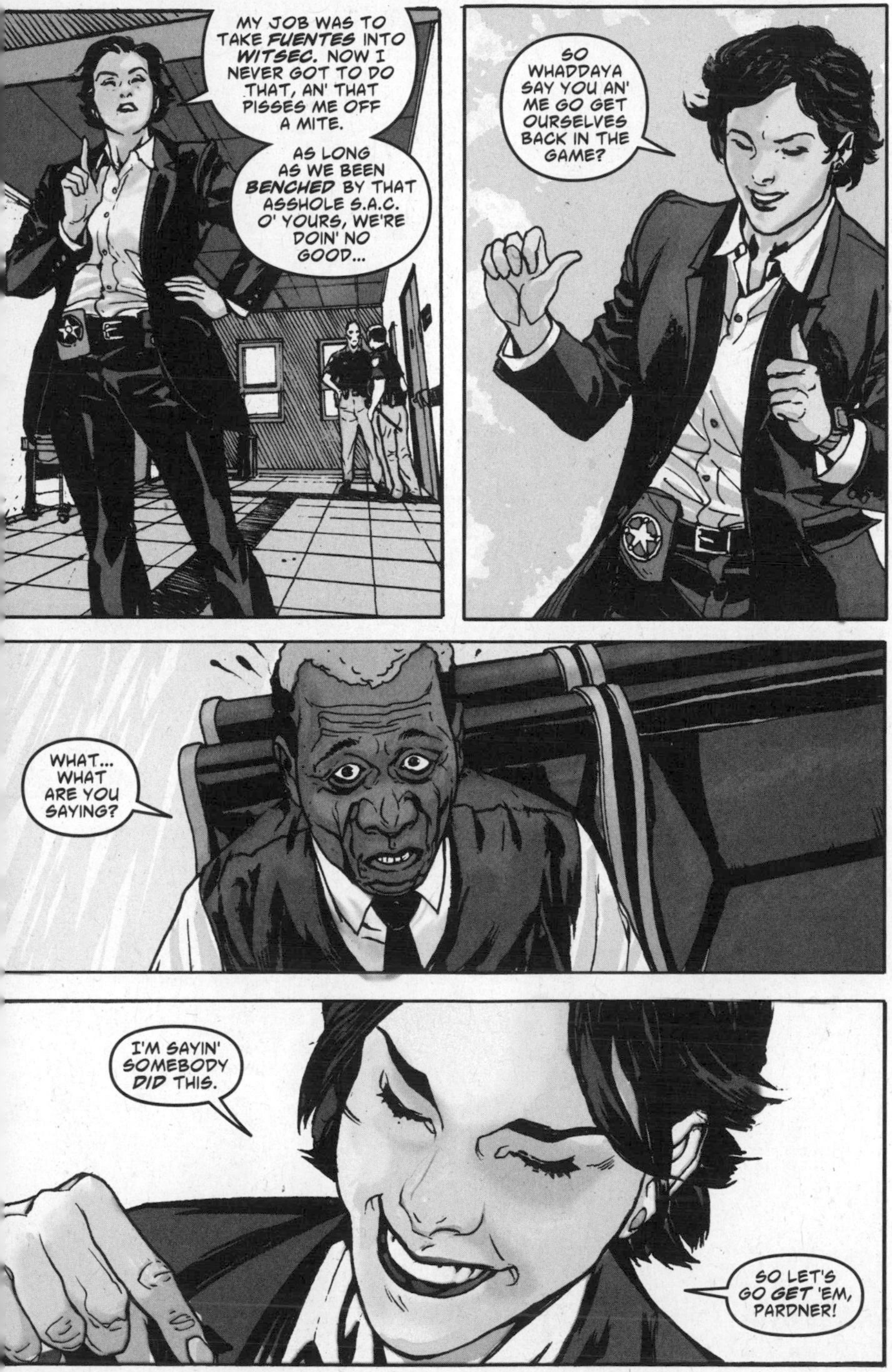
MY JOB WAS TO TAKE FUENTES INTO WITSEC. NOW I NEVER GOT TO DO THAT, AN' THAT PISSES ME OFF A MITE.
AS LONG AS WE BEEN BENCHED BY THAT ASSHOLE S.A.C. O' YOURS, WE'RE DOIN' NO GOOD...
SO WHADDAYA SAY YOU AN' ME GO GET OURSELVES BACK IN THE GAME?
WHAT... WHAT ARE YOU SAYING?
I'M SAYIN' SOMEBODY DID THIS.
SO LET'S GO GET 'EM, PARDNER!

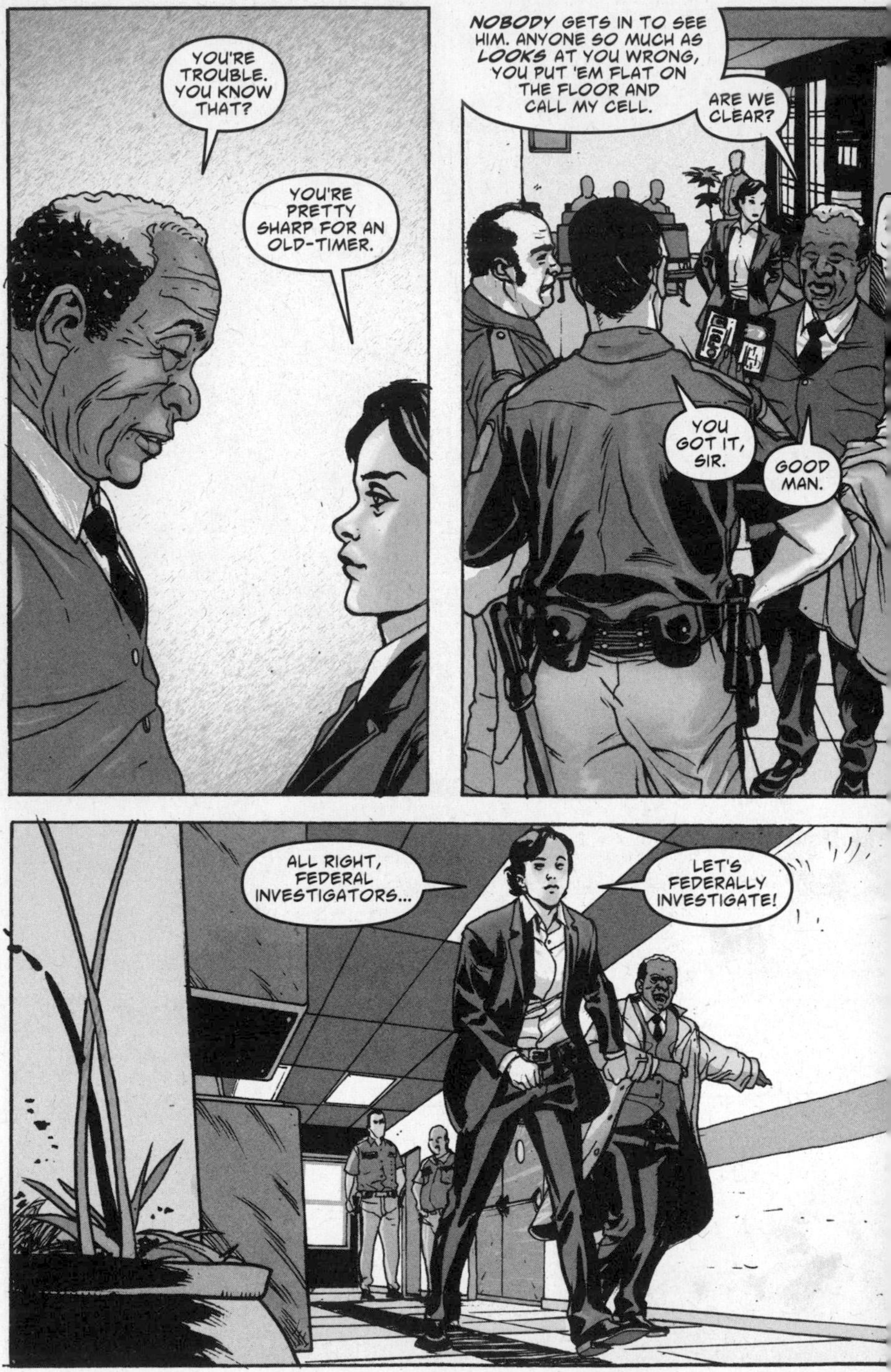
YOU'RE TROUBLE. YOU KNOW THAT?
YOU'RE PRETTY SHARP FOR AN OLD-TIMER.
NOBODY GETS IN TO SEE HIM. ANYONE SO MUCH AS LOOKS AT YOU WRONG, YOU PUT 'EM FLAT ON THE FLOOR AND CALL MY CELL.
ARE WE CLEAR?
YOU GOT IT, SIR.
GOOD MAN.
ALL RIGHT, FEDERAL INVESTIGATORS...
LET'S FEDERALLY INVESTIGATE!

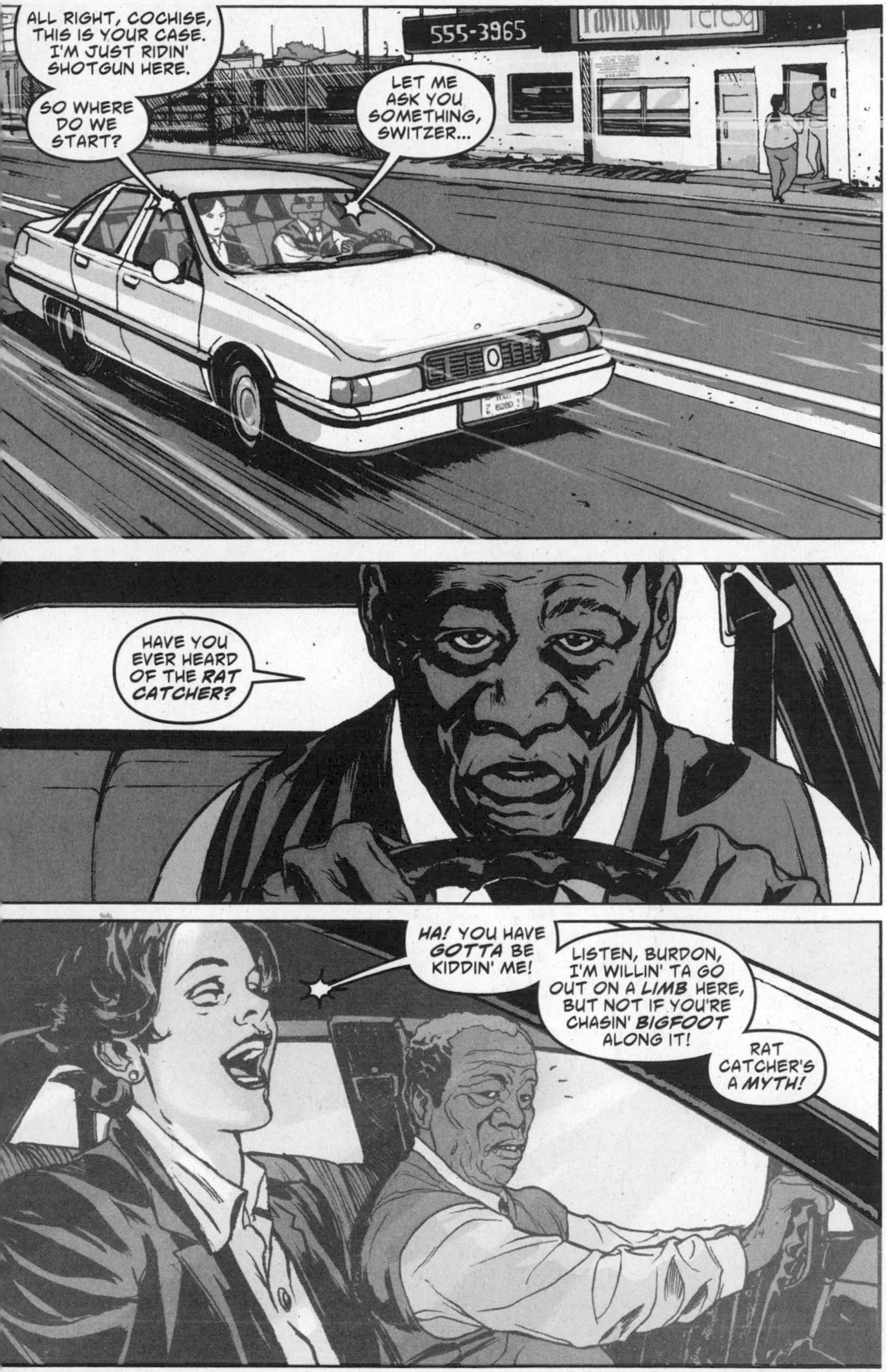

555-3965
ALL RIGHT, COCHISE, THIS IS YOUR CASE. I'M JUST RIDIN' SHOTGUN HERE.
SO WHERE DO WE START?
LET ME ASK YOU SOMETHING, SWITZER...
HAVE YOU EVER HEARD OF THE *RAT CATCHER?*
HA! YOU HAVE *GOTTA* BE KIDDIN' ME!
LISTEN, BURDON, I'M WILLIN' TA GO OUT ON A *LIMB* HERE, BUT NOT IF YOU'RE CHASIN' *BIGFOOT* ALONG IT!
RAT CATCHER'S A *MYTH!*

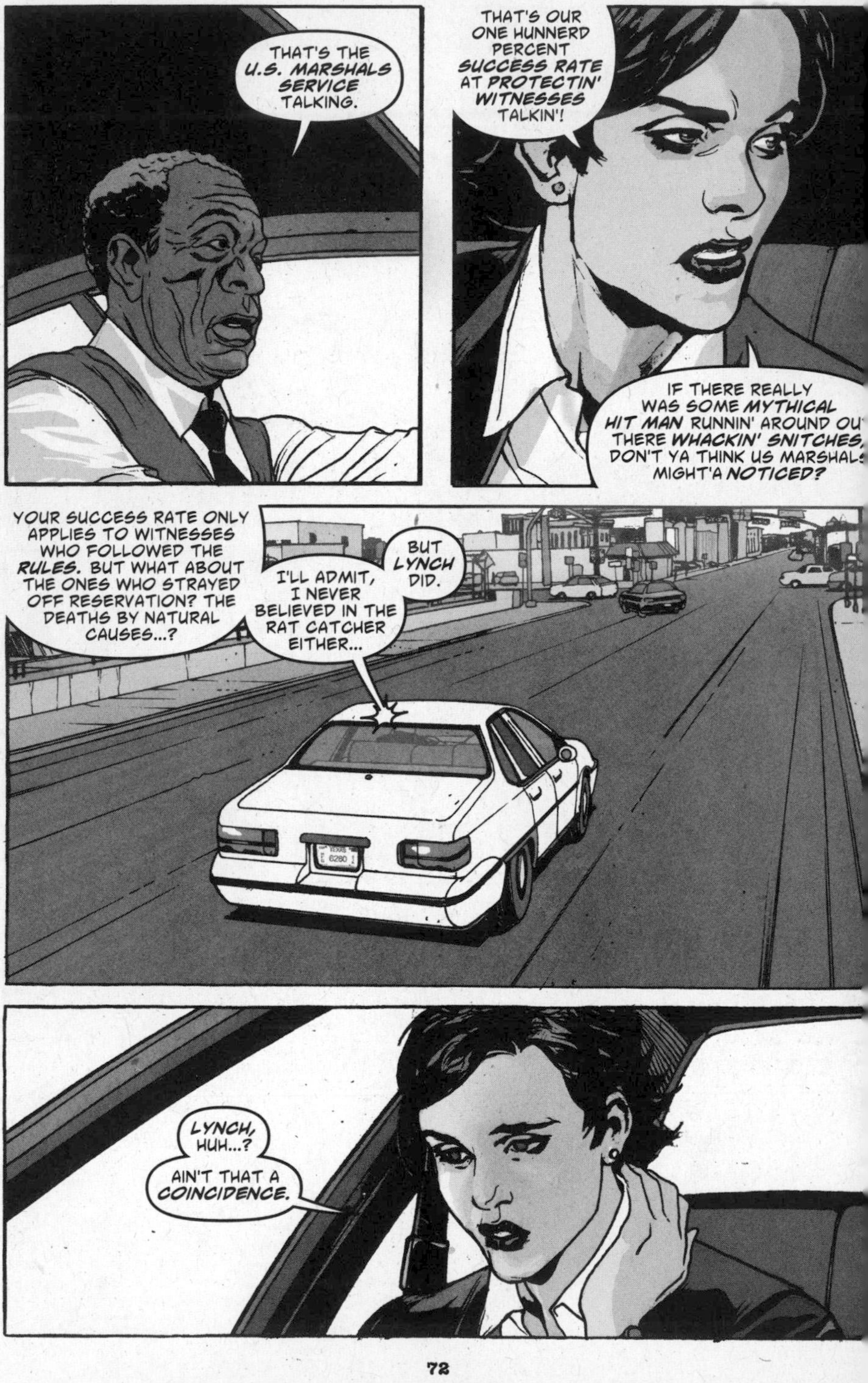
THAT'S THE U.S. MARSHALS SERVICE TALKING.
THAT'S OUR ONE HUNNERD PERCENT SUCCESS RATE AT PROTECTIN' WITNESSES TALKIN'!
IF THERE REALLY WAS SOME MYTHICAL HIT MAN RUNNIN' AROUND OU THERE WHACKIN' SNITCHES, DON'T YA THINK US MARSHAL MIGHT'A NOTICED?
YOUR SUCCESS RATE ONLY APPLIES TO WITNESSES WHO FOLLOWED THE RULES. BUT WHAT ABOUT THE ONES WHO STRAYED OFF RESERVATION? THE DEATHS BY NATURAL CAUSES...?
I'LL ADMIT, I NEVER BELIEVED IN THE RAT CATCHER EITHER...
BUT LYNCH DID.
LYNCH, HUH...?
AIN'T THAT A COINCIDENCE.

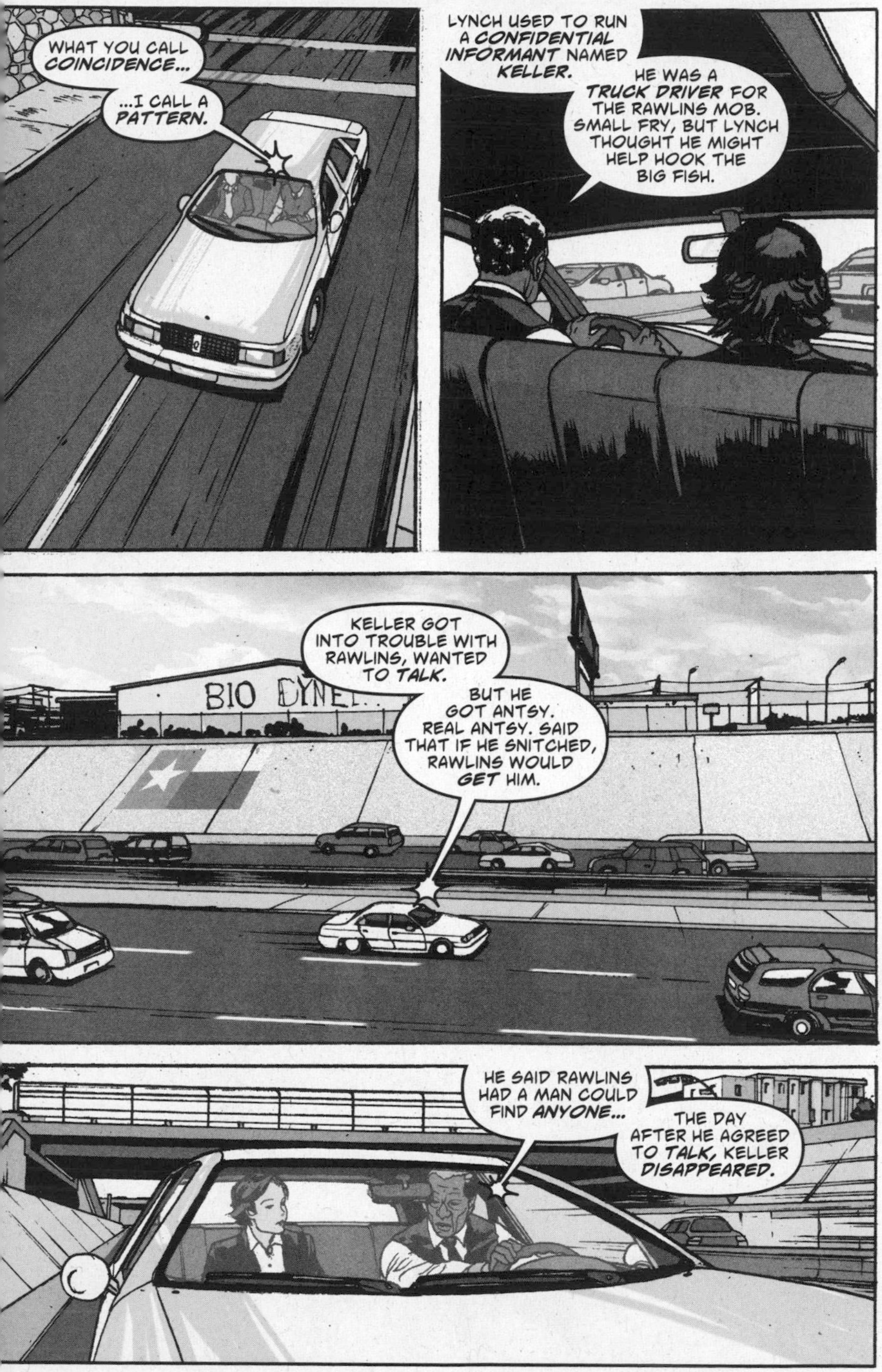
WHAT YOU CALL COINCIDENCE...
...I CALL A PATTERN.
LYNCH USED TO RUN A CONFIDENTIAL INFORMANT NAMED KELLER.
HE WAS A TRUCK DRIVER FOR THE RAWLINS MOB. SMALL FRY, BUT LYNCH THOUGHT HE MIGHT HELP HOOK THE BIG FISH.
KELLER GOT INTO TROUBLE WITH RAWLINS, WANTED TO TALK.
BUT HE GOT ANTSY. REAL ANTSY. SAID THAT IF HE SNITCHED, RAWLINS WOULD GET HIM.
BIO DYNE
HE SAID RAWLINS HAD A MAN COULD FIND ANYONE...
THE DAY AFTER HE AGREED TO TALK, KELLER DISAPPEARED.

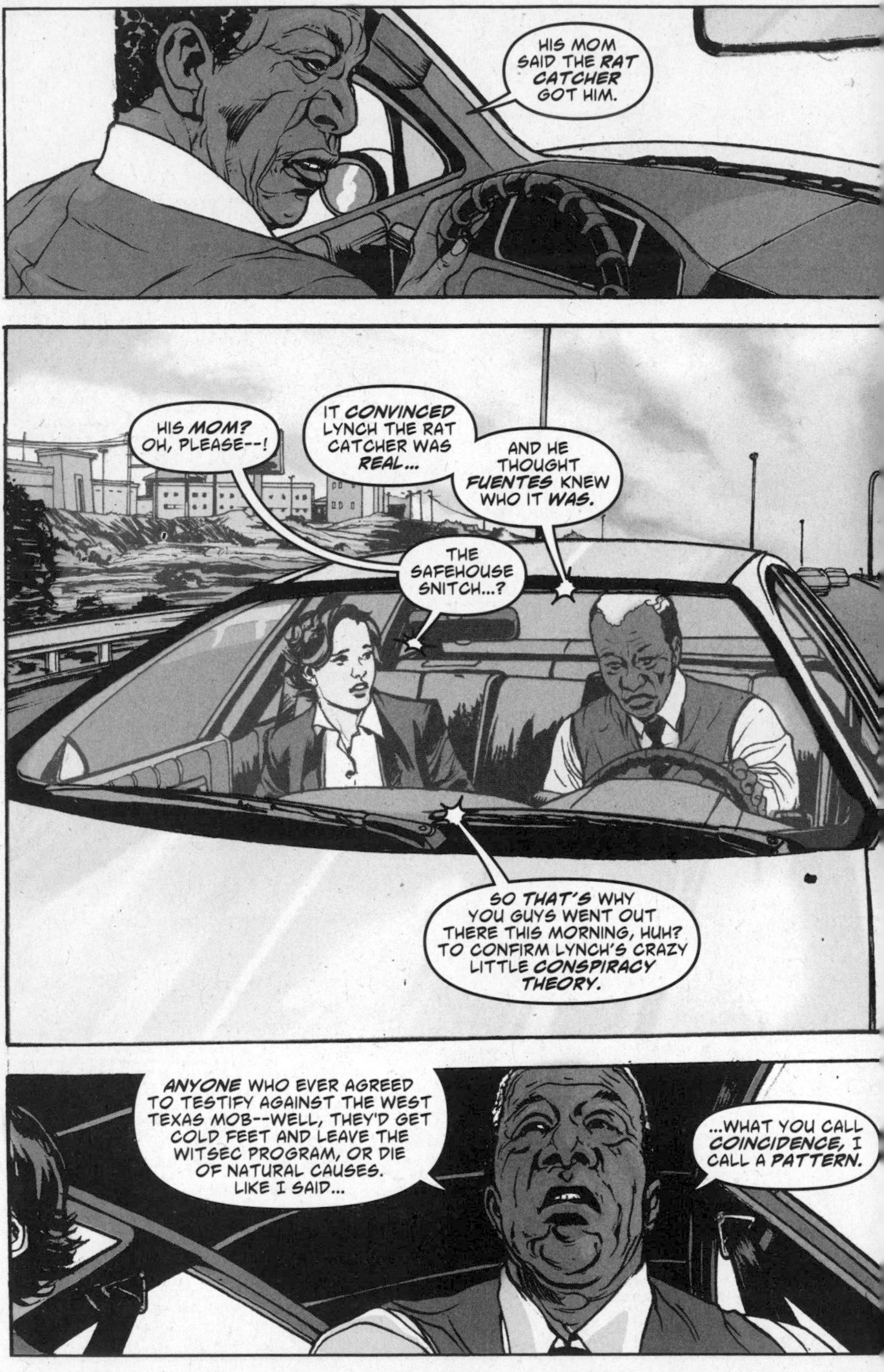
HIS MOM SAID THE RAT CATCHER GOT HIM.
HIS MOM? OH, PLEASE--!
IT CONVINCED LYNCH THE RAT CATCHER WAS REAL...
AND HE THOUGHT FUENTES KNEW WHO IT WAS.
THE SAFEHOUSE SNITCH...?
SO THAT'S WHY YOU GUYS WENT OUT THERE THIS MORNING, HUH? TO CONFIRM LYNCH'S CRAZY LITTLE CONSPIRACY THEORY.
ANYONE WHO EVER AGREED TO TESTIFY AGAINST THE WEST TEXAS MOB--WELL, THEY'D GET COLD FEET AND LEAVE THE WITSEC PROGRAM, OR DIE OF NATURAL CAUSES. LIKE I SAID...
...WHAT YOU CALL COINCIDENCE, I CALL A PATTERN.

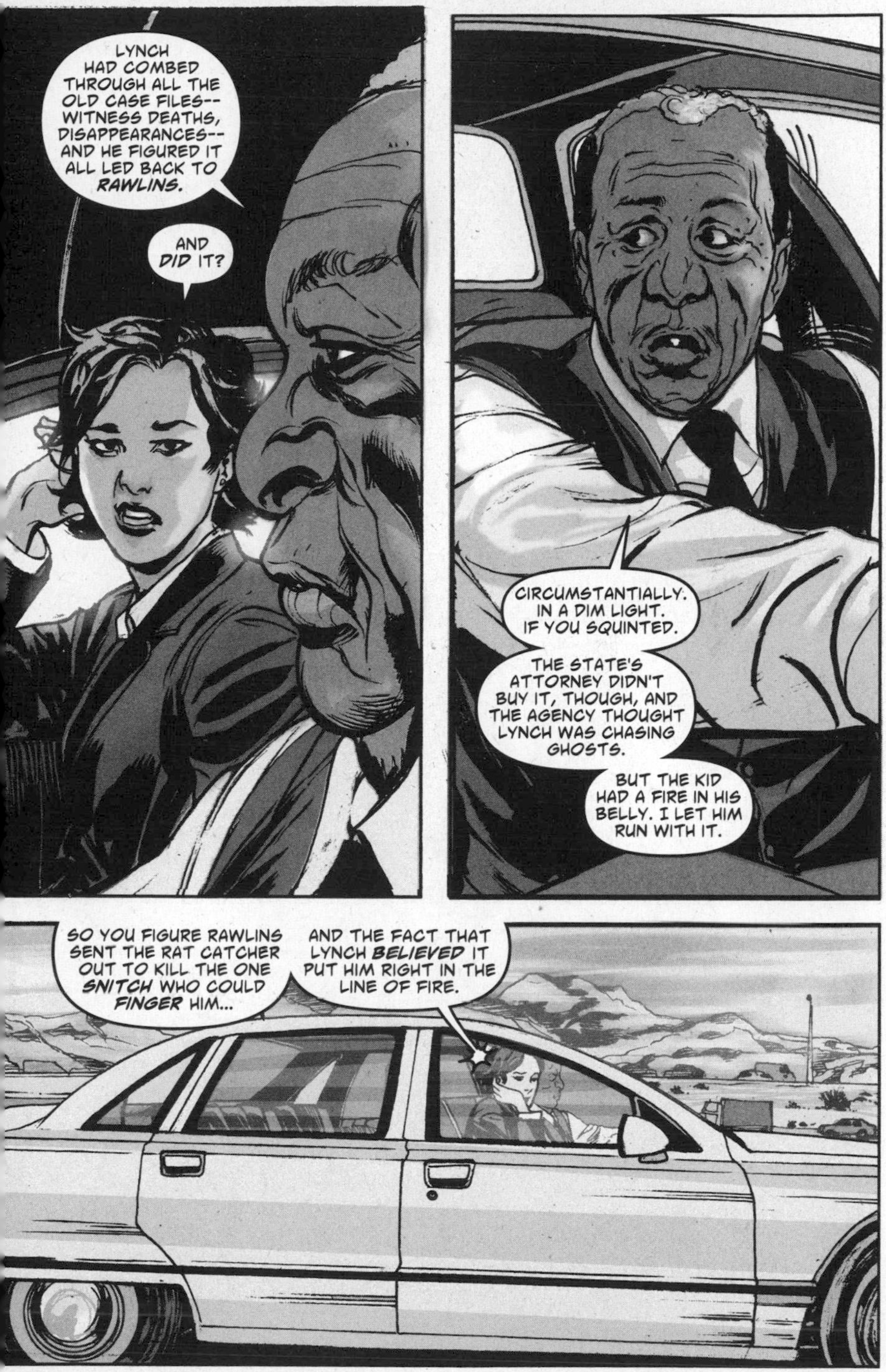
LYNCH HAD COMBED THROUGH ALL THE OLD CASE FILES--WITNESS DEATHS, DISAPPEARANCES--AND HE FIGURED IT ALL LED BACK TO *RAWLINS.*
AND *DID* IT?
CIRCUMSTANTIALLY. IN A DIM LIGHT. IF YOU SQUINTED.
THE STATE'S ATTORNEY DIDN'T BUY IT, THOUGH, AND THE AGENCY THOUGHT LYNCH WAS CHASING GHOSTS.
BUT THE KID HAD A FIRE IN HIS BELLY. I LET HIM RUN WITH IT.
SO YOU FIGURE RAWLINS SENT THE RAT CATCHER OUT TO KILL THE ONE *SNITCH* WHO COULD *FINGER* HIM...
AND THE FACT THAT LYNCH *BELIEVED* IT PUT HIM RIGHT IN THE LINE OF FIRE.

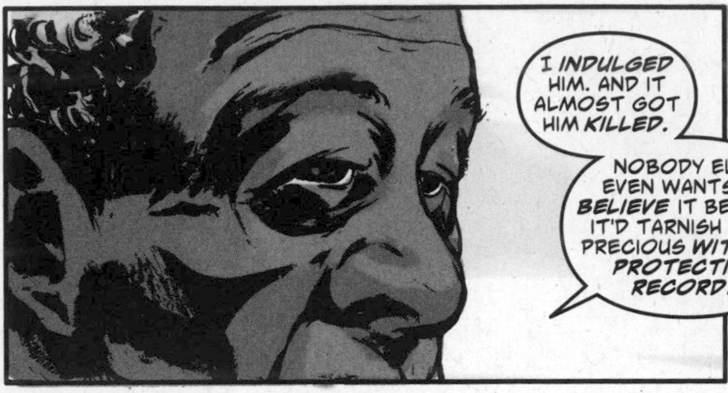
I INDULGED HIM. AND IT ALMOST GOT HIM KILLED.
NOBODY ELSE EVEN WANTS TO BELIEVE IT BECAUSE IT'D TARNISH THEIR PRECIOUS WITNESS PROTECTION RECORD...

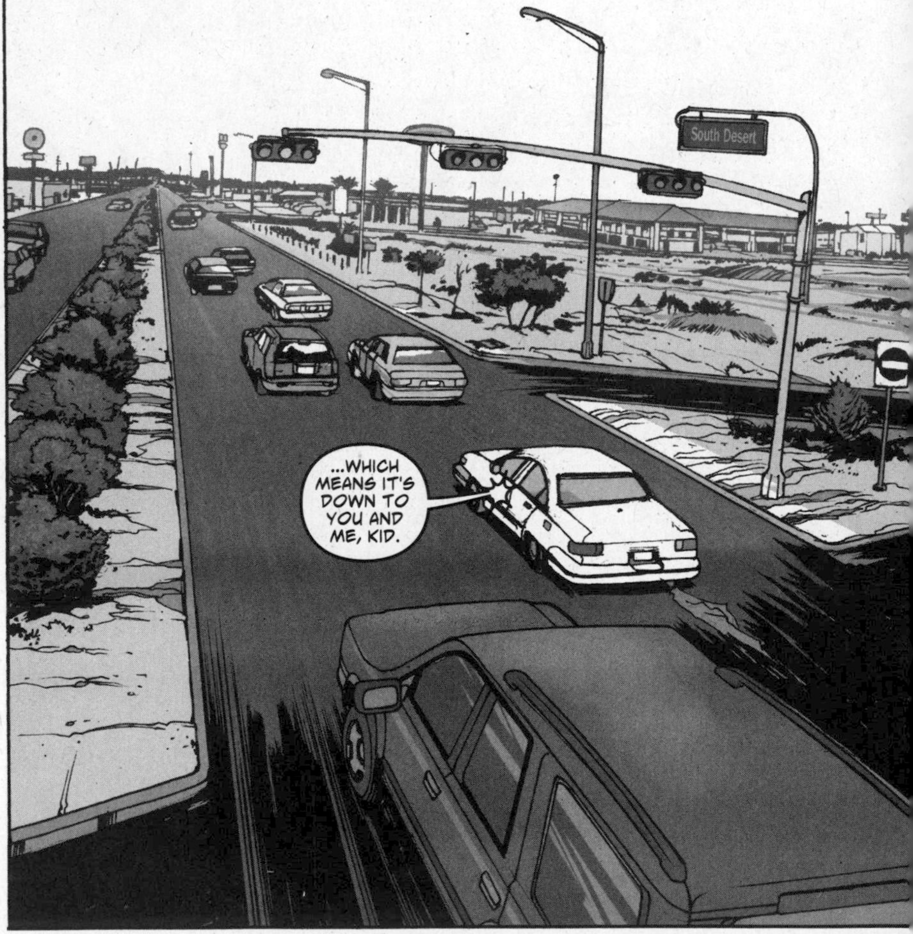
South Desert
...WHICH MEANS IT'S DOWN TO YOU AND ME, KID.

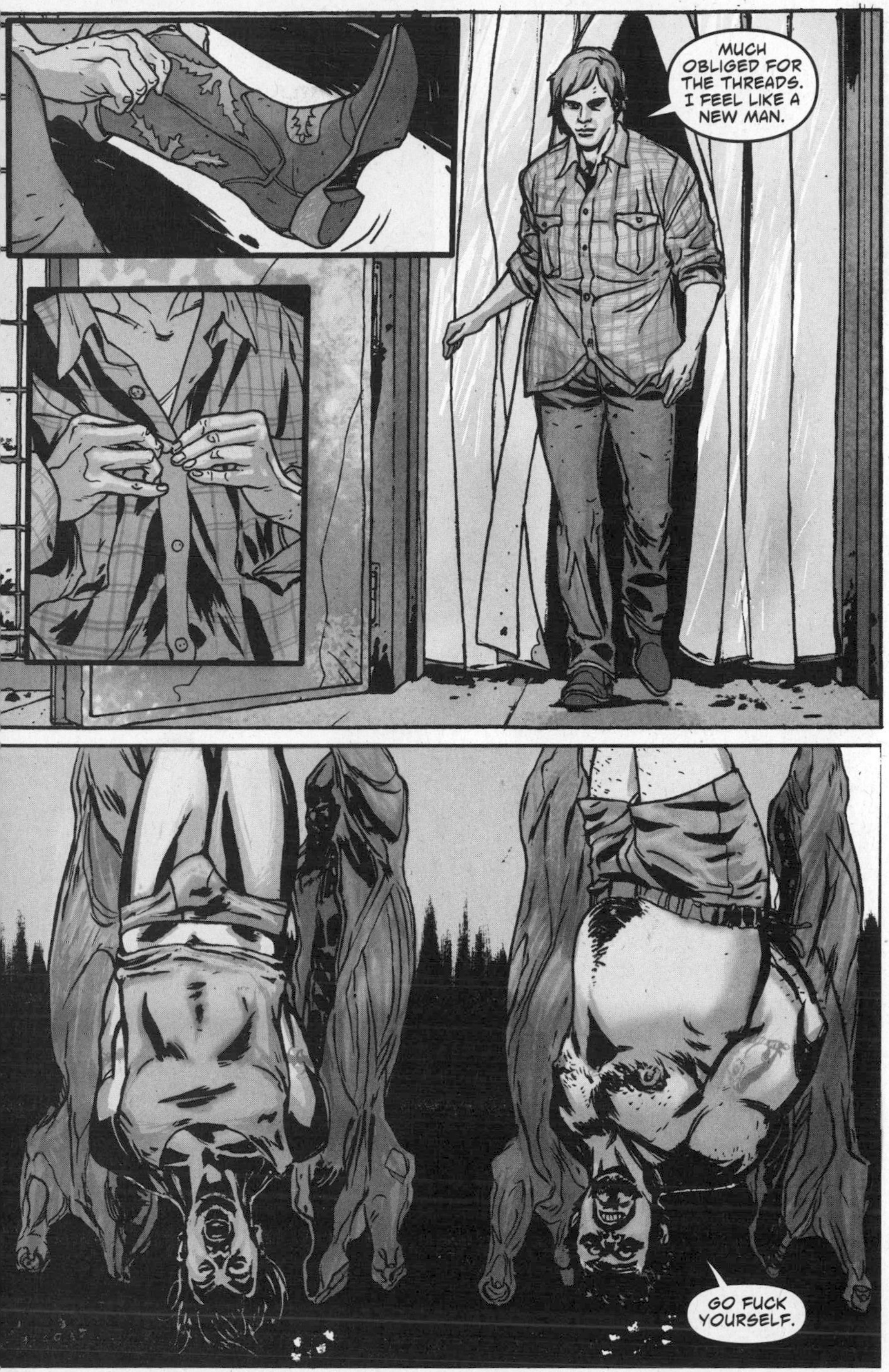
MUCH OBLIGED FOR THE THREADS. I FEEL LIKE A NEW MAN.
GO FUCK YOURSELF.

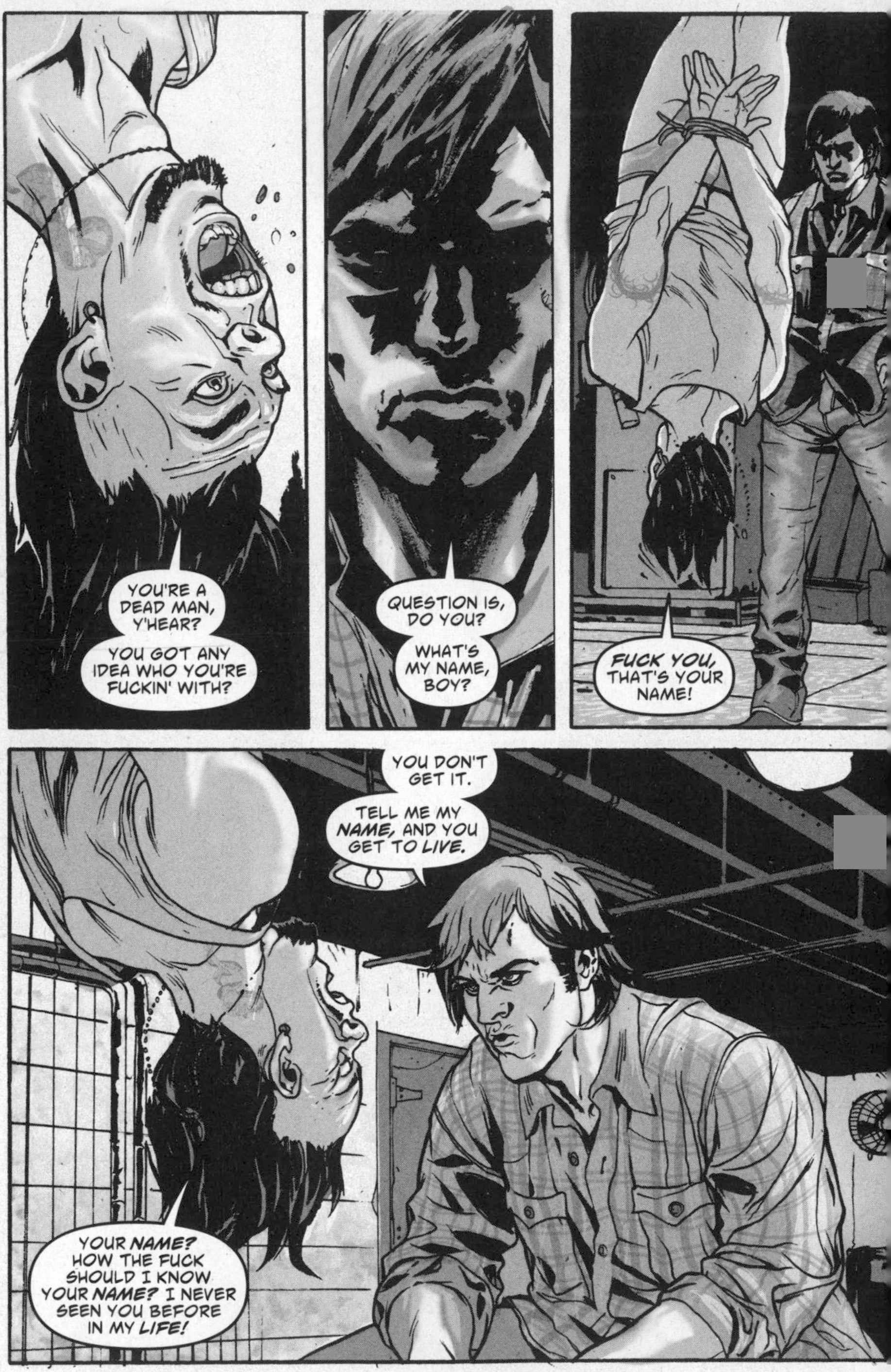

YOU'RE A DEAD MAN, Y'HEAR?
YOU GOT ANY IDEA WHO YOU'RE FUCKIN' WITH?
QUESTION IS, DO YOU?
WHAT'S MY NAME, BOY?
FUCK YOU, THAT'S YOUR NAME!
YOU DON'T GET IT.
TELL ME MY NAME, AND YOU GET TO LIVE.
YOUR NAME? HOW THE FUCK SHOULD I KNOW YOUR NAME? I NEVER SEEN YOU BEFORE IN MY LIFE!

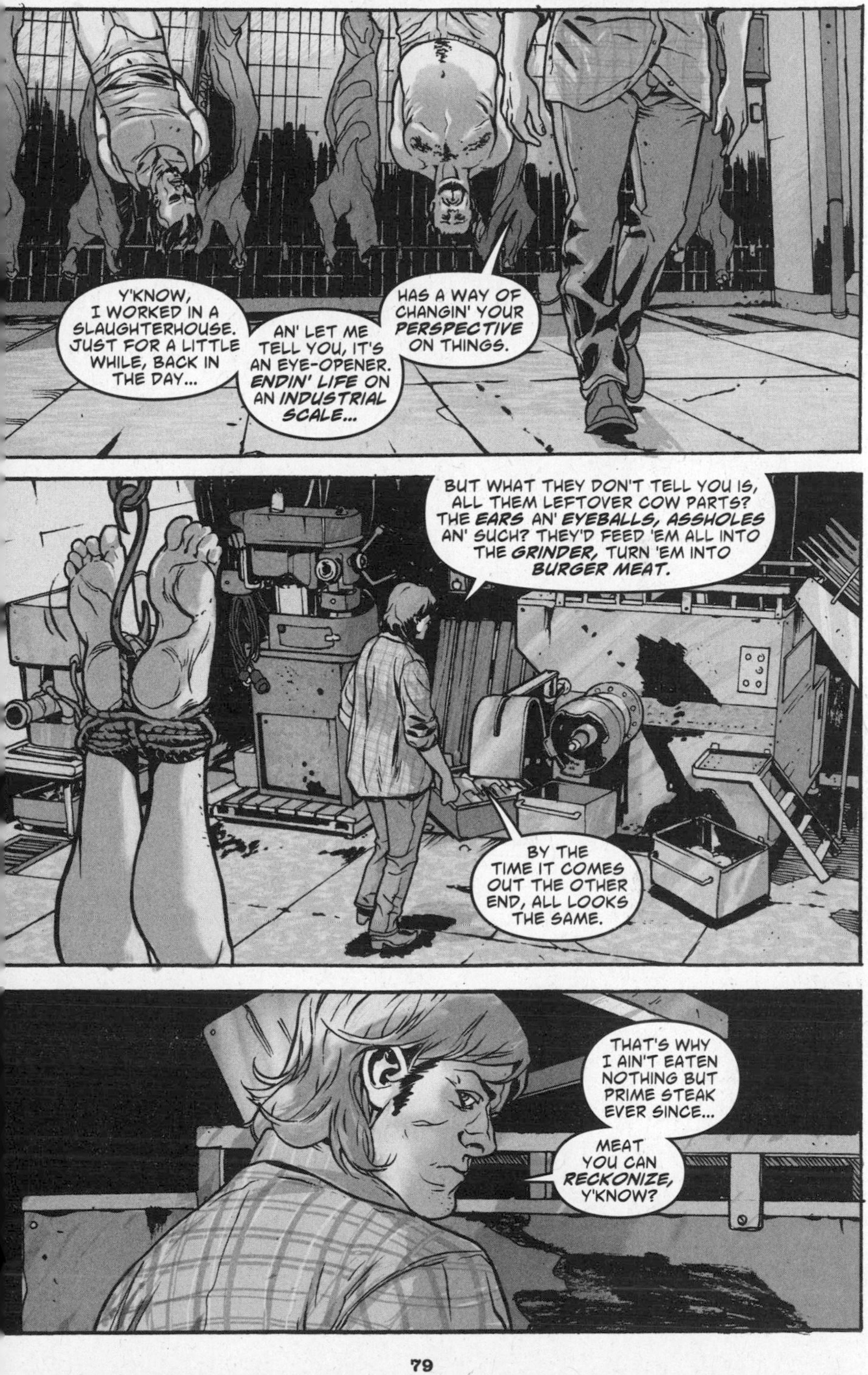
Y'KNOW, I WORKED IN A SLAUGHTERHOUSE. JUST FOR A LITTLE WHILE, BACK IN THE DAY...
AN' LET ME TELL YOU, IT'S AN EYE-OPENER. ENDIN' LIFE ON AN INDUSTRIAL SCALE...
HAS A WAY OF CHANGIN' YOUR PERSPECTIVE ON THINGS.
BUT WHAT THEY DON'T TELL YOU IS, ALL THEM LEFTOVER COW PARTS? THE EARS AN' EYEBALLS, ASSHOLES AN' SUCH? THEY'D FEED 'EM ALL INTO THE GRINDER, TURN 'EM INTO BURGER MEAT.
BY THE TIME IT COMES OUT THE OTHER END, ALL LOOKS THE SAME.
THAT'S WHY I AIN'T EATEN NOTHING BUT PRIME STEAK EVER SINCE...
MEAT YOU CAN RECKONIZE, Y'KNOW?

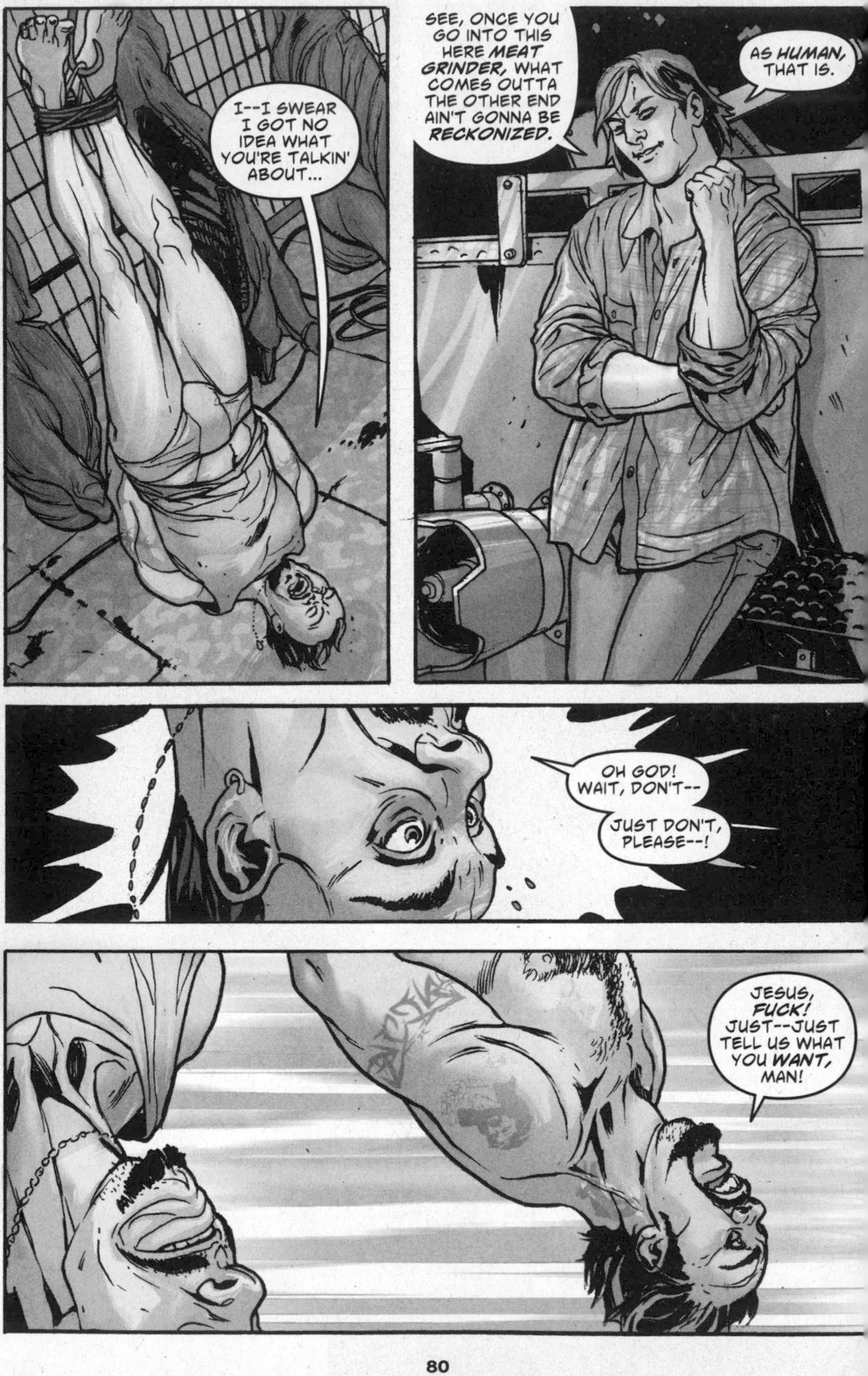
I--I SWEAR I GOT NO IDEA WHAT YOU'RE TALKIN' ABOUT...
SEE, ONCE YOU GO INTO THIS HERE MEAT GRINDER, WHAT COMES OUTTA THE OTHER END AIN'T GONNA BE RECKONIZED.
AS HUMAN, THAT IS.
OH GOD! WAIT, DON'T--
JUST DON'T, PLEASE--!
JESUS, FUCK! JUST--JUST TELL US WHAT YOU WANT, MAN!

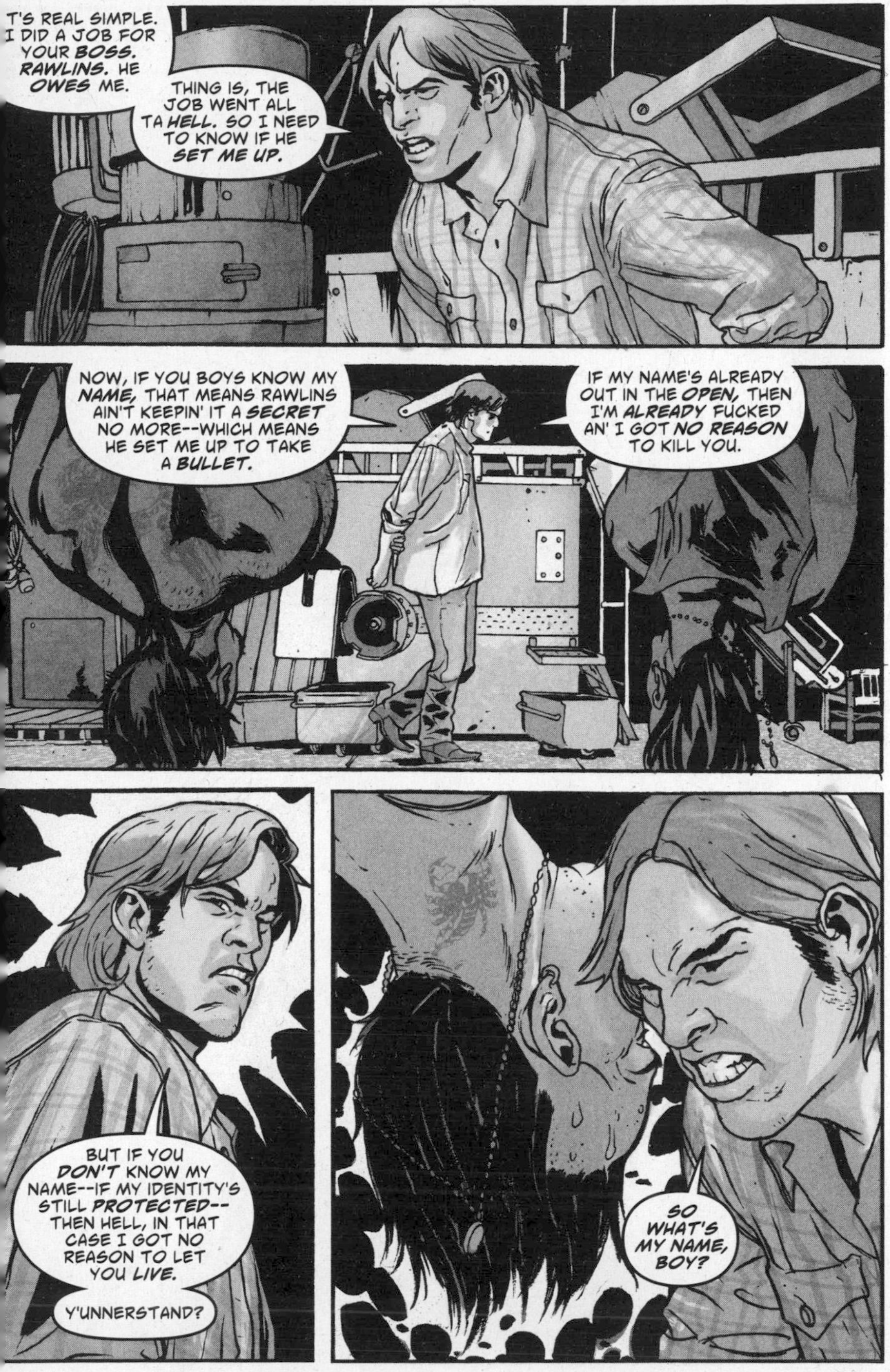
T'S REAL SIMPLE. I DID A JOB FOR YOUR BOSS. RAWLINS. HE OWES ME.
THING IS, THE JOB WENT ALL TA HELL. SO I NEED TO KNOW IF HE SET ME UP.
NOW, IF YOU BOYS KNOW MY NAME, THAT MEANS RAWLINS AIN'T KEEPIN' IT A SECRET NO MORE--WHICH MEANS HE SET ME UP TO TAKE A BULLET.
IF MY NAME'S ALREADY OUT IN THE OPEN, THEN I'M ALREADY FUCKED AN' I GOT NO REASON TO KILL YOU.
BUT IF YOU DON'T KNOW MY NAME--IF MY IDENTITY'S STILL PROTECTED--THEN HELL, IN THAT CASE I GOT NO REASON TO LET YOU LIVE.
Y'UNNERSTAND?
SO WHAT'S MY NAME, BOY?

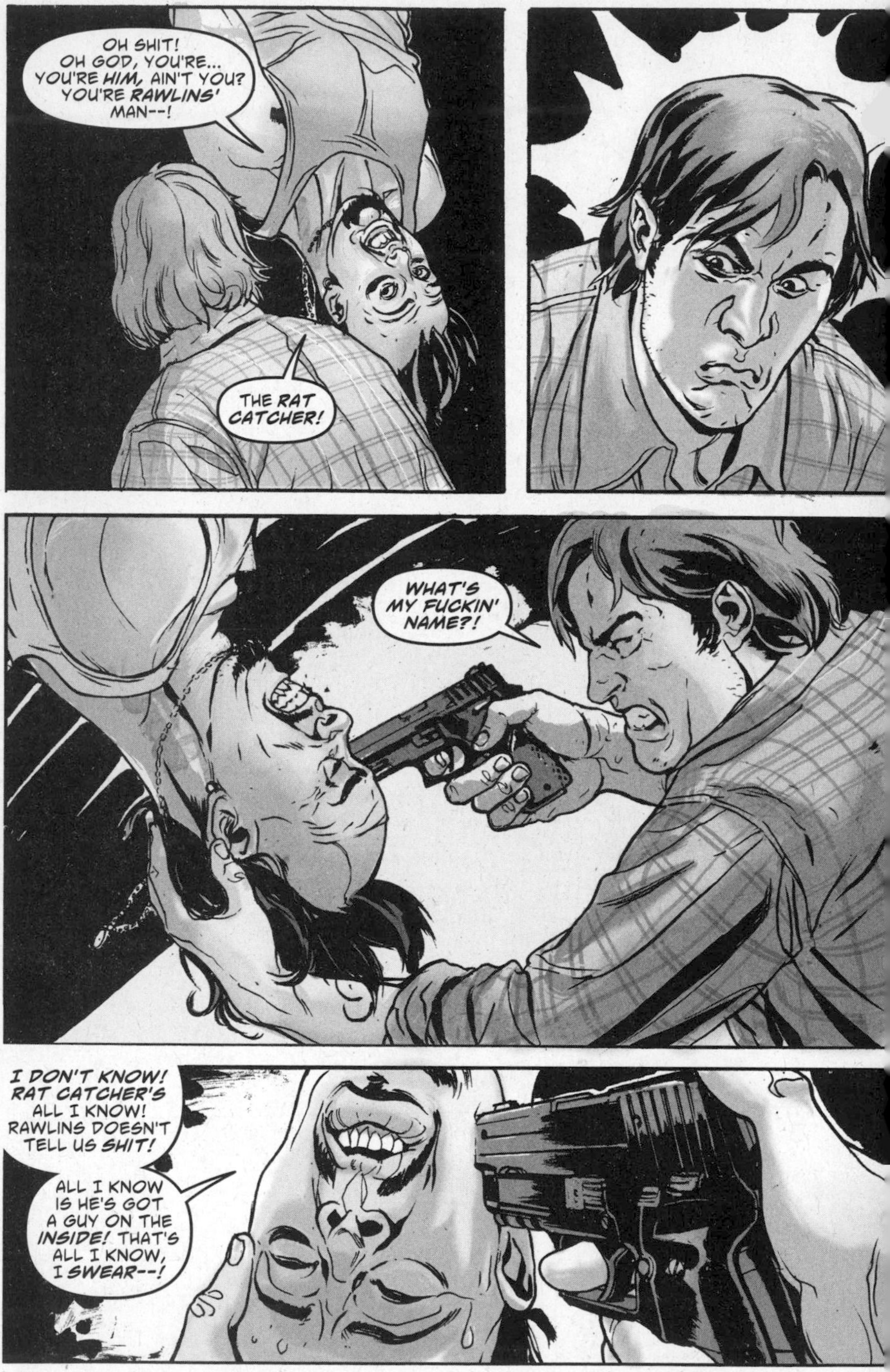
OH SHIT! OH GOD, YOU'RE... YOU'RE *HIM,* AIN'T YOU? YOU'RE *RAWLINS'* MAN--!
THE *RAT CATCHER!*
WHAT'S MY FUCKIN' NAME?!
I DON'T KNOW! RAT CATCHER'S ALL I KNOW! RAWLINS DOESN'T TELL US *SHIT!*
ALL I KNOW IS HE'S GOT A GUY ON THE *INSIDE!* THAT'S ALL I KNOW, I *SWEAR--!*

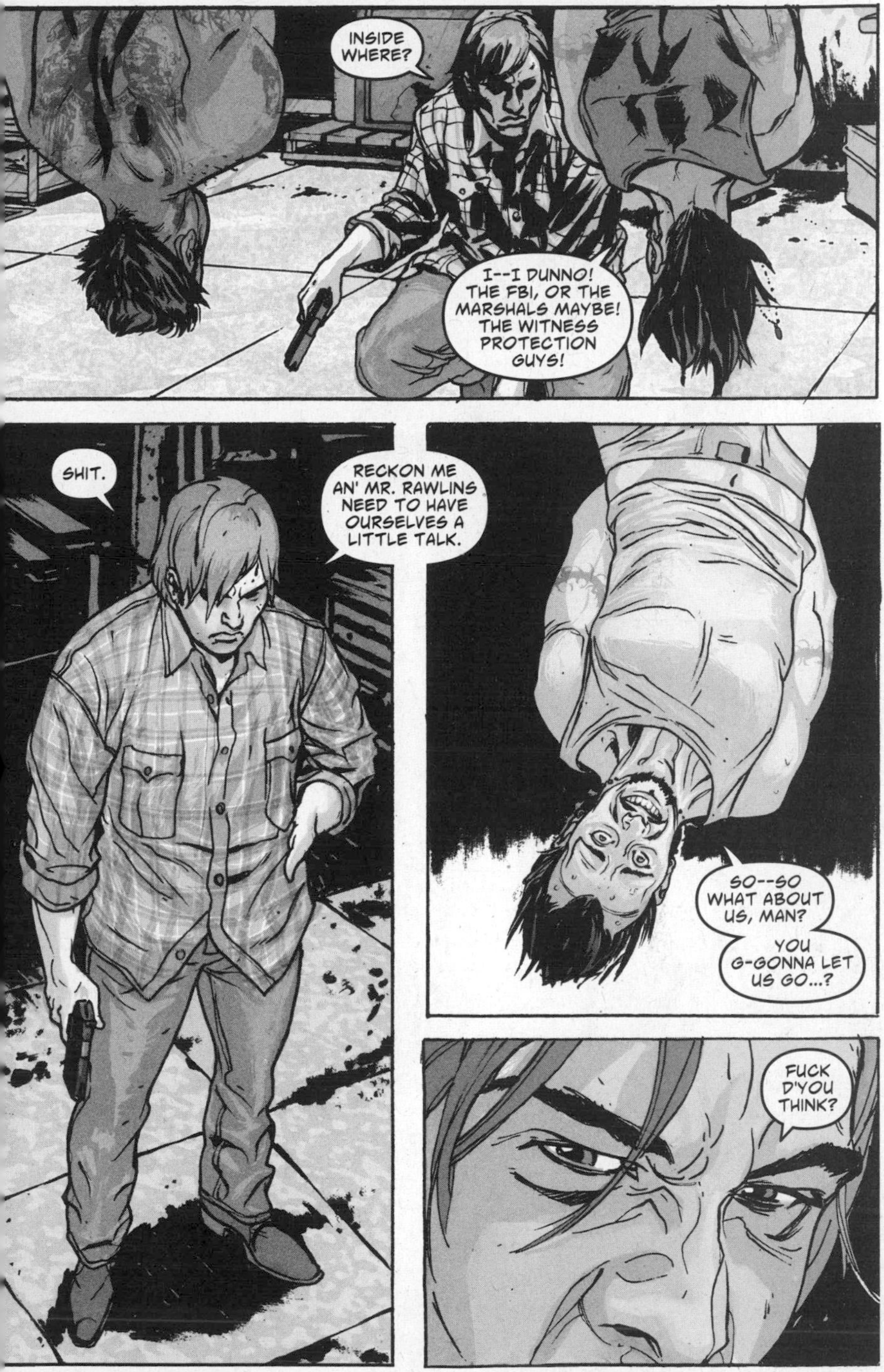
INSIDE WHERE?
I--I DUNNO! THE FBI, OR THE MARSHALS MAYBE! THE WITNESS PROTECTION GUYS!
SHIT.
RECKON ME AN' MR. RAWLINS NEED TO HAVE OURSELVES A LITTLE TALK.
SO--SO WHAT ABOUT US, MAN?
YOU G-GONNA LET US GO...?
FUCK D'YOU THINK?

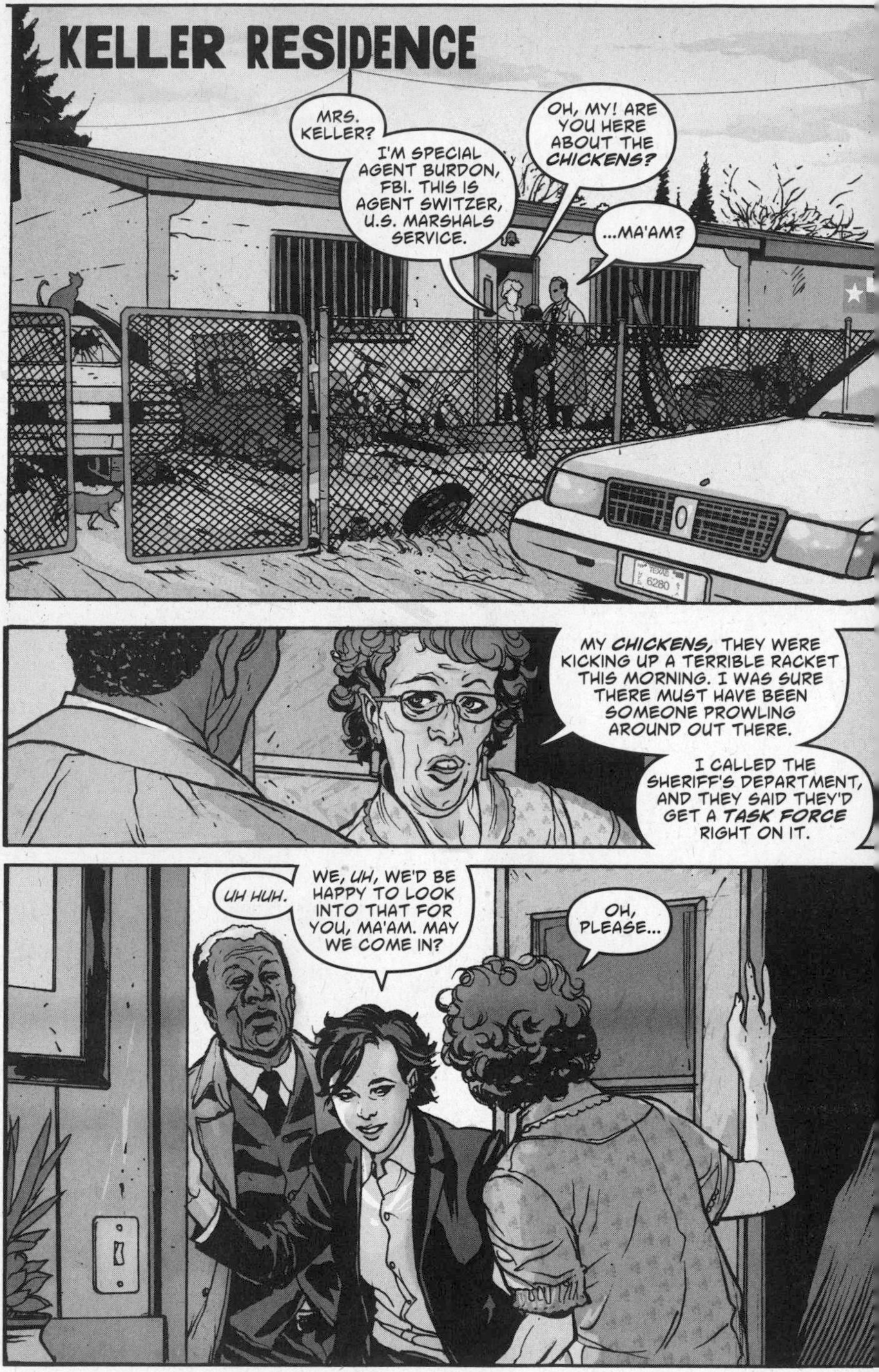
KELLER RESIDENCE
MRS. KELLER?
I'M SPECIAL AGENT BURDON, FBI. THIS IS AGENT SWITZER, U.S. MARSHALS SERVICE.
OH, MY! ARE YOU HERE ABOUT THE CHICKENS?
...MA'AM?
TEXAS
6280
MY CHICKENS, THEY WERE KICKING UP A TERRIBLE RACKET THIS MORNING. I WAS SURE THERE MUST HAVE BEEN SOMEONE PROWLING AROUND OUT THERE.
I CALLED THE SHERIFF'S DEPARTMENT, AND THEY SAID THEY'D GET A TASK FORCE RIGHT ON IT.
UH HUH.
WE, UH, WE'D BE HAPPY TO LOOK INTO THAT FOR YOU, MA'AM. MAY WE COME IN?
OH, PLEASE...

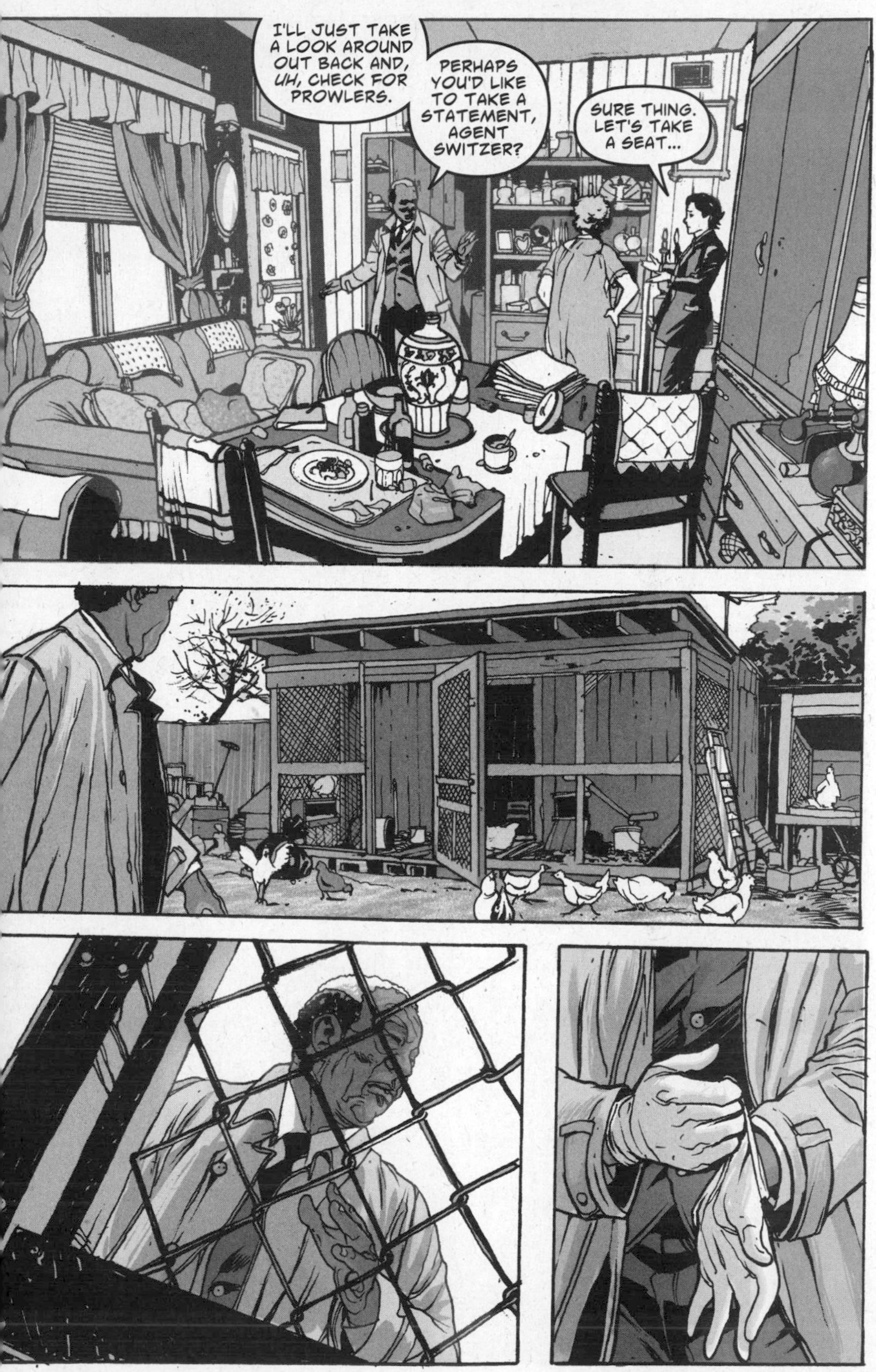
I'LL JUST TAKE A LOOK AROUND OUT BACK AND, UH, CHECK FOR PROWLERS.
PERHAPS YOU'D LIKE TO TAKE A STATEMENT, AGENT SWITZER?
SURE THING. LET'S TAKE A SEAT...

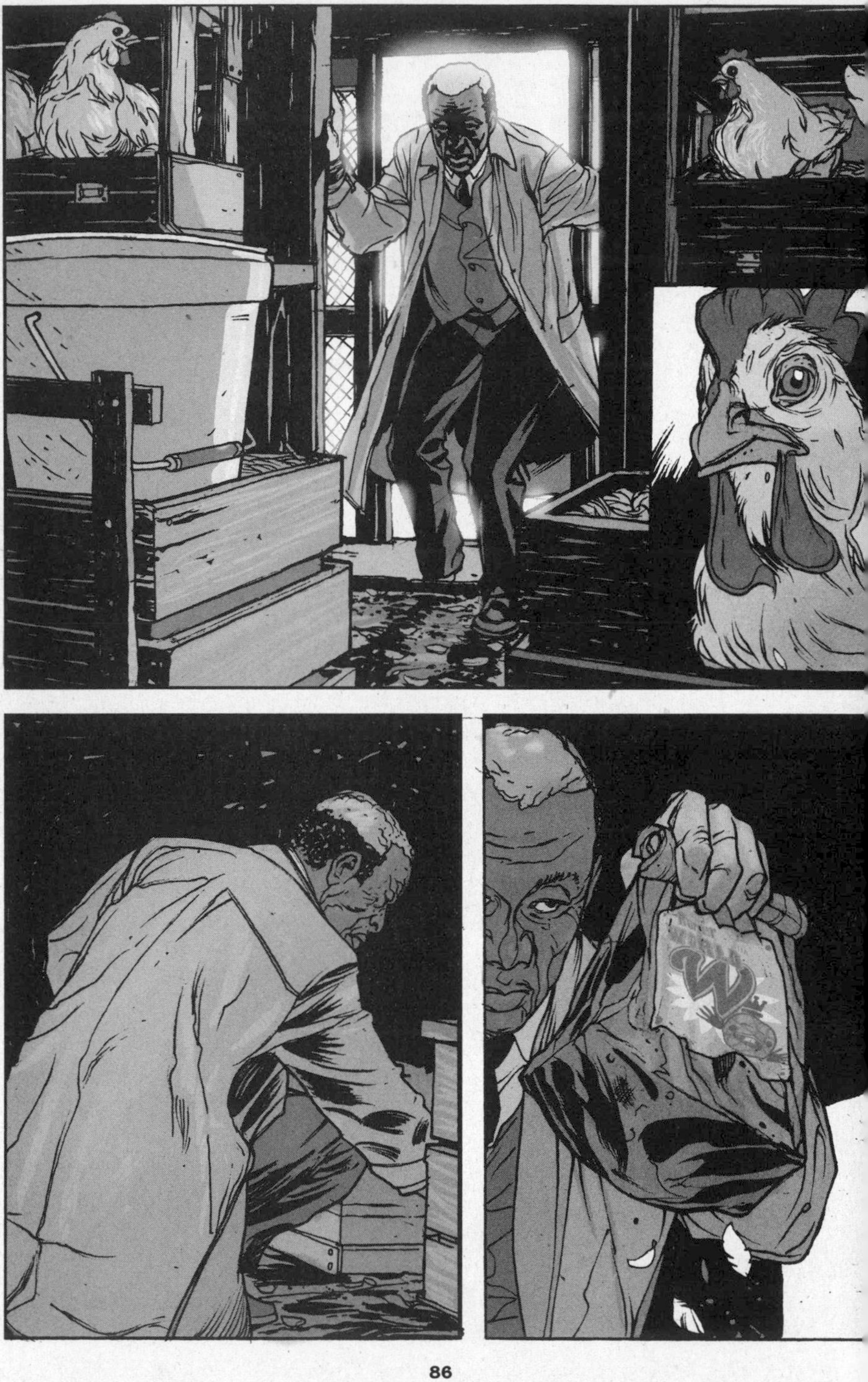

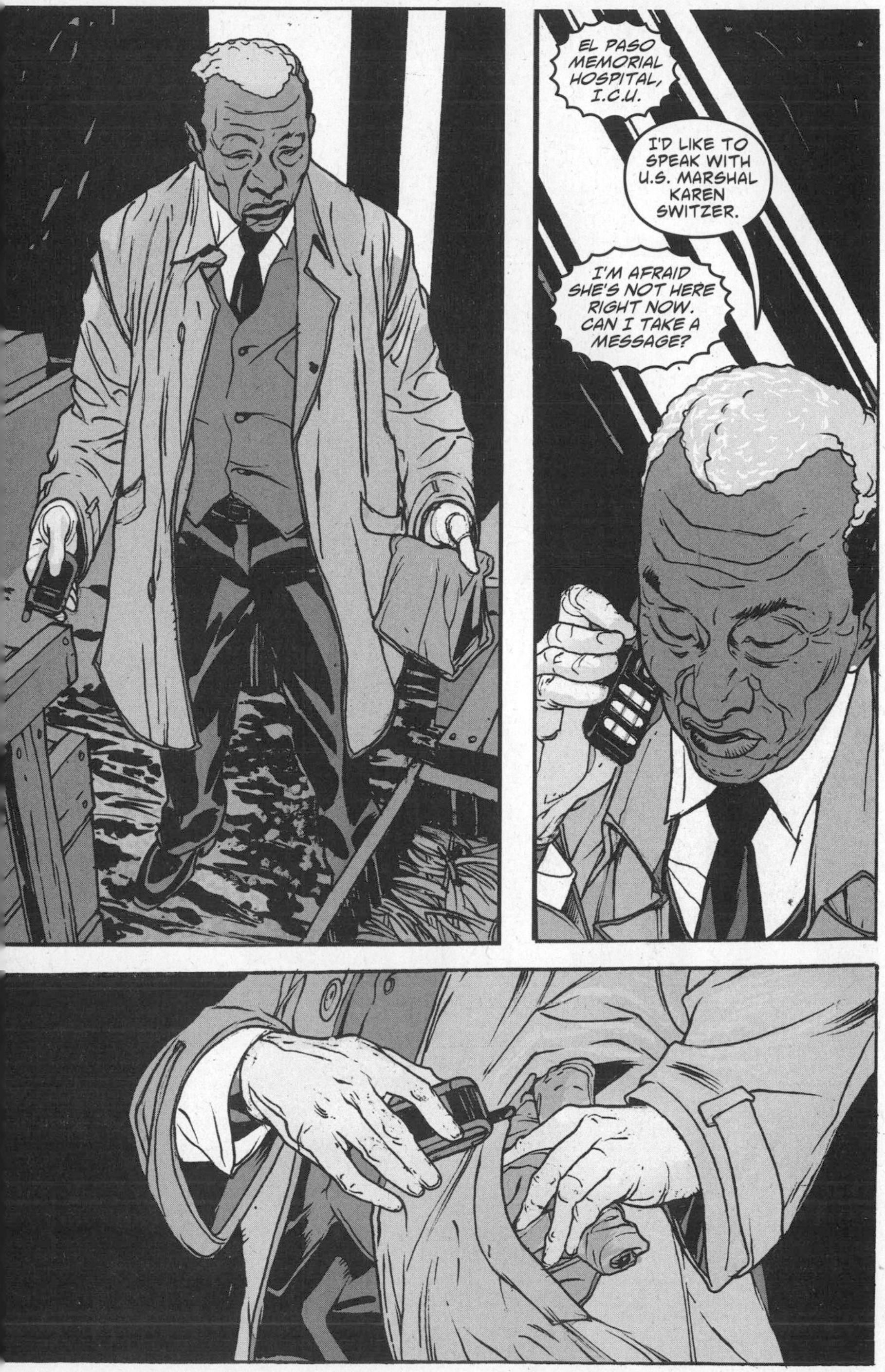
EL PASO MEMORIAL HOSPITAL, I.C.U.
I'D LIKE TO SPEAK WITH U.S. MARSHAL KAREN SWITZER.
I'M AFRAID SHE'S NOT HERE RIGHT NOW. CAN I TAKE A MESSAGE?

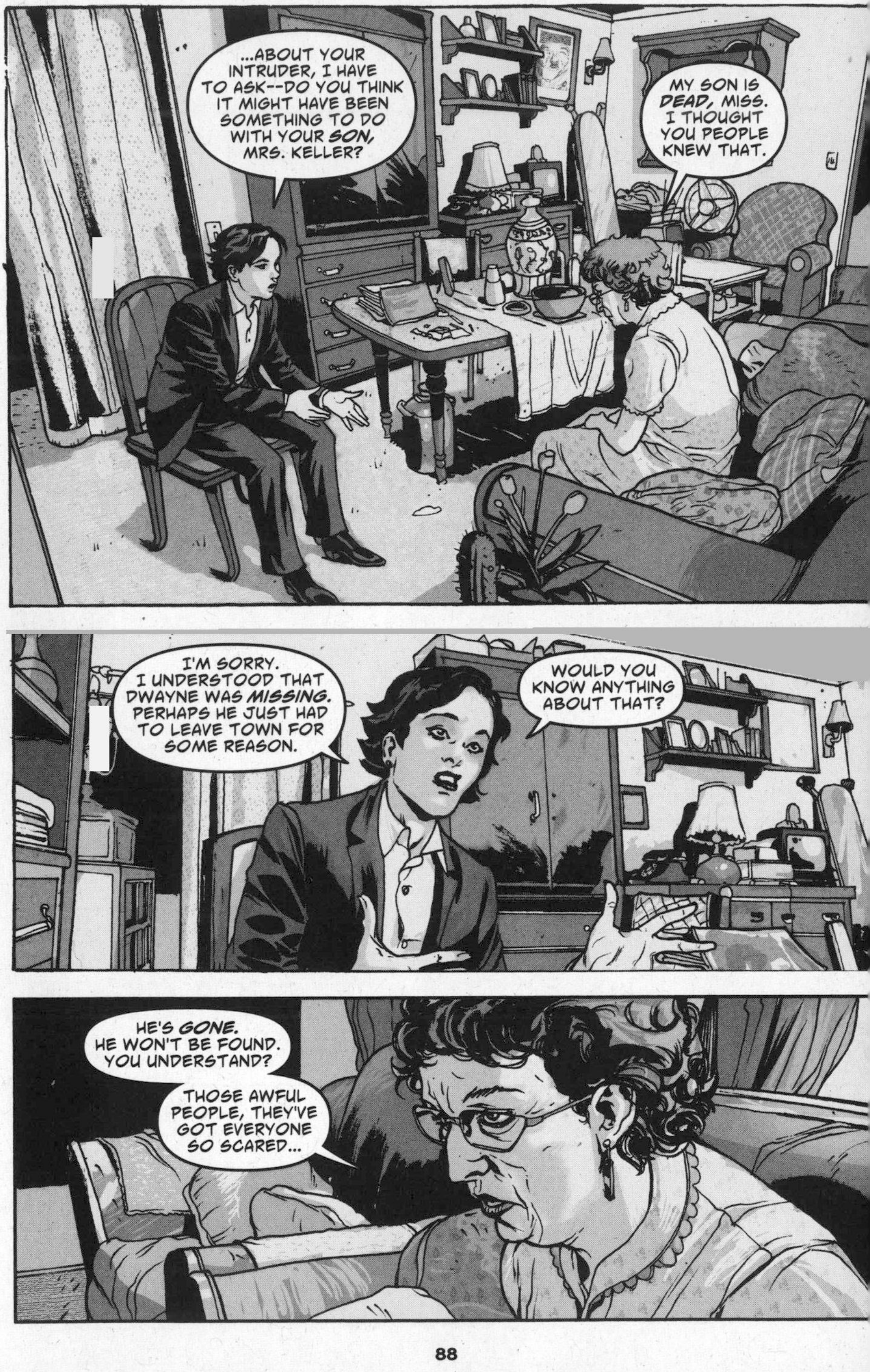
...ABOUT YOUR INTRUDER, I HAVE TO ASK--DO YOU THINK IT MIGHT HAVE BEEN SOMETHING TO DO WITH YOUR SON, MRS. KELLER?
MY SON IS DEAD, MISS. I THOUGHT YOU PEOPLE KNEW THAT.
I'M SORRY. I UNDERSTOOD THAT DWAYNE WAS MISSING. PERHAPS HE JUST HAD TO LEAVE TOWN FOR SOME REASON.
WOULD YOU KNOW ANYTHING ABOUT THAT?
HE'S GONE. HE WON'T BE FOUND. YOU UNDERSTAND?
THOSE AWFUL PEOPLE, THEY'VE GOT EVERYONE SO SCARED...

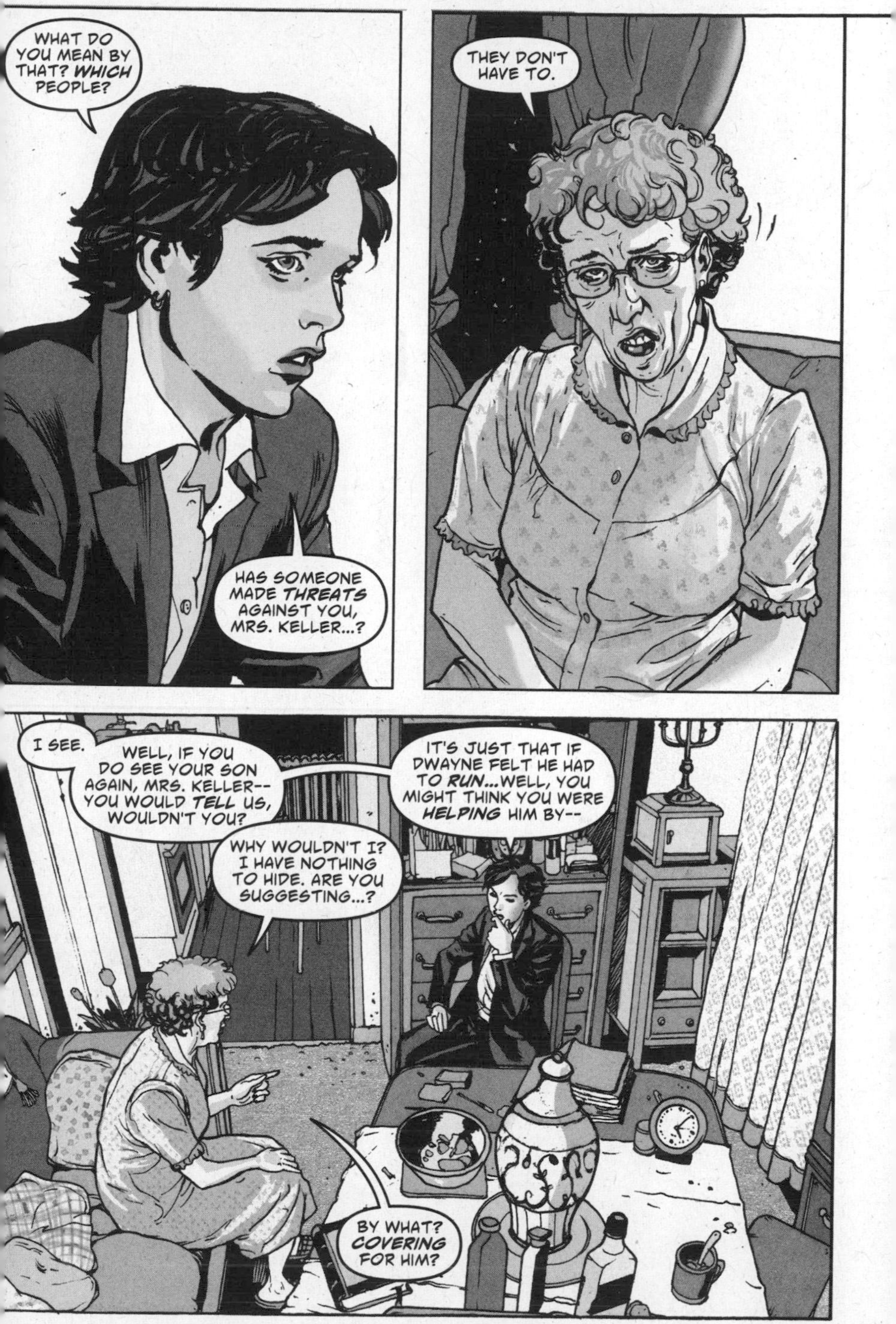
WHAT DO YOU MEAN BY THAT? WHICH PEOPLE?
HAS SOMEONE MADE THREATS AGAINST YOU, MRS. KELLER...?
THEY DON'T HAVE TO.
I SEE.
WELL, IF YOU DO SEE YOUR SON AGAIN, MRS. KELLER-- YOU WOULD TELL US, WOULDN'T YOU?
WHY WOULDN'T I? I HAVE NOTHING TO HIDE. ARE YOU SUGGESTING...?
IT'S JUST THAT IF DWAYNE FELT HE HAD TO RUN...WELL, YOU MIGHT THINK YOU WERE HELPING HIM BY--
BY WHAT? COVERING FOR HIM?

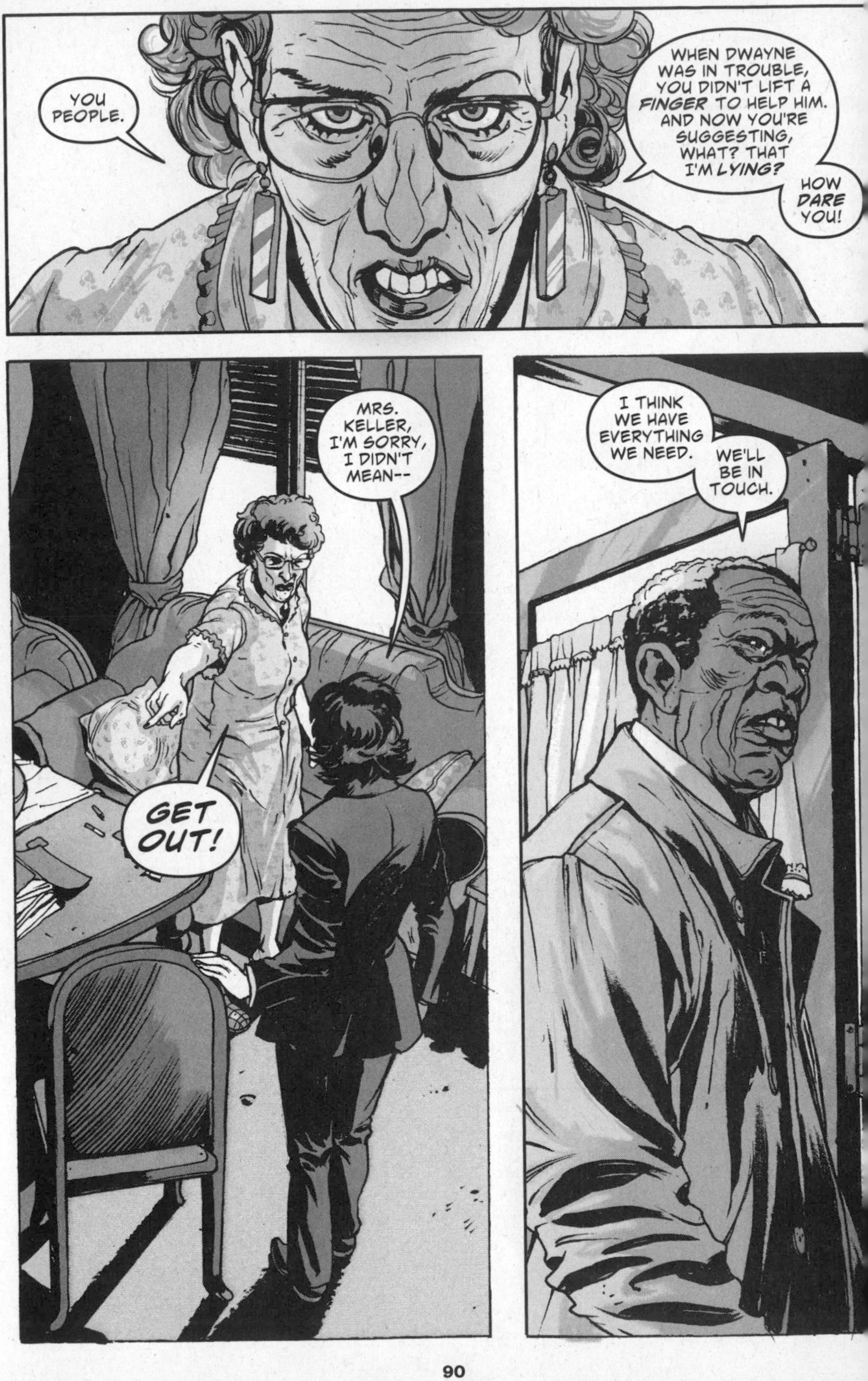
YOU PEOPLE.
WHEN DWAYNE WAS IN TROUBLE, YOU DIDN'T LIFT A FINGER TO HELP HIM. AND NOW YOU'RE SUGGESTING, WHAT? THAT I'M LYING?
HOW DARE YOU!
MRS. KELLER, I'M SORRY, I DIDN'T MEAN--
GET OUT!
I THINK WE HAVE EVERYTHING WE NEED.
WE'LL BE IN TOUCH.

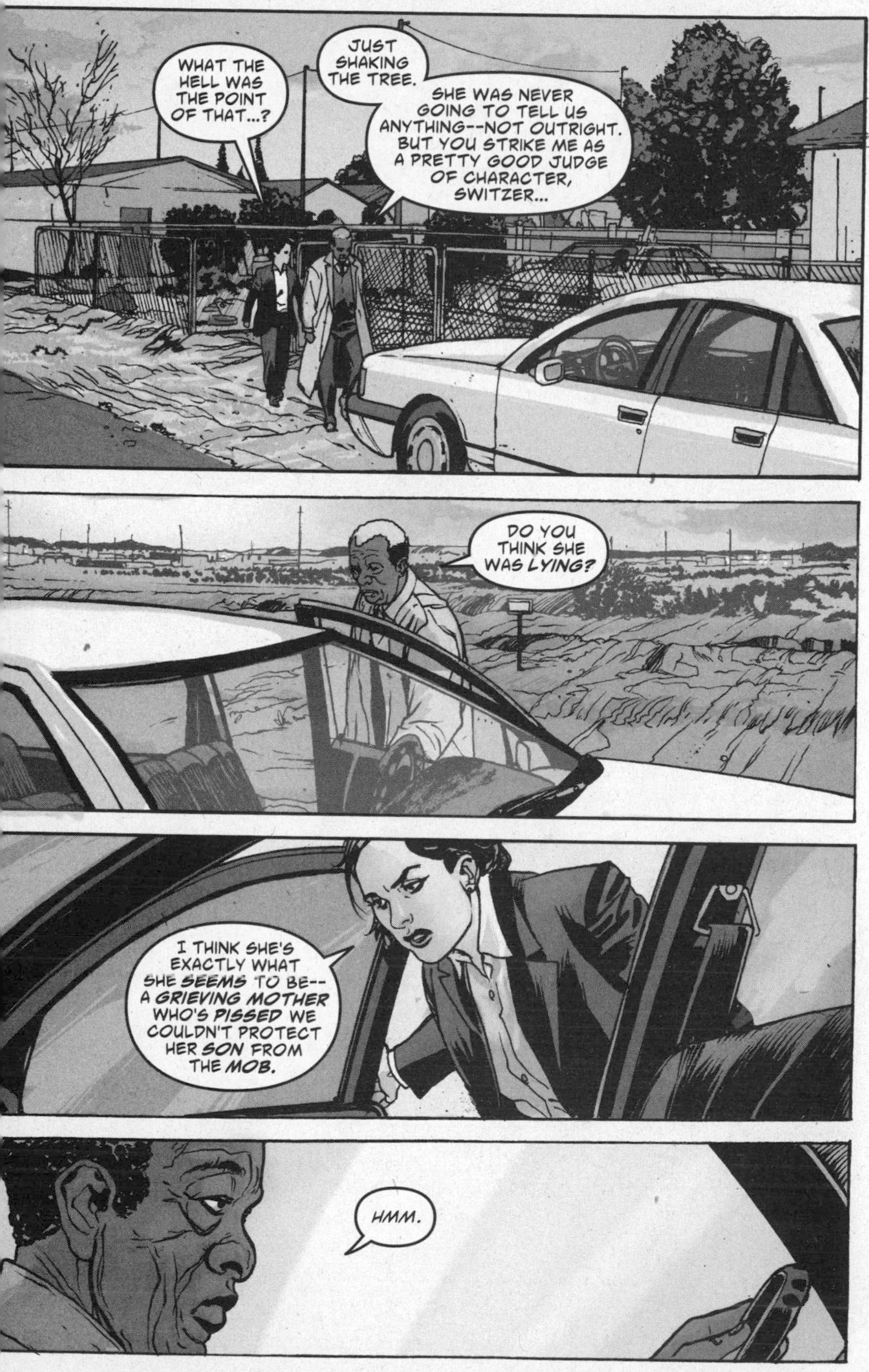
WHAT THE HELL WAS THE POINT OF THAT...?
JUST SHAKING THE TREE.
SHE WAS NEVER GOING TO TELL US ANYTHING--NOT OUTRIGHT. BUT YOU STRIKE ME AS A PRETTY GOOD JUDGE OF CHARACTER, SWITZER...
DO YOU THINK SHE WAS *LYING?*
I THINK SHE'S EXACTLY WHAT SHE *SEEMS* TO BE--A *GRIEVING MOTHER* WHO'S *PISSED* WE COULDN'T PROTECT HER *SON* FROM THE *MOB.*
HMM.

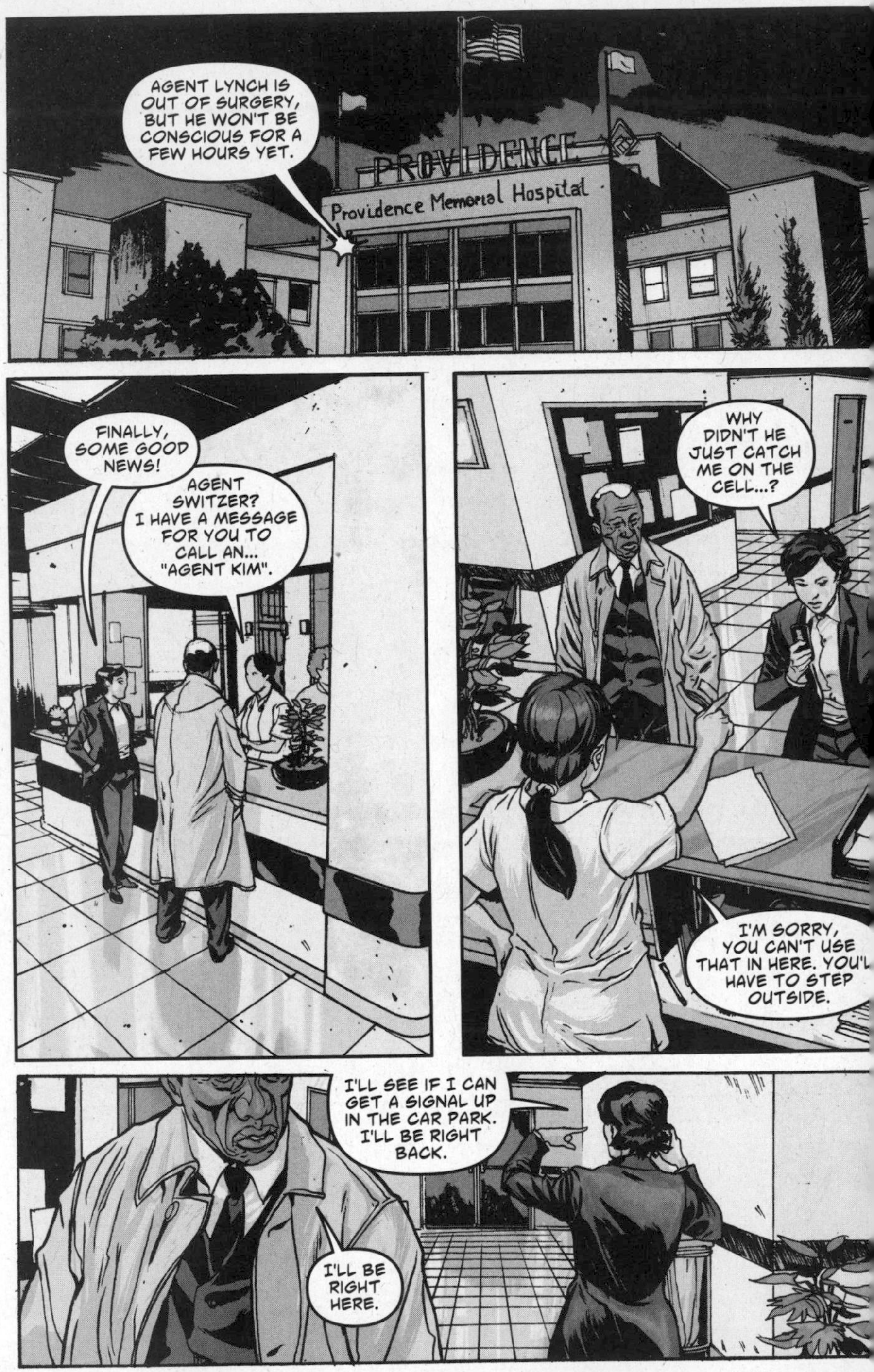
PROVIDENCE
Providence Memorial Hospital
AGENT LYNCH IS OUT OF SURGERY, BUT HE WON'T BE CONSCIOUS FOR A FEW HOURS YET.
FINALLY, SOME GOOD NEWS!
AGENT SWITZER? I HAVE A MESSAGE FOR YOU TO CALL AN... "AGENT KIM".
WHY DIDN'T HE JUST CATCH ME ON THE CELL...?
I'M SORRY, YOU CAN'T USE THAT IN HERE. YOU'L HAVE TO STEP OUTSIDE.
I'LL SEE IF I CAN GET A SIGNAL UP IN THE CAR PARK. I'LL BE RIGHT BACK.
I'LL BE RIGHT HERE.

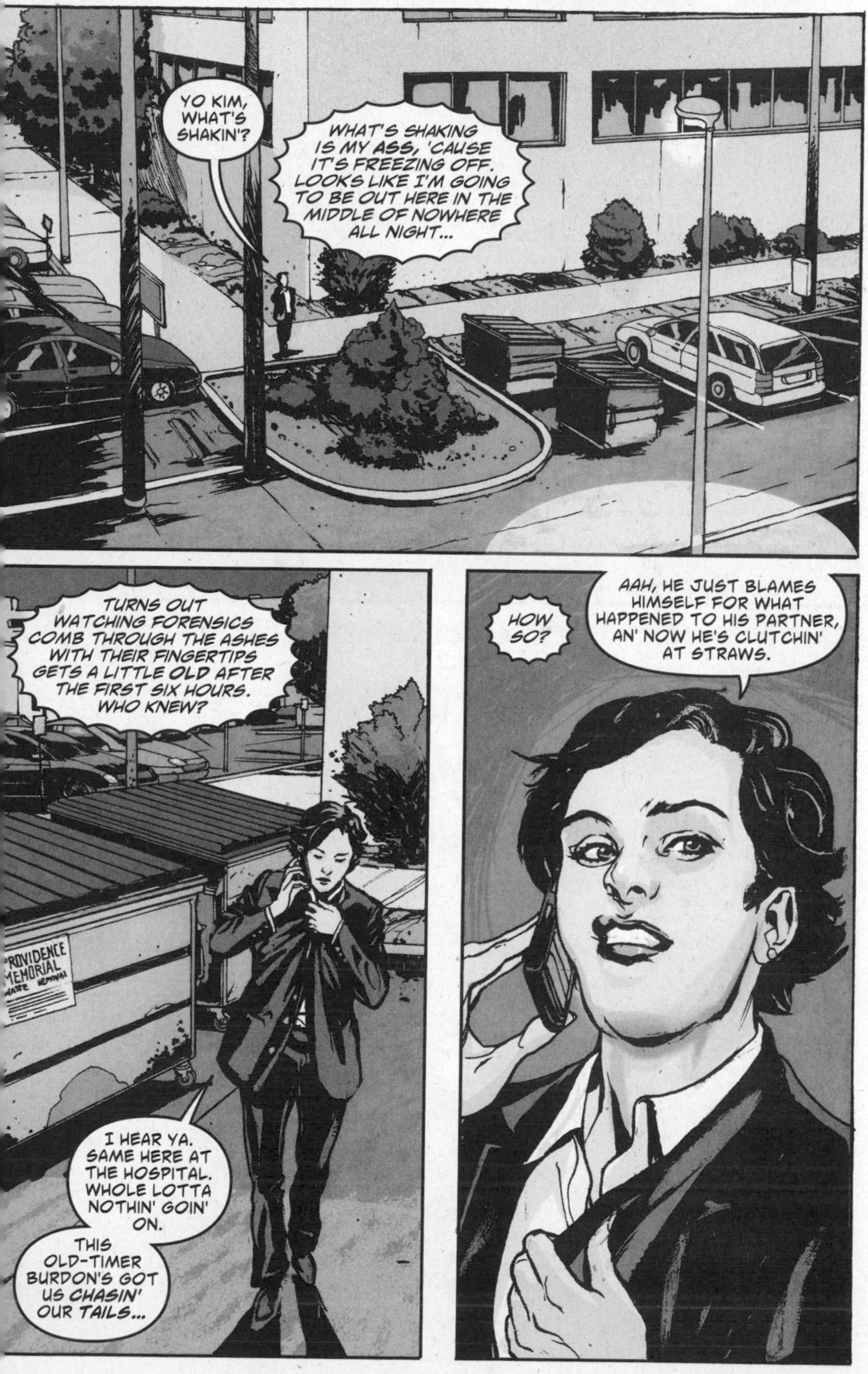
YO KIM, WHAT'S SHAKIN'?
WHAT'S SHAKING IS MY ASS, 'CAUSE IT'S FREEZING OFF. LOOKS LIKE I'M GOING TO BE OUT HERE IN THE MIDDLE OF NOWHERE ALL NIGHT...
TURNS OUT WATCHING FORENSICS COMB THROUGH THE ASHES WITH THEIR FINGERTIPS GETS A LITTLE OLD AFTER THE FIRST SIX HOURS. WHO KNEW?
PROVIDENCE MEMORIAL
I HEAR YA. SAME HERE AT THE HOSPITAL. WHOLE LOTTA NOTHIN' GOIN' ON.
THIS OLD-TIMER BURDON'S GOT US CHASIN' OUR TAILS...
HOW SO?
AAH, HE JUST BLAMES HIMSELF FOR WHAT HAPPENED TO HIS PARTNER, AN' NOW HE'S CLUTCHIN' AT STRAWS.

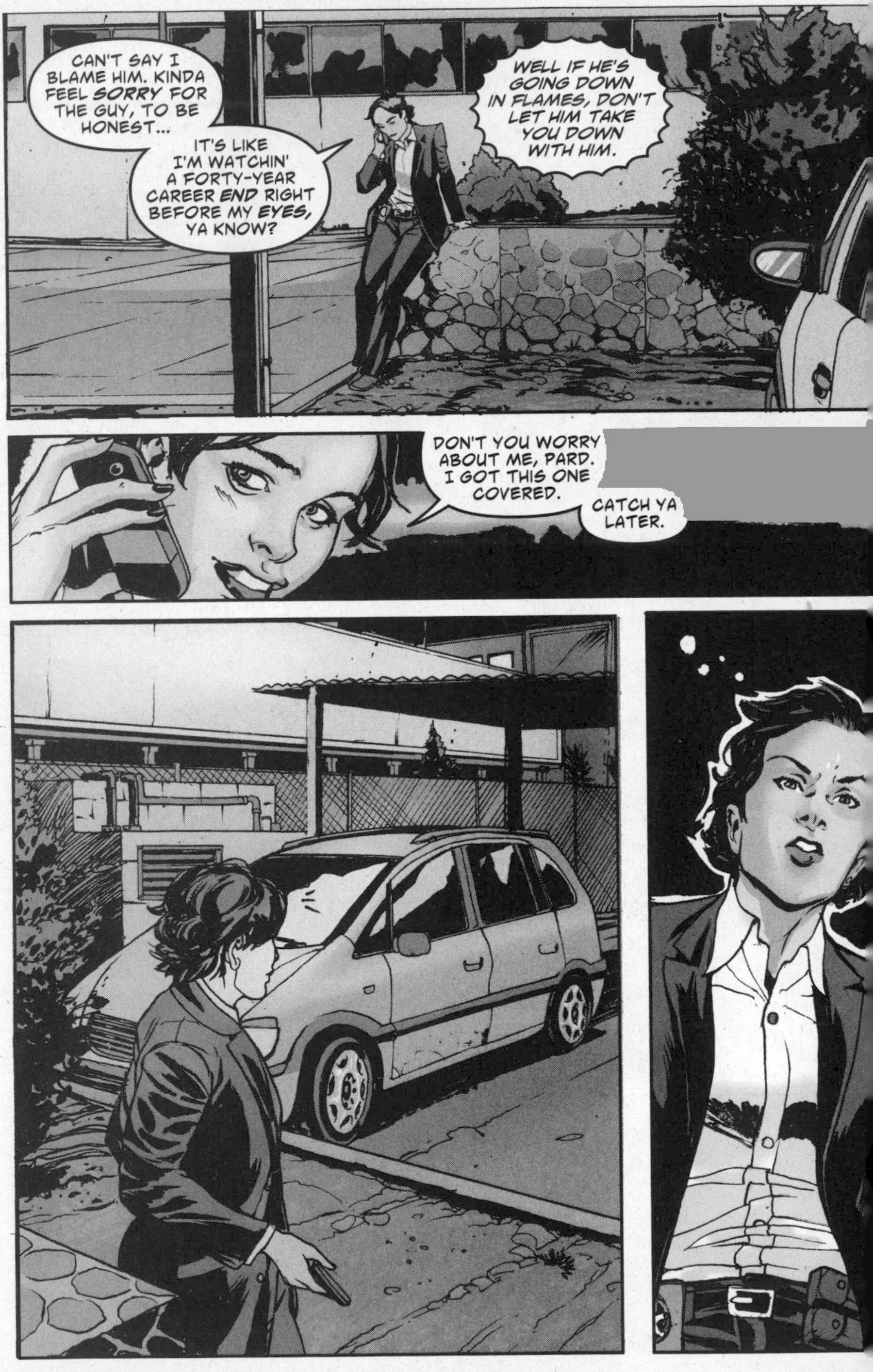
CAN'T SAY I BLAME HIM. KINDA FEEL SORRY FOR THE GUY, TO BE HONEST...
IT'S LIKE I'M WATCHIN' A FORTY-YEAR CAREER END RIGHT BEFORE MY EYES, YA KNOW?
WELL IF HE'S GOING DOWN IN FLAMES, DON'T LET HIM TAKE YOU DOWN WITH HIM.
DON'T YOU WORRY ABOUT ME, PARD. I GOT THIS ONE COVERED.
CATCH YA LATER.

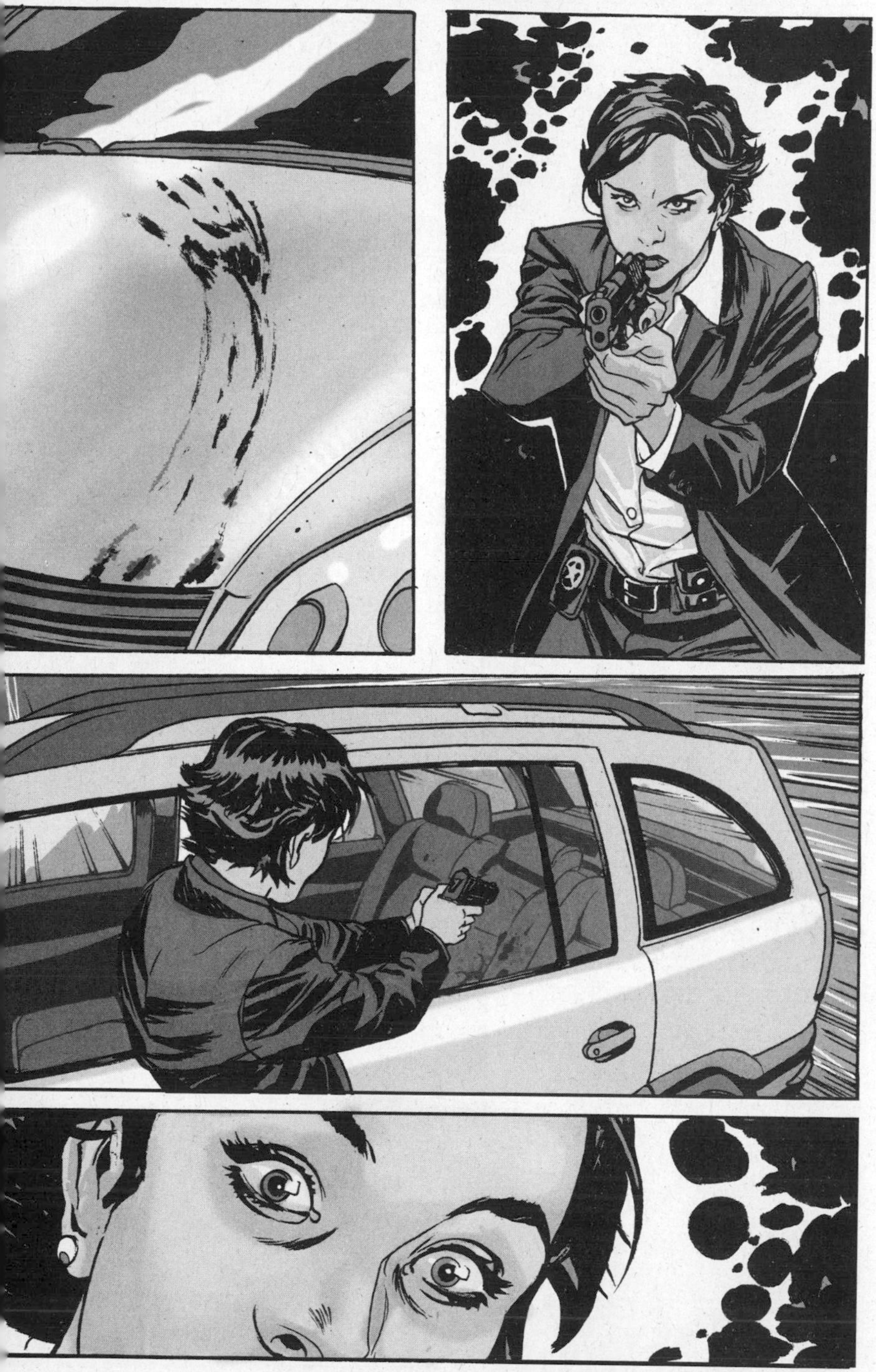

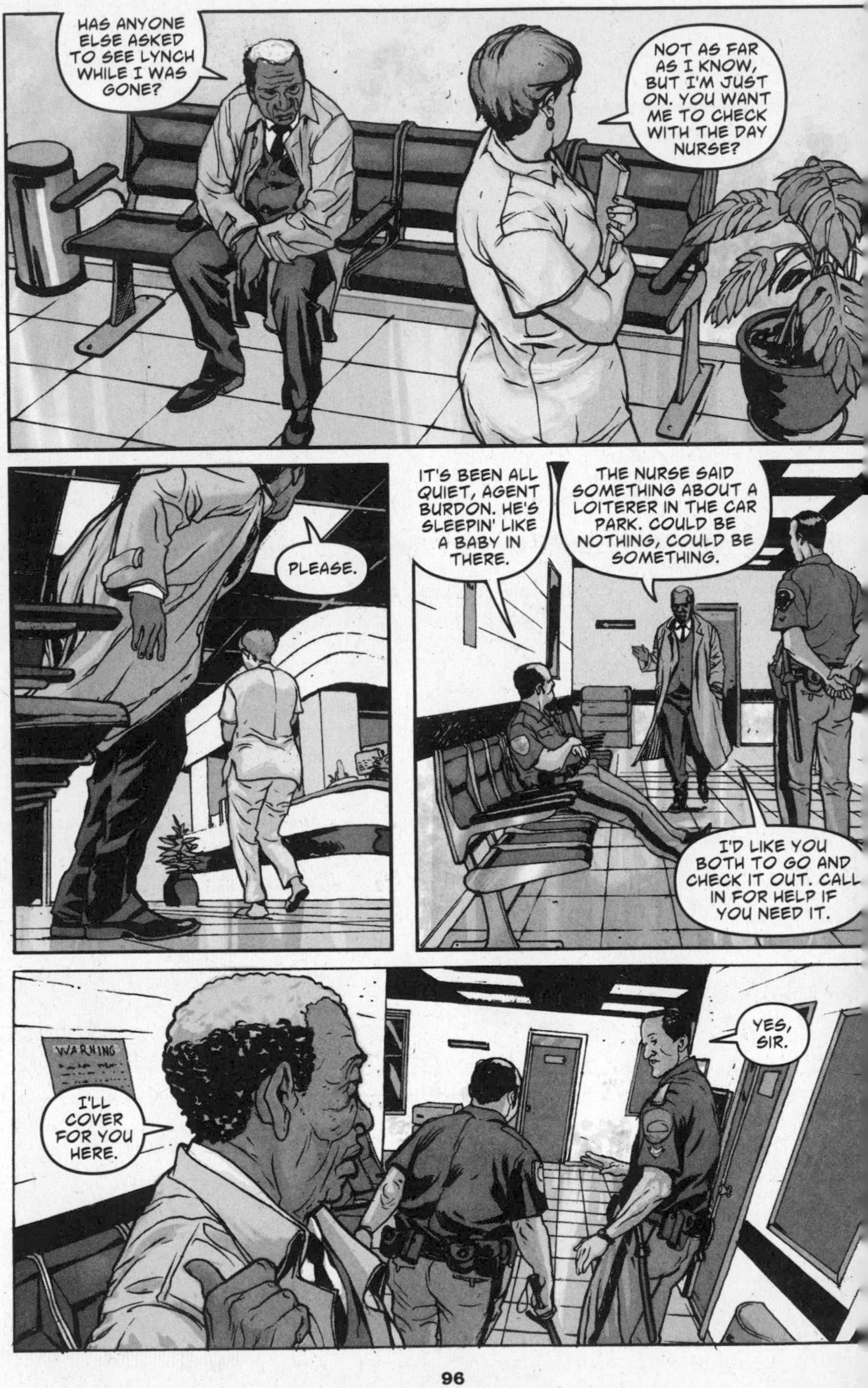
HAS ANYONE ELSE ASKED TO SEE LYNCH WHILE I WAS GONE?
NOT AS FAR AS I KNOW, BUT I'M JUST ON. YOU WANT ME TO CHECK WITH THE DAY NURSE?
PLEASE.
IT'S BEEN ALL QUIET, AGENT BURDON. HE'S SLEEPIN' LIKE A BABY IN THERE.
THE NURSE SAID SOMETHING ABOUT A LOITERER IN THE CAR PARK. COULD BE NOTHING, COULD BE SOMETHING.
I'D LIKE YOU BOTH TO GO AND CHECK IT OUT. CALL IN FOR HELP IF YOU NEED IT.
WARNING
I'LL COVER FOR YOU HERE.
YES, SIR.

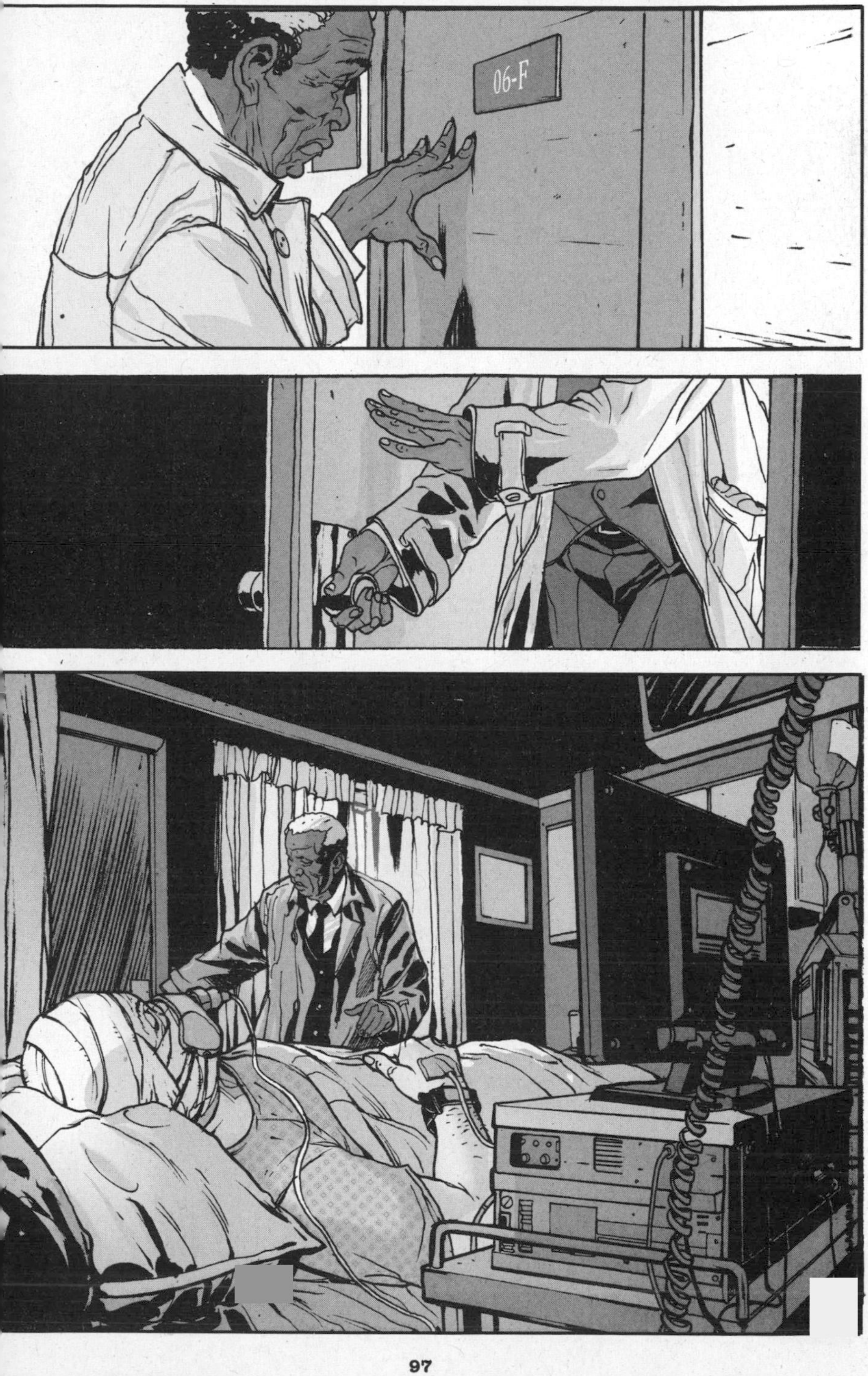
06-F

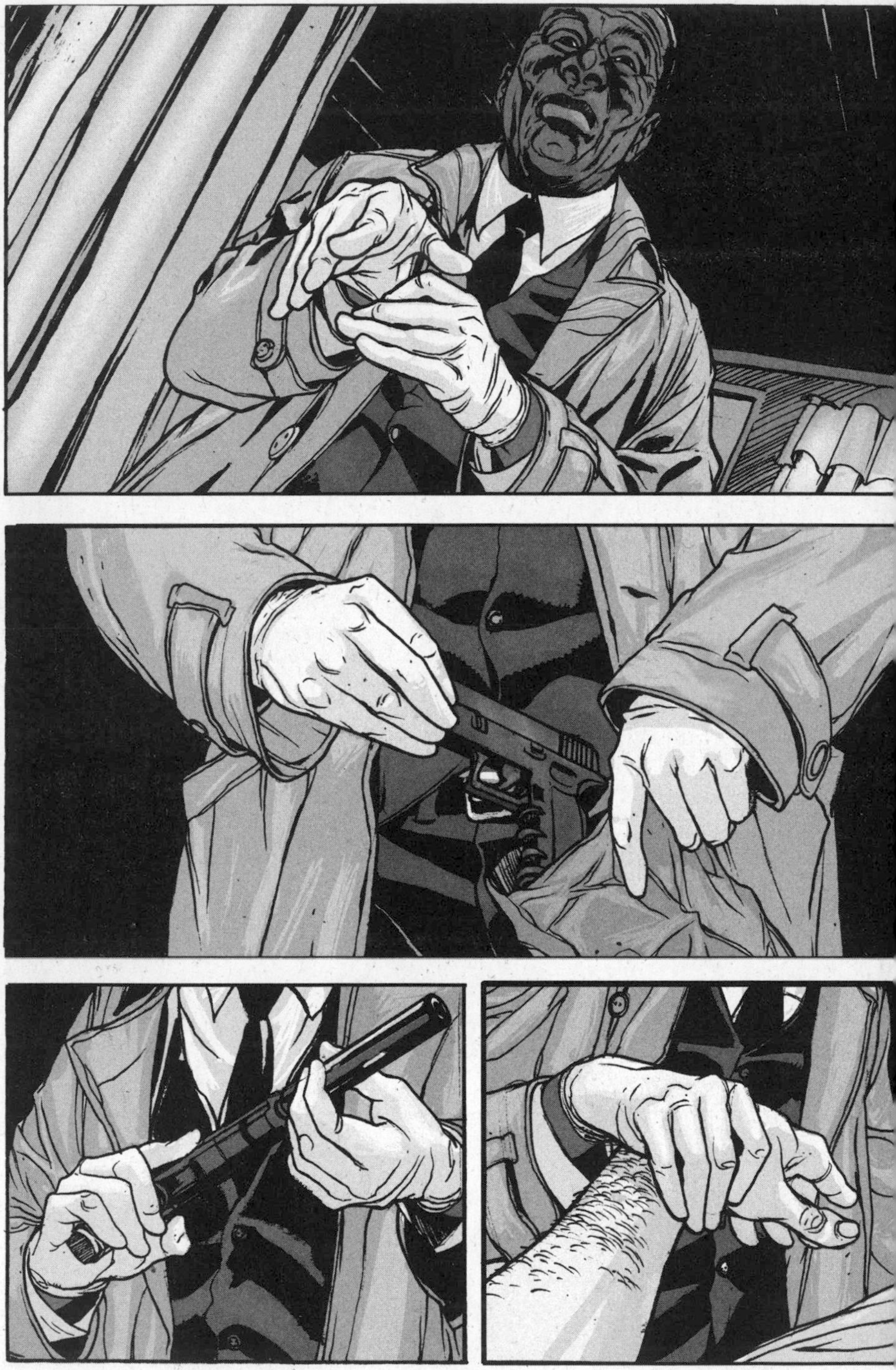

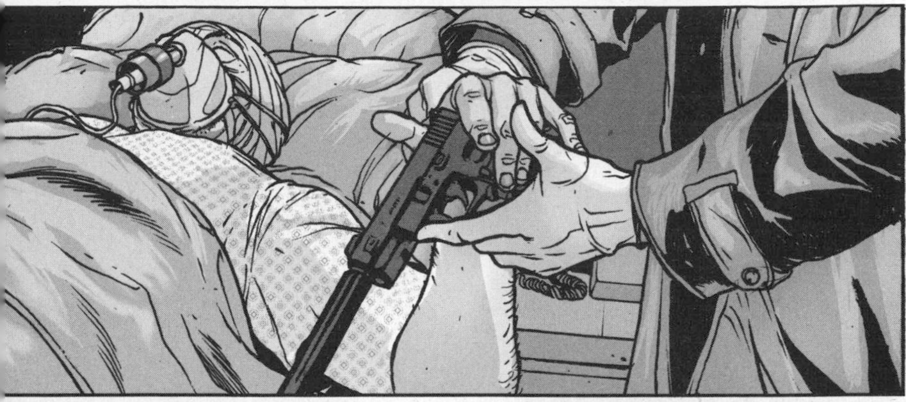

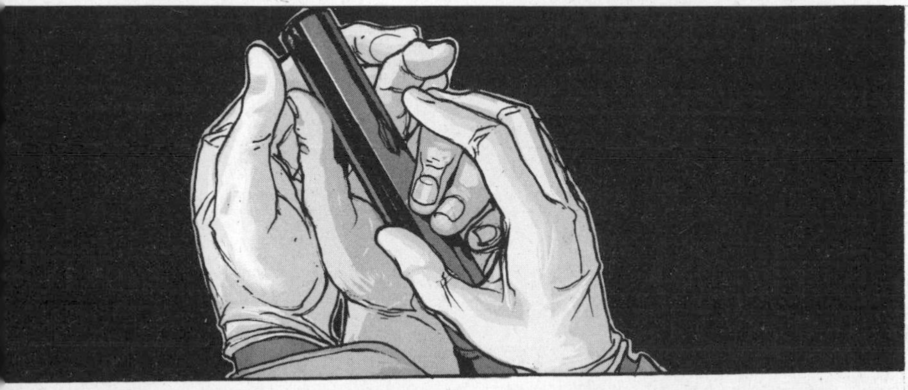

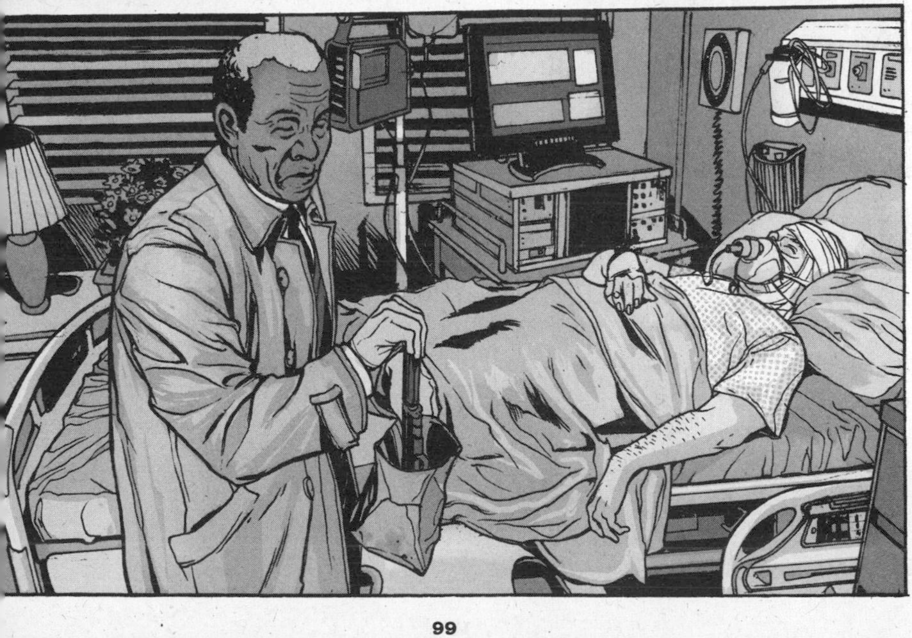

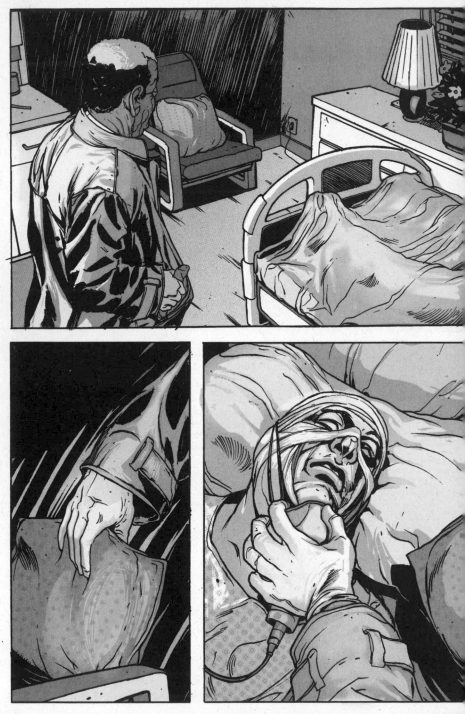

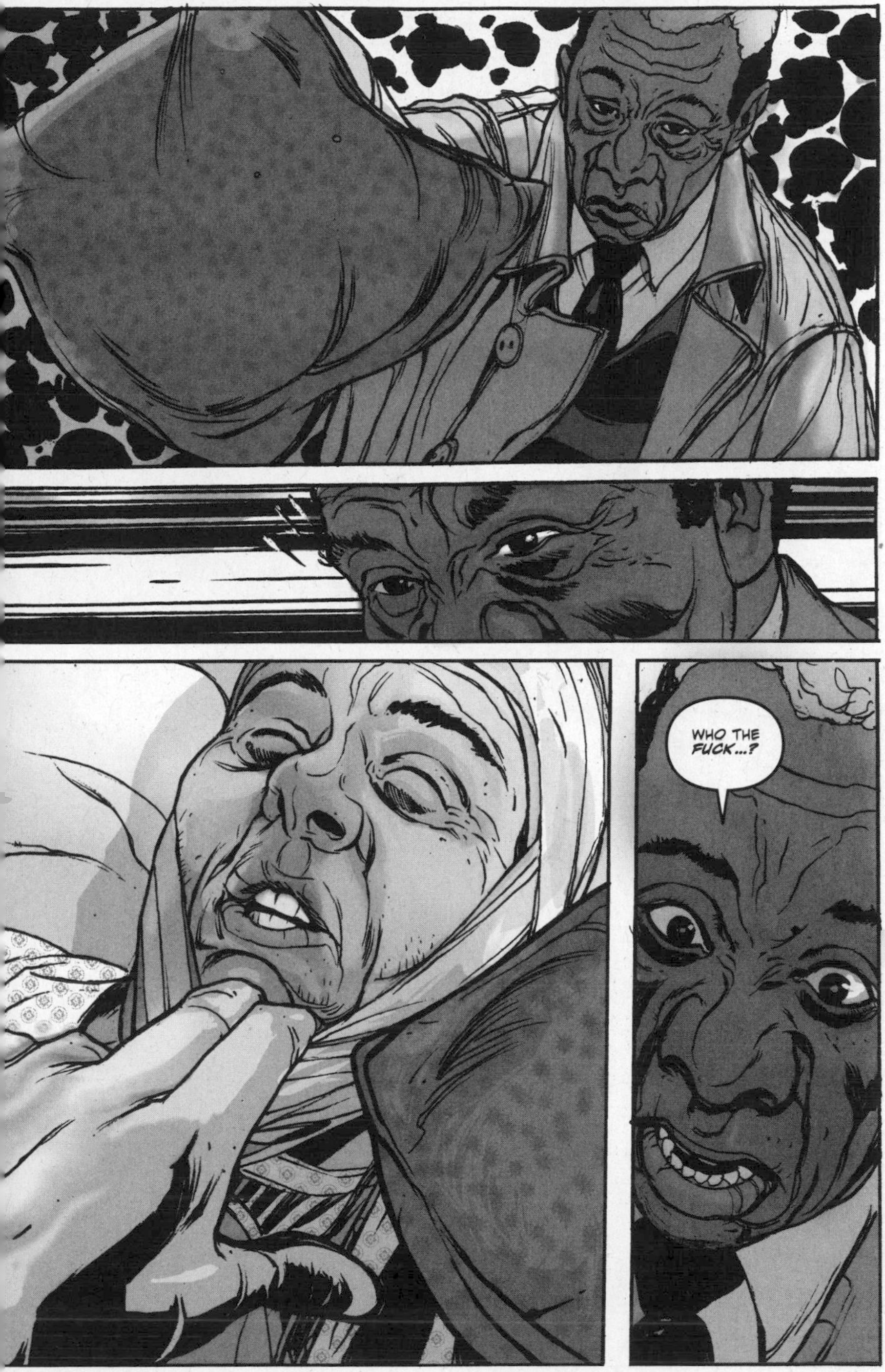
WHO THE FUCK...?

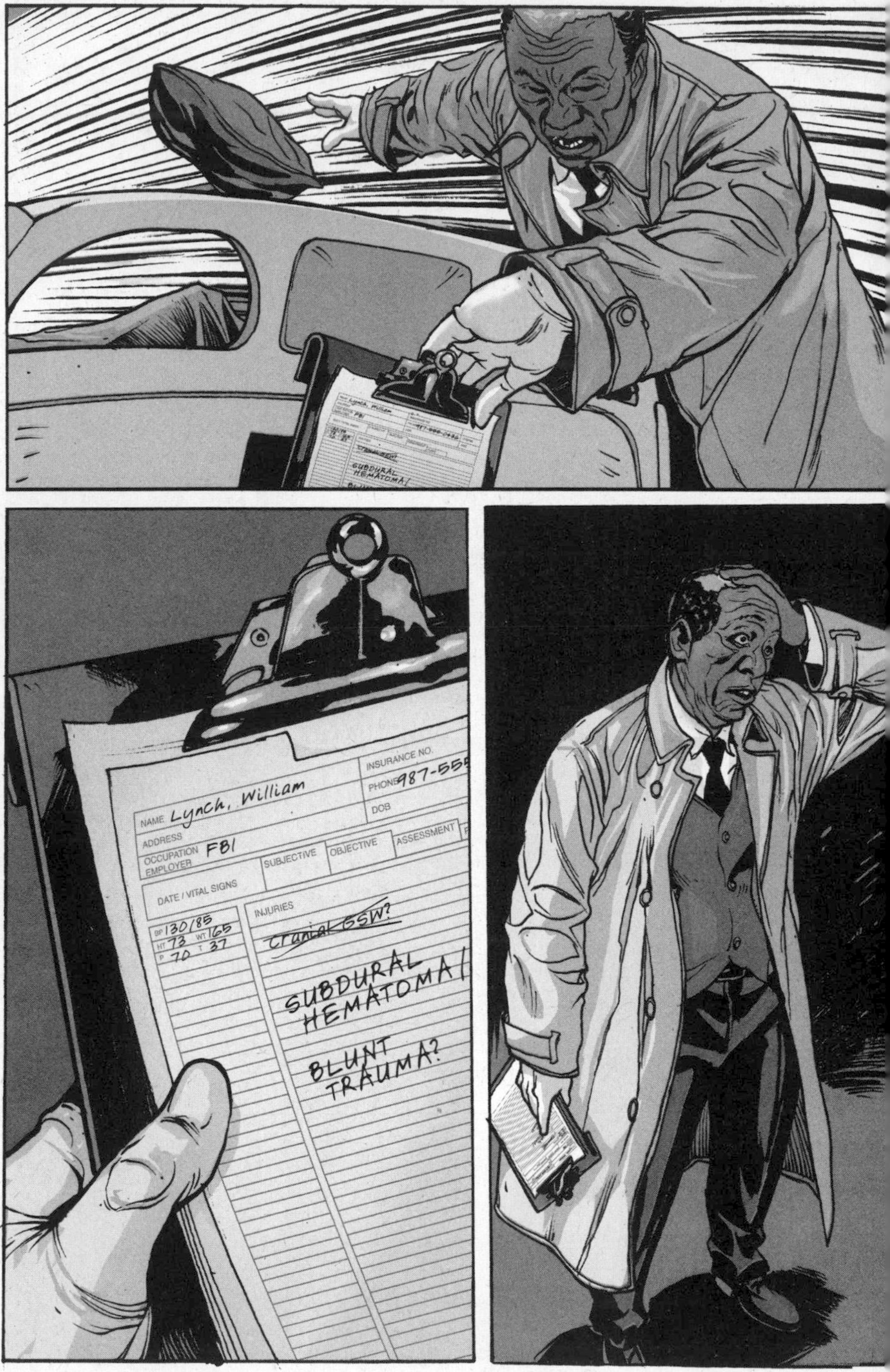
INSURANCE NO.
PHONE 987-555
NAME Lynch, William
DOB
ADDRESS
OCCUPATION EMPLOYER FBI
SUBJECTIVE
OBJECTIVE
ASSESSMENT
DATE / VITAL SIGNS
BP 130/85
HT 73 WT 165
P 70 T 37
INJURIES
~~Cranial GSW?~~
SUBDURAL HEMATOMA!
BLUNT TRAUMA?

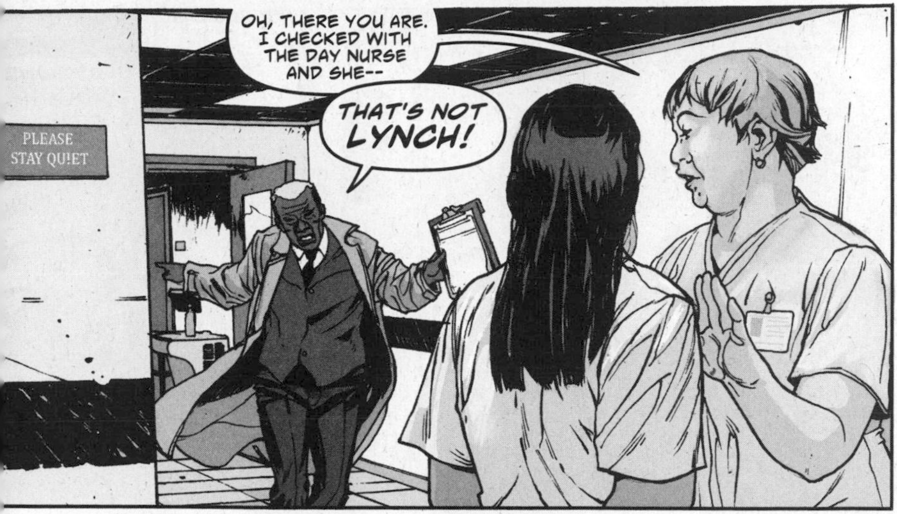
PLEASE STAY QU!ET
OH, THERE YOU ARE. I CHECKED WITH THE DAY NURSE AND SHE--
THAT'S NOT LYNCH!

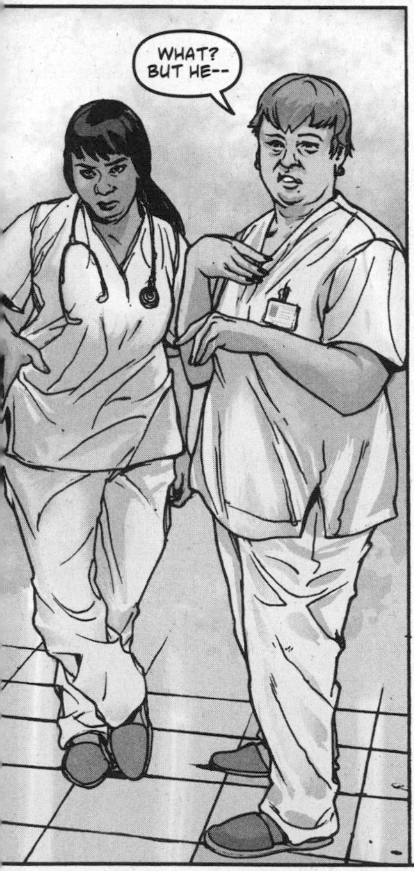
WHAT? BUT HE--

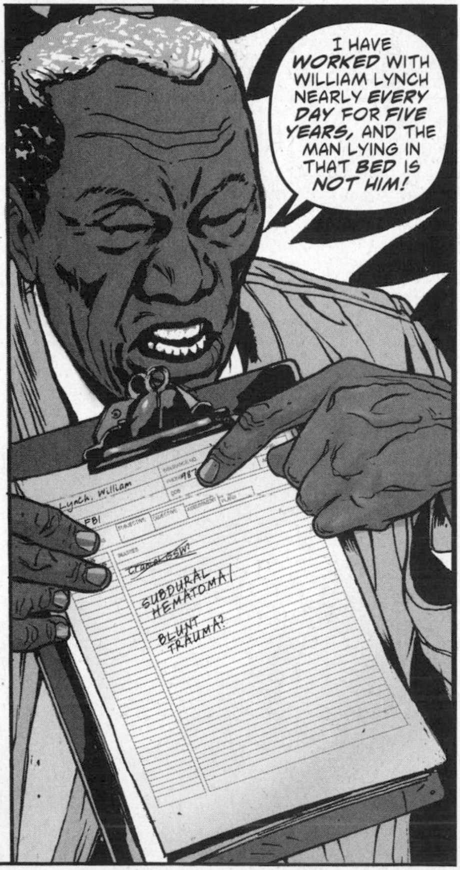
I HAVE WORKED WITH WILLIAM LYNCH NEARLY EVERY DAY FOR FIVE YEARS, AND THE MAN LYING IN THAT BED IS NOT HIM!
Lynch, William
FBI
SUBDURAL HEMATOMA/
BLUNT TRAUMA?

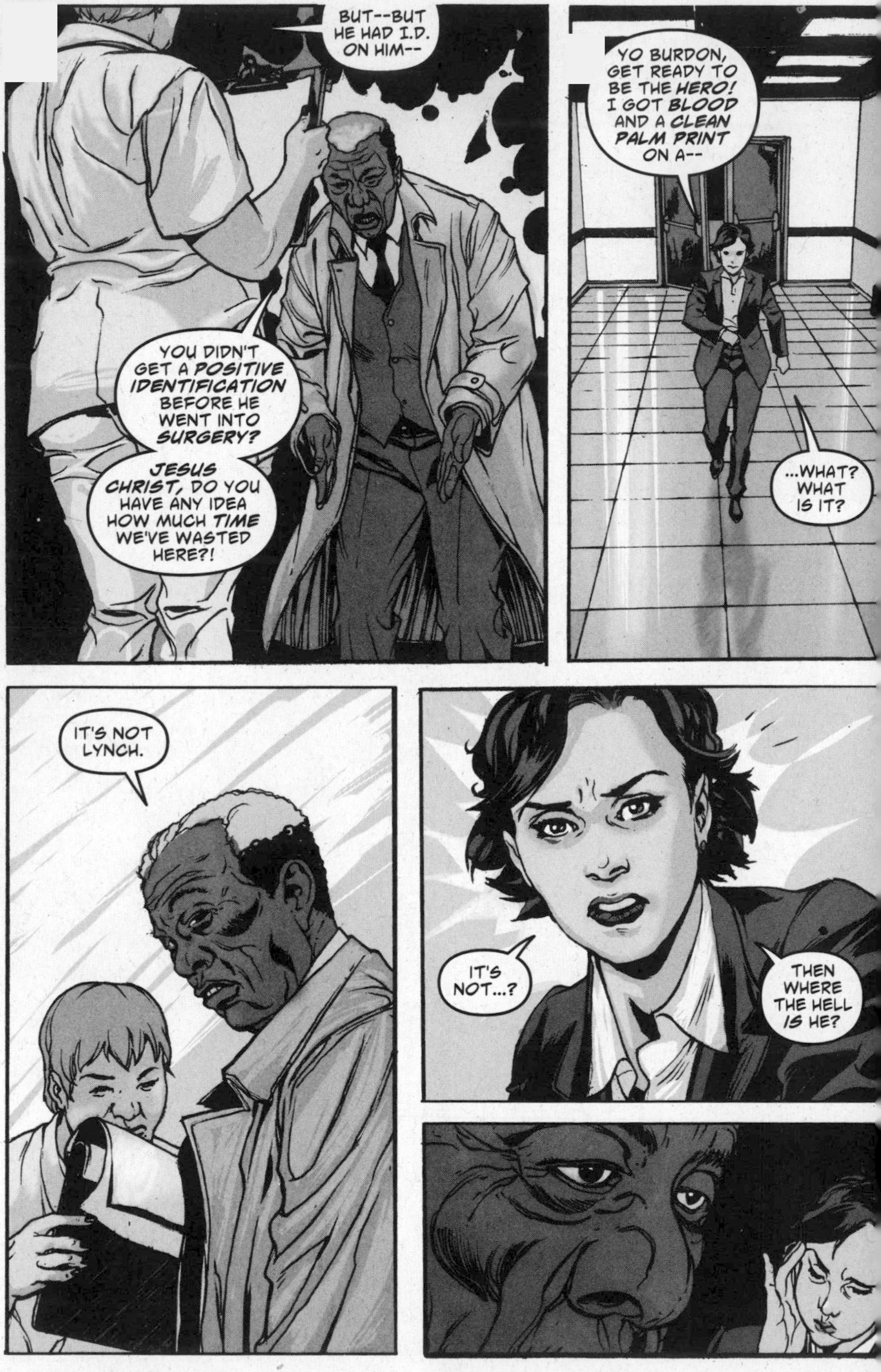

BUT--BUT HE HAD I.D. ON HIM--
YOU DIDN'T GET A POSITIVE IDENTIFICATION BEFORE HE WENT INTO SURGERY?
JESUS CHRIST, DO YOU HAVE ANY IDEA HOW MUCH TIME WE'VE WASTED HERE?!
YO BURDON, GET READY TO BE THE HERO! I GOT BLOOD AND A CLEAN PALM PRINT ON A--
...WHAT? WHAT IS IT?
IT'S NOT LYNCH.
IT'S NOT...?
THEN WHERE THE HELL IS HE?

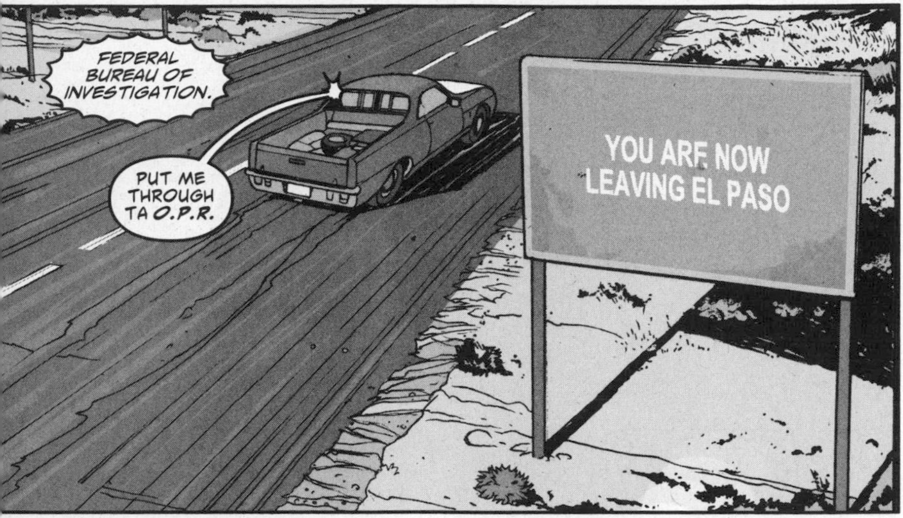

FEDERAL BUREAU OF INVESTIGATION.
PUT ME THROUGH TA O.P.R.
YOU ARE NOW LEAVING EL PASO

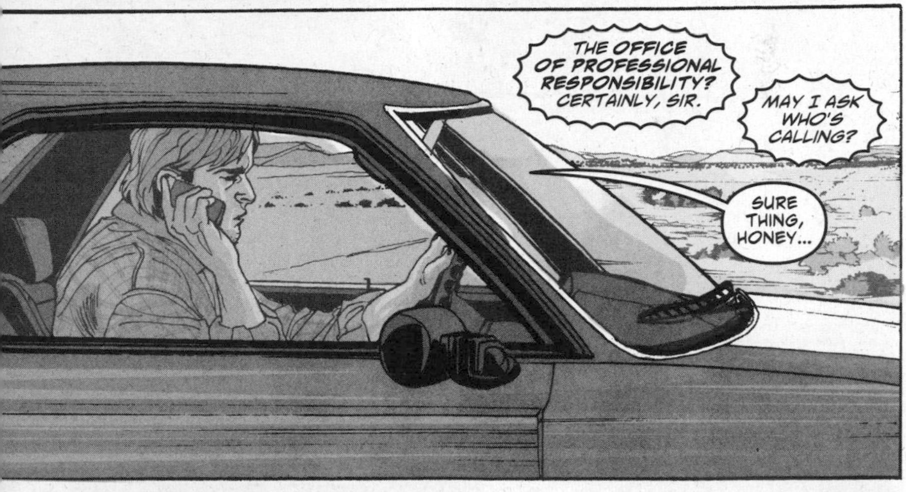

THE OFFICE OF PROFESSIONAL RESPONSIBILITY? CERTAINLY, SIR.
MAY I ASK WHO'S CALLING?
SURE THING, HONEY...

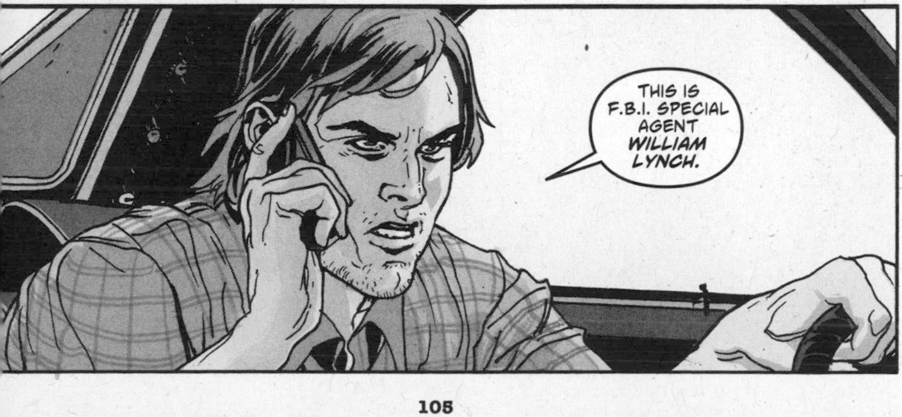

THIS IS F.B.I. SPECIAL AGENT WILLIAM LYNCH.

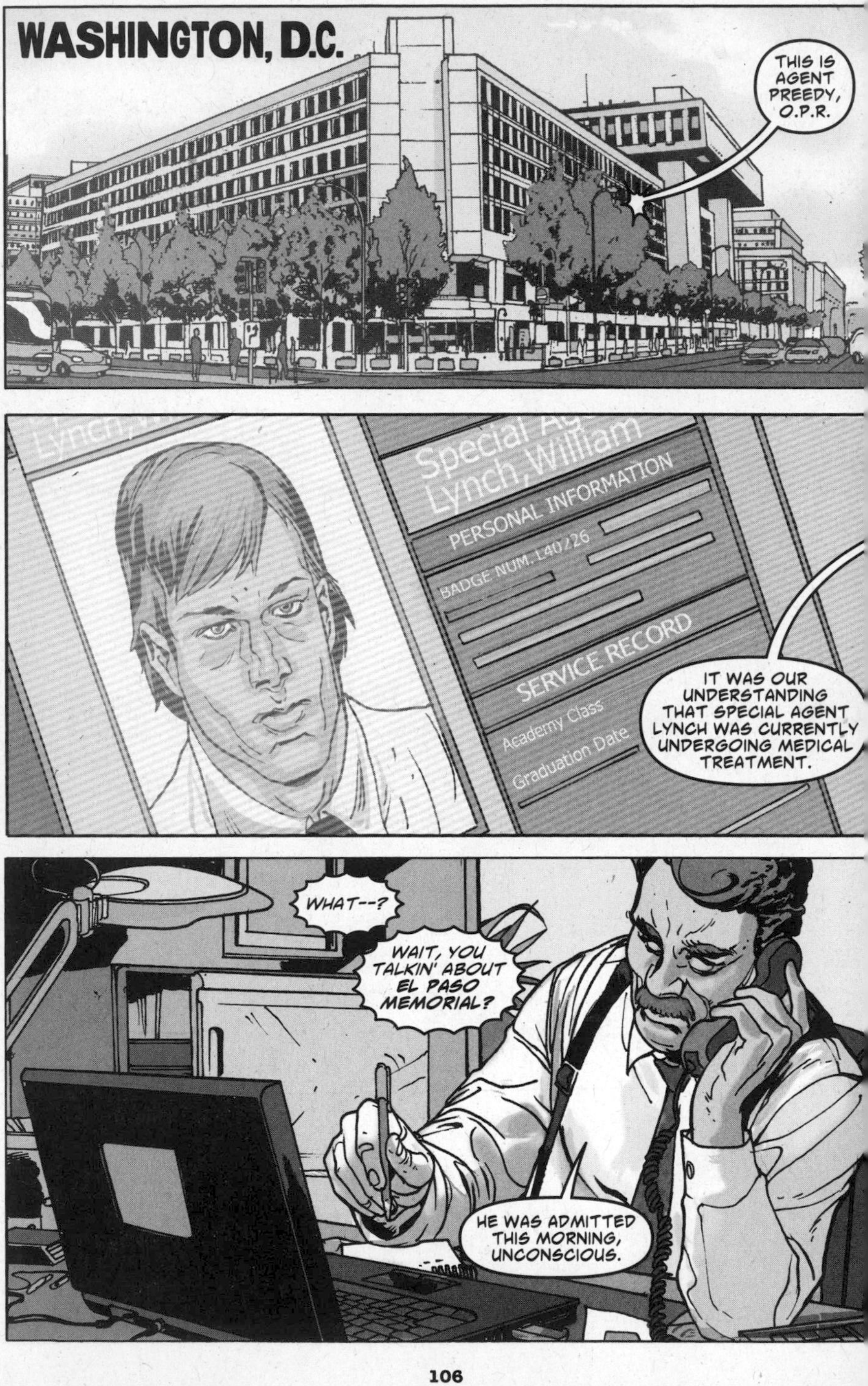
WASHINGTON, D.C.
THIS IS AGENT PREEDY, O.P.R.
Special Agent
Lynch, William
PERSONAL INFORMATION
BADGE NUM. L40226
SERVICE RECORD
Academy Class
Graduation Date
IT WAS OUR UNDERSTANDING THAT SPECIAL AGENT LYNCH WAS CURRENTLY UNDERGOING MEDICAL TREATMENT.
WHAT--?
WAIT, YOU TALKIN' ABOUT EL PASO MEMORIAL?
HE WAS ADMITTED THIS MORNING, UNCONSCIOUS.

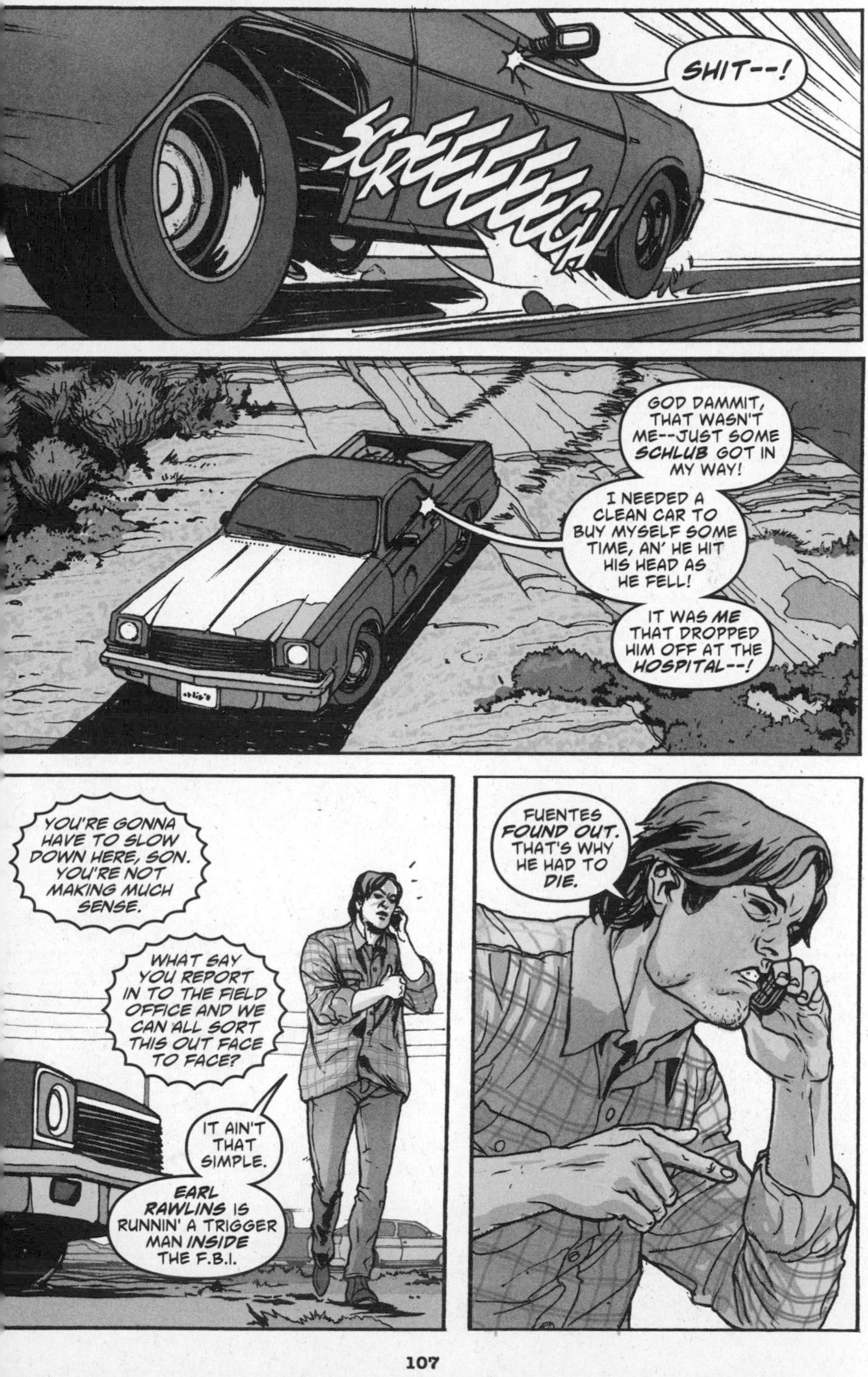
SHIT--!
SCREEEEEECH
GOD DAMMIT, THAT WASN'T ME--JUST SOME SCHLUB GOT IN MY WAY!
I NEEDED A CLEAN CAR TO BUY MYSELF SOME TIME, AN' HE HIT HIS HEAD AS HE FELL!
IT WAS ME THAT DROPPED HIM OFF AT THE HOSPITAL--!
YOU'RE GONNA HAVE TO SLOW DOWN HERE, SON. YOU'RE NOT MAKING MUCH SENSE.
WHAT SAY YOU REPORT IN TO THE FIELD OFFICE AND WE CAN ALL SORT THIS OUT FACE TO FACE?
IT AIN'T THAT SIMPLE.
EARL RAWLINS IS RUNNIN' A TRIGGER MAN INSIDE THE F.B.I.
FUENTES FOUND OUT. THAT'S WHY HE HAD TO DIE.

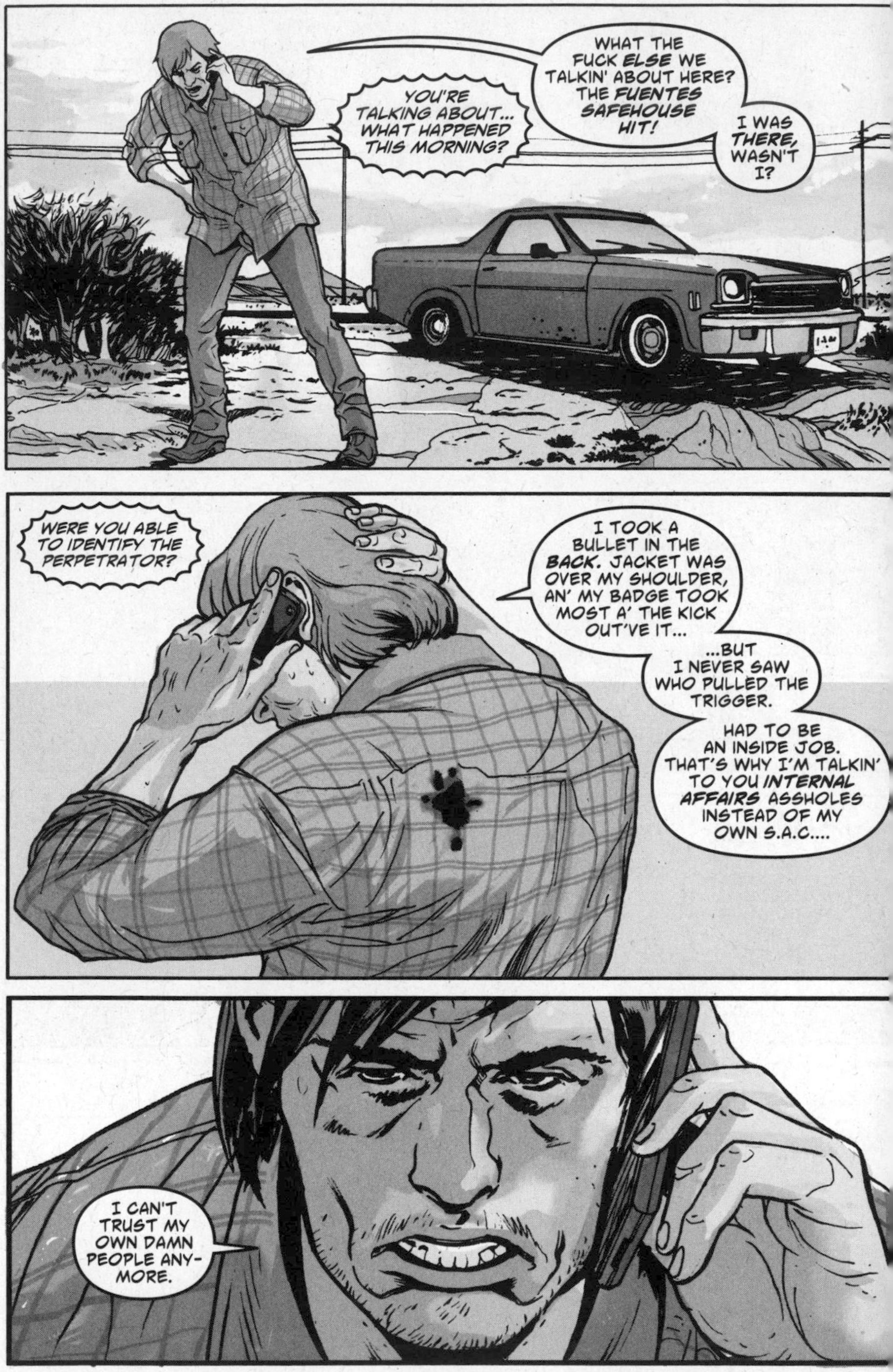
WHAT THE FUCK ELSE WE TALKIN' ABOUT HERE? THE FUENTES SAFEHOUSE HIT!
YOU'RE TALKING ABOUT... WHAT HAPPENED THIS MORNING?
I WAS THERE, WASN'T I?
WERE YOU ABLE TO IDENTIFY THE PERPETRATOR?
I TOOK A BULLET IN THE BACK. JACKET WAS OVER MY SHOULDER, AN' MY BADGE TOOK MOST A' THE KICK OUT'VE IT...
...BUT I NEVER SAW WHO PULLED THE TRIGGER.
HAD TO BE AN INSIDE JOB. THAT'S WHY I'M TALKIN' TO YOU INTERNAL AFFAIRS ASSHOLES INSTEAD OF MY OWN S.A.C....
I CAN'T TRUST MY OWN DAMN PEOPLE ANYMORE.

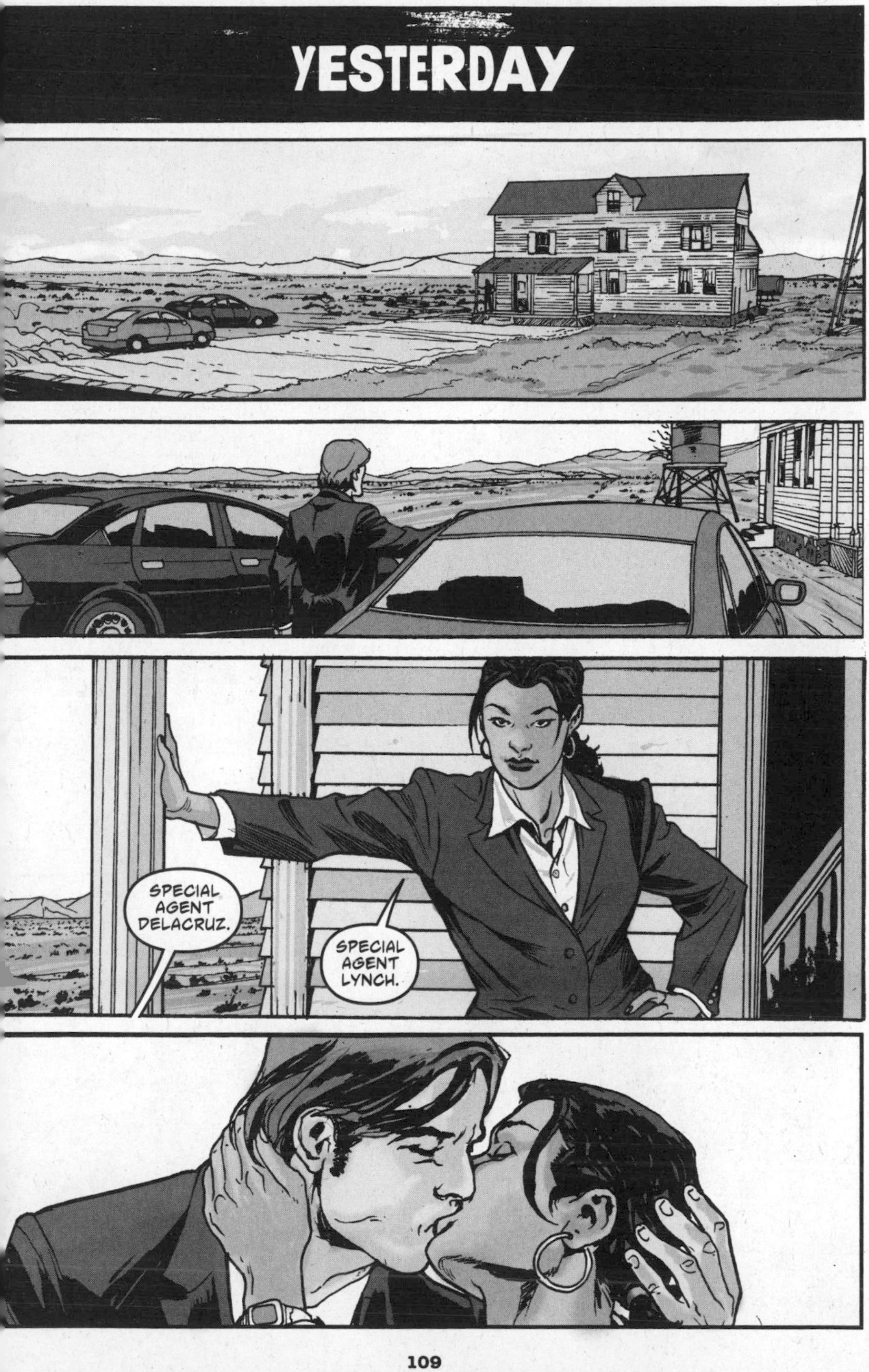
YESTERDAY
SPECIAL AGENT DELACRUZ.
SPECIAL AGENT LYNCH.

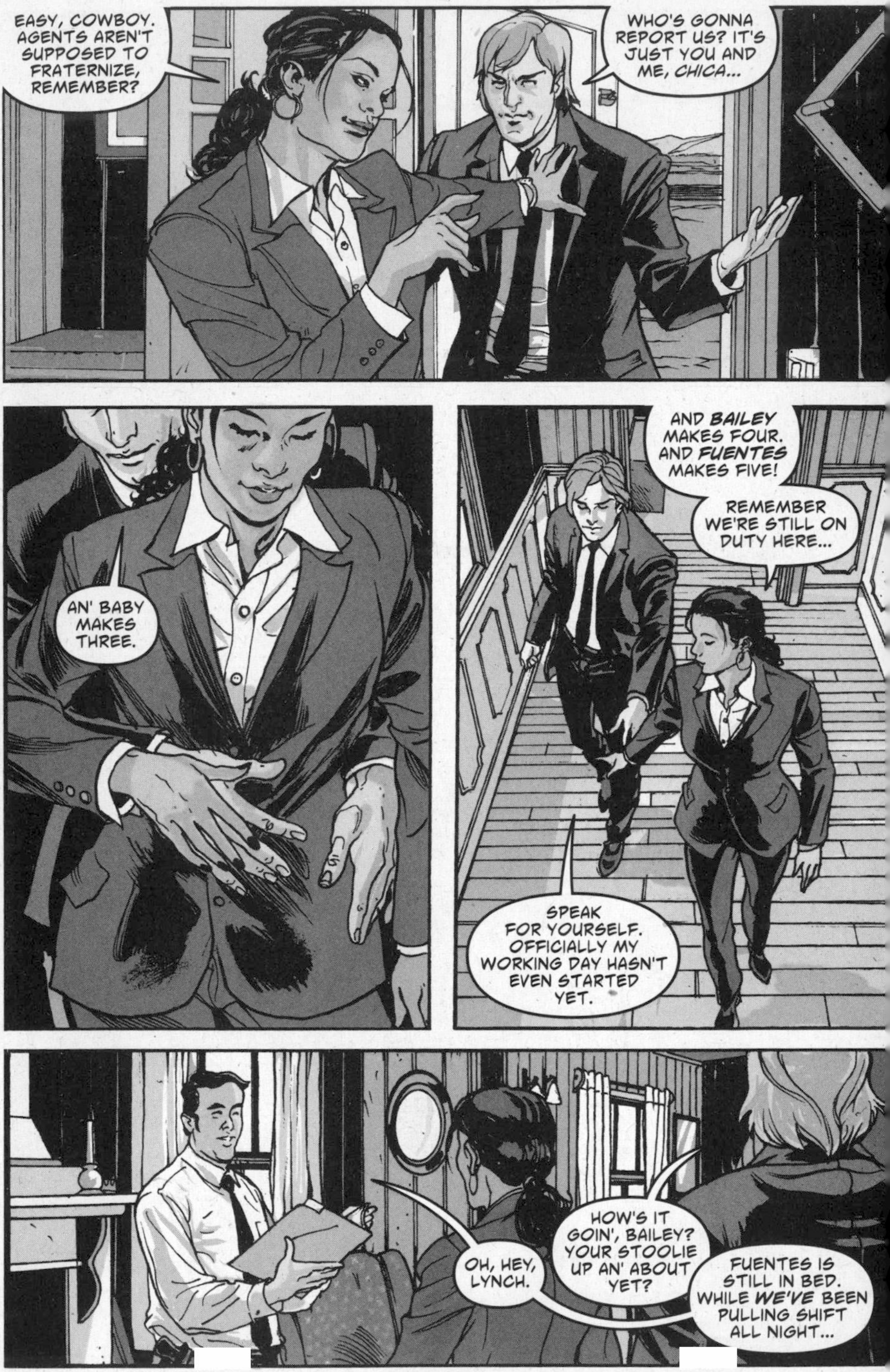
EASY, COWBOY. AGENTS AREN'T SUPPOSED TO FRATERNIZE, REMEMBER?
WHO'S GONNA REPORT US? IT'S JUST YOU AND ME, CHICA...
AN' BABY MAKES THREE.
AND BAILEY MAKES FOUR. AND FUENTES MAKES FIVE!
REMEMBER WE'RE STILL ON DUTY HERE...
SPEAK FOR YOURSELF. OFFICIALLY MY WORKING DAY HASN'T EVEN STARTED YET.
OH, HEY, LYNCH.
HOW'S IT GOIN', BAILEY? YOUR STOOLIE UP AN' ABOUT YET?
FUENTES IS STILL IN BED. WHILE WE'VE BEEN PULLING SHIFT ALL NIGHT...

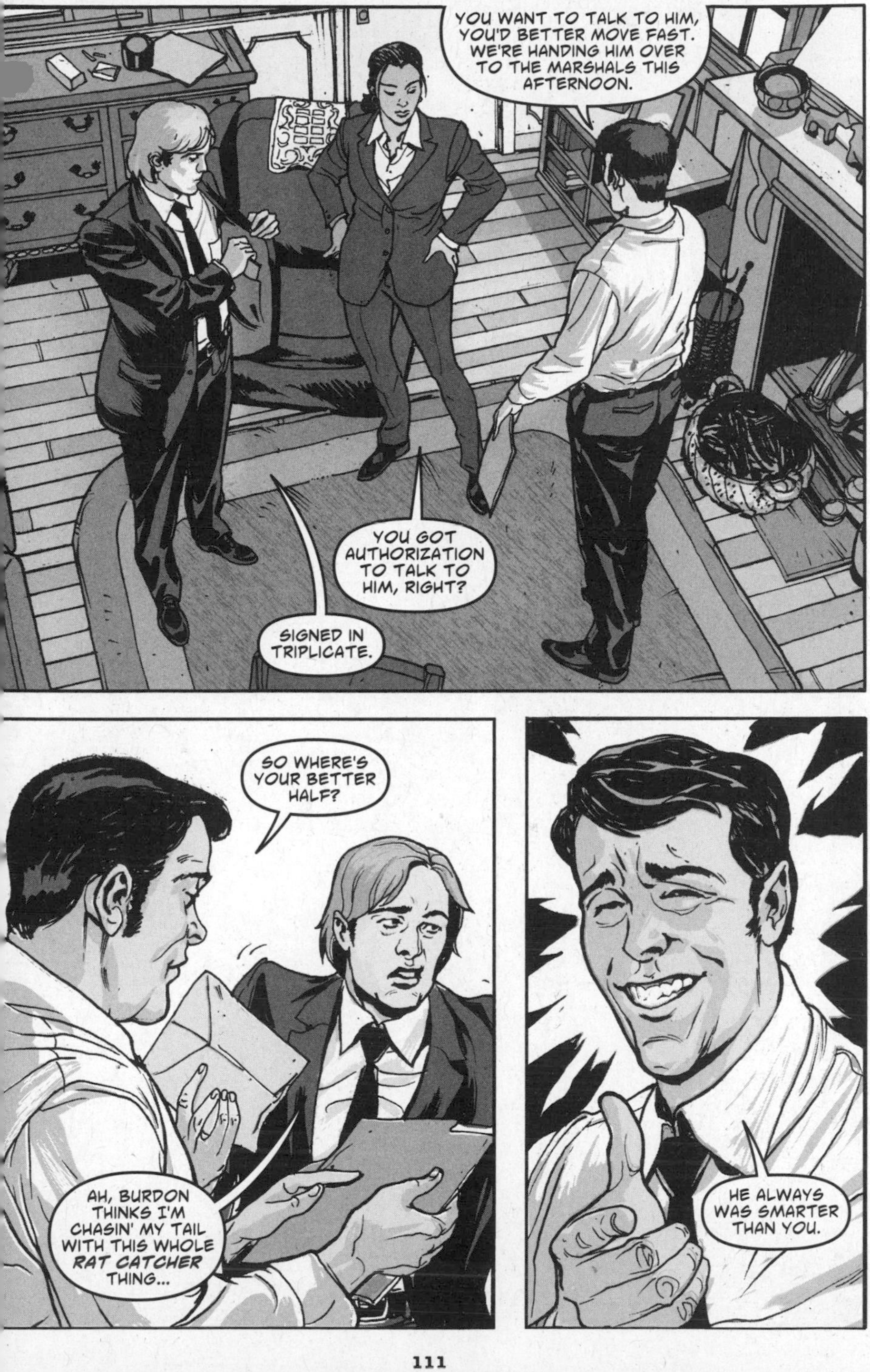
YOU WANT TO TALK TO HIM, YOU'D BETTER MOVE FAST. WE'RE HANDING HIM OVER TO THE MARSHALS THIS AFTERNOON.
YOU GOT AUTHORIZATION TO TALK TO HIM, RIGHT?
SIGNED IN TRIPLICATE.
SO WHERE'S YOUR BETTER HALF?
AH, BURDON THINKS I'M CHASIN' MY TAIL WITH THIS WHOLE *RAT CATCHER* THING...
HE ALWAYS WAS SMARTER THAN YOU.

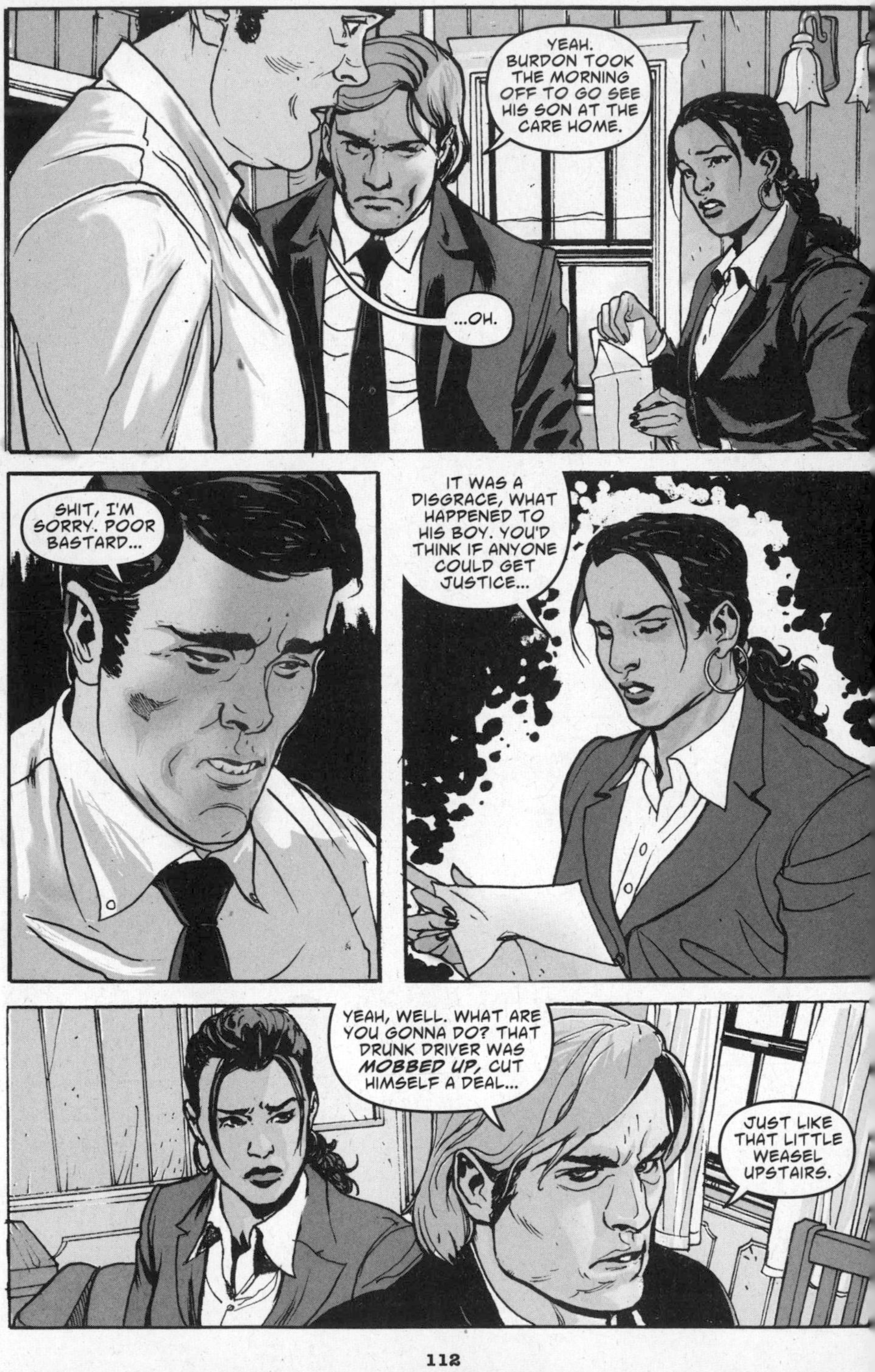
YEAH. BURDON TOOK THE MORNING OFF TO GO SEE HIS SON AT THE CARE HOME.
...OH.
SHIT, I'M SORRY. POOR BASTARD...
IT WAS A DISGRACE, WHAT HAPPENED TO HIS BOY. YOU'D THINK IF ANYONE COULD GET JUSTICE...
YEAH, WELL. WHAT ARE YOU GONNA DO? THAT DRUNK DRIVER WAS *MOBBED UP*, CUT HIMSELF A DEAL...
JUST LIKE THAT LITTLE WEASEL UPSTAIRS.

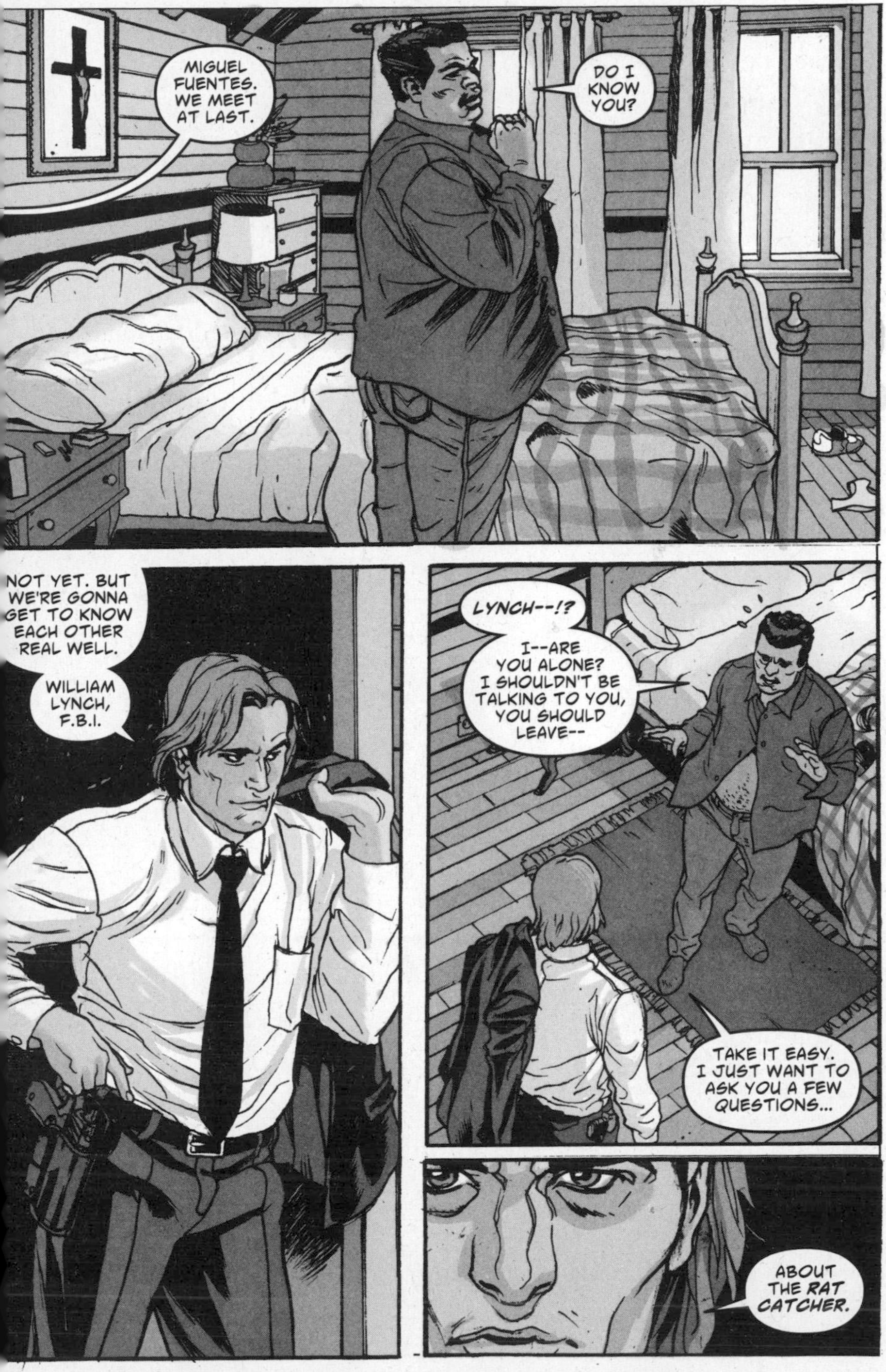
MIGUEL FUENTES. WE MEET AT LAST.
DO I KNOW YOU?
NOT YET. BUT WE'RE GONNA GET TO KNOW EACH OTHER REAL WELL.
WILLIAM LYNCH, F.B.I.
LYNCH--!?
I--ARE YOU ALONE? I SHOULDN'T BE TALKING TO YOU, YOU SHOULD LEAVE--
TAKE IT EASY. I JUST WANT TO ASK YOU A FEW QUESTIONS...
ABOUT THE RAT CATCHER.

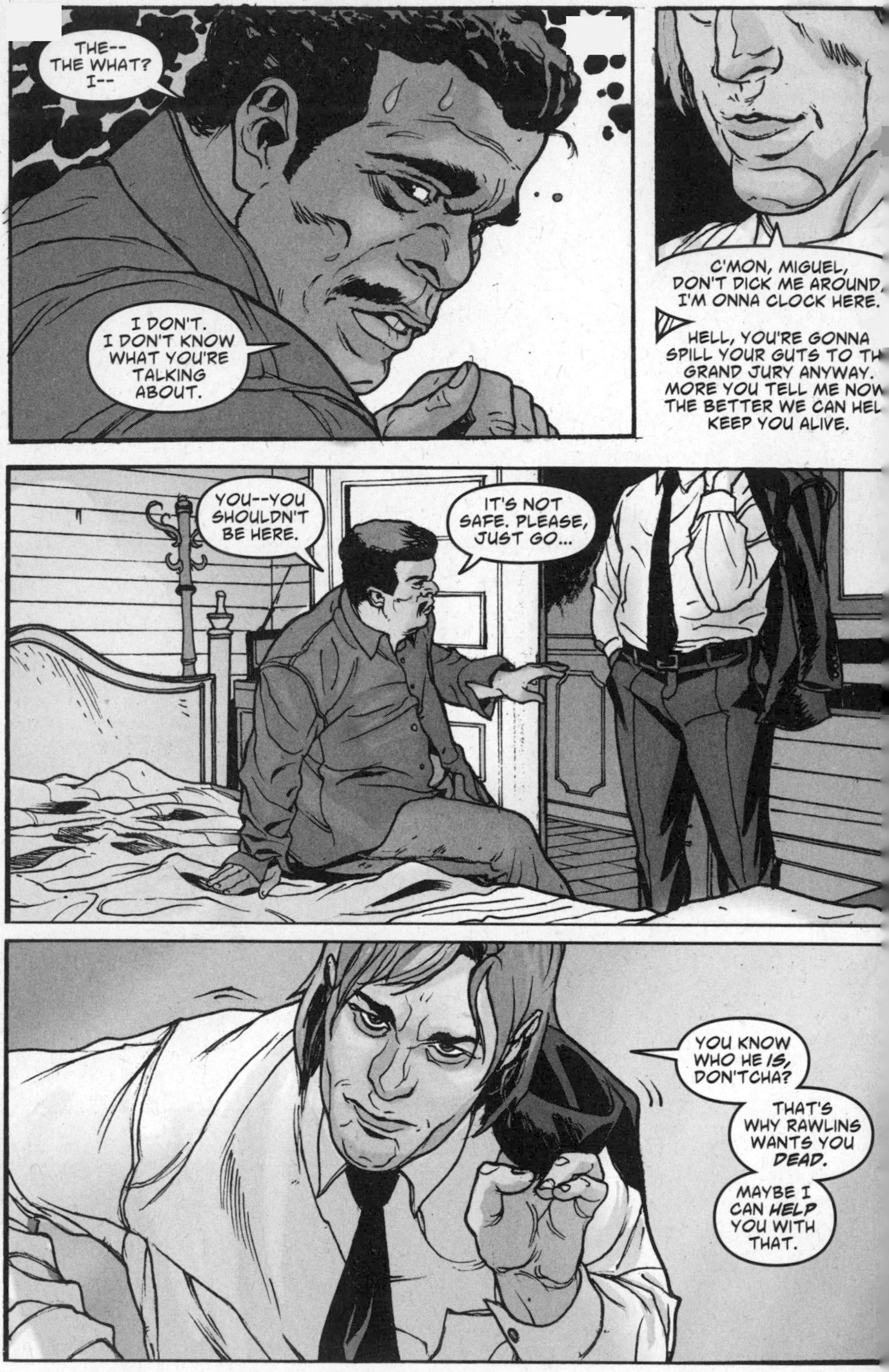
THE-- THE WHAT? I--
I DON'T. I DON'T KNOW WHAT YOU'RE TALKING ABOUT.
C'MON, MIGUEL, DON'T DICK ME AROUND, I'M ONNA CLOCK HERE.
HELL, YOU'RE GONNA SPILL YOUR GUTS TO TH GRAND JURY ANYWAY. MORE YOU TELL ME NOW THE BETTER WE CAN HEL KEEP YOU ALIVE.
YOU--YOU SHOULDN'T BE HERE.
IT'S NOT SAFE. PLEASE, JUST GO...
YOU KNOW WHO HE *IS*, DON'TCHA?
THAT'S WHY RAWLINS WANTS YOU *DEAD*.
MAYBE I CAN *HELP* YOU WITH THAT.

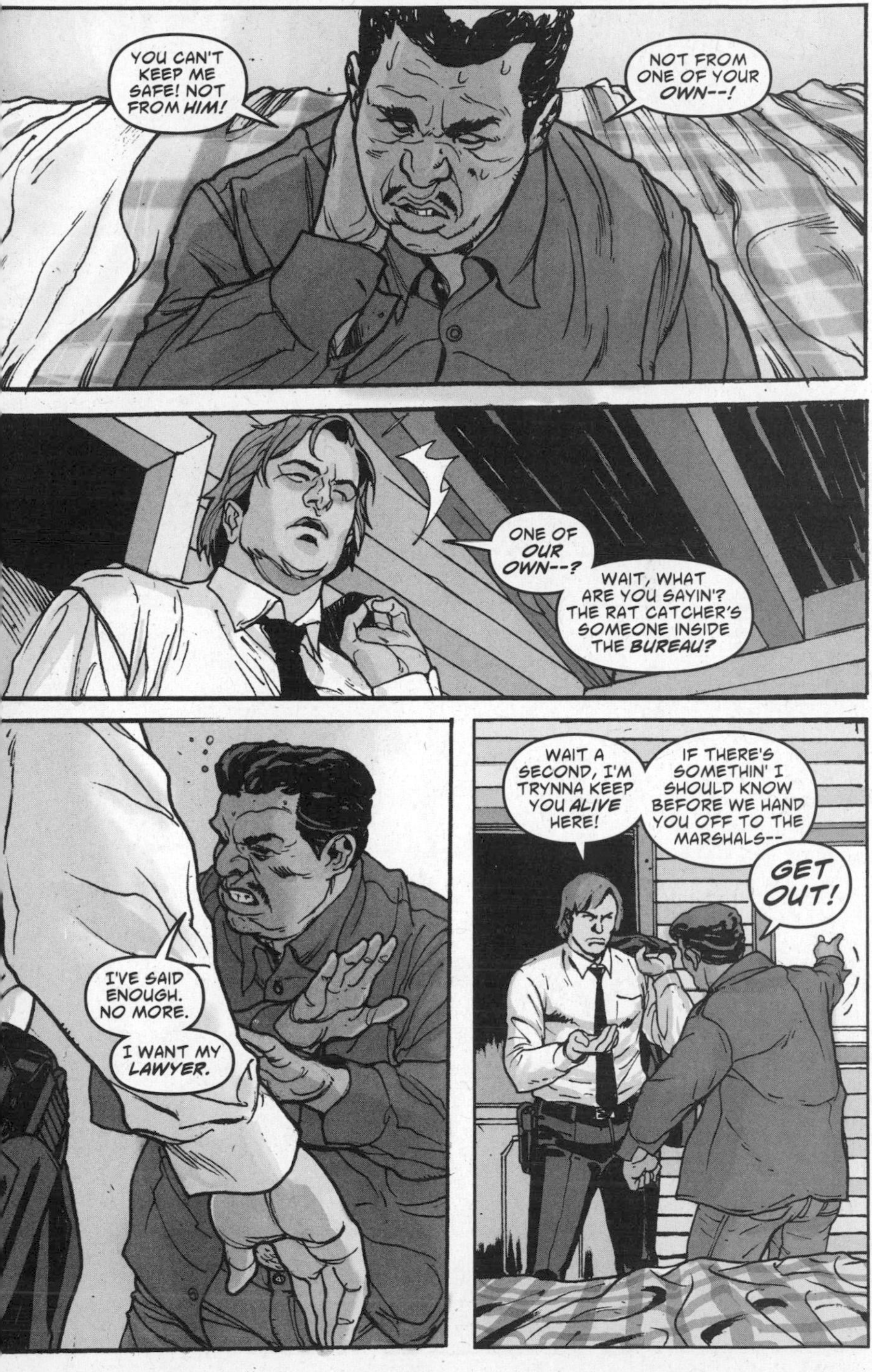
YOU CAN'T KEEP ME SAFE! NOT FROM HIM!
NOT FROM ONE OF YOUR OWN--!
ONE OF OUR OWN--?
WAIT, WHAT ARE YOU SAYIN'? THE RAT CATCHER'S SOMEONE INSIDE THE BUREAU?
I'VE SAID ENOUGH. NO MORE.
I WANT MY LAWYER.
WAIT A SECOND, I'M TRYNNA KEEP YOU ALIVE HERE!
IF THERE'S SOMETHIN' I SHOULD KNOW BEFORE WE HAND YOU OFF TO THE MARSHALS--
GET OUT!

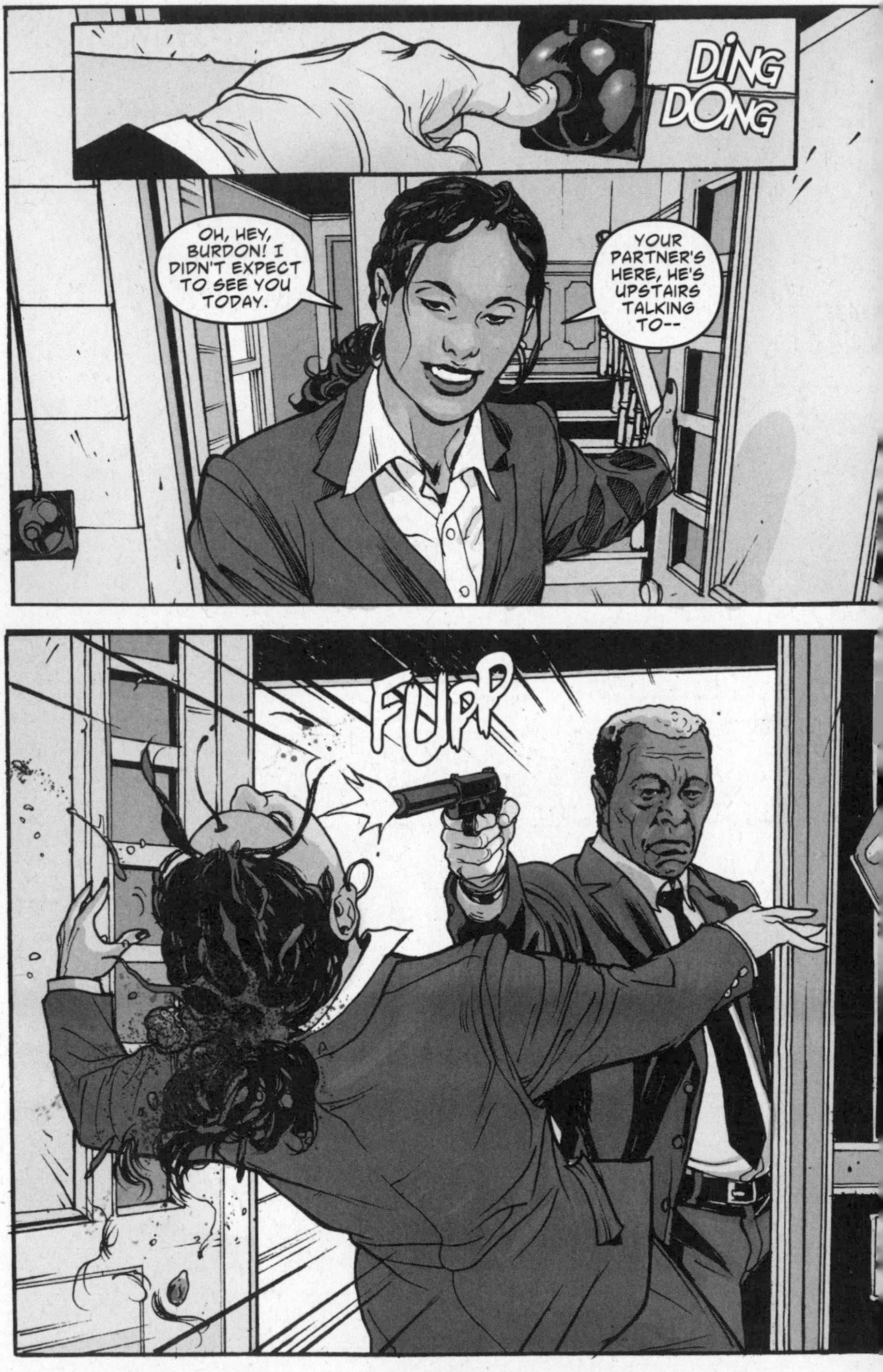
DING DONG
OH, HEY, BURDON! I DIDN'T EXPECT TO SEE YOU TODAY.
YOUR PARTNER'S HERE, HE'S UPSTAIRS TALKING TO--
FUPP

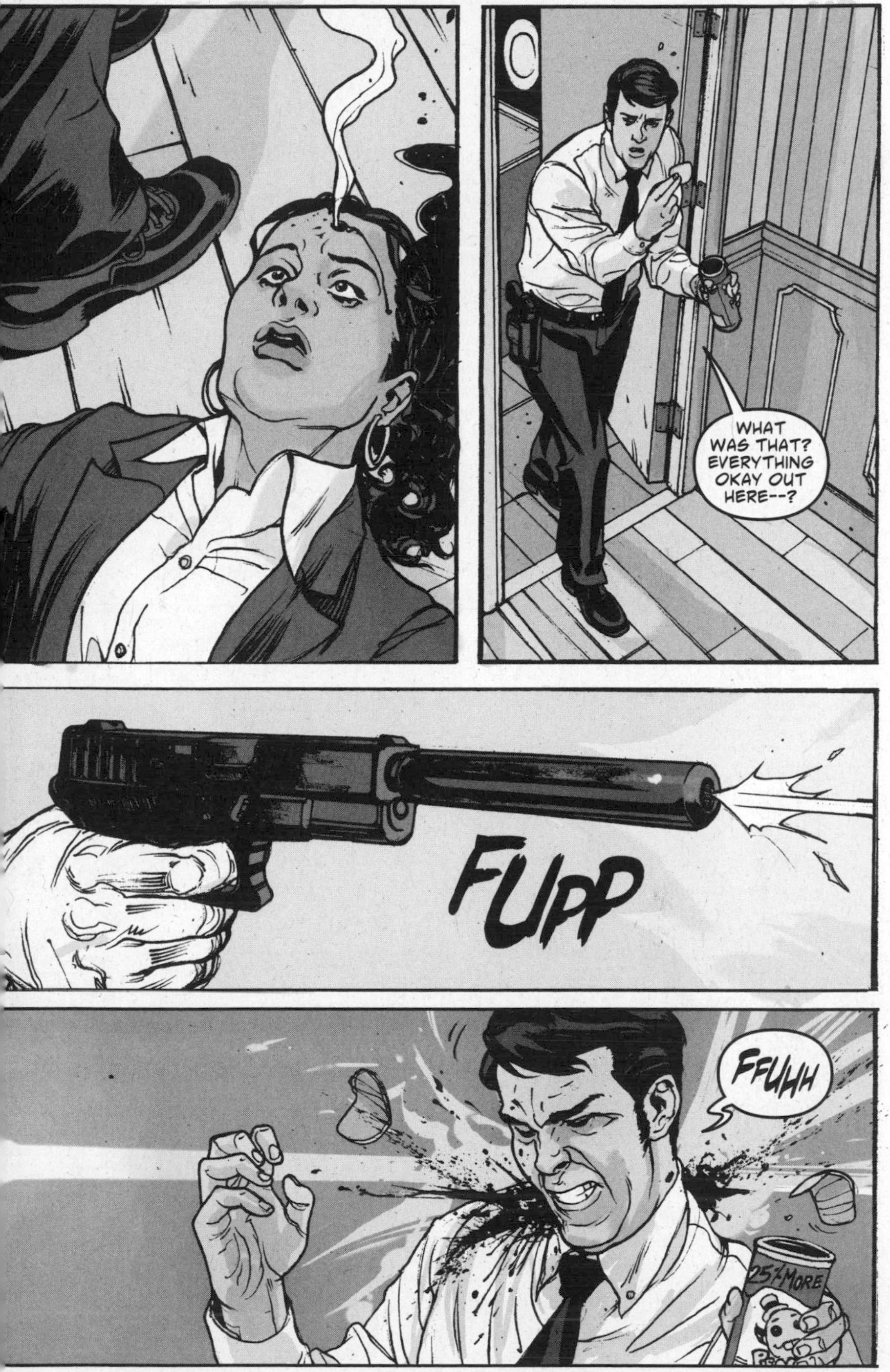
WHAT WAS THAT? EVERYTHING OKAY OUT HERE--?
FUPP
FFUHH
25% MORE

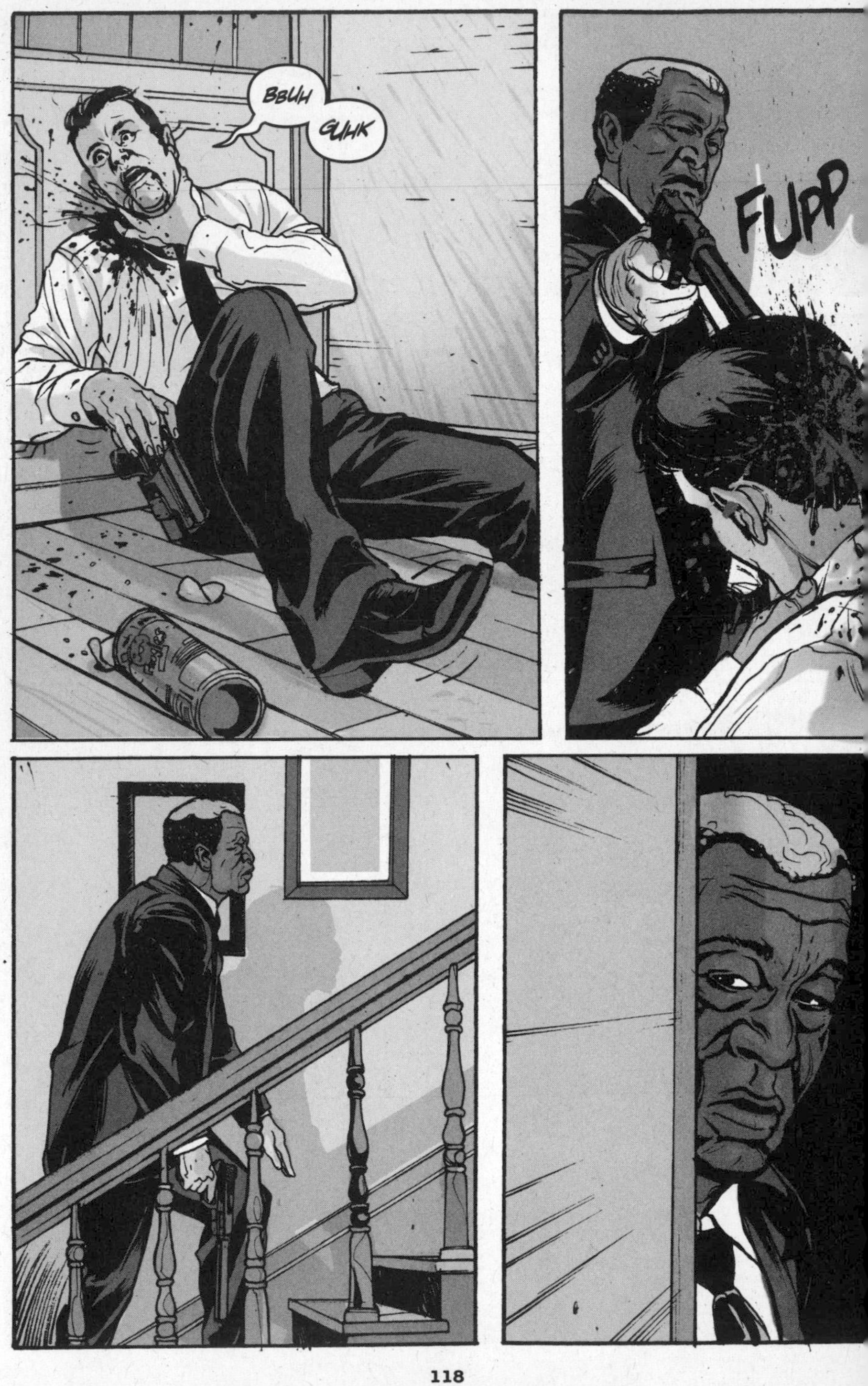
BBUH
GUHK
FUPP

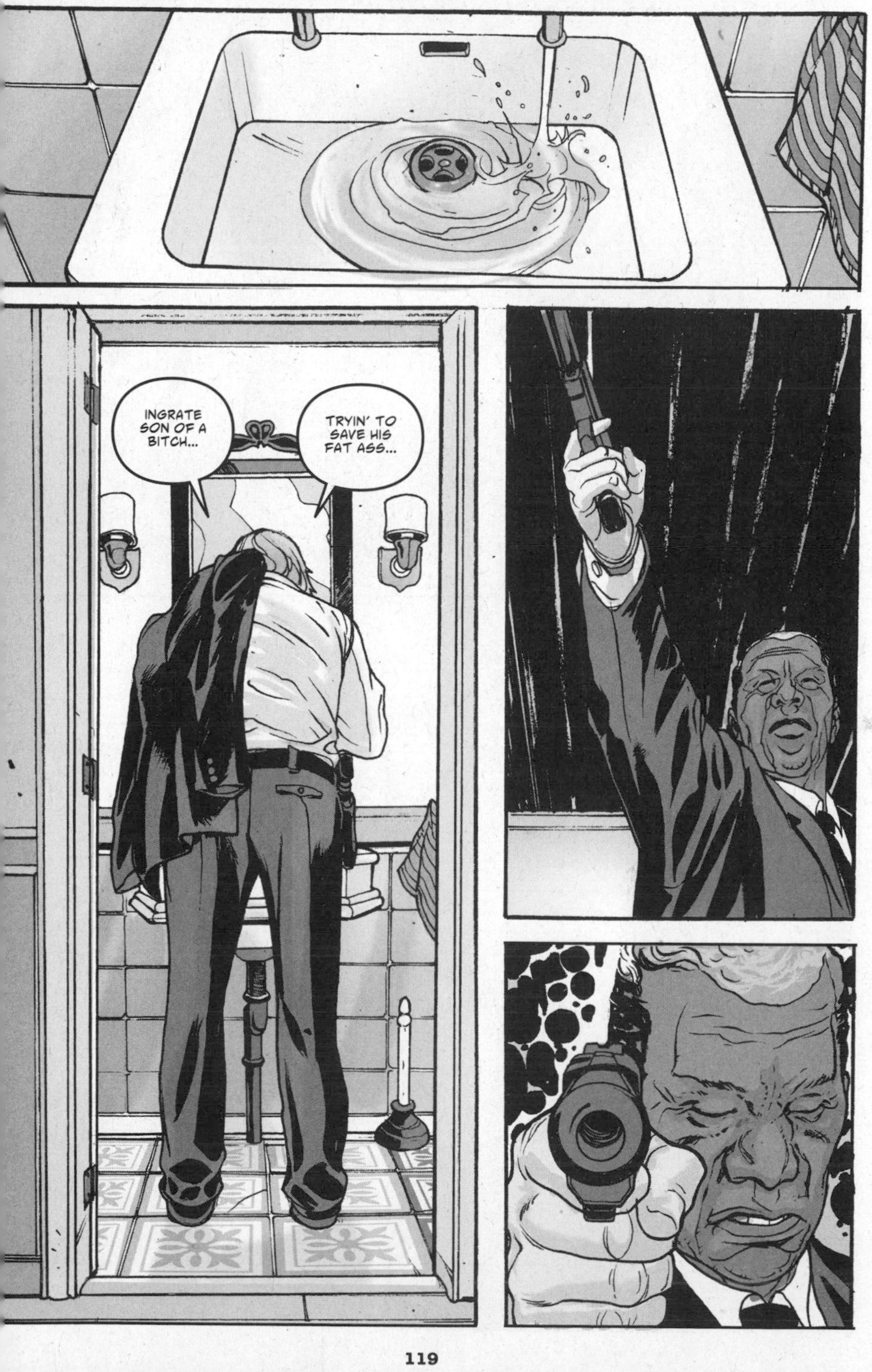
INGRATE SON OF A BITCH...
TRYIN' TO SAVE HIS FAT ASS...

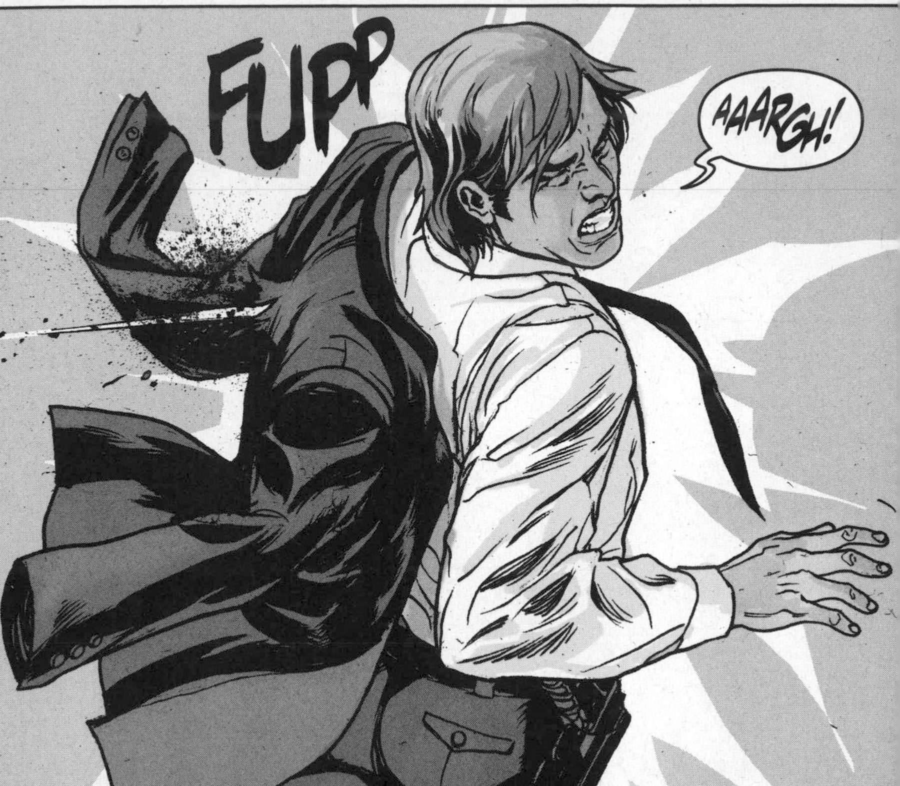
FUPP
AAARGH!

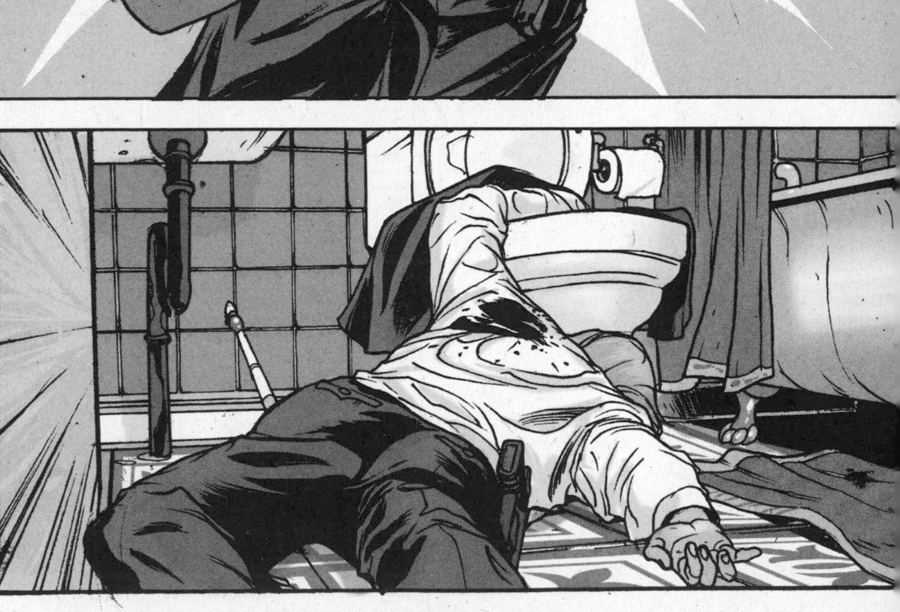

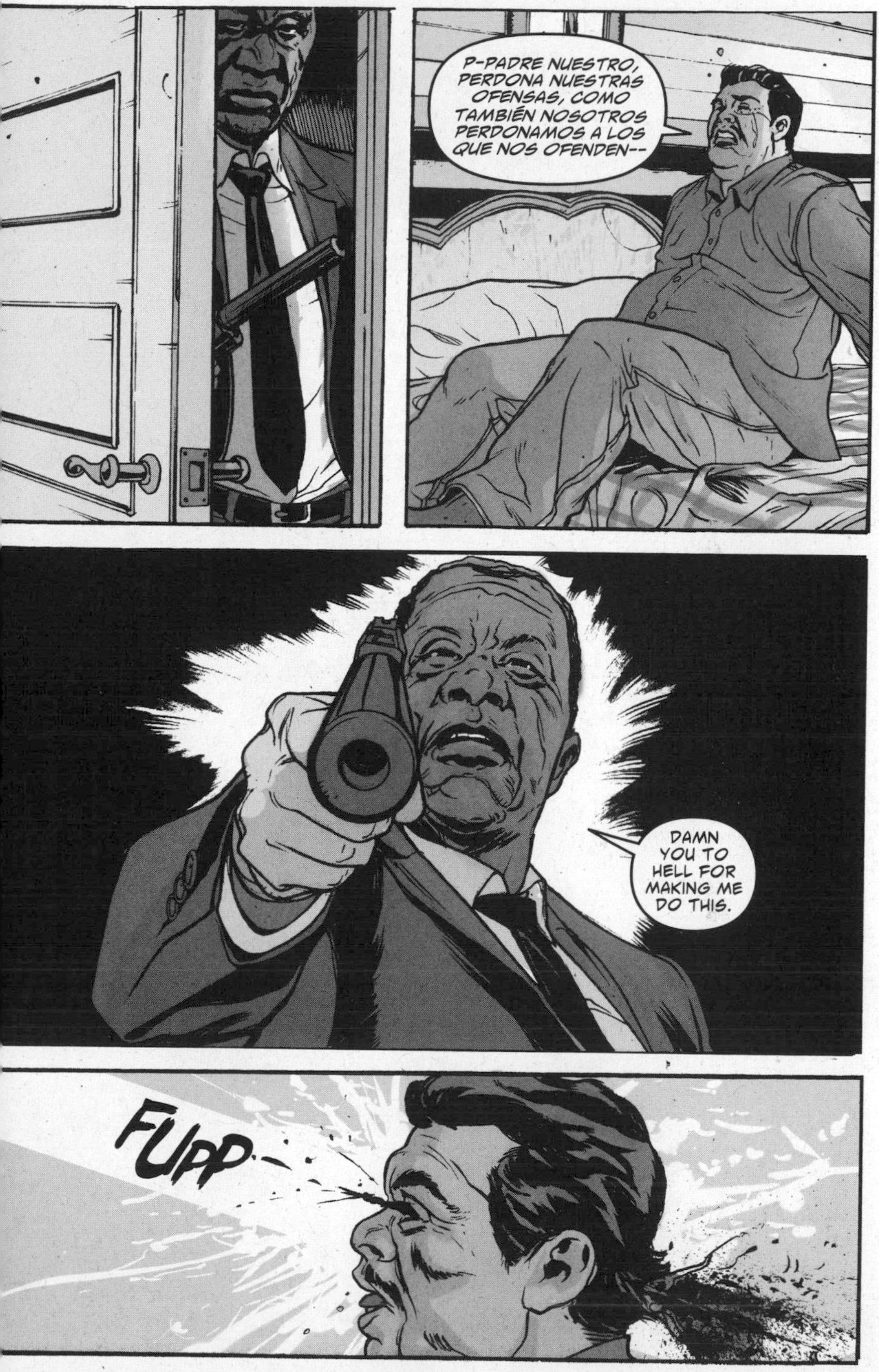
P-PADRE NUESTRO, PERDONA NUESTRAS OFENSAS, COMO TAMBIÉN NOSOTROS PERDONAMOS A LOS QUE NOS OFENDEN--
DAMN YOU TO HELL FOR MAKING ME DO THIS.
FUPP--

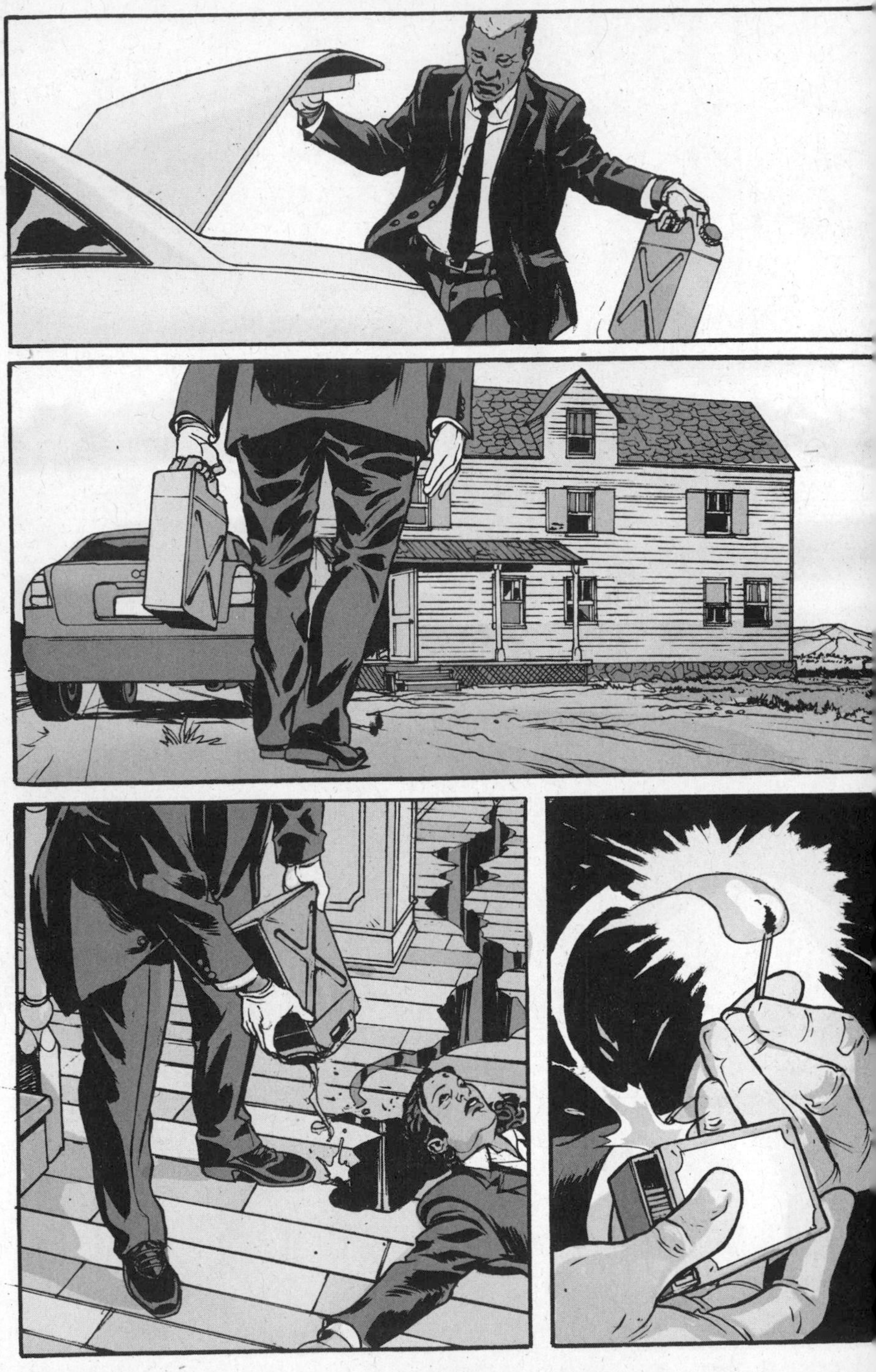

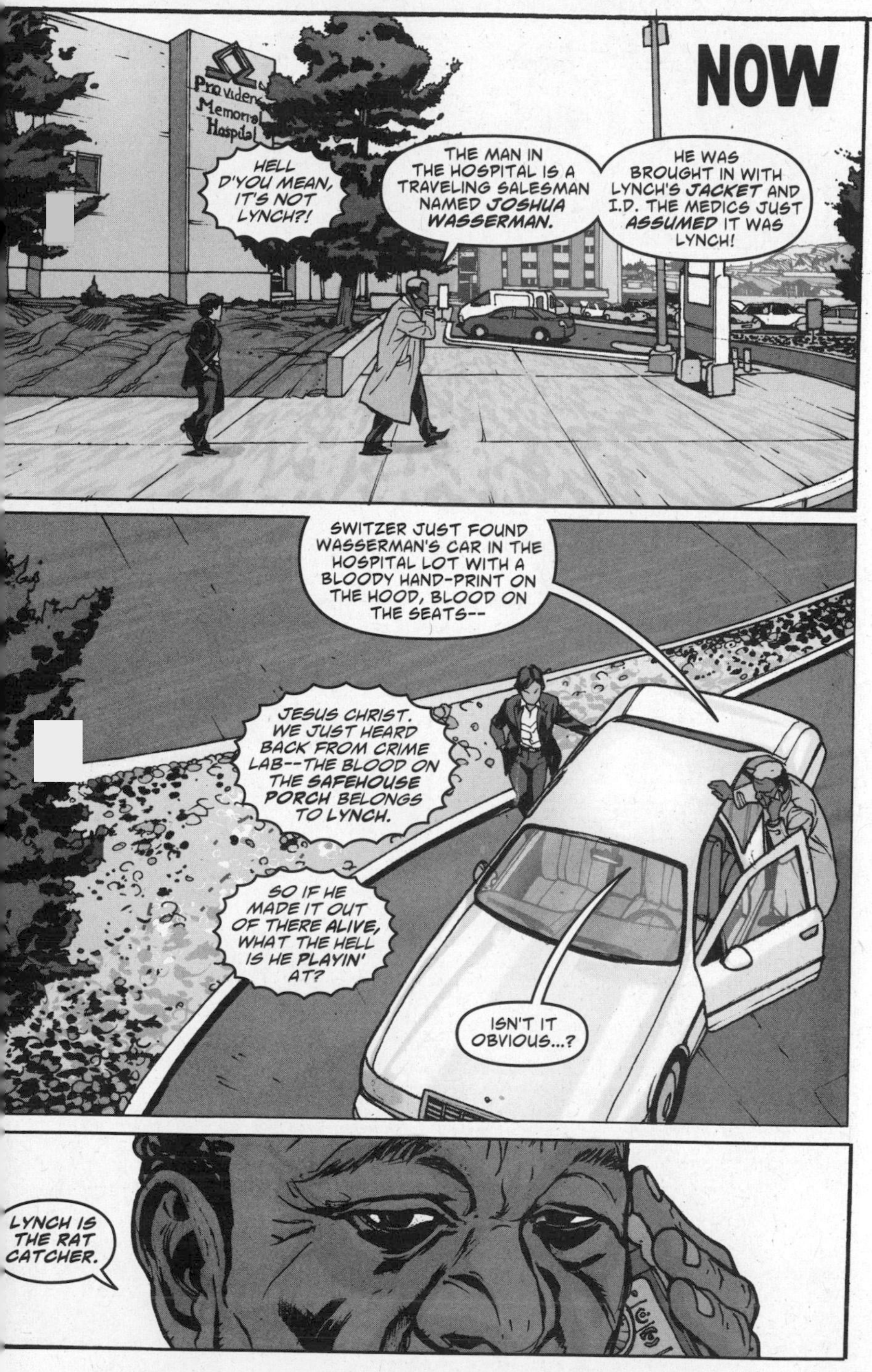
NOW
Providence Memorial Hospital
HELL D'YOU MEAN, IT'S NOT LYNCH?!
THE MAN IN THE HOSPITAL IS A TRAVELING SALESMAN NAMED JOSHUA WASSERMAN.
HE WAS BROUGHT IN WITH LYNCH'S JACKET AND I.D. THE MEDICS JUST ASSUMED IT WAS LYNCH!
SWITZER JUST FOUND WASSERMAN'S CAR IN THE HOSPITAL LOT WITH A BLOODY HAND-PRINT ON THE HOOD, BLOOD ON THE SEATS--
JESUS CHRIST. WE JUST HEARD BACK FROM CRIME LAB--THE BLOOD ON THE SAFEHOUSE PORCH BELONGS TO LYNCH.
SO IF HE MADE IT OUT OF THERE ALIVE, WHAT THE HELL IS HE PLAYIN' AT?
ISN'T IT OBVIOUS...?
LYNCH IS THE RAT CATCHER.

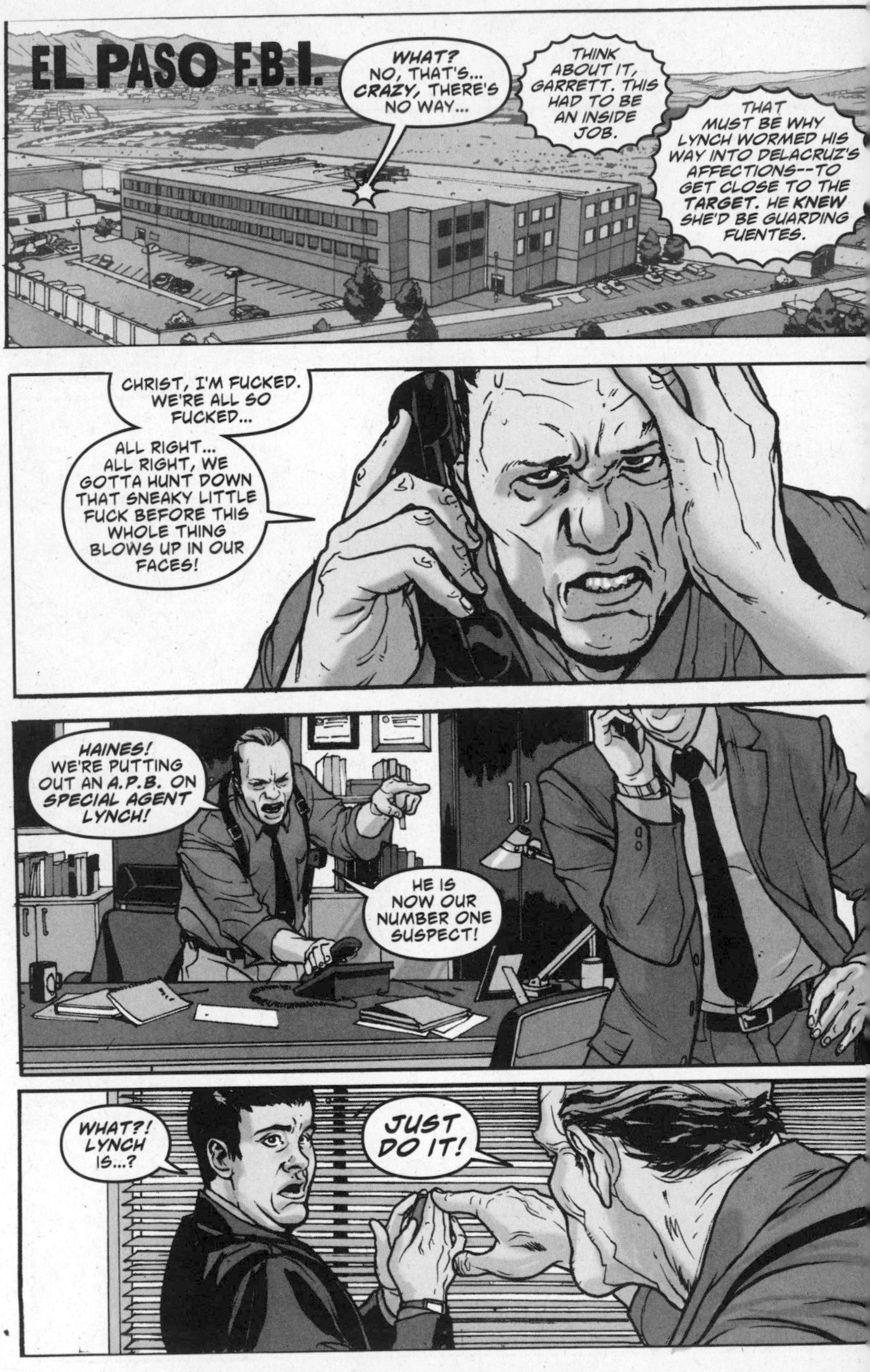
EL PASO F.B.I.
WHAT? NO, THAT'S... CRAZY, THERE'S NO WAY...
THINK ABOUT IT, GARRETT. THIS HAD TO BE AN INSIDE JOB.
THAT MUST BE WHY LYNCH WORMED HIS WAY INTO DELACRUZ'S AFFECTIONS--TO GET CLOSE TO THE TARGET. HE KNEW SHE'D BE GUARDING FUENTES.
CHRIST, I'M FUCKED. WE'RE ALL SO FUCKED...
ALL RIGHT... ALL RIGHT, WE GOTTA HUNT DOWN THAT SNEAKY LITTLE FUCK BEFORE THIS WHOLE THING BLOWS UP IN OUR FACES!
HAINES! WE'RE PUTTING OUT AN A.P.B. ON SPECIAL AGENT LYNCH!
HE IS NOW OUR NUMBER ONE SUSPECT!
WHAT?! LYNCH IS...?
JUST DO IT!

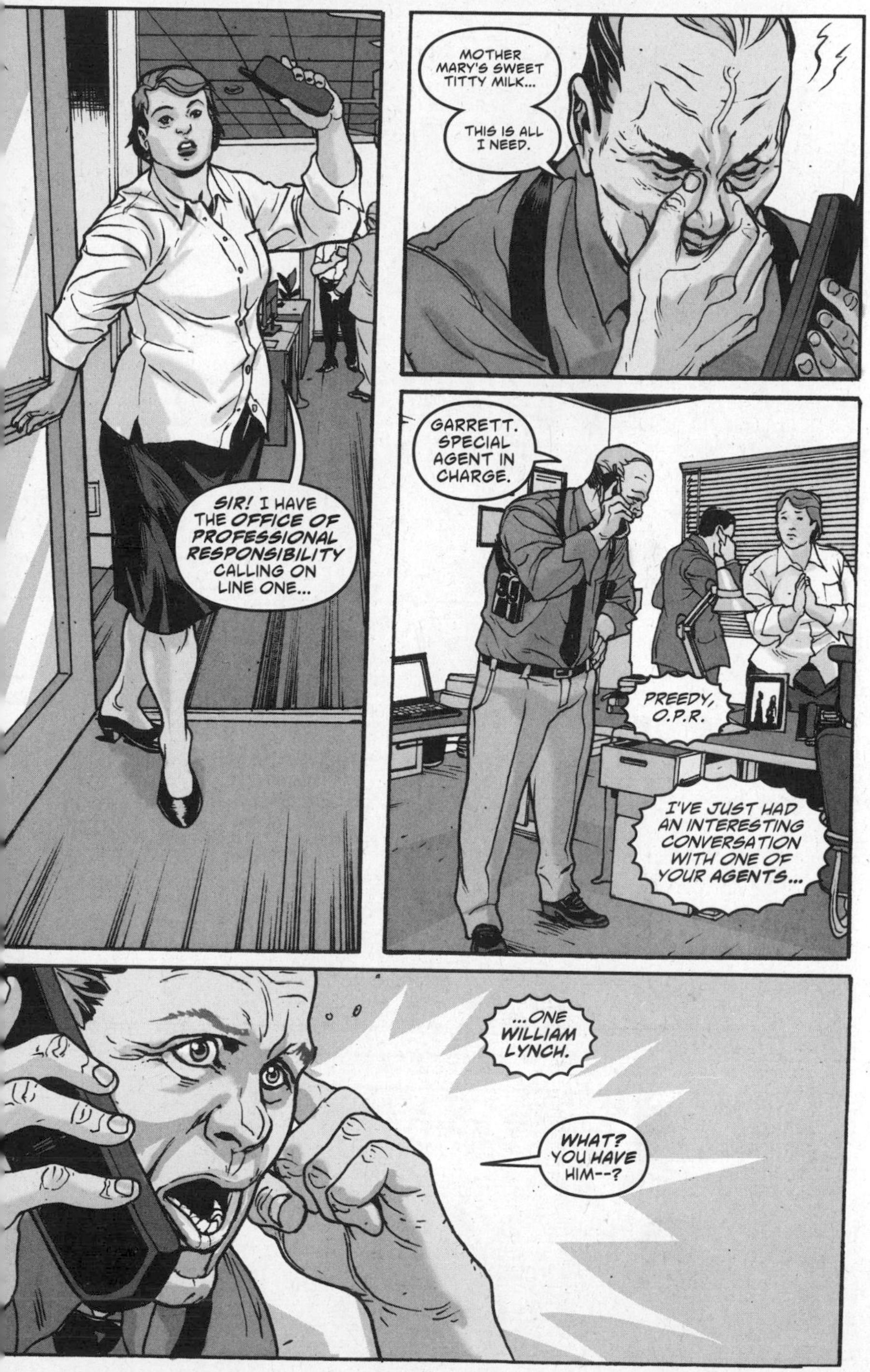
SIR! I HAVE THE OFFICE OF PROFESSIONAL RESPONSIBILITY CALLING ON LINE ONE...
MOTHER MARY'S SWEET TITTY MILK...
THIS IS ALL I NEED.
GARRETT. SPECIAL AGENT IN CHARGE.
PREEDY, O.P.R.
I'VE JUST HAD AN INTERESTING CONVERSATION WITH ONE OF YOUR AGENTS...
...ONE WILLIAM LYNCH.
WHAT? YOU HAVE HIM--?

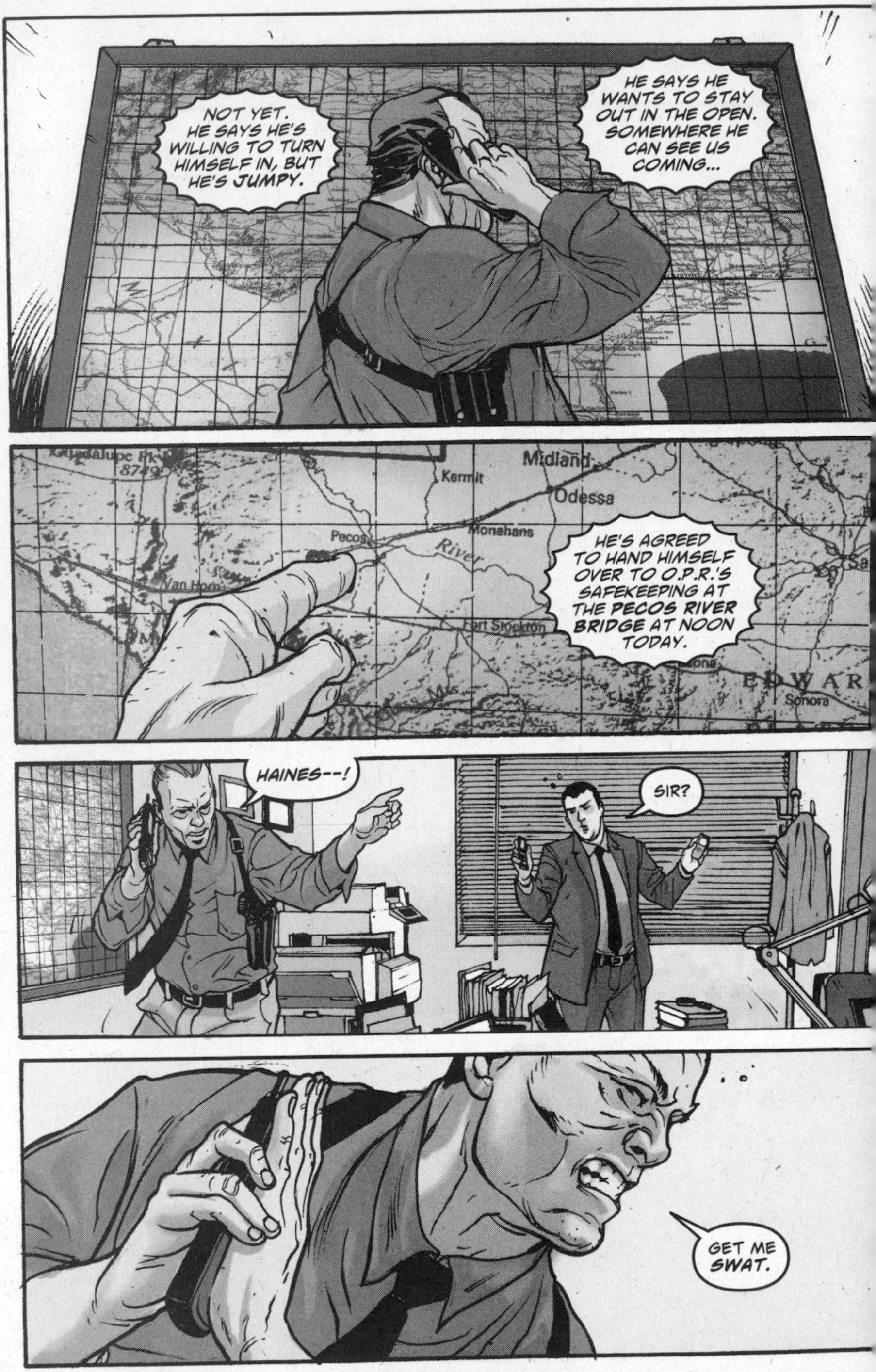
NOT YET. HE SAYS HE'S WILLING TO TURN HIMSELF IN, BUT HE'S JUMPY.
HE SAYS HE WANTS TO STAY OUT IN THE OPEN. SOMEWHERE HE CAN SEE US COMING...
Midland
Kermit
Odessa
Pecos
Monahans
River
Van Horn
Fort Stockton
Sonora
EDWAR
HE'S AGREED TO HAND HIMSELF OVER TO O.P.R.'S SAFEKEEPING AT THE PECOS RIVER BRIDGE AT NOON TODAY.
HAINES--!
SIR?
GET ME SWAT.

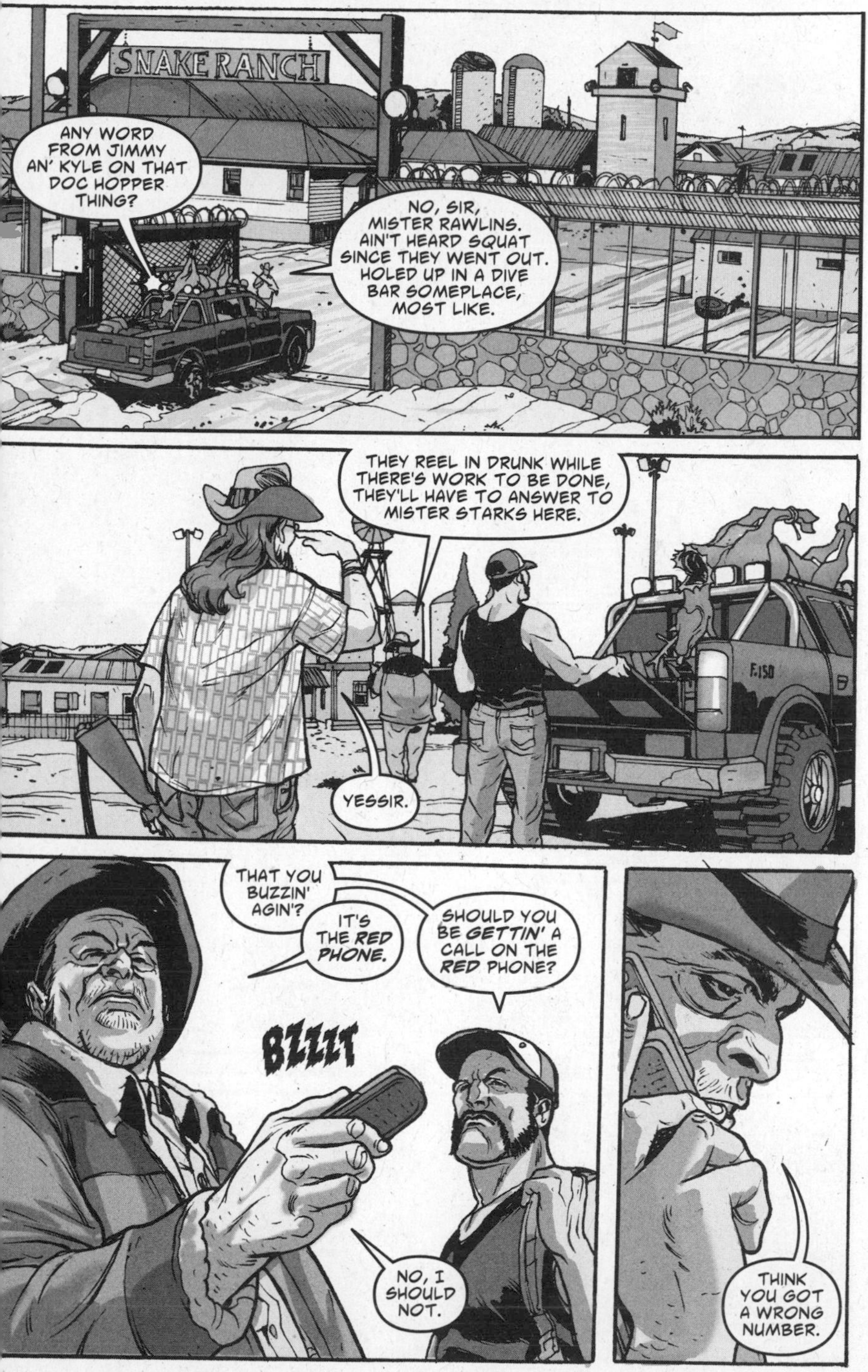
SNAKE RANCH
ANY WORD FROM JIMMY AN' KYLE ON THAT DOC HOPPER THING?
NO, SIR, MISTER RAWLINS. AIN'T HEARD SQUAT SINCE THEY WENT OUT. HOLED UP IN A DIVE BAR SOMEPLACE, MOST LIKE.
THEY REEL IN DRUNK WHILE THERE'S WORK TO BE DONE, THEY'LL HAVE TO ANSWER TO MISTER STARKS HERE.
YESSIR.
F-150
THAT YOU BUZZIN' AGIN?
IT'S THE *RED PHONE.*
SHOULD YOU BE *GETTIN'* A CALL ON THE *RED* PHONE?
BZZZT
NO, I SHOULD NOT.
THINK YOU GOT A WRONG NUMBER.

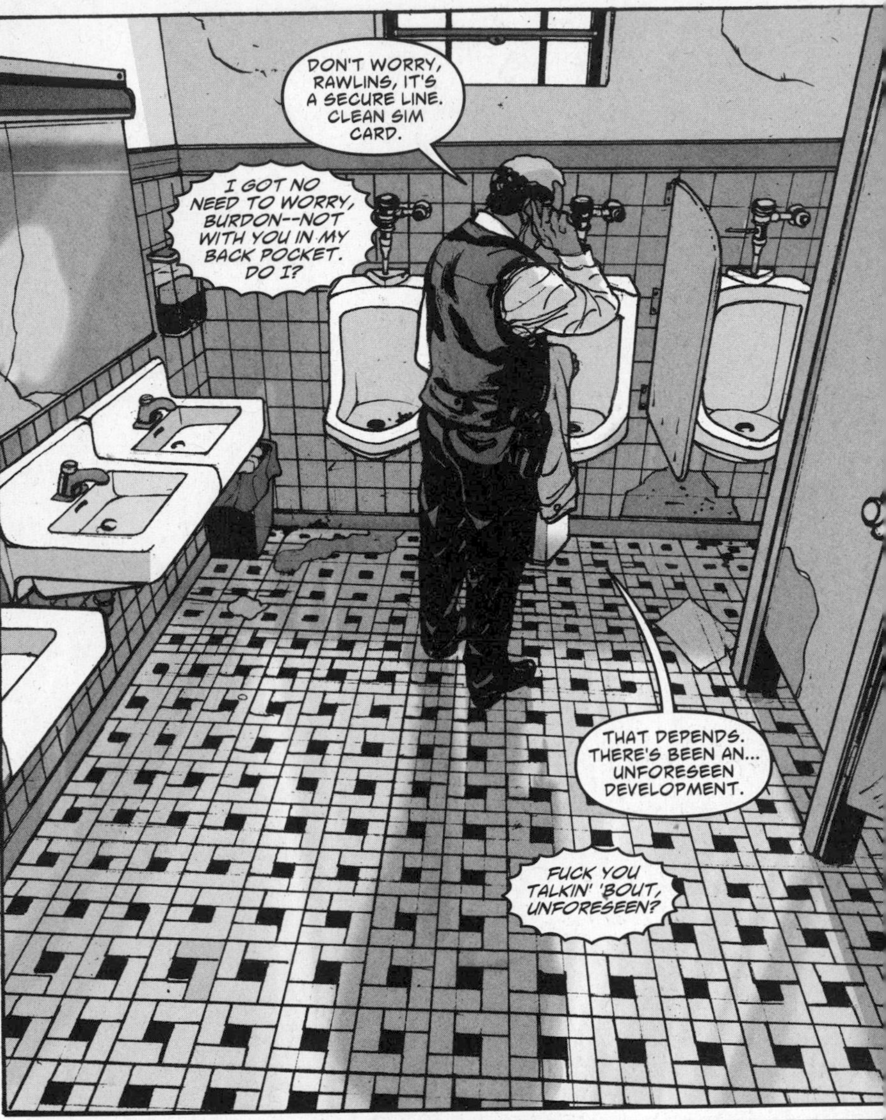
DON'T WORRY, RAWLINS, IT'S A SECURE LINE. CLEAN SIM CARD.
I GOT NO NEED TO WORRY, BURDON--NOT WITH YOU IN MY BACK POCKET. DO I?
THAT DEPENDS. THERE'S BEEN AN... UNFORESEEN DEVELOPMENT.
FUCK YOU TALKIN' 'BOUT, UNFORESEEN?

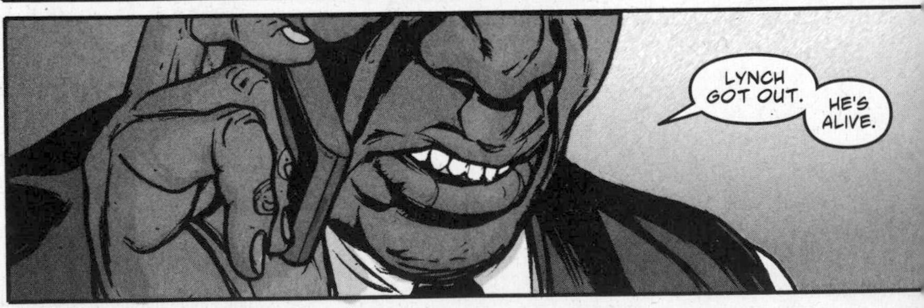
LYNCH GOT OUT.
HE'S ALIVE.

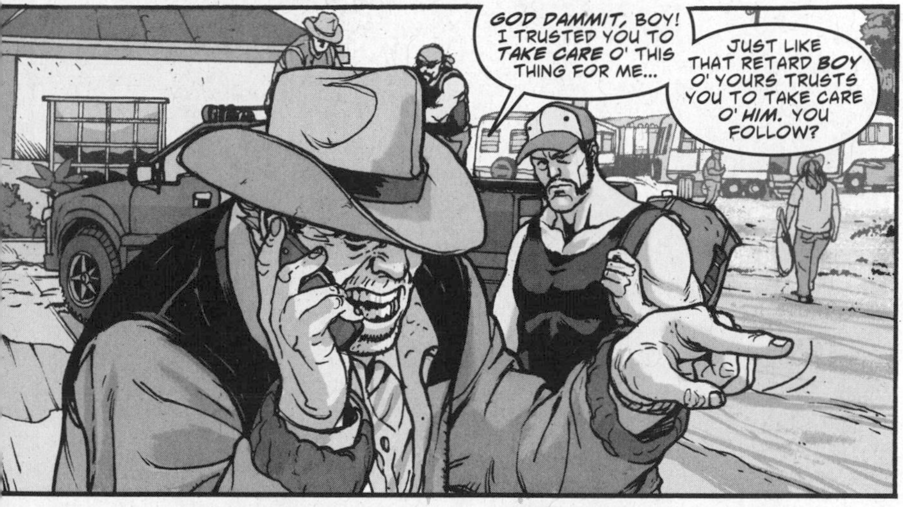
GOD DAMMIT, BOY! I TRUSTED YOU TO TAKE CARE O' THIS THING FOR ME...
JUST LIKE THAT RETARD BOY O' YOURS TRUSTS YOU TO TAKE CARE O' HIM. YOU FOLLOW?

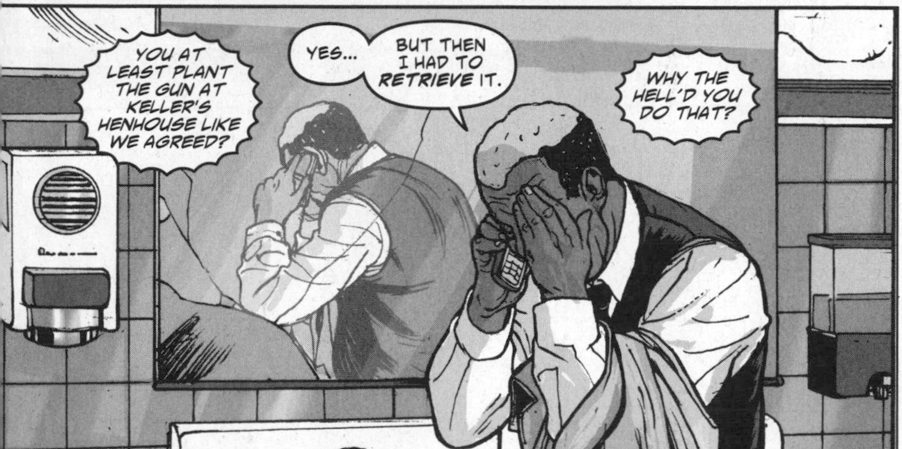
YOU AT LEAST PLANT THE GUN AT KELLER'S HENHOUSE LIKE WE AGREED?
YES...
BUT THEN I HAD TO RETRIEVE IT.
WHY THE HELL'D YOU DO THAT?

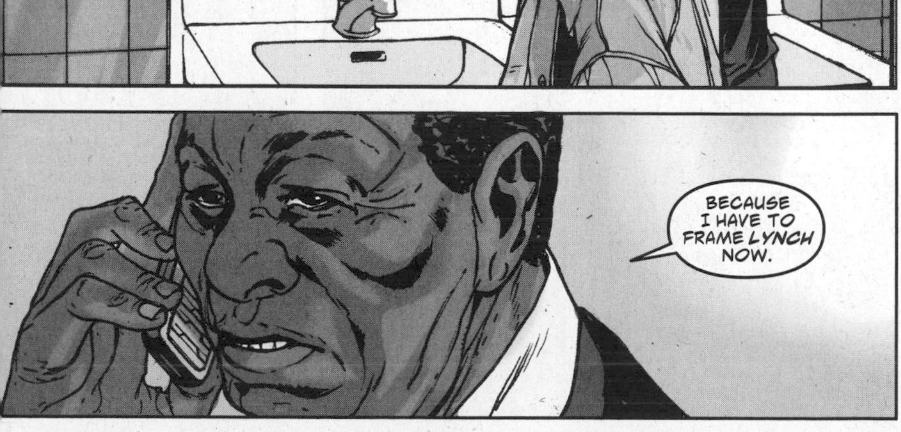
BECAUSE I HAVE TO FRAME LYNCH NOW.

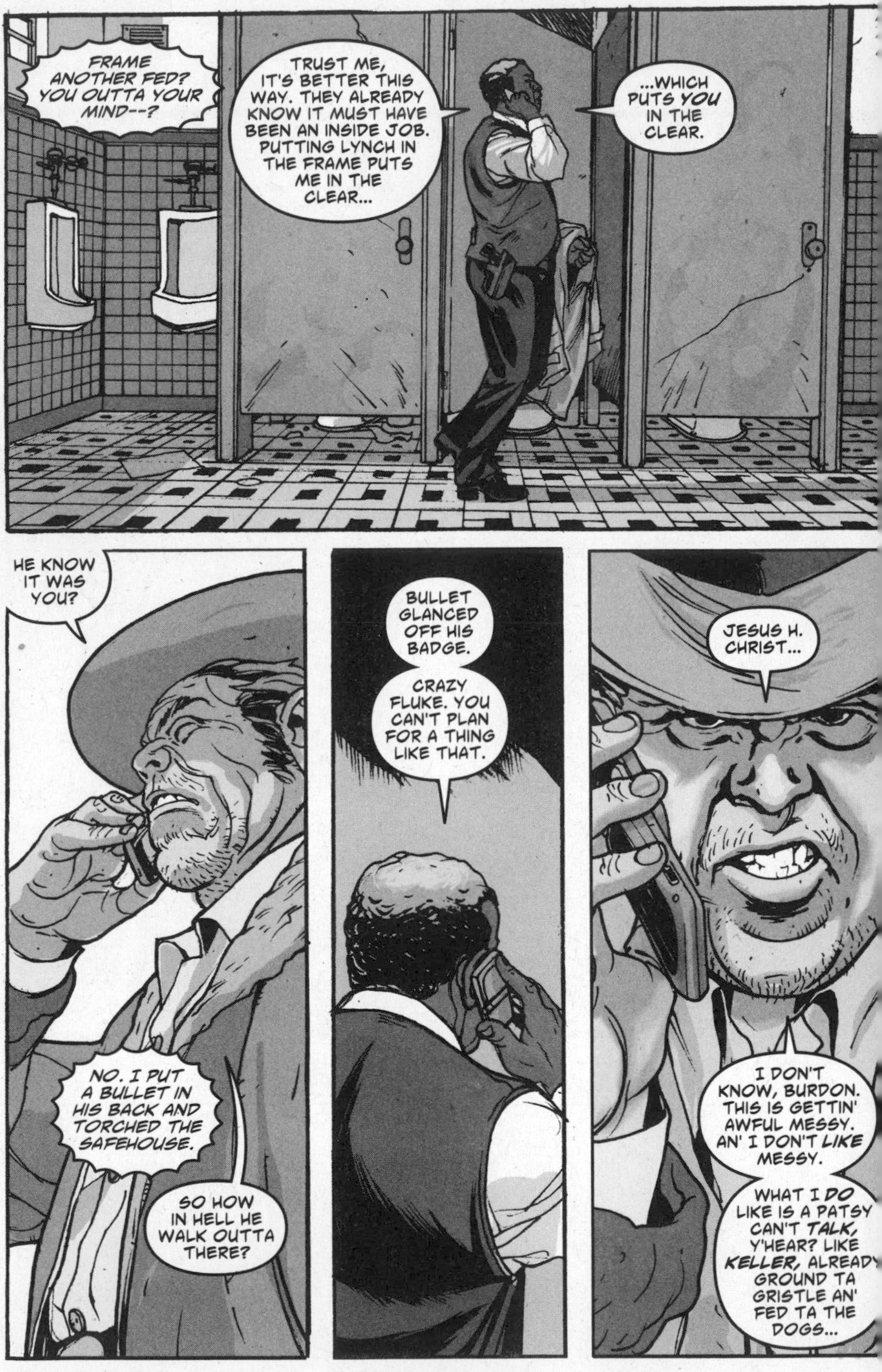

FRAME ANOTHER FED? YOU OUTTA YOUR MIND--?
TRUST ME, IT'S BETTER THIS WAY. THEY ALREADY KNOW IT MUST HAVE BEEN AN INSIDE JOB. PUTTING LYNCH IN THE FRAME PUTS ME IN THE CLEAR...
...WHICH PUTS YOU IN THE CLEAR.
HE KNOW IT WAS YOU?
NO. I PUT A BULLET IN HIS BACK AND TORCHED THE SAFEHOUSE.
SO HOW IN HELL HE WALK OUTTA THERE?
BULLET GLANCED OFF HIS BADGE.
CRAZY FLUKE. YOU CAN'T PLAN FOR A THING LIKE THAT.
JESUS H. CHRIST...
I DON'T KNOW, BURDON. THIS IS GETTIN' AWFUL MESSY. AN' I DON'T LIKE MESSY.
WHAT I DO LIKE IS A PATSY CAN'T TALK, Y'HEAR? LIKE KELLER, ALREADY GROUND TA GRISTLE AN' FED TA THE DOGS...

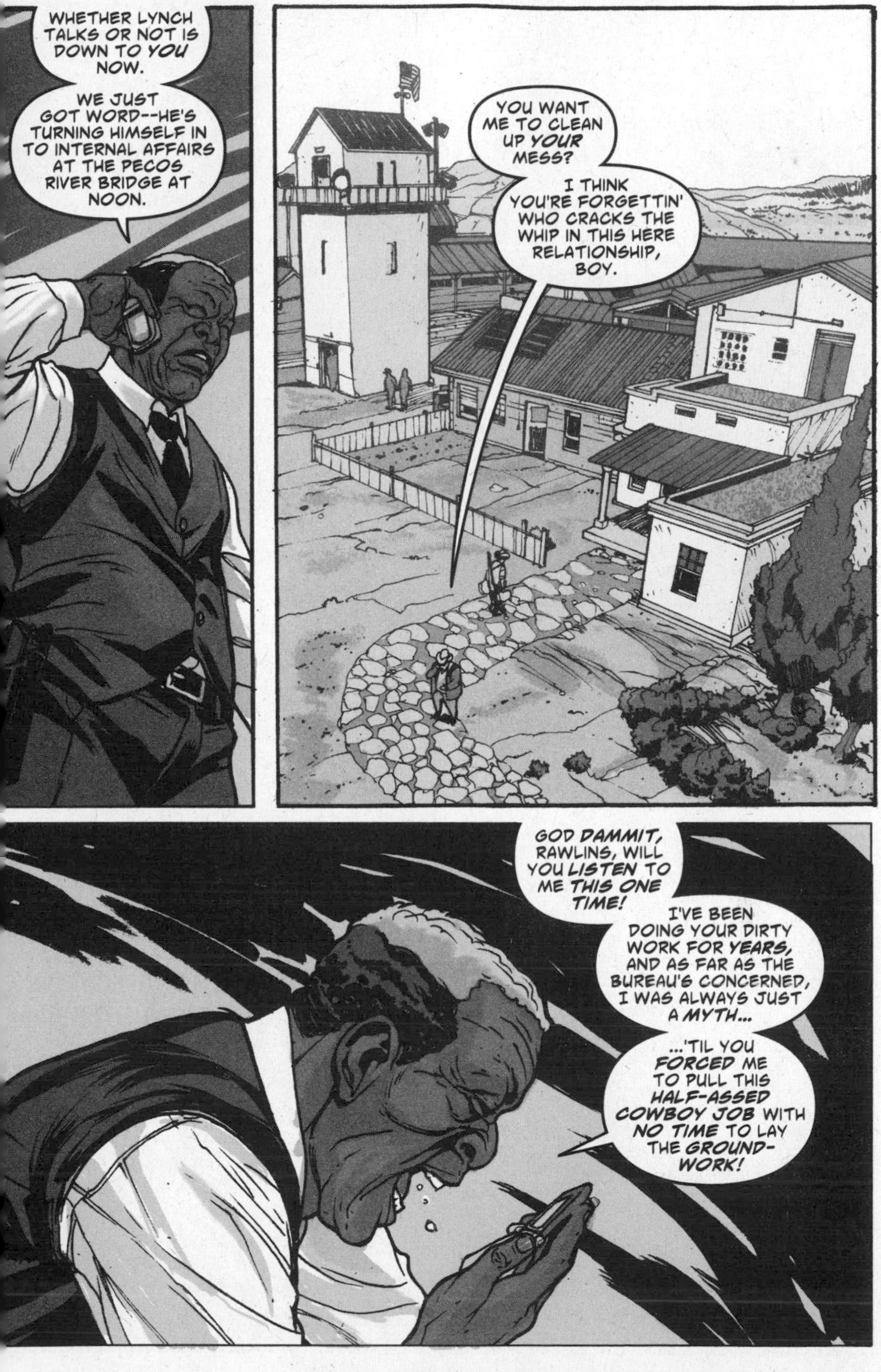
WHETHER LYNCH TALKS OR NOT IS DOWN TO YOU NOW.
WE JUST GOT WORD--HE'S TURNING HIMSELF IN TO INTERNAL AFFAIRS AT THE PECOS RIVER BRIDGE AT NOON.
YOU WANT ME TO CLEAN UP YOUR MESS?
I THINK YOU'RE FORGETTIN' WHO CRACKS THE WHIP IN THIS HERE RELATIONSHIP, BOY.
GOD DAMMIT, RAWLINS, WILL YOU LISTEN TO ME THIS ONE TIME!
I'VE BEEN DOING YOUR DIRTY WORK FOR YEARS, AND AS FAR AS THE BUREAU'S CONCERNED, I WAS ALWAYS JUST A MYTH...
...'TIL YOU FORCED ME TO PULL THIS HALF-ASSED COWBOY JOB WITH NO TIME TO LAY THE GROUND-WORK!

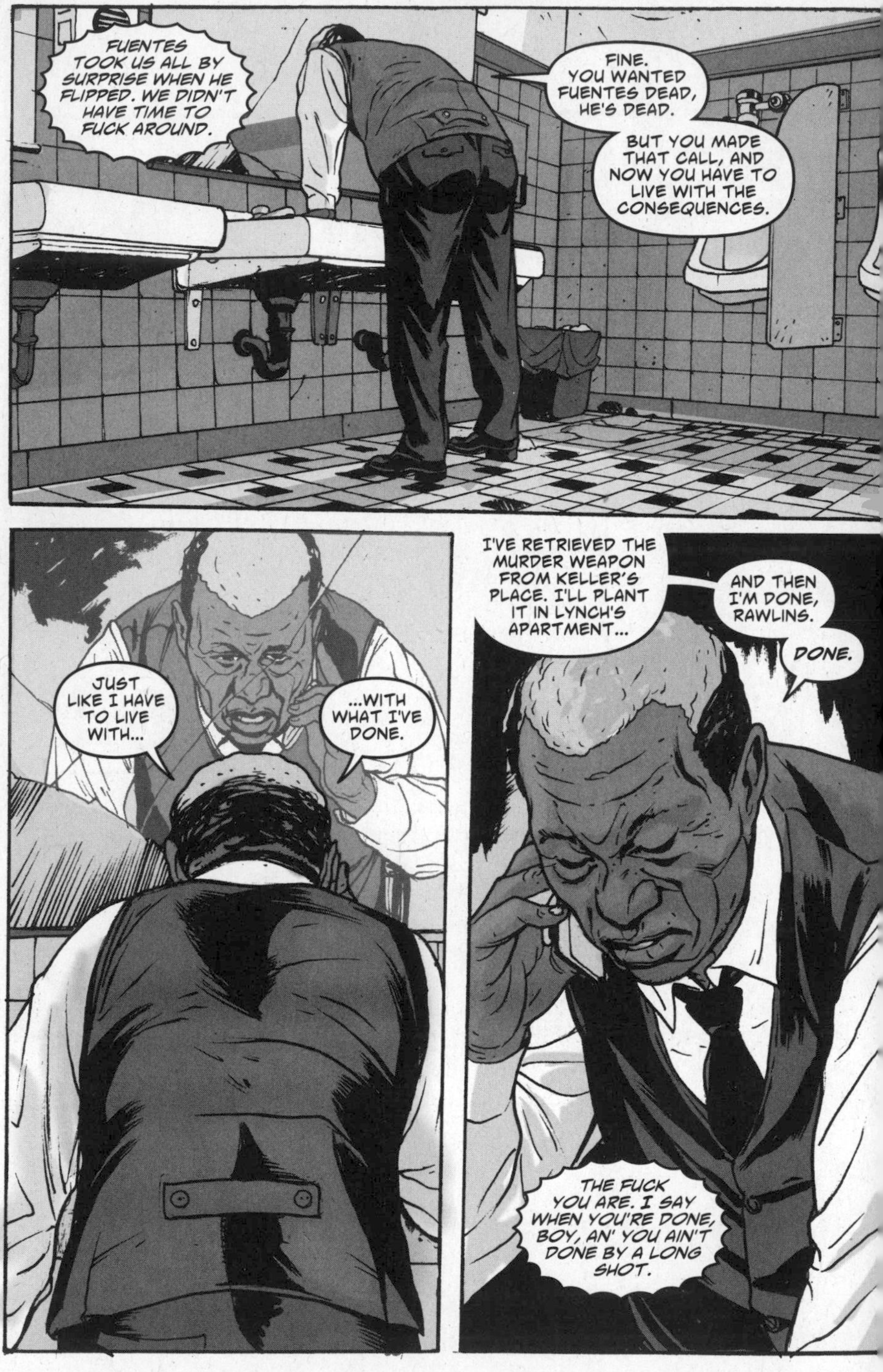
FUENTES TOOK US ALL BY SURPRISE WHEN HE FLIPPED. WE DIDN'T HAVE TIME TO FUCK AROUND.
FINE. YOU WANTED FUENTES DEAD, HE'S DEAD.
BUT YOU MADE THAT CALL, AND NOW YOU HAVE TO LIVE WITH THE CONSEQUENCES.
JUST LIKE I HAVE TO LIVE WITH...
...WITH WHAT I'VE DONE.
I'VE RETRIEVED THE MURDER WEAPON FROM KELLER'S PLACE. I'LL PLANT IT IN LYNCH'S APARTMENT...
AND THEN I'M DONE, RAWLINS.
DONE.
THE FUCK YOU ARE. I SAY WHEN YOU'RE DONE, BOY, AN' YOU AIN'T DONE BY A LONG SHOT.

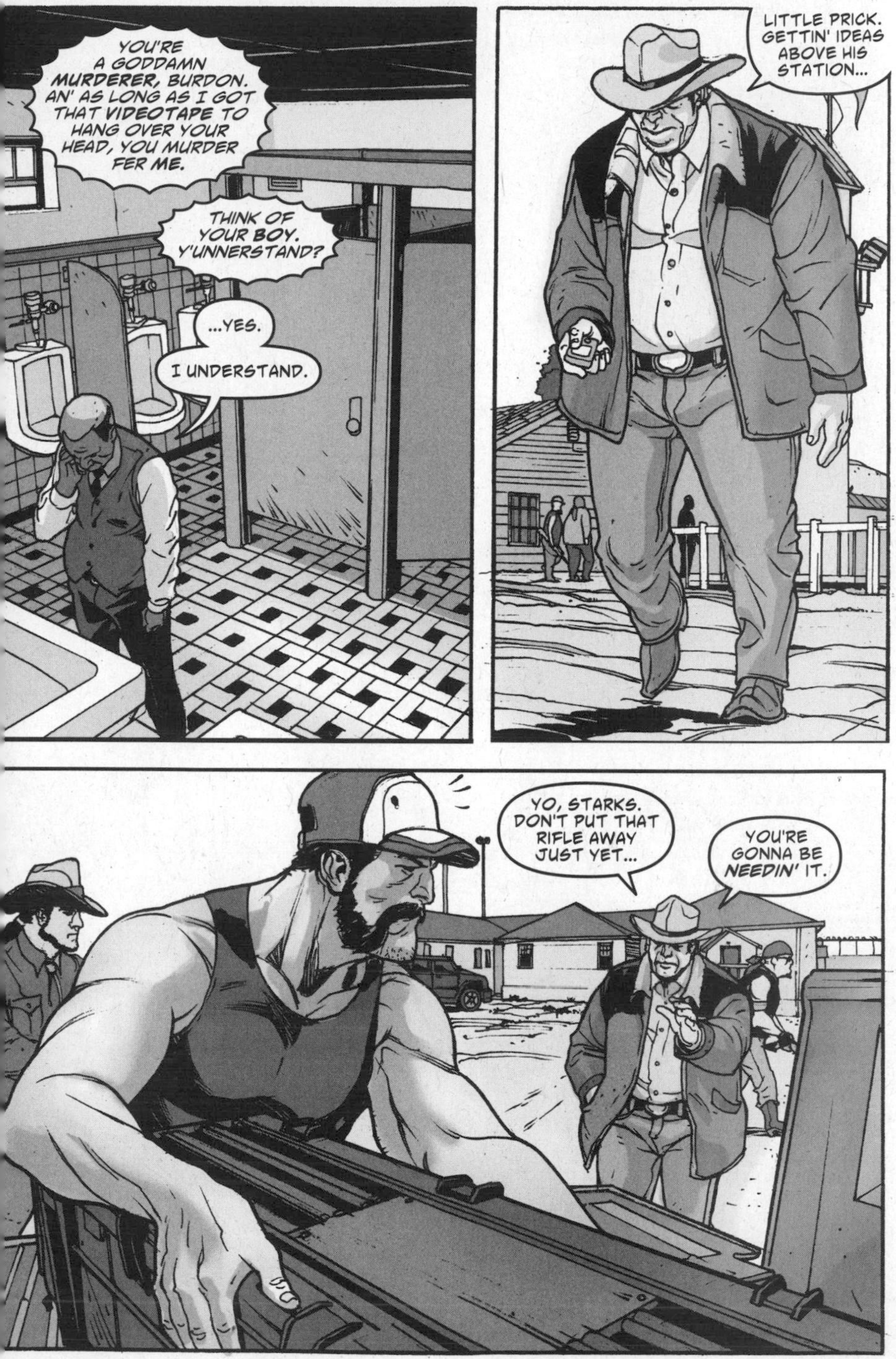
YOU'RE A GODDAMN MURDERER, BURDON. AN' AS LONG AS I GOT THAT VIDEOTAPE TO HANG OVER YOUR HEAD, YOU MURDER FER ME.
THINK OF YOUR BOY. Y'UNNERSTAND?
...YES.
I UNDERSTAND.
LITTLE PRICK. GETTIN' IDEAS ABOVE HIS STATION...
YO, STARKS. DON'T PUT THAT RIFLE AWAY JUST YET...
YOU'RE GONNA BE NEEDIN' IT.

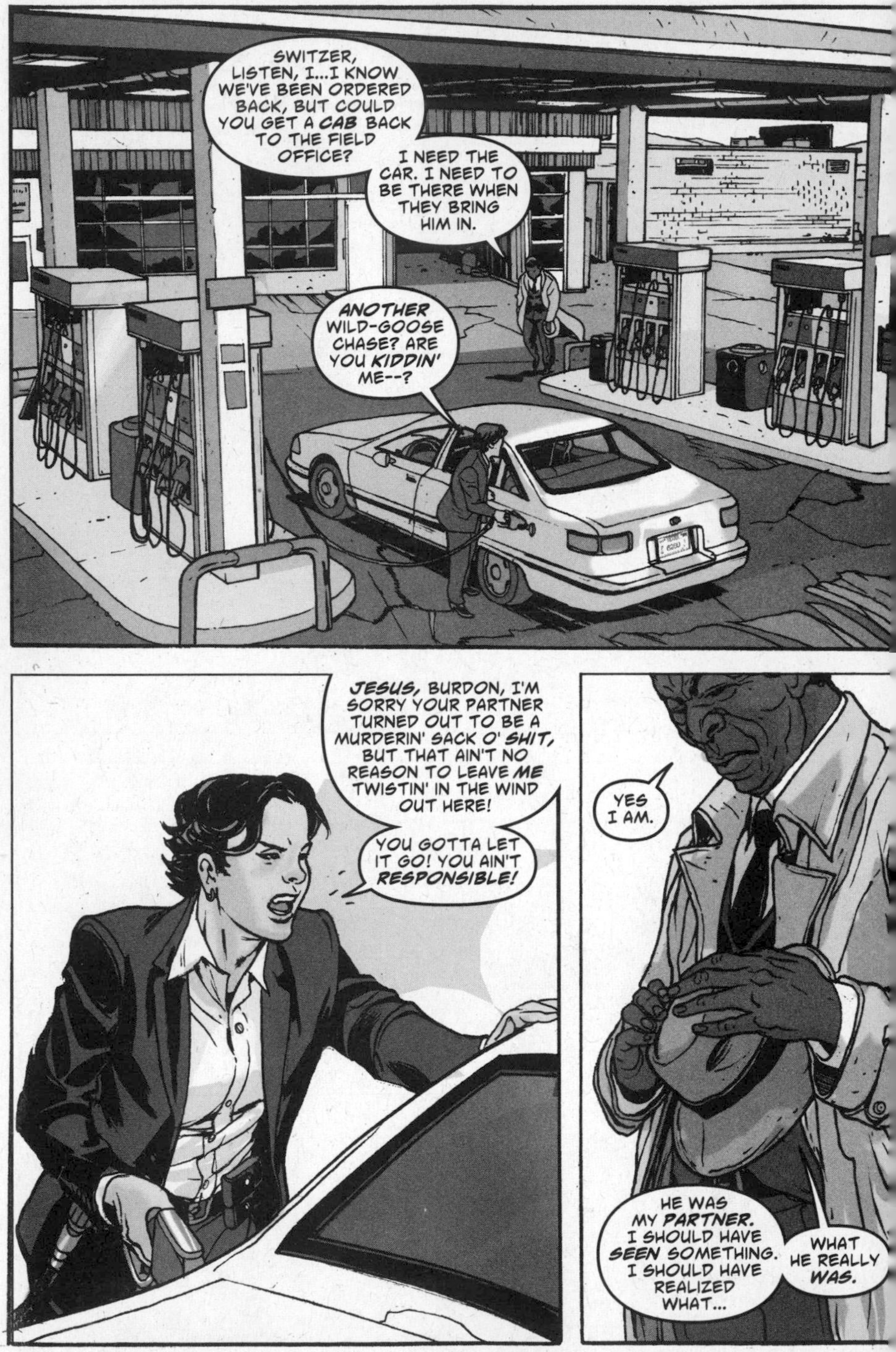
SWITZER, LISTEN, I...I KNOW WE'VE BEEN ORDERED BACK, BUT COULD YOU GET A CAB BACK TO THE FIELD OFFICE?
I NEED THE CAR. I NEED TO BE THERE WHEN THEY BRING HIM IN.
ANOTHER WILD-GOOSE CHASE? ARE YOU KIDDIN' ME--?
JESUS, BURDON, I'M SORRY YOUR PARTNER TURNED OUT TO BE A MURDERIN' SACK O' SHIT, BUT THAT AIN'T NO REASON TO LEAVE ME TWISTIN' IN THE WIND OUT HERE!
YOU GOTTA LET IT GO! YOU AIN'T RESPONSIBLE!
YES I AM.
HE WAS MY PARTNER. I SHOULD HAVE SEEN SOMETHING. I SHOULD HAVE REALIZED WHAT...
WHAT HE REALLY WAS.

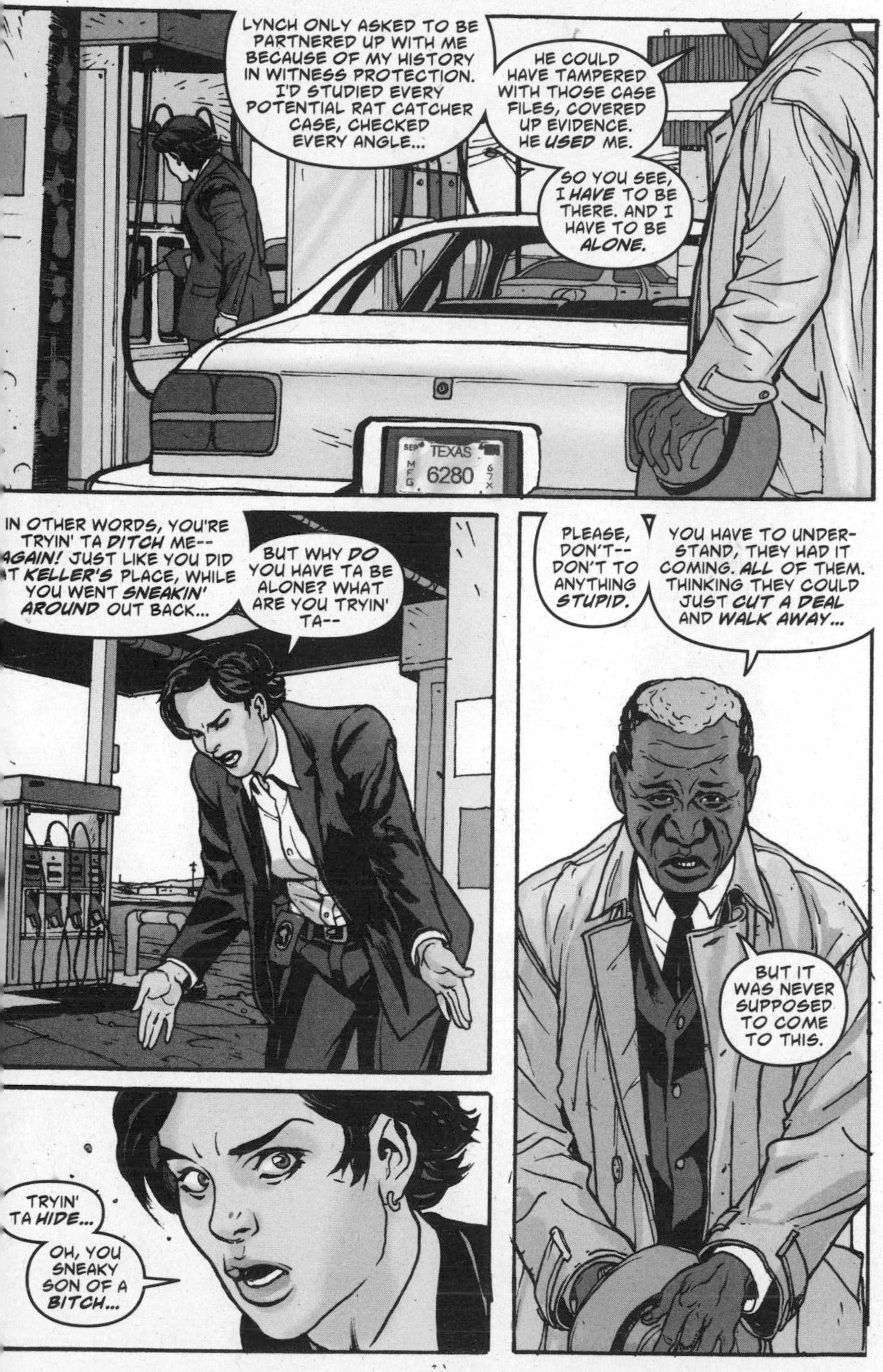
LYNCH ONLY ASKED TO BE PARTNERED UP WITH ME BECAUSE OF MY HISTORY IN WITNESS PROTECTION. I'D STUDIED EVERY POTENTIAL RAT CATCHER CASE, CHECKED EVERY ANGLE...
HE COULD HAVE TAMPERED WITH THOSE CASE FILES, COVERED UP EVIDENCE. HE *USED* ME.
SO YOU SEE, I *HAVE* TO BE THERE. AND I HAVE TO BE *ALONE.*
TEXAS
6280
IN OTHER WORDS, YOU'RE TRYIN' TA *DITCH* ME-- *AGAIN!* JUST LIKE YOU DID T *KELLER'S* PLACE, WHILE YOU WENT *SNEAKIN' AROUND* OUT BACK...
BUT WHY *DO* YOU HAVE TA BE ALONE? WHAT ARE YOU TRYIN' TA--
TRYIN' TA *HIDE*...
OH, YOU SNEAKY SON OF A *BITCH*...
PLEASE, DON'T-- DON'T TO ANYTHING *STUPID.*
YOU HAVE TO UNDERSTAND, THEY HAD IT COMING. *ALL* OF THEM. THINKING THEY COULD JUST *CUT A DEAL* AND *WALK AWAY*...
BUT IT WAS NEVER SUPPOSED TO COME TO THIS.

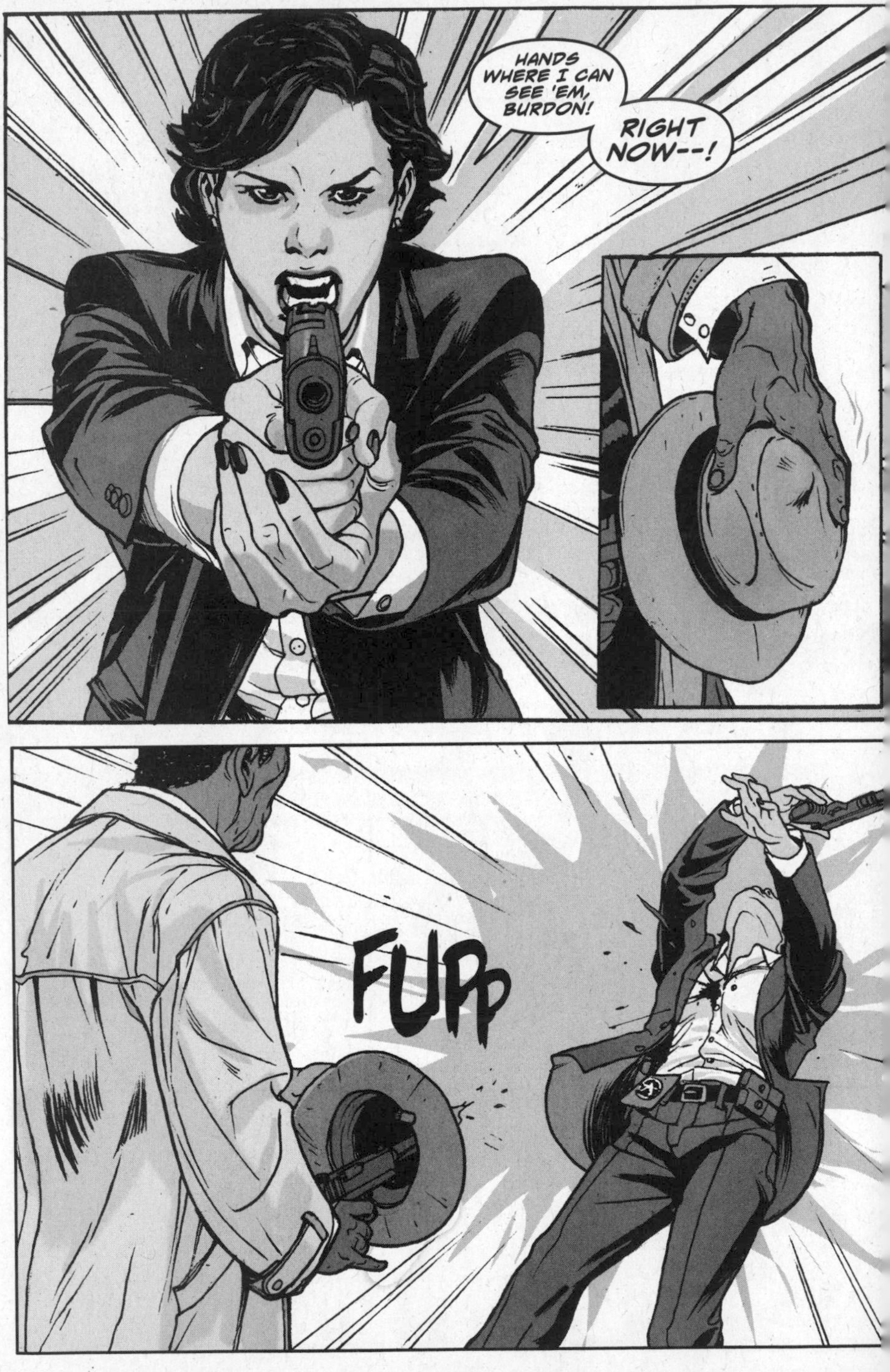
HANDS WHERE I CAN SEE 'EM, BURDON!
RIGHT NOW--!
FUPP

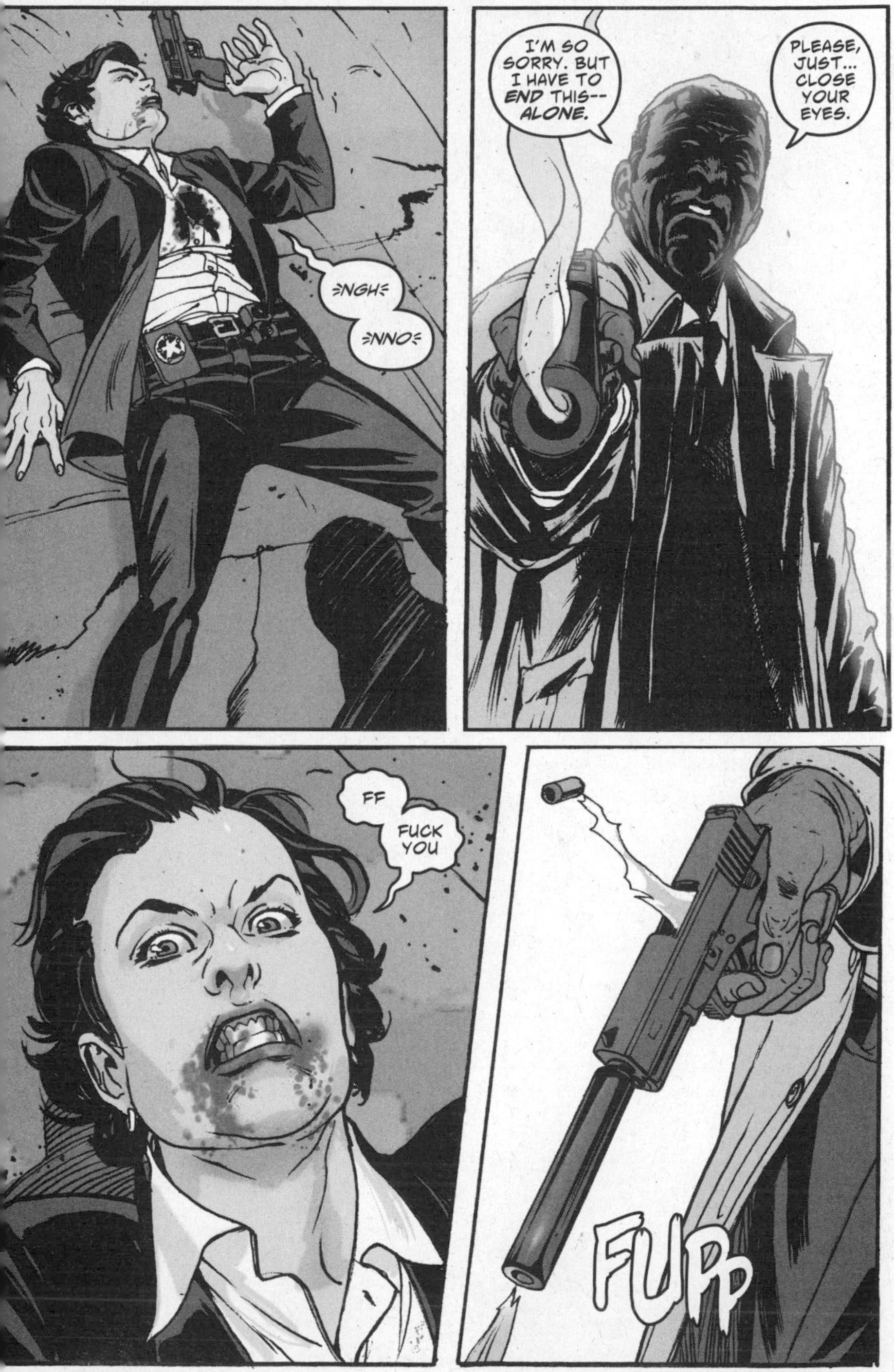
NGH
NNO
I'M SO SORRY. BUT I HAVE TO END THIS-- ALONE.
PLEASE, JUST... CLOSE YOUR EYES.
FF
FUCK YOU
FUPP

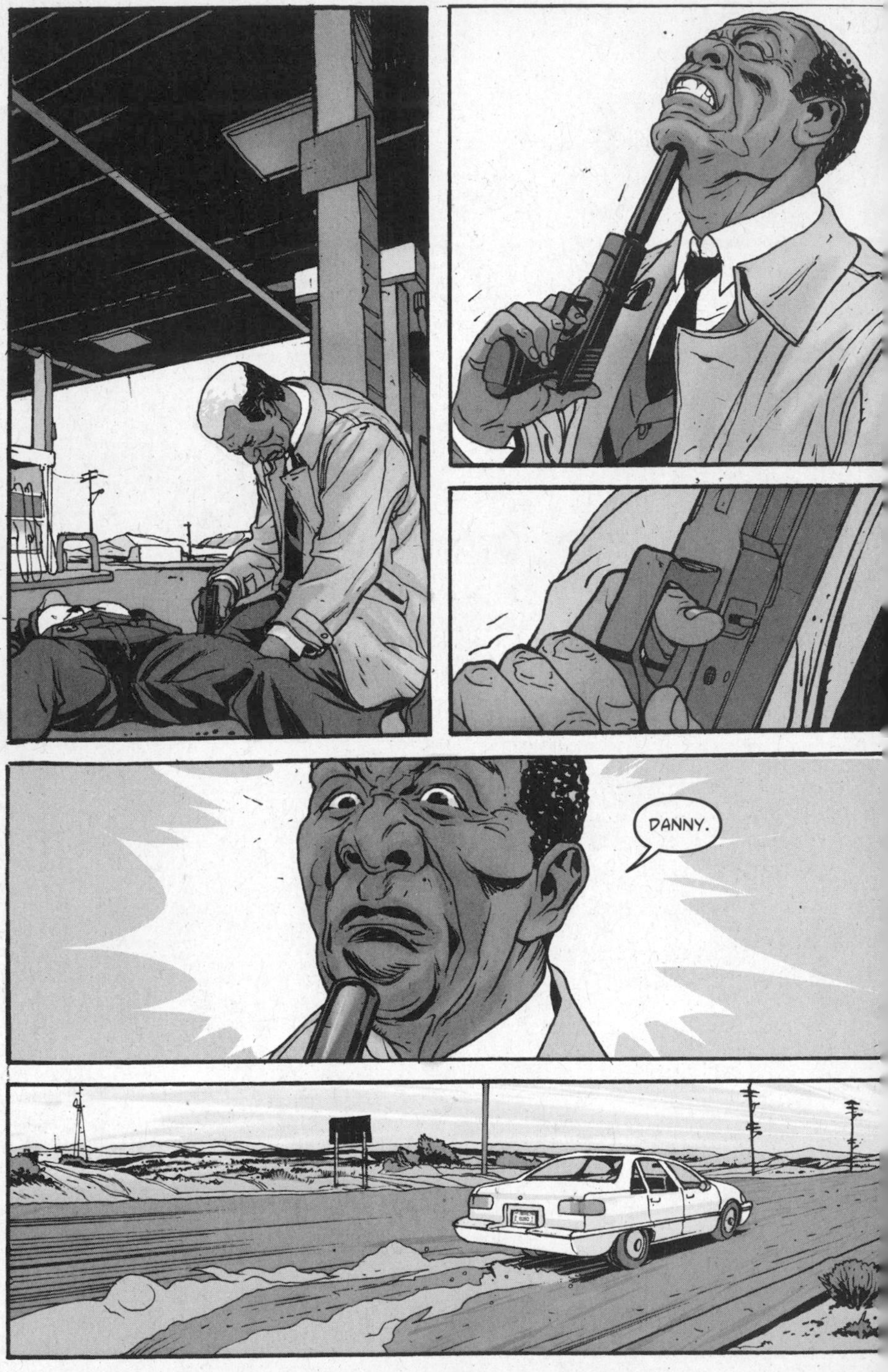
DANNY.

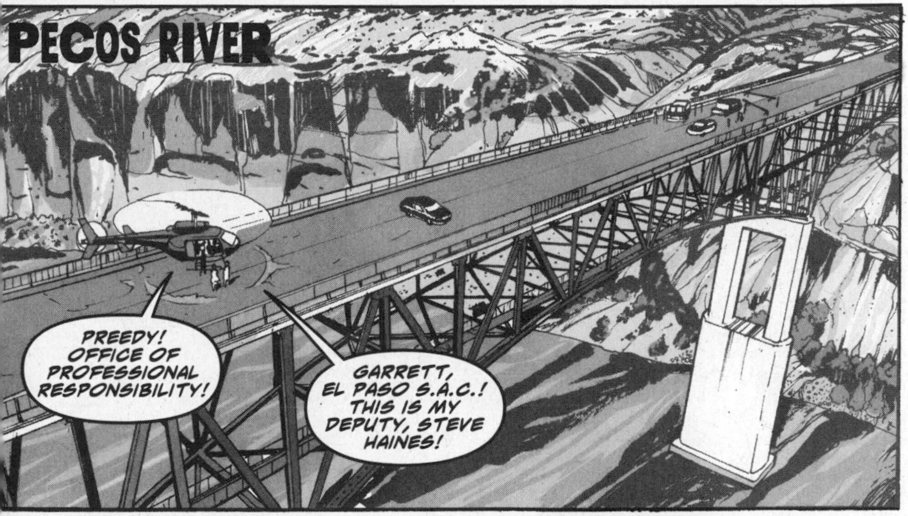
PECOS RIVER
PREEDY! OFFICE OF PROFESSIONAL RESPONSIBILITY!
GARRETT, EL PASO S.A.C.! THIS IS MY DEPUTY, STEVE HAINES!

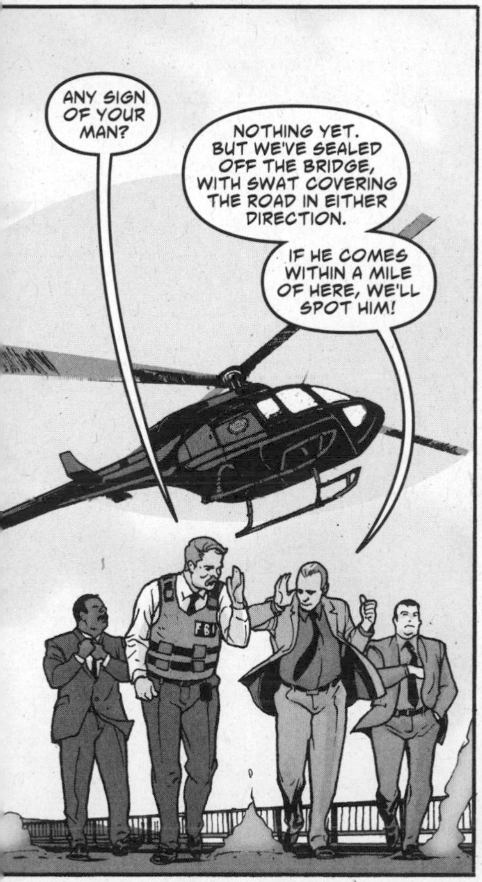
ANY SIGN OF YOUR MAN?
NOTHING YET. BUT WE'VE SEALED OFF THE BRIDGE, WITH SWAT COVERING THE ROAD IN EITHER DIRECTION.
IF HE COMES WITHIN A MILE OF HERE, WE'LL SPOT HIM!
FBI

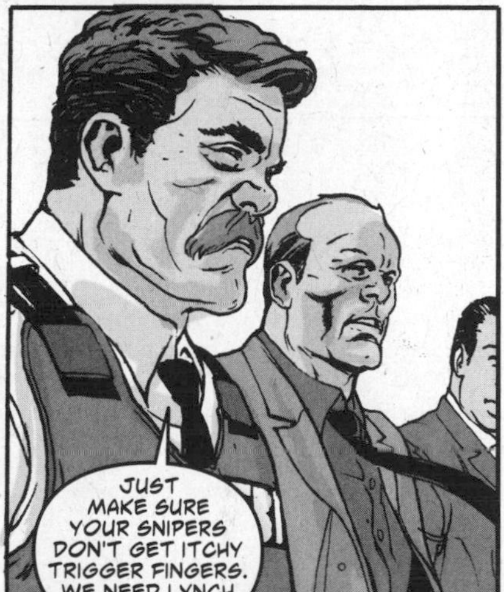
JUST MAKE SURE YOUR SNIPERS DON'T GET ITCHY TRIGGER FINGERS. WE NEED LYNCH ALIVE!

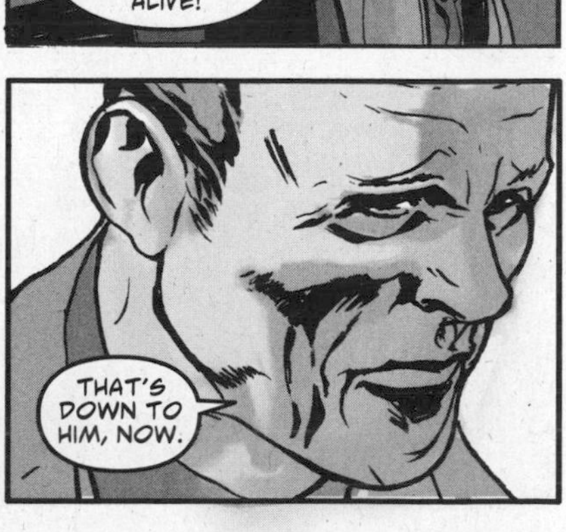
THAT'S DOWN TO HIM, NOW.

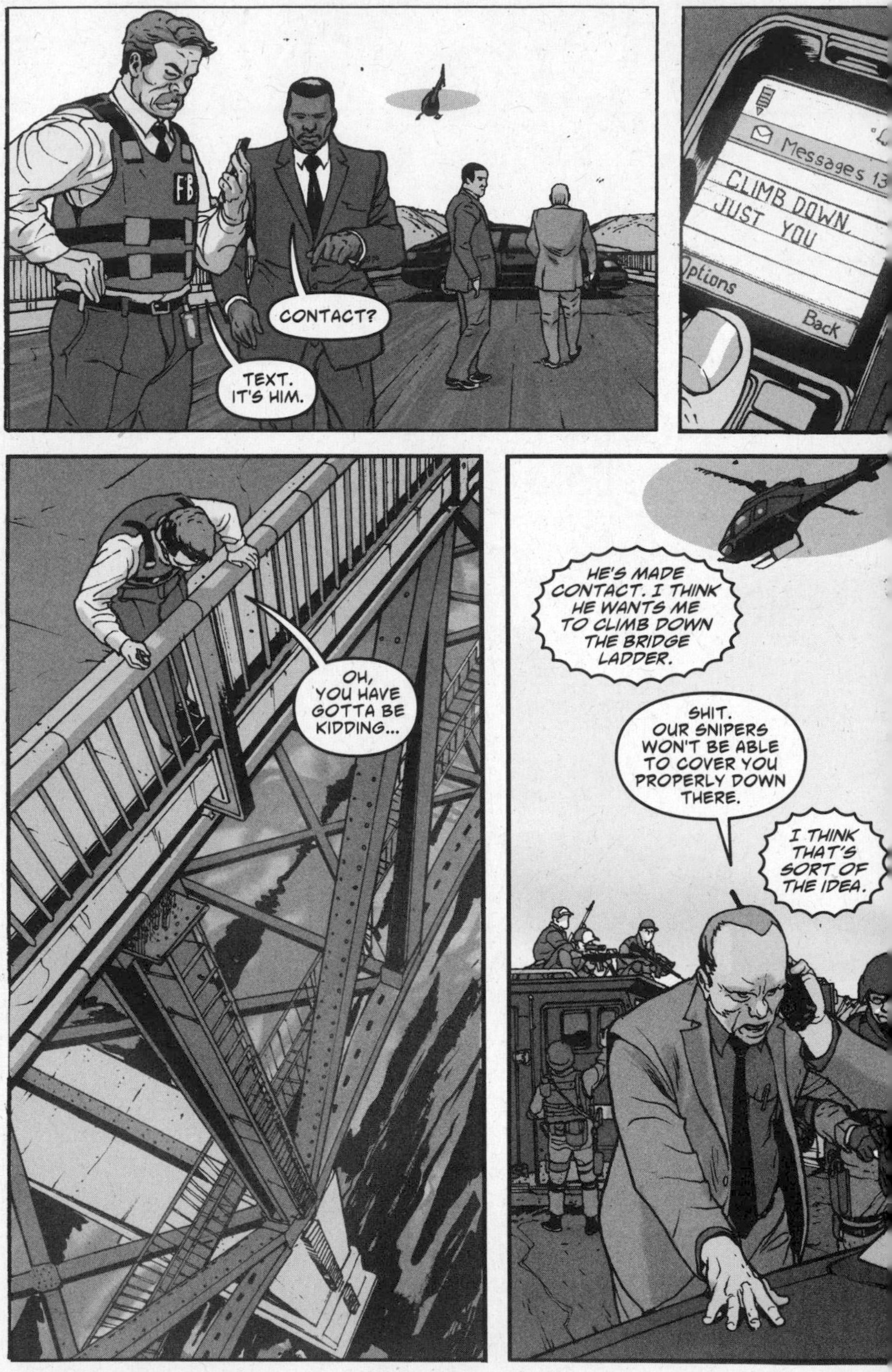
CONTACT?
TEXT. IT'S HIM.
Messages
CLIMB DOWN. JUST YOU
Options
Back
OH, YOU HAVE GOTTA BE KIDDING...
HE'S MADE CONTACT. I THINK HE WANTS ME TO CLIMB DOWN THE BRIDGE LADDER.
SHIT. OUR SNIPERS WON'T BE ABLE TO COVER YOU PROPERLY DOWN THERE.
I THINK THAT'S SORT OF THE IDEA.

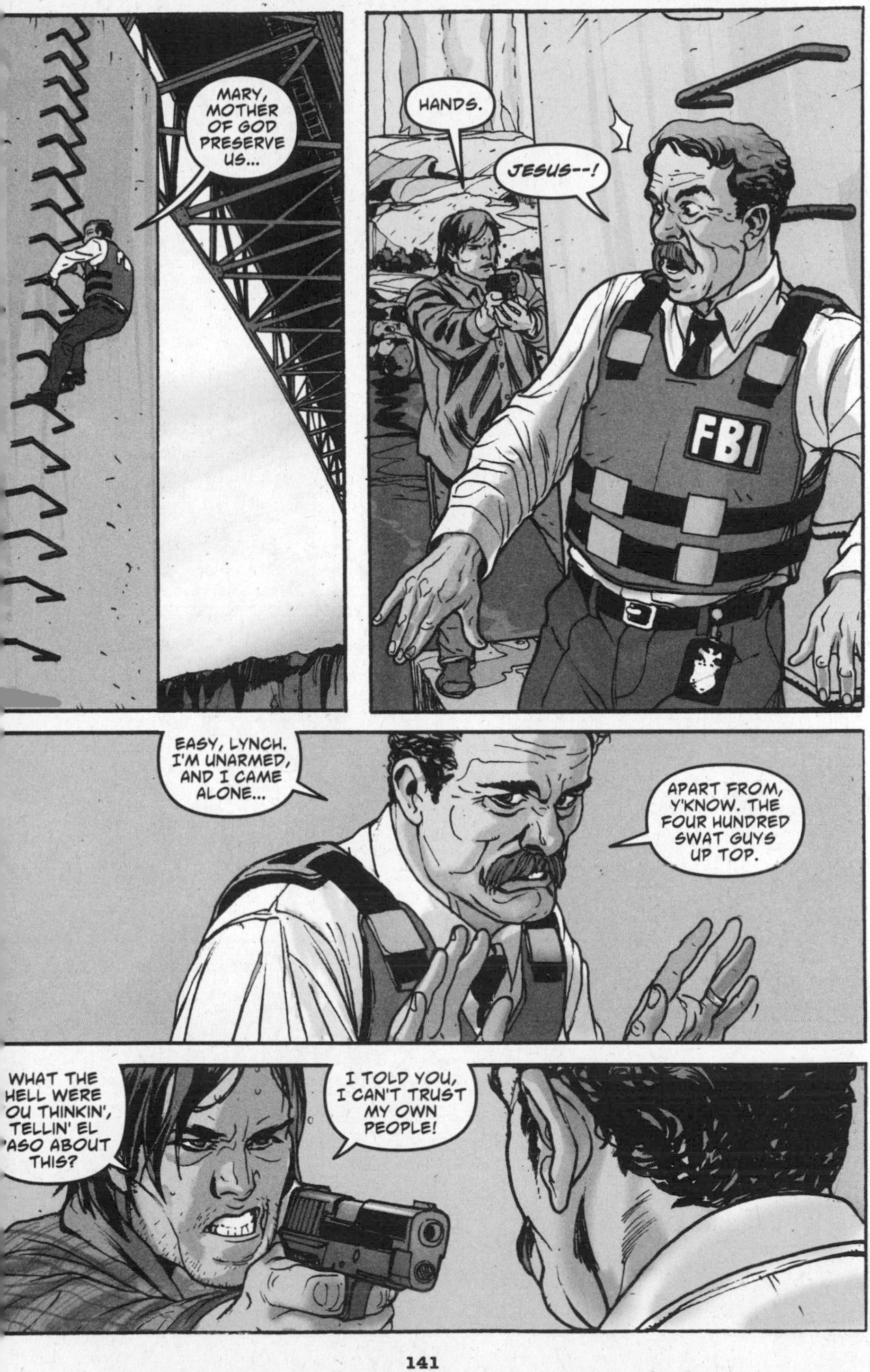
MARY, MOTHER OF GOD PRESERVE US...
HANDS.
JESUS--!
EASY, LYNCH. I'M UNARMED, AND I CAME ALONE...
APART FROM, Y'KNOW. THE FOUR HUNDRED SWAT GUYS UP TOP.
WHAT THE HELL WERE 'OU THINKIN', TELLIN' EL 'ASO ABOUT THIS?
I TOLD YOU, I CAN'T TRUST MY OWN PEOPLE!

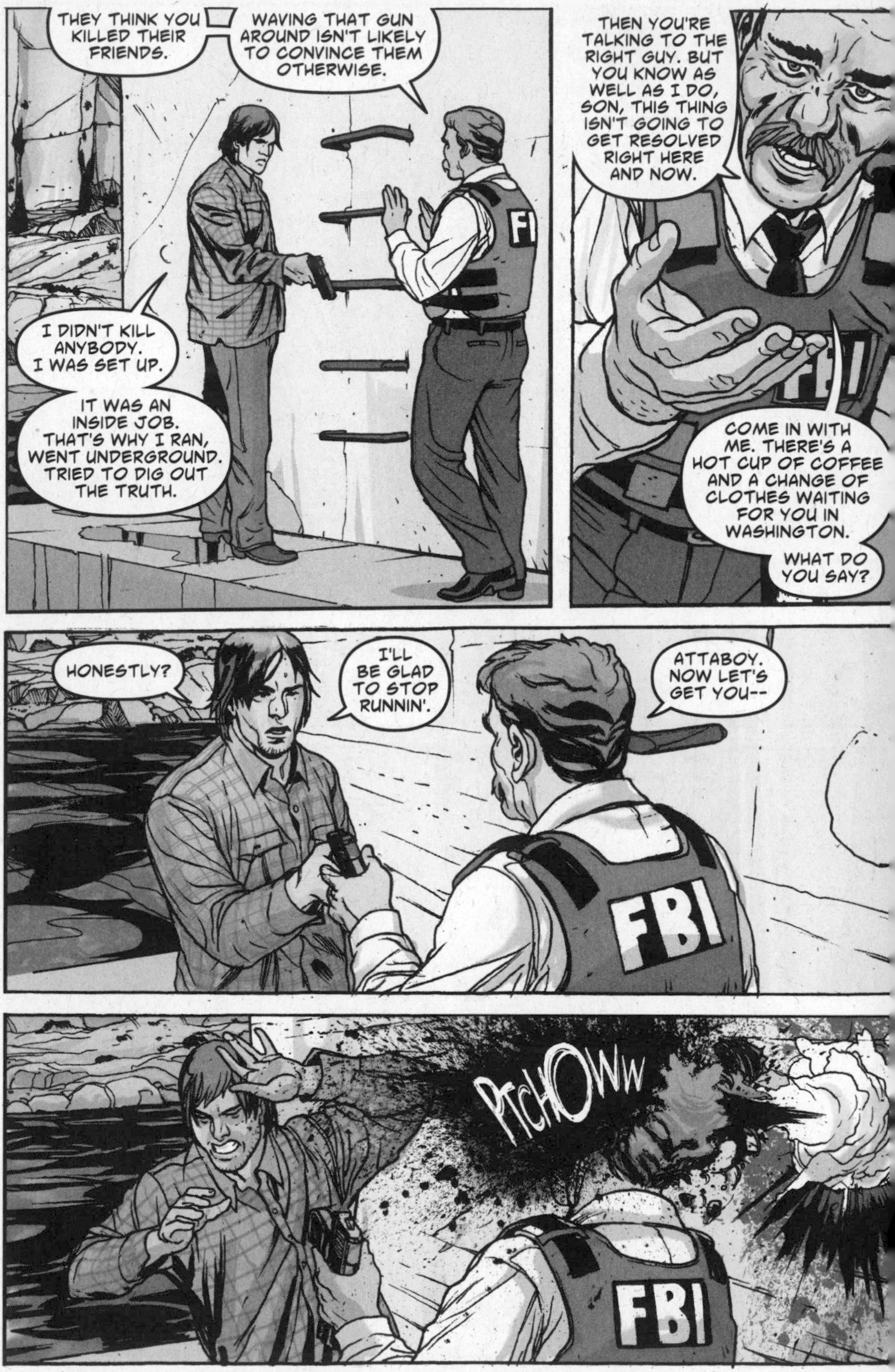
THEY THINK YOU KILLED THEIR FRIENDS.
WAVING THAT GUN AROUND ISN'T LIKELY TO CONVINCE THEM OTHERWISE.
I DIDN'T KILL ANYBODY. I WAS SET UP.
IT WAS AN INSIDE JOB. THAT'S WHY I RAN, WENT UNDERGROUND. TRIED TO DIG OUT THE TRUTH.
FBI
THEN YOU'RE TALKING TO THE RIGHT GUY. BUT YOU KNOW AS WELL AS I DO, SON, THIS THING ISN'T GOING TO GET RESOLVED RIGHT HERE AND NOW.
COME IN WITH ME. THERE'S A HOT CUP OF COFFEE AND A CHANGE OF CLOTHES WAITING FOR YOU IN WASHINGTON.
WHAT DO YOU SAY?
HONESTLY?
I'LL BE GLAD TO STOP RUNNIN'.
ATTABOY. NOW LET'S GET YOU--
FBI
PTCHOWW
FBI

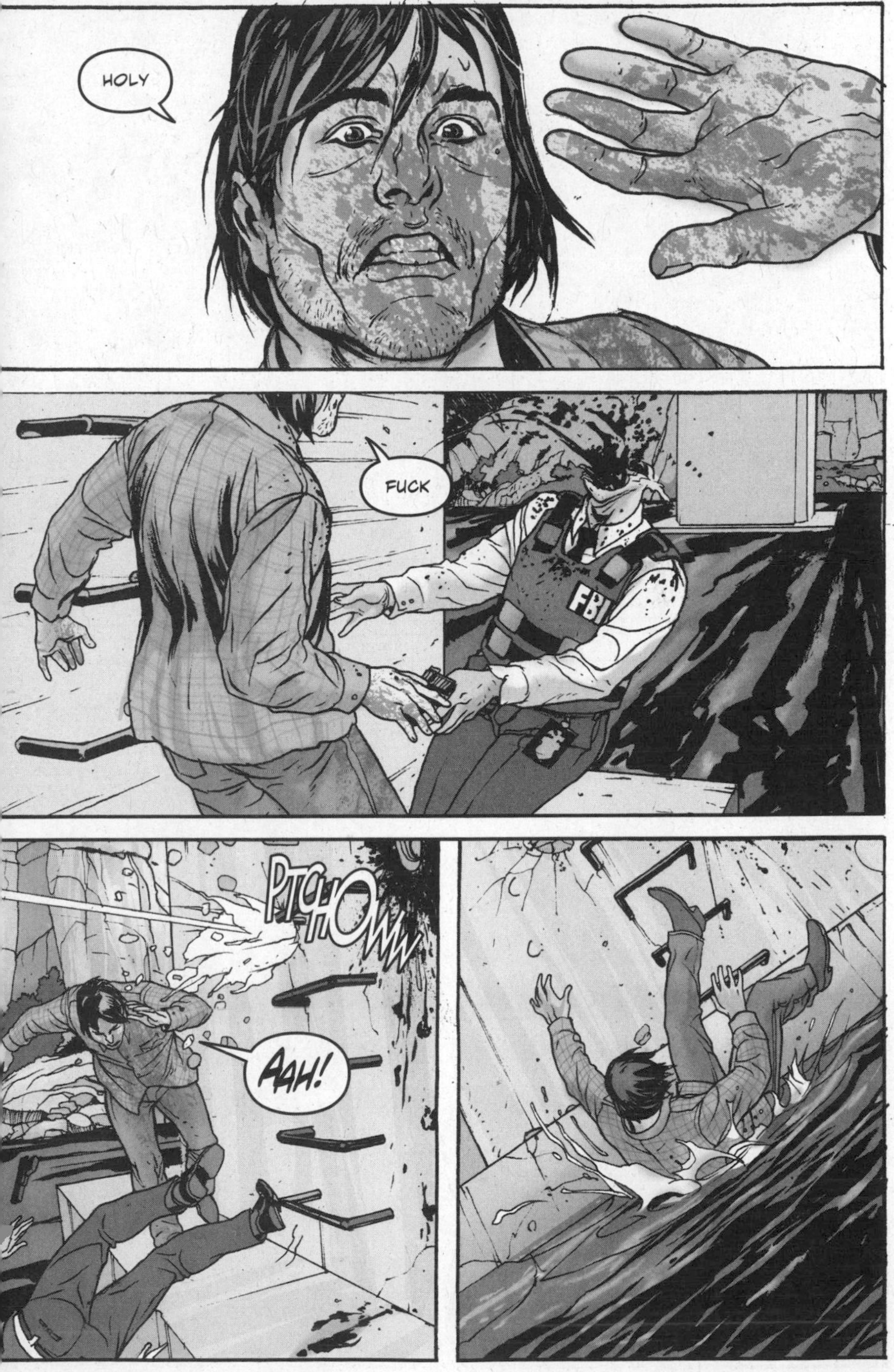
HOLY
FUCK
PTCHOWW
AAH!

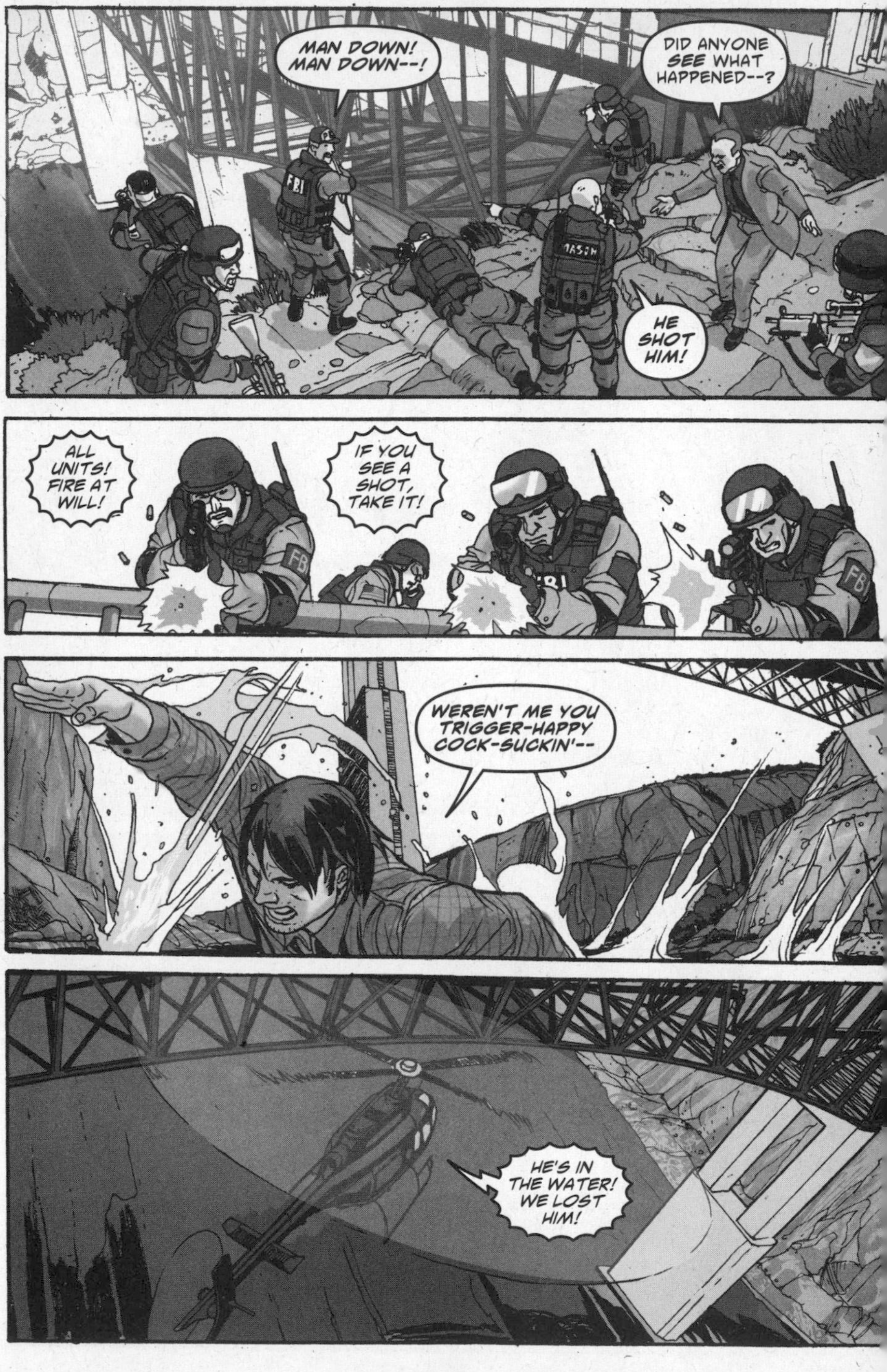
MAN DOWN! MAN DOWN--!
DID ANYONE SEE WHAT HAPPENED--?
HE SHOT HIM!
ALL UNITS! FIRE AT WILL!
IF YOU SEE A SHOT, TAKE IT!
WEREN'T ME YOU TRIGGER-HAPPY COCK-SUCKIN'--
HE'S IN THE WATER! WE LOST HIM!

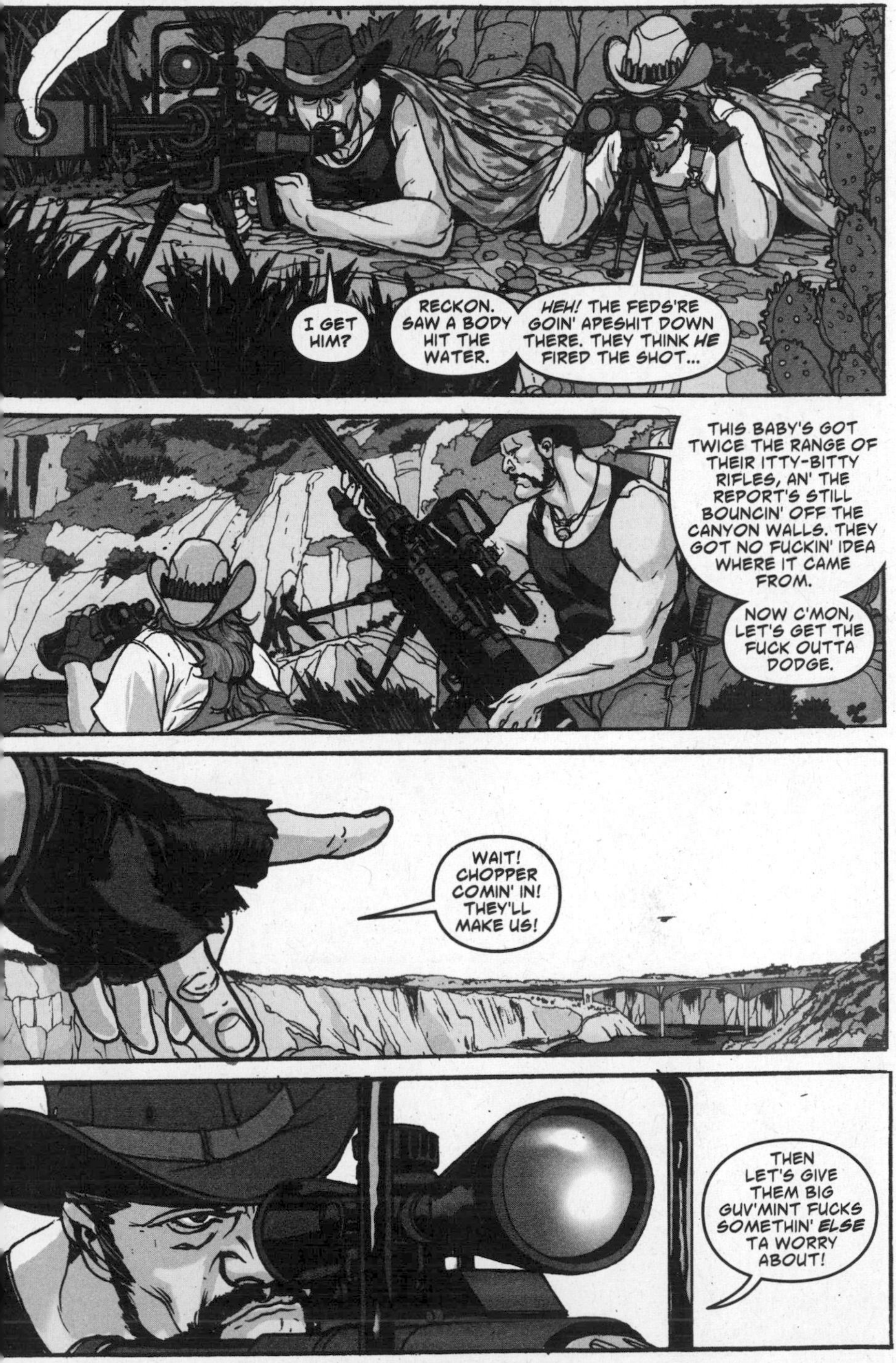
I GET HIM?
RECKON. SAW A BODY HIT THE WATER.
HEH! THE FEDS'RE GOIN' APESHIT DOWN THERE. THEY THINK HE FIRED THE SHOT...
THIS BABY'S GOT TWICE THE RANGE OF THEIR ITTY-BITTY RIFLES, AN' THE REPORT'S STILL BOUNCIN' OFF THE CANYON WALLS. THEY GOT NO FUCKIN' IDEA WHERE IT CAME FROM.
NOW C'MON, LET'S GET THE FUCK OUTTA DODGE.
WAIT! CHOPPER COMIN' IN! THEY'LL MAKE US!
THEN LET'S GIVE THEM BIG GUV'MINT FUCKS SOMETHIN' ELSE TA WORRY ABOUT!

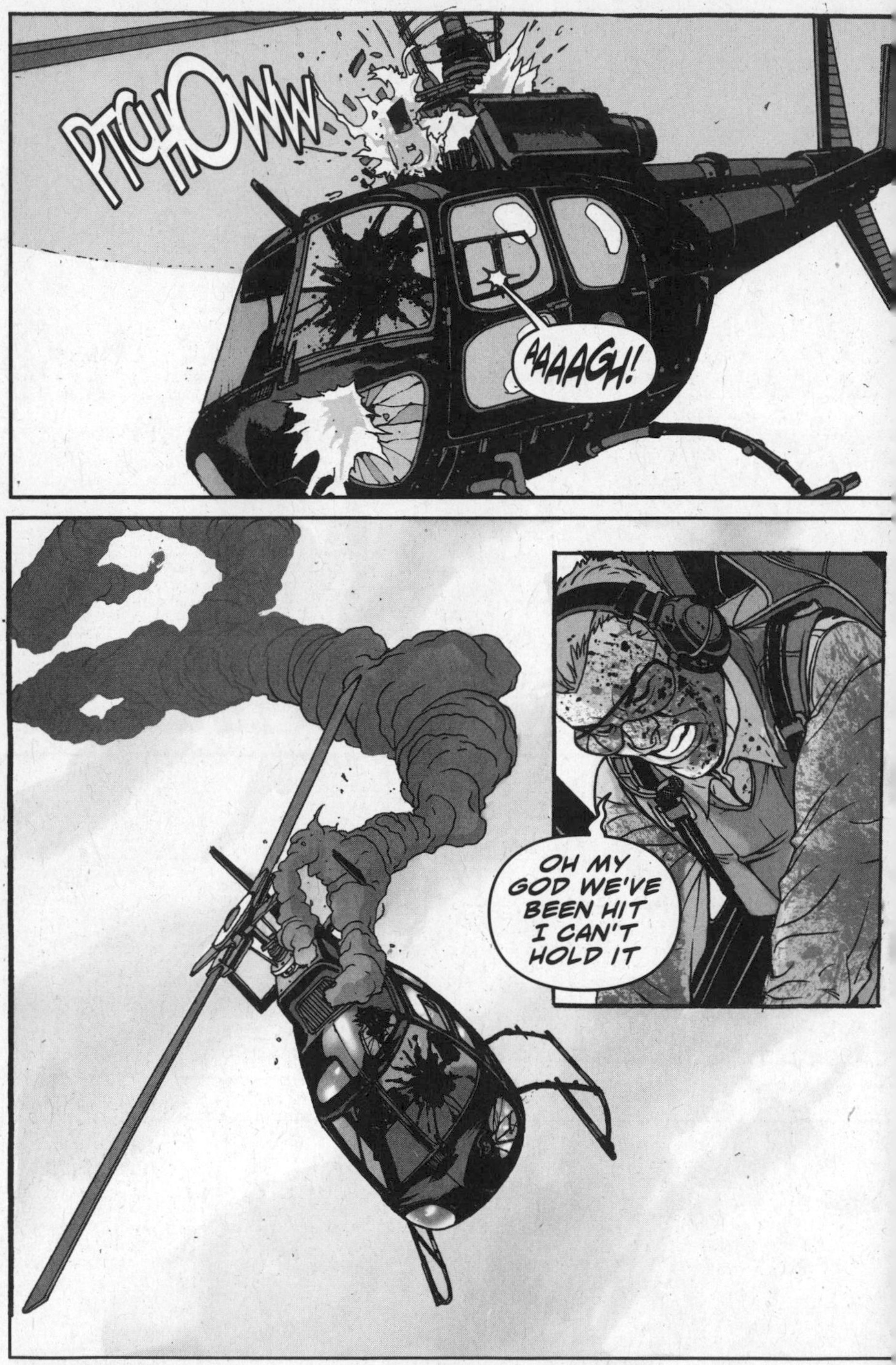
PTCHOWW
AAAAGH!
OH MY GOD WE'VE BEEN HIT I CAN'T HOLD IT

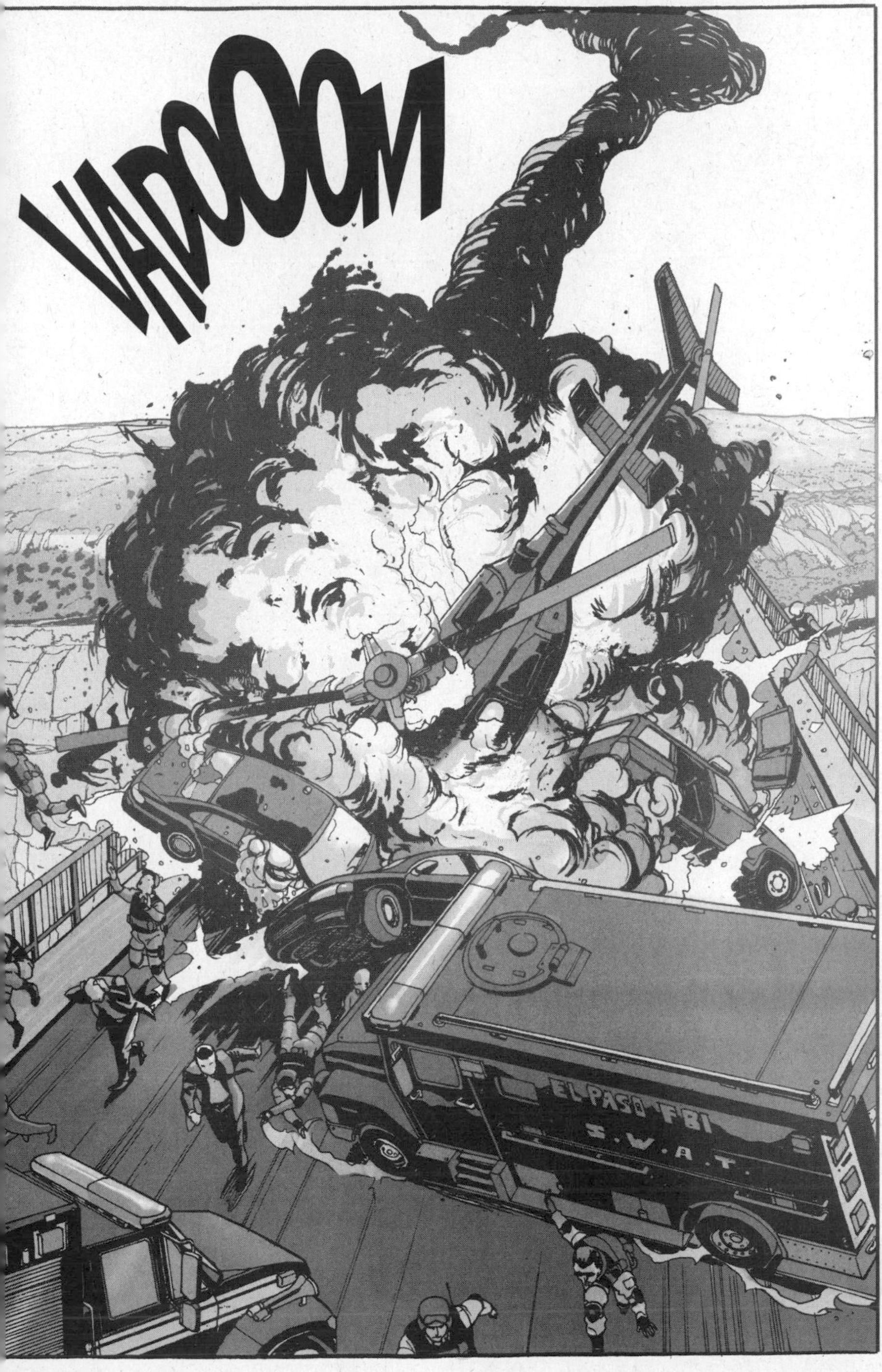
VADOOOM
EL PASO FBI
S.W.A.T.

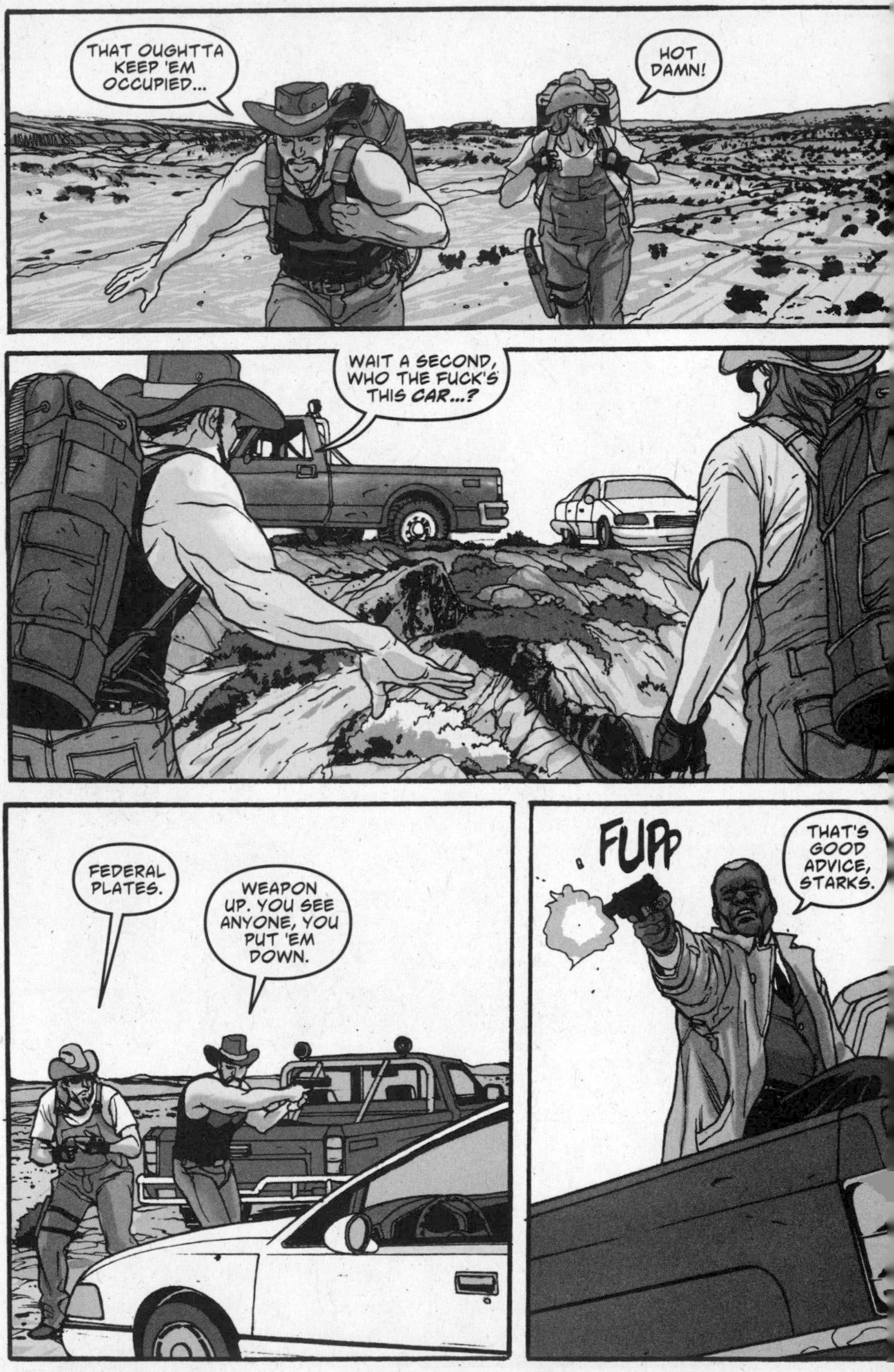
THAT OUGHTTA KEEP 'EM OCCUPIED...
HOT DAMN!
WAIT A SECOND, WHO THE FUCK'S THIS CAR...?
FEDERAL PLATES.
WEAPON UP. YOU SEE ANYONE, YOU PUT 'EM DOWN.
FUPP
THAT'S GOOD ADVICE, STARKS.

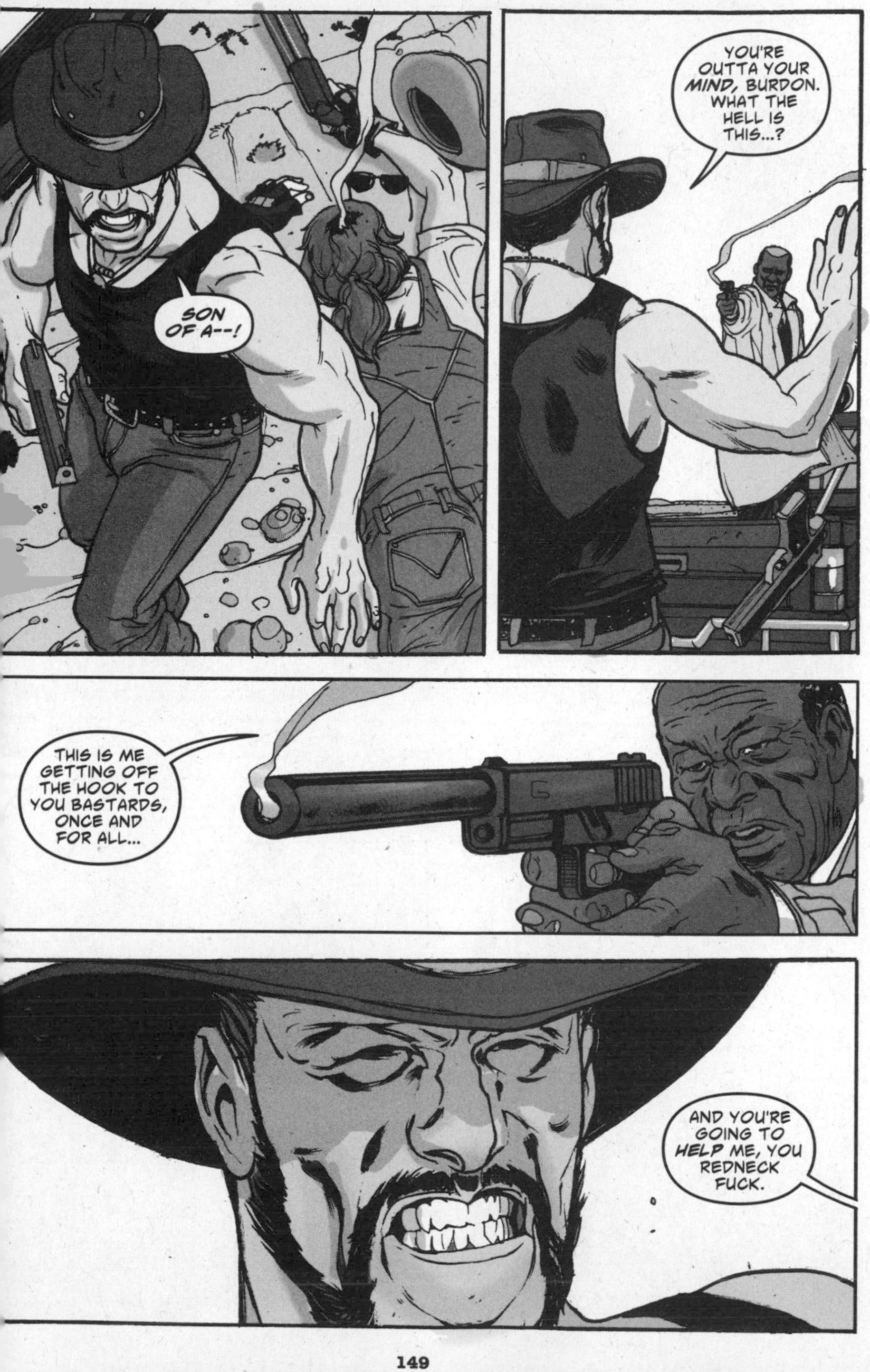
SON OF A--!
YOU'RE OUTTA YOUR MIND, BURDON. WHAT THE HELL IS THIS...?
THIS IS ME GETTING OFF THE HOOK TO YOU BASTARDS, ONCE AND FOR ALL...
AND YOU'RE GOING TO HELP ME, YOU REDNECK FUCK.

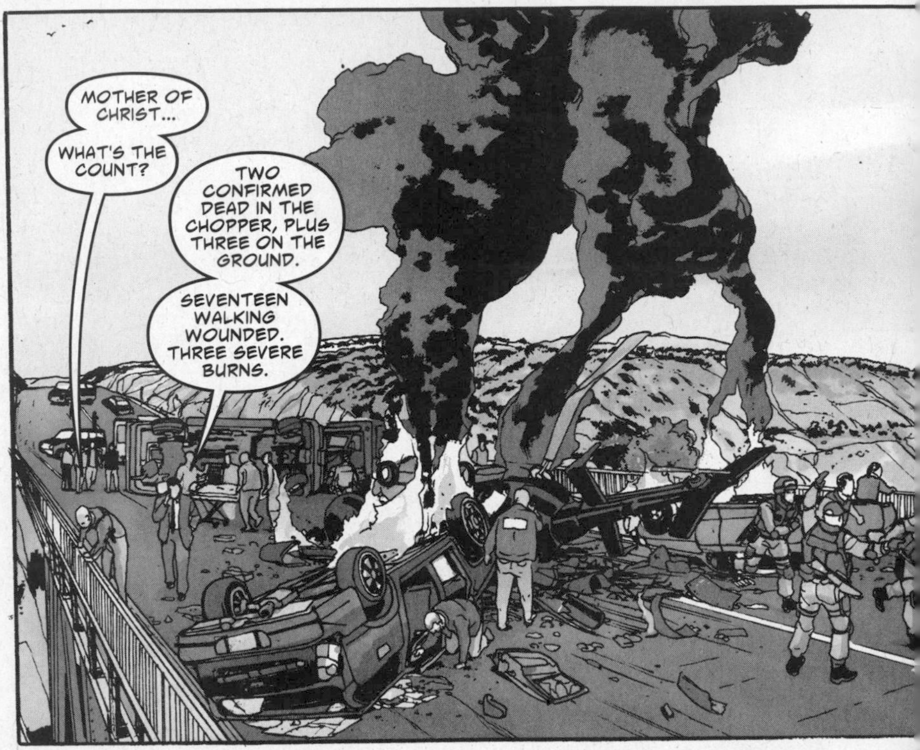
MOTHER OF CHRIST...
WHAT'S THE COUNT?
TWO CONFIRMED DEAD IN THE CHOPPER, PLUS THREE ON THE GROUND.
SEVENTEEN WALKING WOUNDED. THREE SEVERE BURNS.

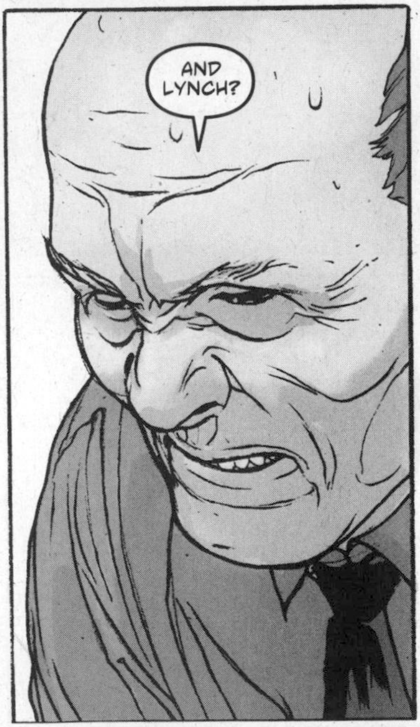
AND LYNCH?

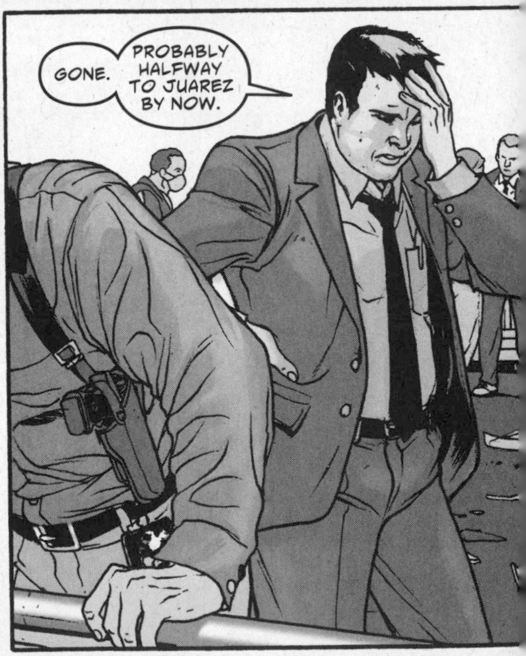
GONE.
PROBABLY HALFWAY TO JUAREZ BY NOW.

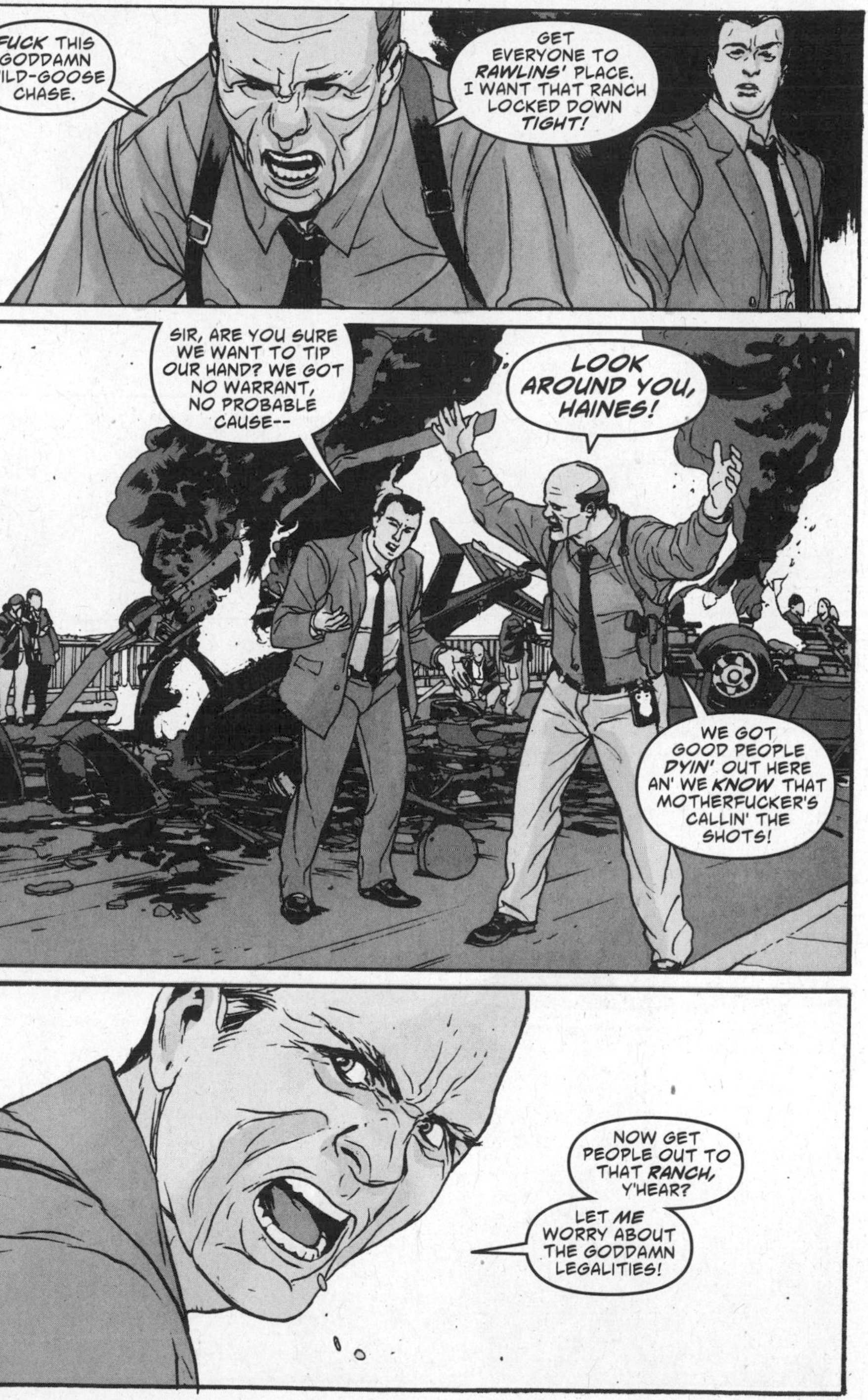
FUCK THIS GODDAMN WILD-GOOSE CHASE.
GET EVERYONE TO RAWLINS' PLACE. I WANT THAT RANCH LOCKED DOWN TIGHT!
SIR, ARE YOU SURE WE WANT TO TIP OUR HAND? WE GOT NO WARRANT, NO PROBABLE CAUSE--
LOOK AROUND YOU, HAINES!
WE GOT GOOD PEOPLE DYIN' OUT HERE AN' WE KNOW THAT MOTHERFUCKER'S CALLIN' THE SHOTS!
NOW GET PEOPLE OUT TO THAT RANCH, Y'HEAR?
LET ME WORRY ABOUT THE GODDAMN LEGALITIES!

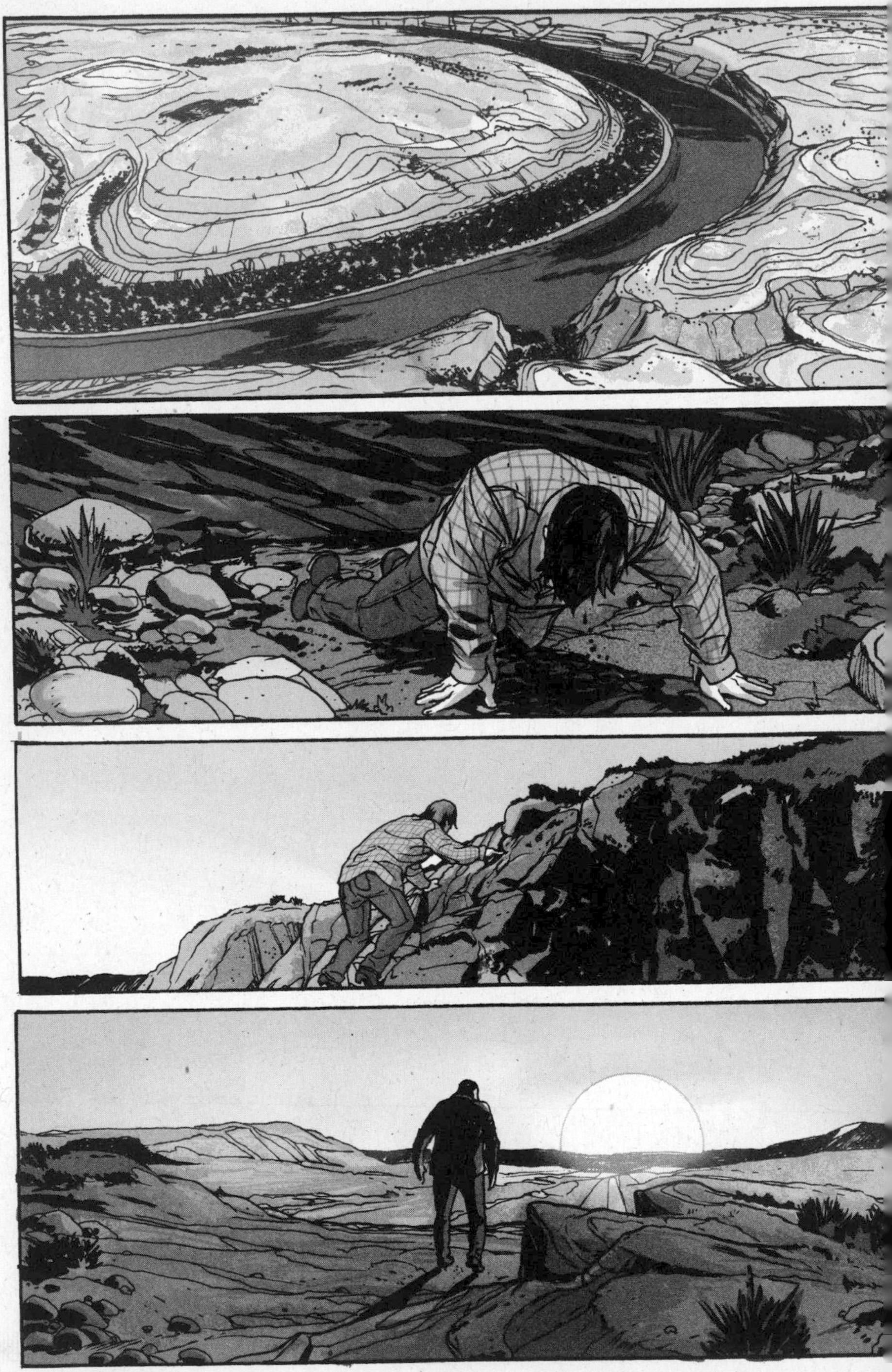

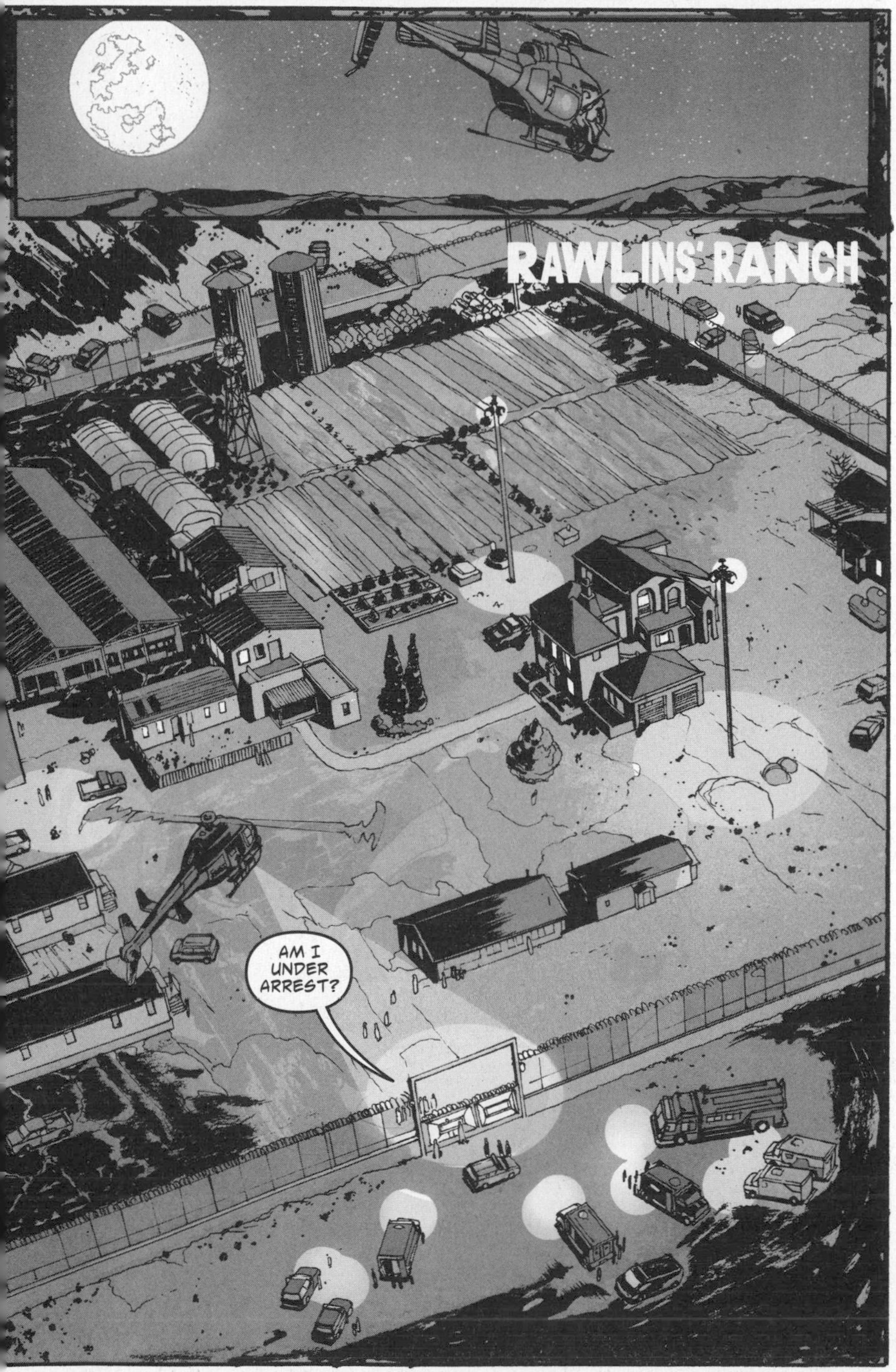
RAWLINS' RANCH
AM I UNDER ARREST?

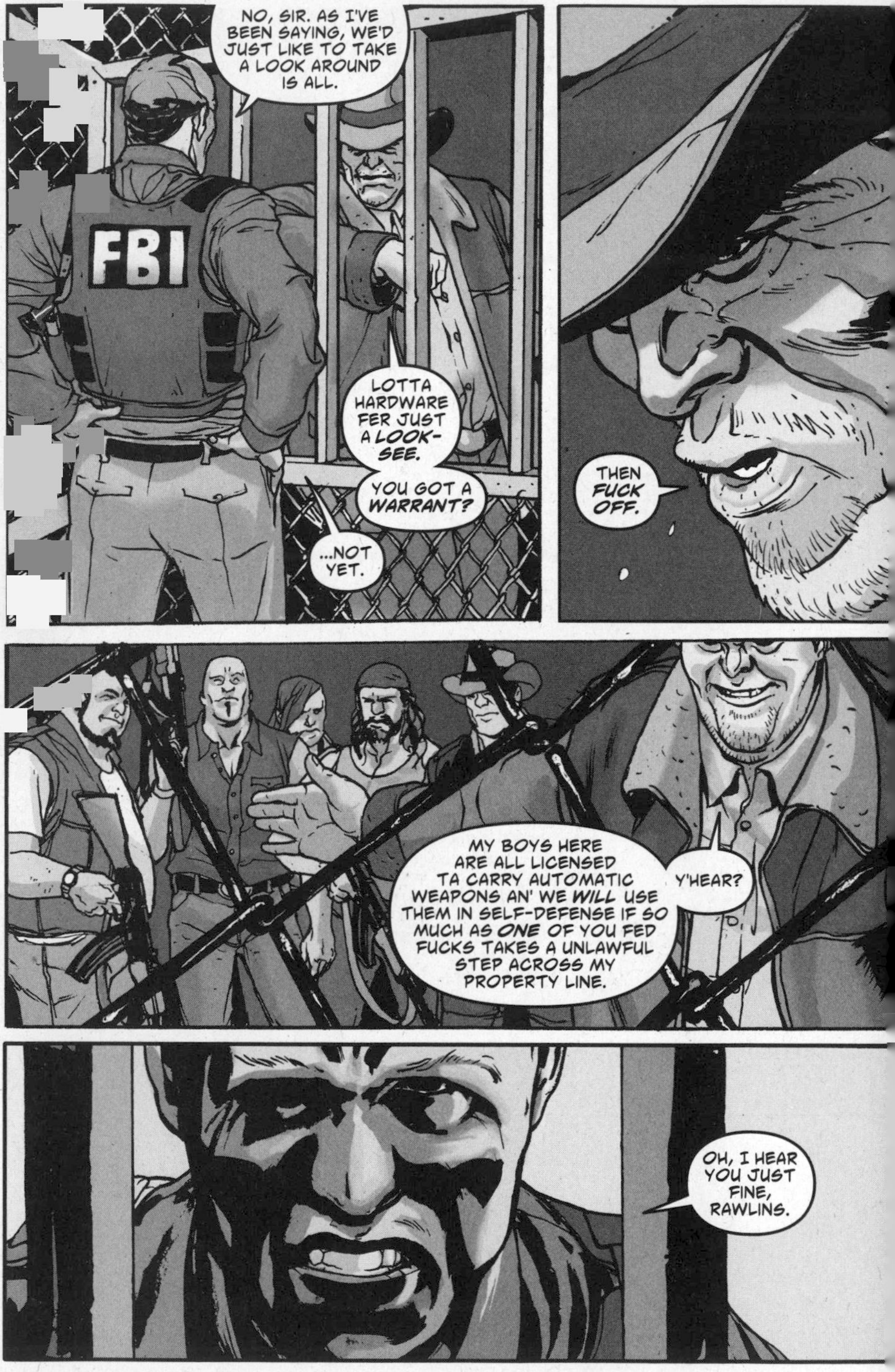
NO, SIR. AS I'VE BEEN SAYING, WE'D JUST LIKE TO TAKE A LOOK AROUND IS ALL.
FBI
LOTTA HARDWARE FER JUST A LOOK-SEE.
YOU GOT A WARRANT?
...NOT YET.
THEN FUCK OFF.
MY BOYS HERE ARE ALL LICENSED TA CARRY AUTOMATIC WEAPONS AN' WE WILL USE THEM IN SELF-DEFENSE IF SO MUCH AS ONE OF YOU FED FUCKS TAKES A UNLAWFUL STEP ACROSS MY PROPERTY LINE.
Y'HEAR?
OH, I HEAR YOU JUST FINE, RAWLINS.

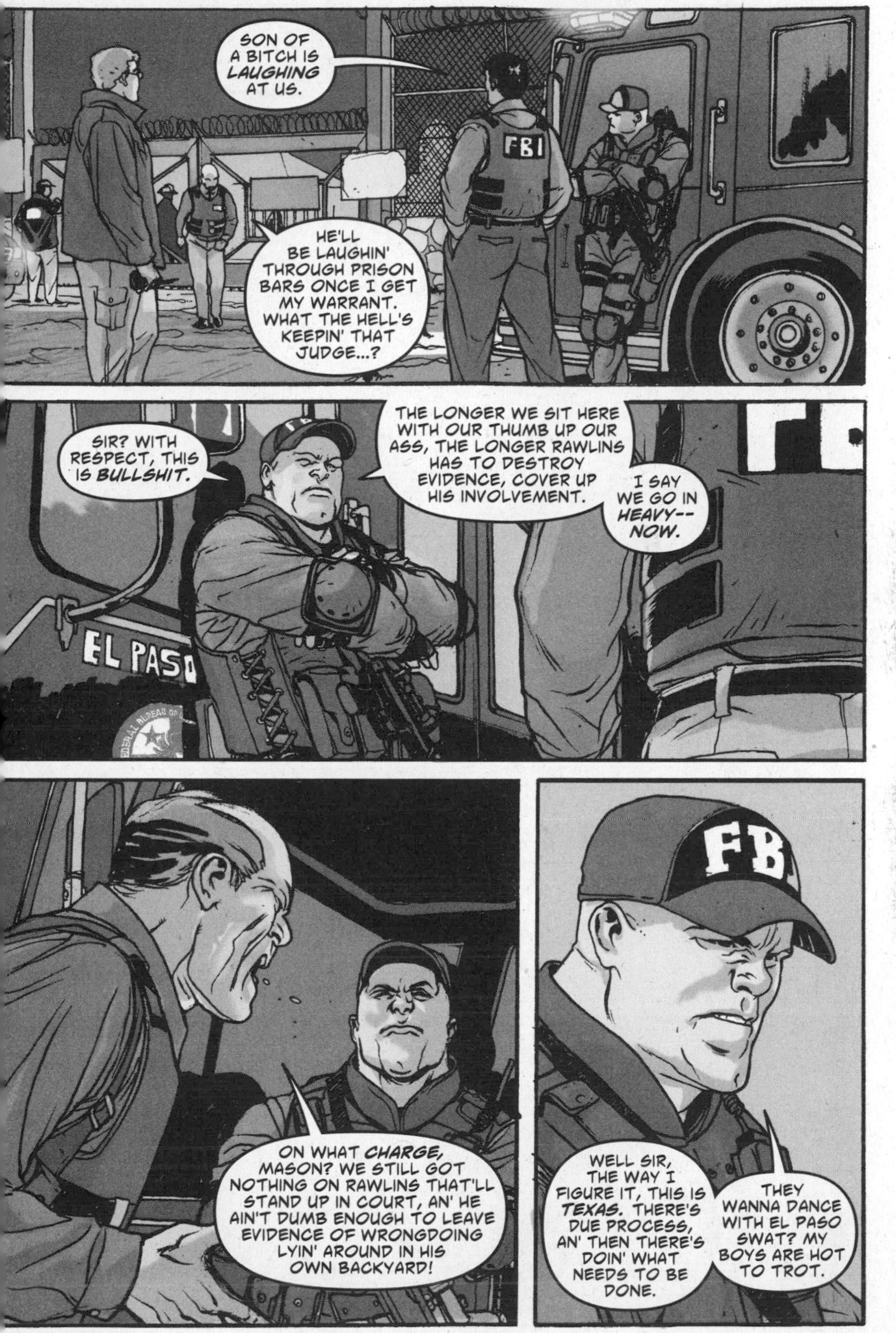
SON OF A BITCH IS *LAUGHING* AT US.
HE'LL BE LAUGHIN' THROUGH PRISON BARS ONCE I GET MY WARRANT. WHAT THE HELL'S KEEPIN' THAT JUDGE...?
FBI
SIR? WITH RESPECT, THIS IS *BULLSHIT.*
THE LONGER WE SIT HERE WITH OUR THUMB UP OUR ASS, THE LONGER RAWLINS HAS TO DESTROY EVIDENCE, COVER UP HIS INVOLVEMENT.
I SAY WE GO IN *HEAVY*-- *NOW.*
EL PASO
ON WHAT *CHARGE,* MASON? WE STILL GOT NOTHING ON RAWLINS THAT'LL STAND UP IN COURT, AN' HE AIN'T DUMB ENOUGH TO LEAVE EVIDENCE OF WRONGDOING LYIN' AROUND IN HIS OWN BACKYARD!
WELL SIR, THE WAY I FIGURE IT, THIS IS *TEXAS.* THERE'S DUE PROCESS, AN' THEN THERE'S DOIN' WHAT NEEDS TO BE DONE.
THEY WANNA DANCE WITH EL PASO SWAT? MY BOYS ARE HOT TO TROT.

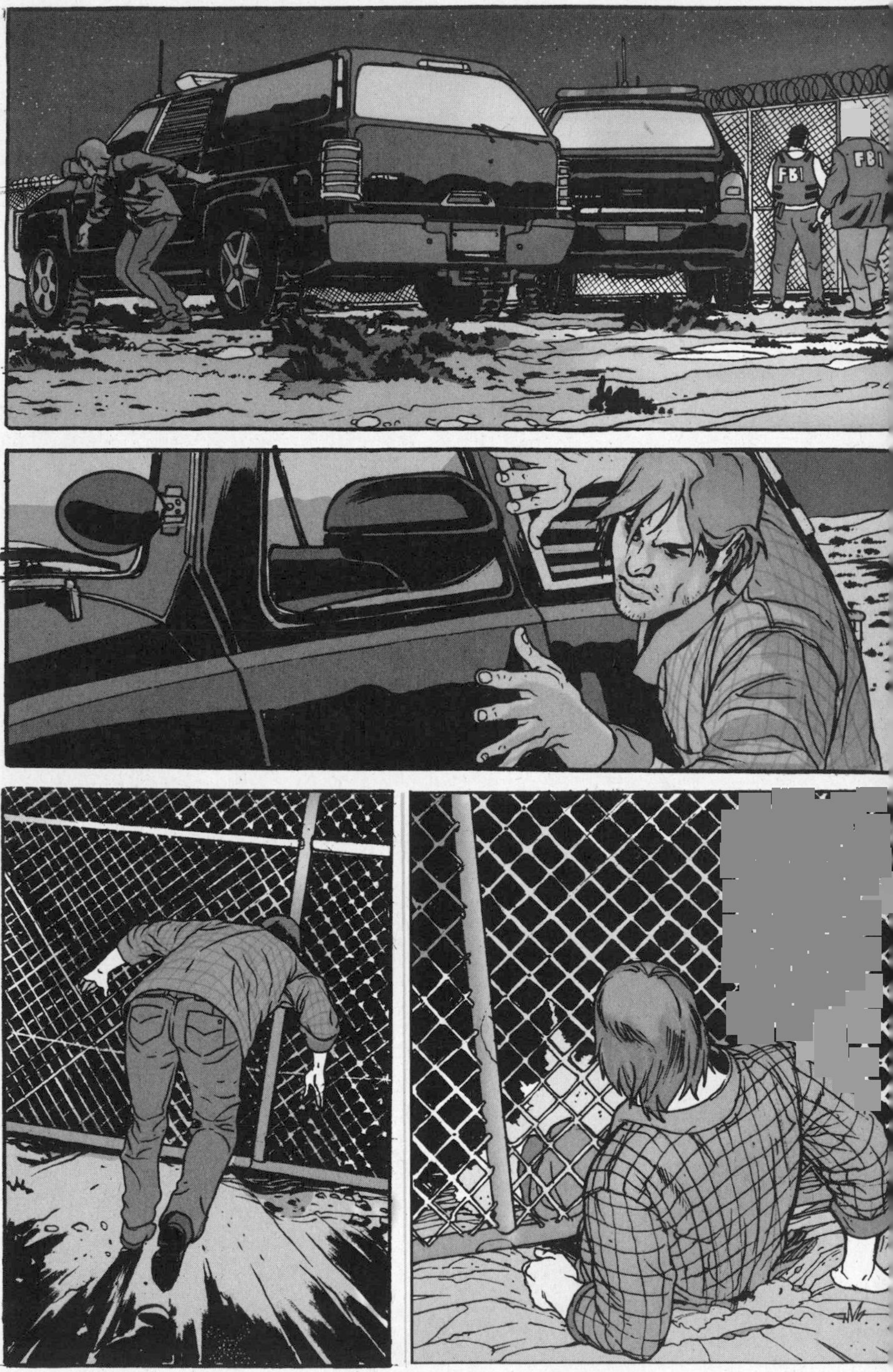
FBI
FBI

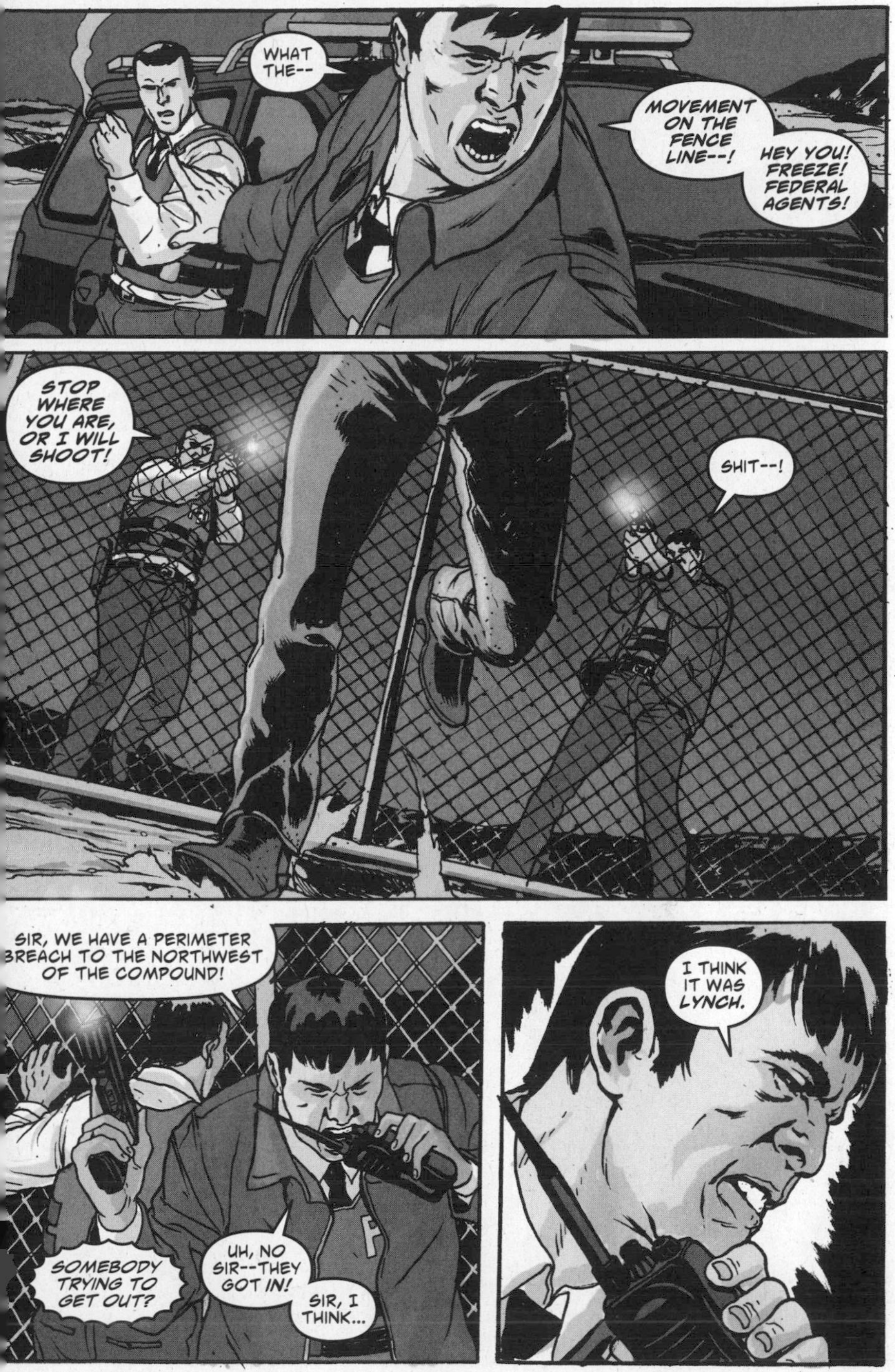
WHAT THE--
MOVEMENT ON THE FENCE LINE--!
HEY YOU! FREEZE! FEDERAL AGENTS!
STOP WHERE YOU ARE, OR I WILL SHOOT!
SHIT--!
SIR, WE HAVE A PERIMETER BREACH TO THE NORTHWEST OF THE COMPOUND!
SOMEBODY TRYING TO GET OUT?
UH, NO SIR--THEY GOT IN!
SIR, I THINK...
I THINK IT WAS LYNCH.

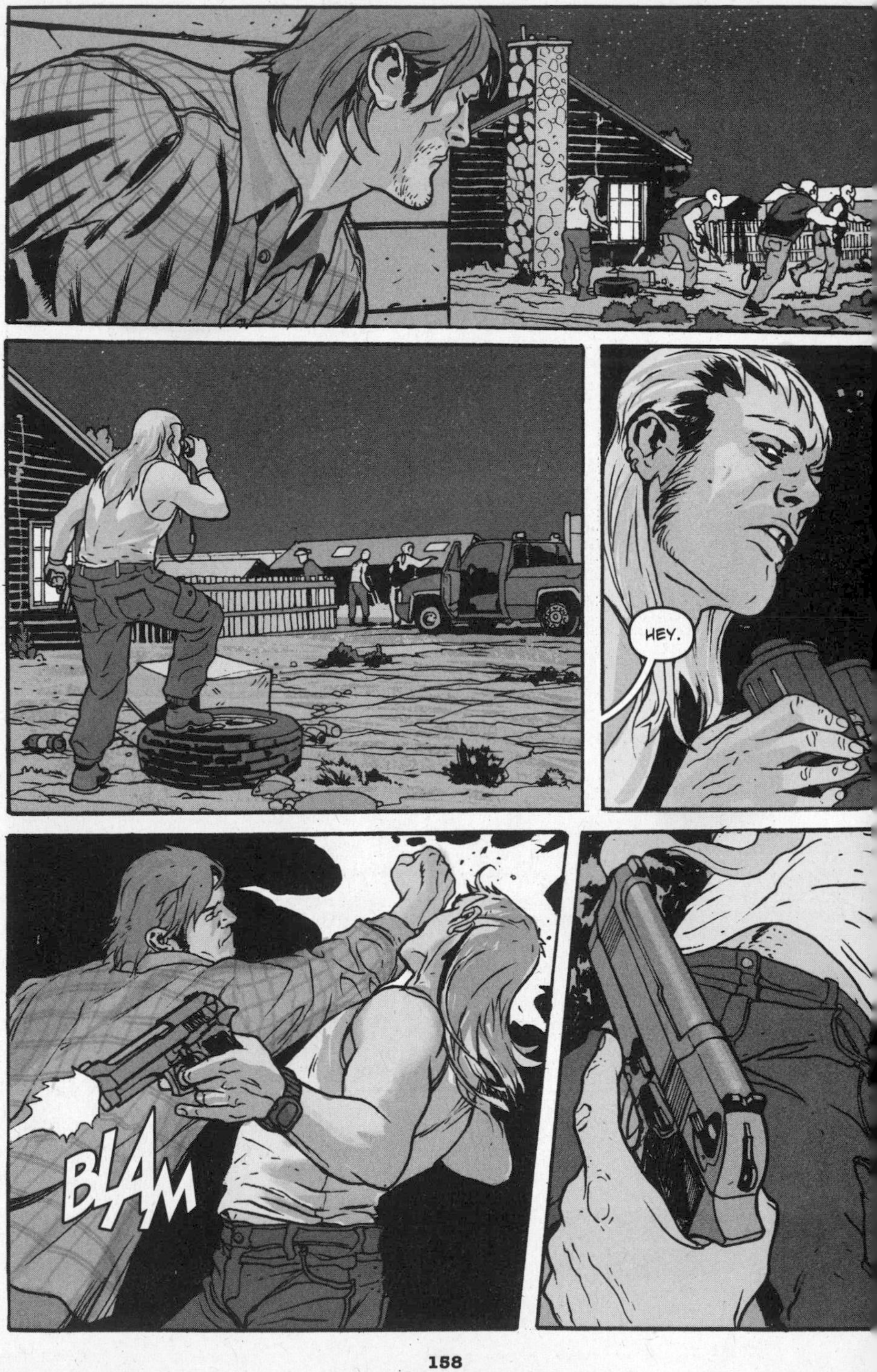
HEY.
BLAM

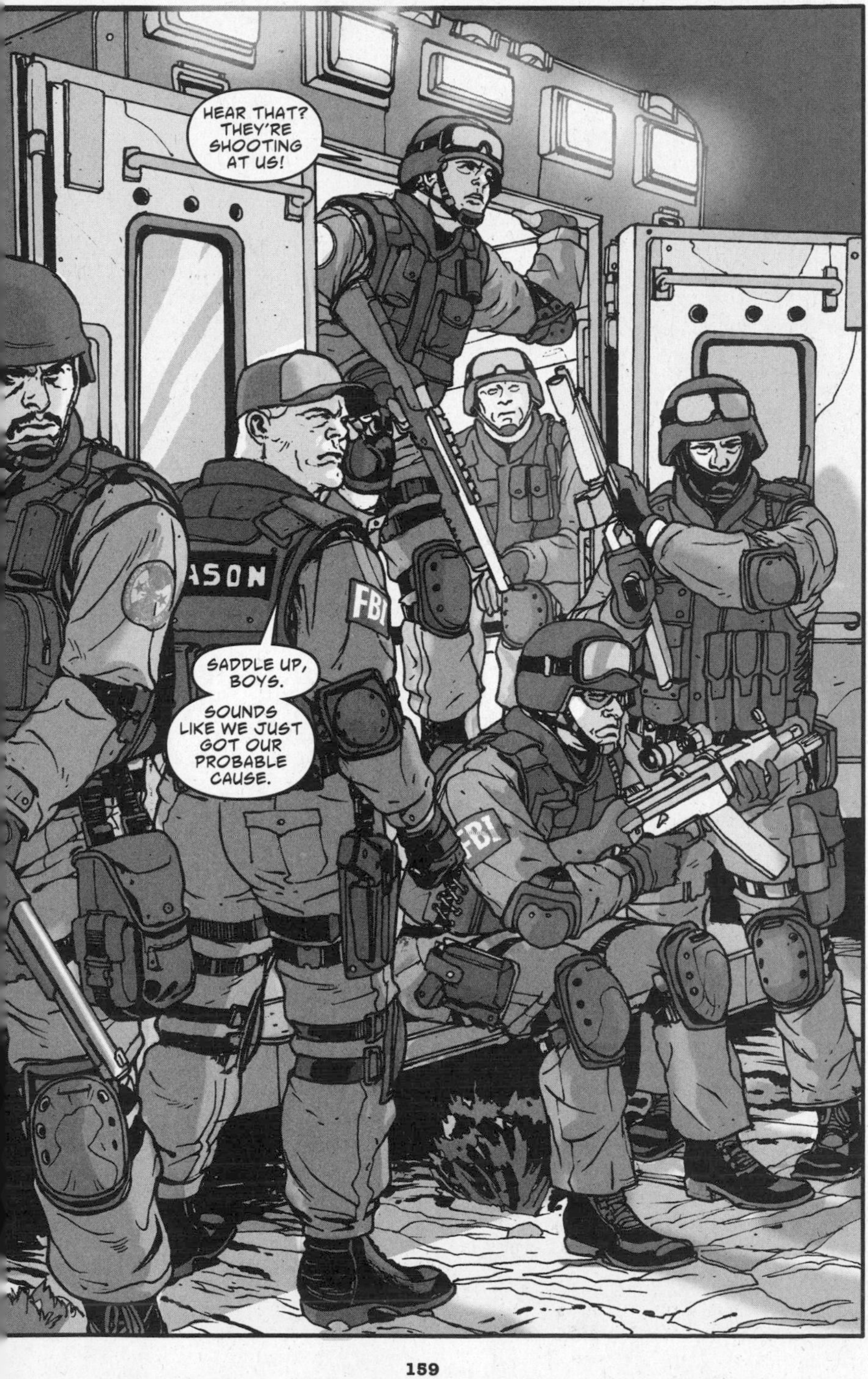
HEAR THAT? THEY'RE SHOOTING AT US!
ASON
FBI
SADDLE UP, BOYS.
SOUNDS LIKE WE JUST GOT OUR PROBABLE CAUSE.
FBI

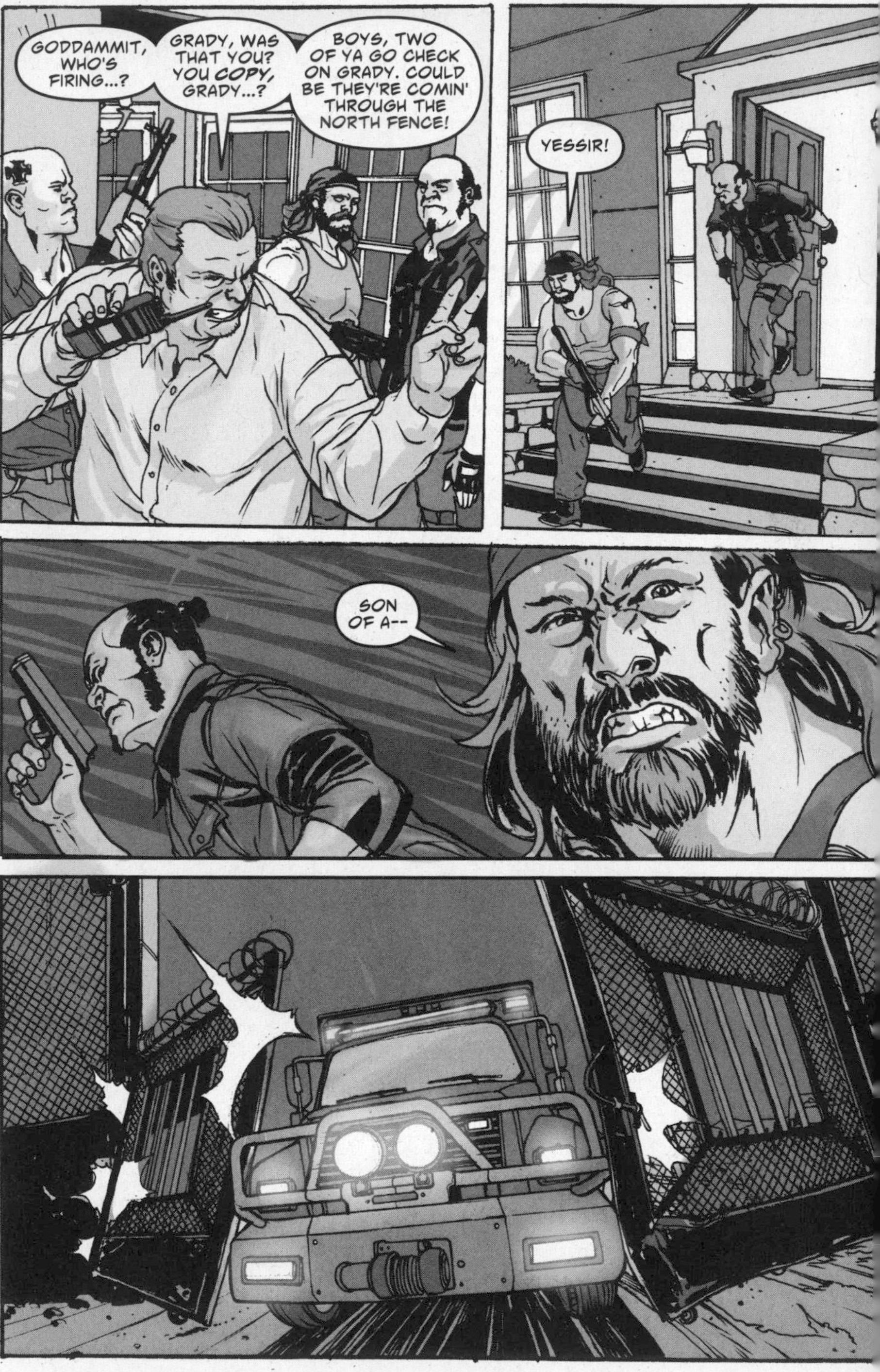
GODDAMMIT, WHO'S FIRING...?
GRADY, WAS THAT YOU? YOU COPY, GRADY...?
BOYS, TWO OF YA GO CHECK ON GRADY. COULD BE THEY'RE COMIN' THROUGH THE NORTH FENCE!
YESSIR!
SON OF A--

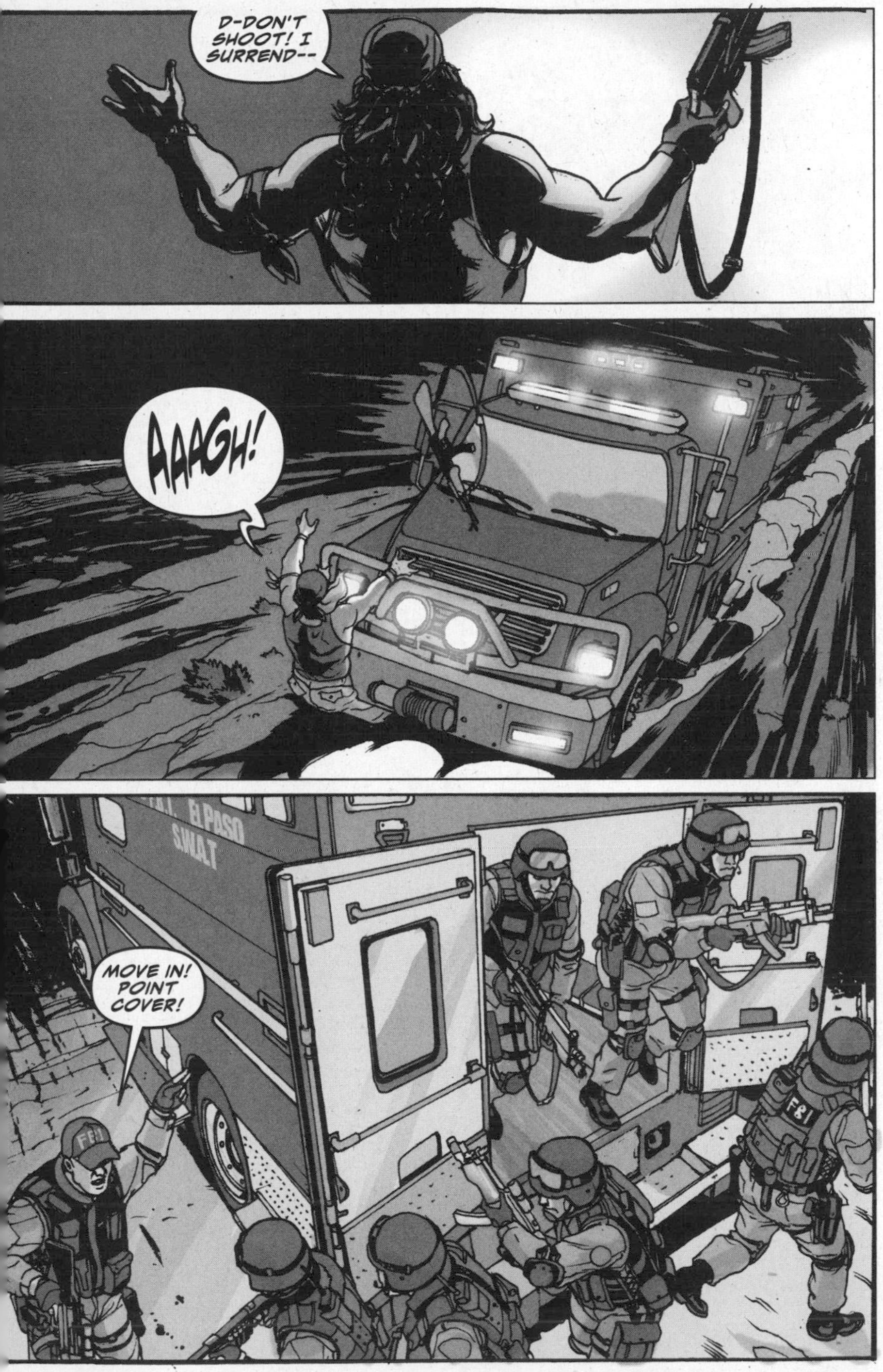
D-DON'T SHOOT! I SURREND--
AAAGH!
F.B.I. EL PASO S.W.A.T
MOVE IN! POINT COVER!
FBI

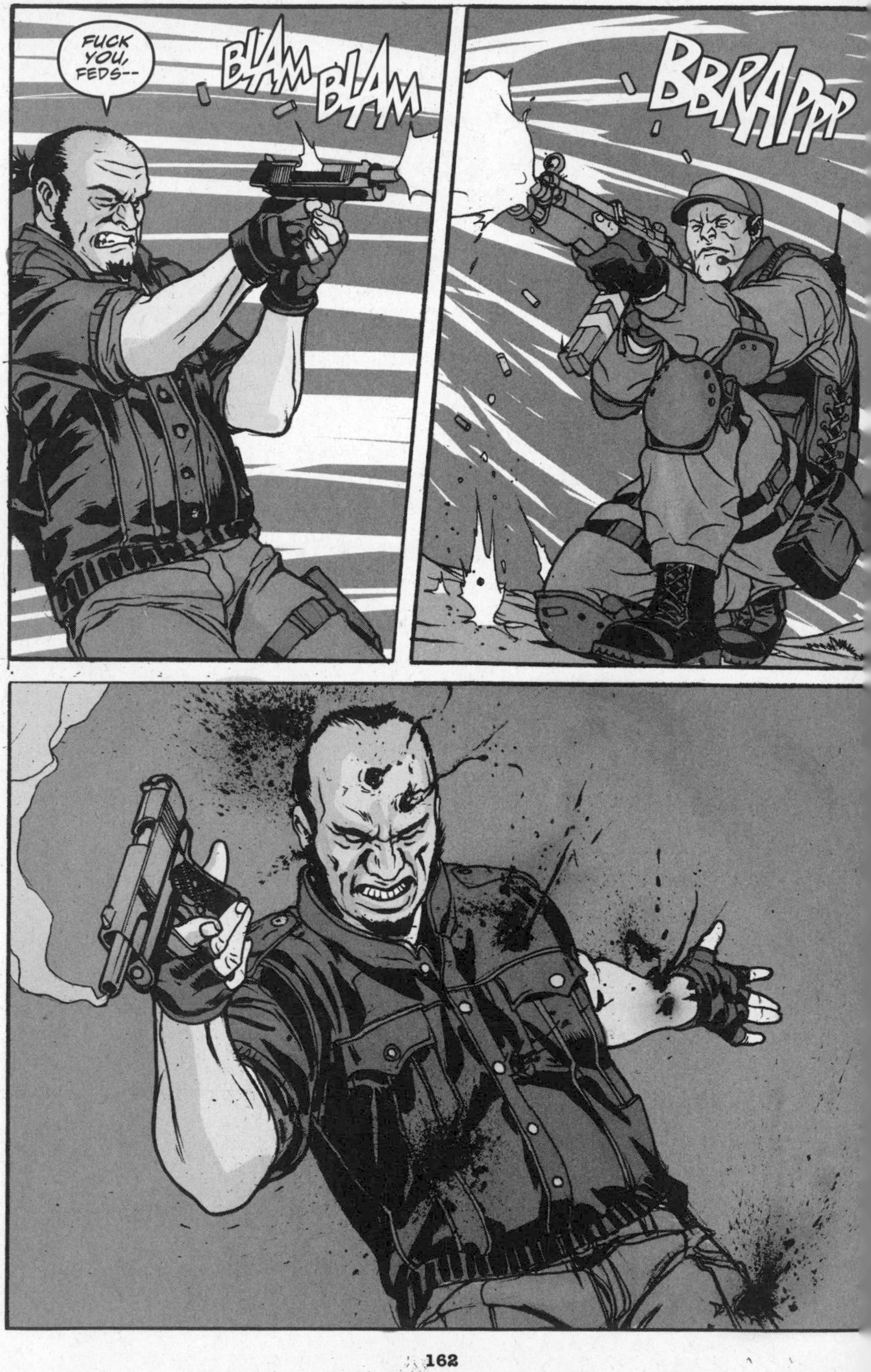
FUCK YOU, FEDS--
BLAM BLAM
BBRAPPP

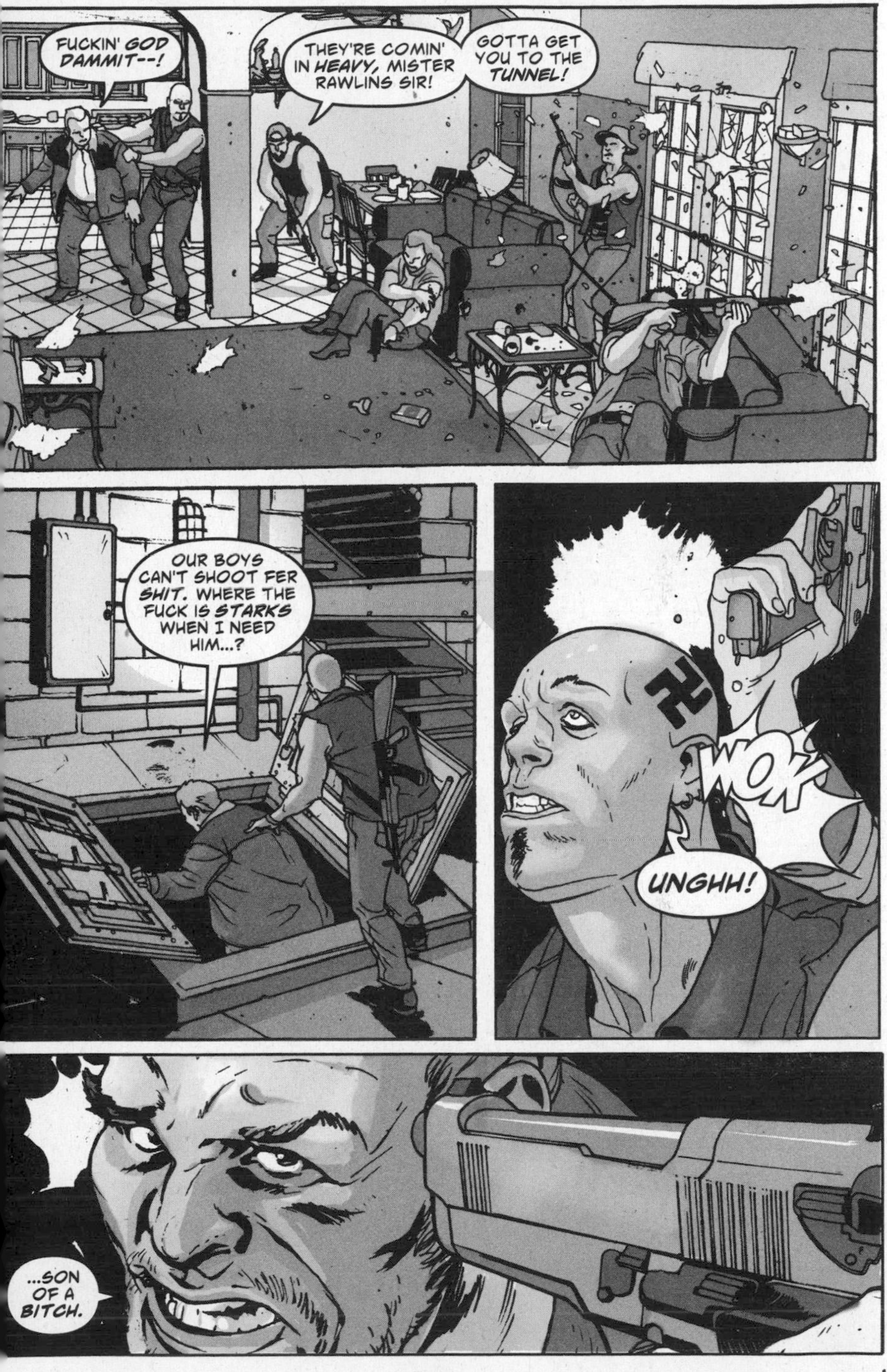
FUCKIN' GOD DAMMIT--!
THEY'RE COMIN' IN HEAVY, MISTER RAWLINS SIR!
GOTTA GET YOU TO THE TUNNEL!
OUR BOYS CAN'T SHOOT FER SHIT. WHERE THE FUCK IS STARKS WHEN I NEED HIM...?
WOK
UNGHH!
...SON OF A BITCH.

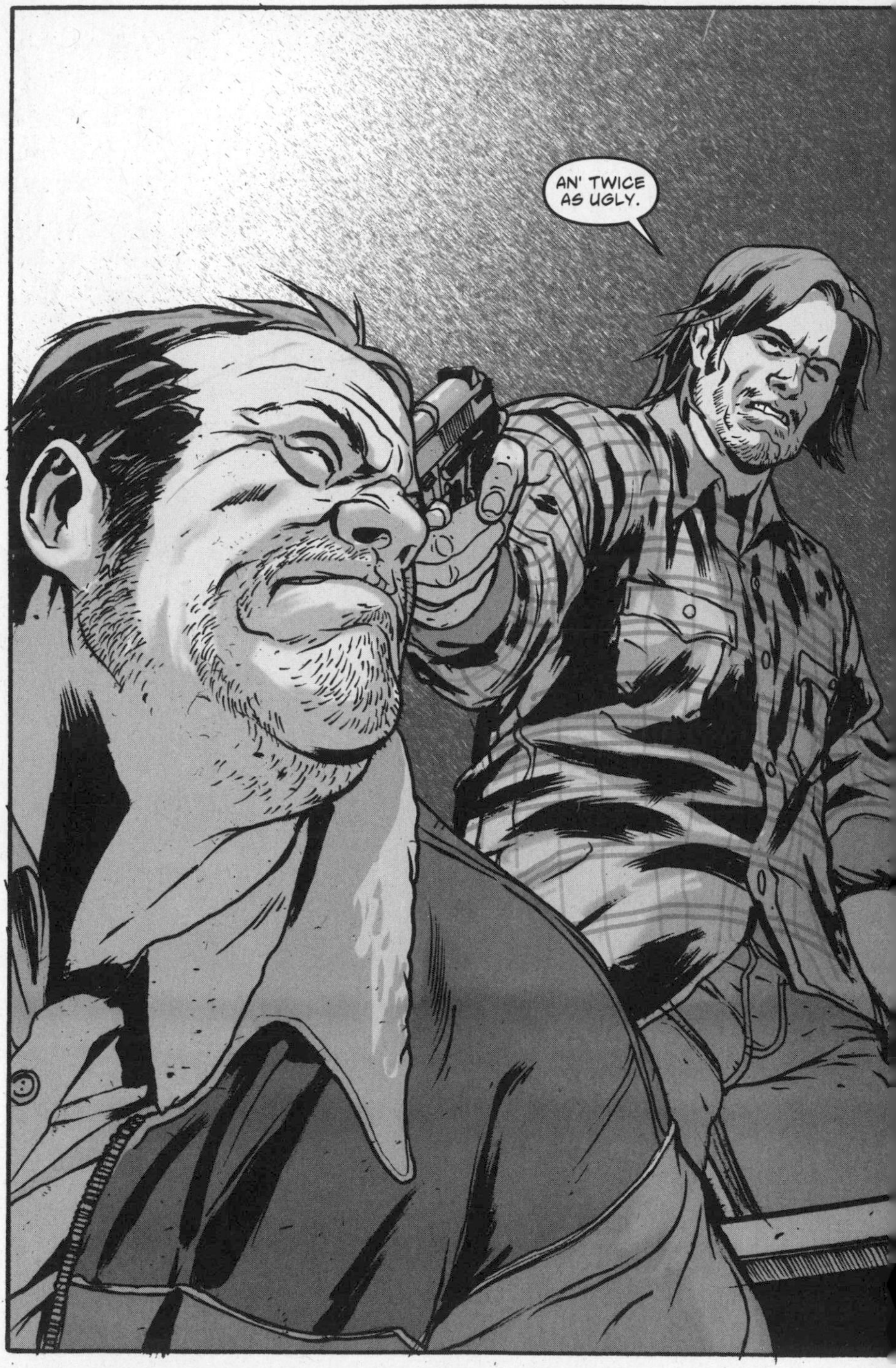
AN' TWICE AS UGLY.

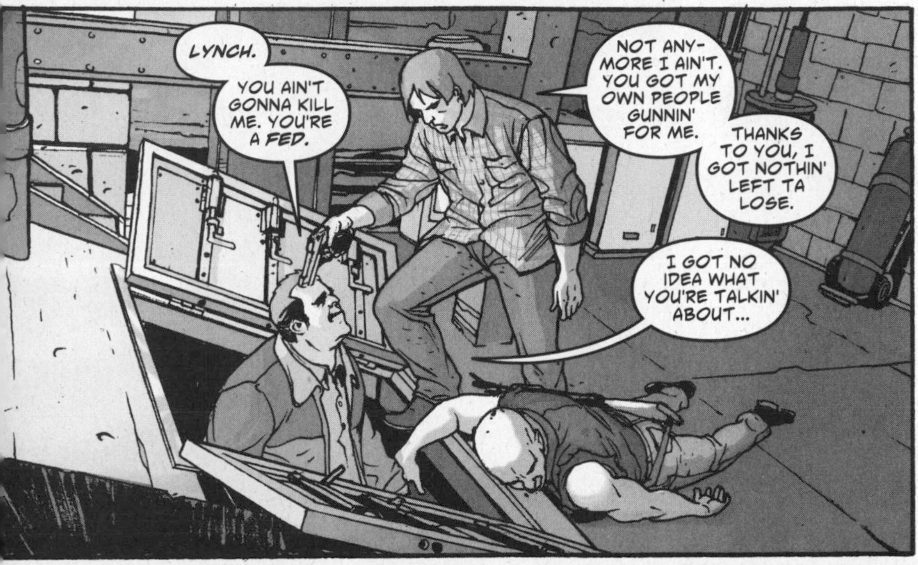
LYNCH.
YOU AIN'T GONNA KILL ME. YOU'RE A FED.
NOT ANY-MORE I AIN'T. YOU GOT MY OWN PEOPLE GUNNIN' FOR ME.
THANKS TO YOU, I GOT NOTHIN' LEFT TA LOSE.
I GOT NO IDEA WHAT YOU'RE TALKIN' ABOUT...

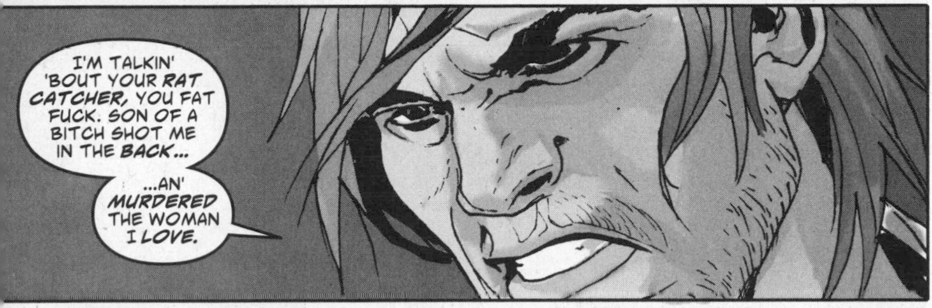
I'M TALKIN' 'BOUT YOUR RAT CATCHER, YOU FAT FUCK. SON OF A BITCH SHOT ME IN THE BACK...
...AN' MURDERED THE WOMAN I LOVE.

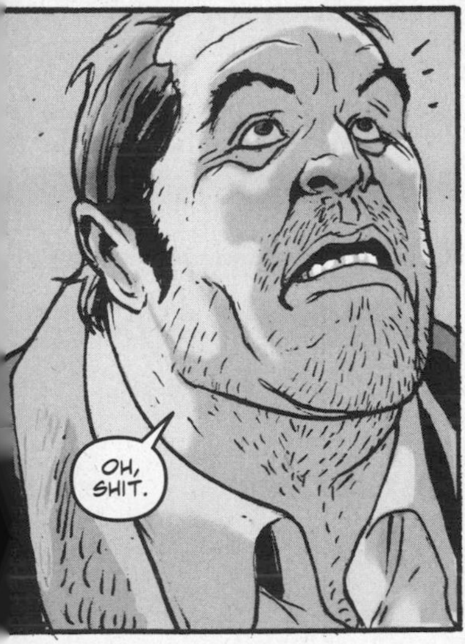
OH, SHIT.

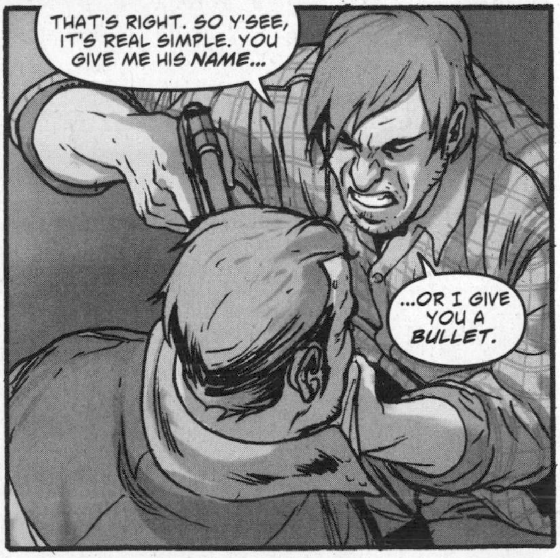
THAT'S RIGHT. SO Y'SEE, IT'S REAL SIMPLE. YOU GIVE ME HIS NAME...
...OR I GIVE YOU A BULLET.

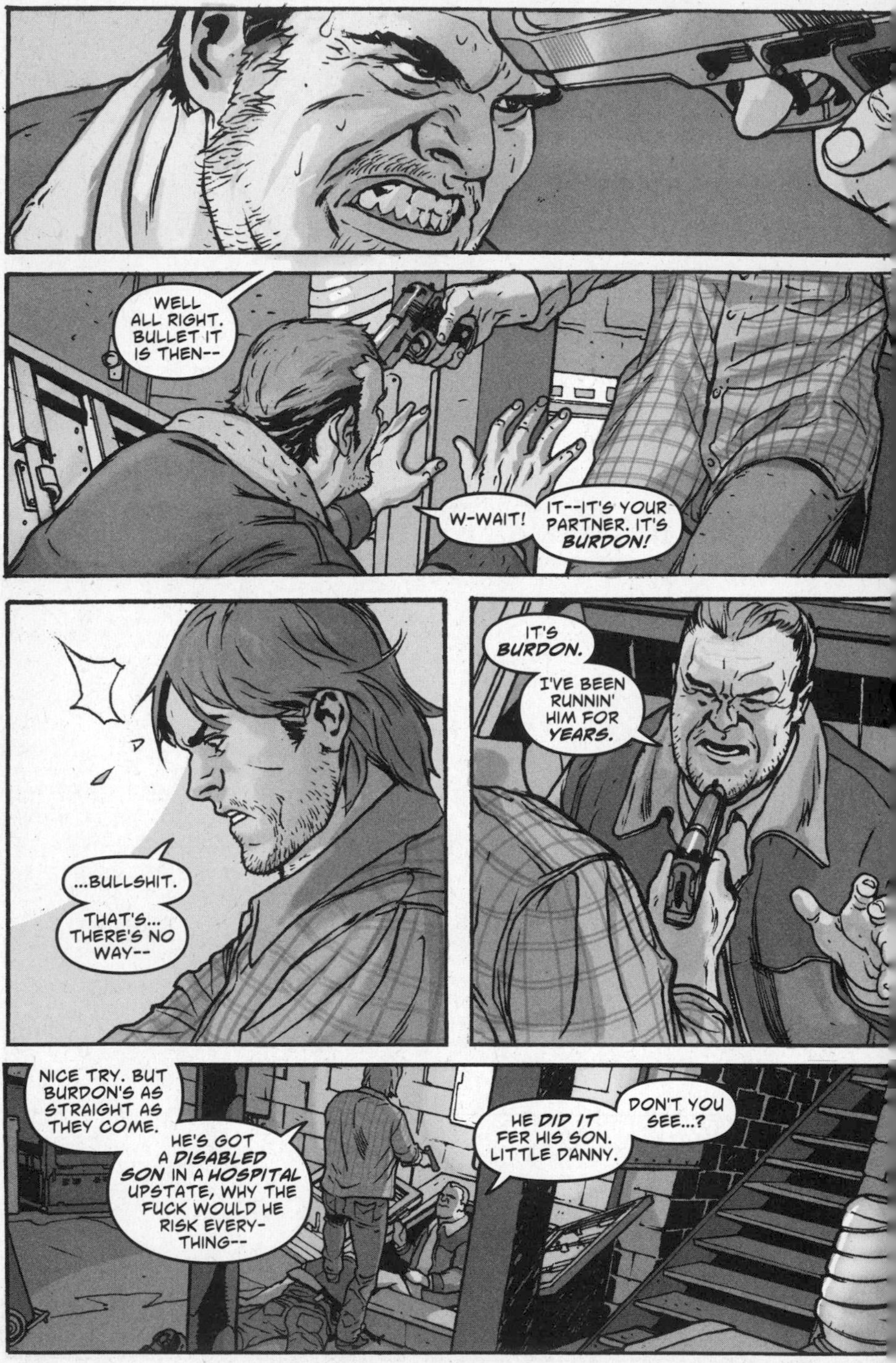
WELL ALL RIGHT. BULLET IT IS THEN--
W-WAIT!
IT--IT'S YOUR PARTNER. IT'S BURDON!
...BULLSHIT.
THAT'S... THERE'S NO WAY--
IT'S BURDON.
I'VE BEEN RUNNIN' HIM FOR YEARS.
NICE TRY. BUT BURDON'S AS STRAIGHT AS THEY COME.
HE'S GOT A DISABLED SON IN A HOSPITAL UPSTATE, WHY THE FUCK WOULD HE RISK EVERY-THING--
DON'T YOU SEE...?
HE DID IT FER HIS SON. LITTLE DANNY.

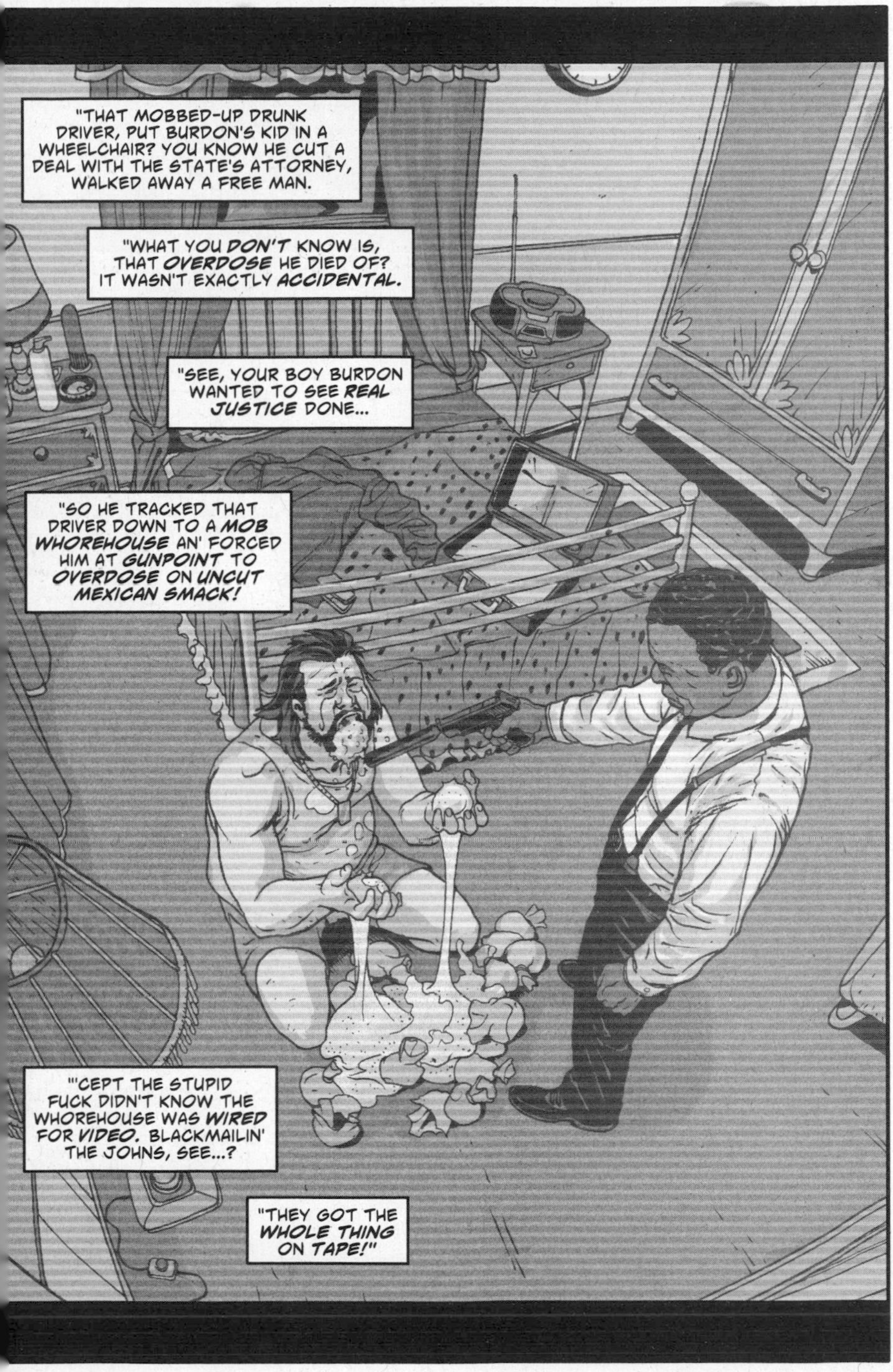
"THAT MOBBED-UP DRUNK DRIVER, PUT BURDON'S KID IN A WHEELCHAIR? YOU KNOW HE CUT A DEAL WITH THE STATE'S ATTORNEY, WALKED AWAY A FREE MAN.
"WHAT YOU *DON'T* KNOW IS, THAT *OVERDOSE* HE DIED OF? IT WASN'T EXACTLY *ACCIDENTAL.*
"SEE, YOUR BOY BURDON WANTED TO SEE *REAL JUSTICE* DONE...
"SO HE TRACKED THAT DRIVER DOWN TO A *MOB WHOREHOUSE* AN' FORCED HIM AT *GUNPOINT* TO *OVERDOSE* ON *UNCUT MEXICAN SMACK!*
"'CEPT THE STUPID FUCK DIDN'T KNOW THE WHOREHOUSE WAS *WIRED* FOR *VIDEO.* BLACKMAILIN' THE JOHNS, SEE...?
"THEY GOT THE *WHOLE THING* ON *TAPE!*"

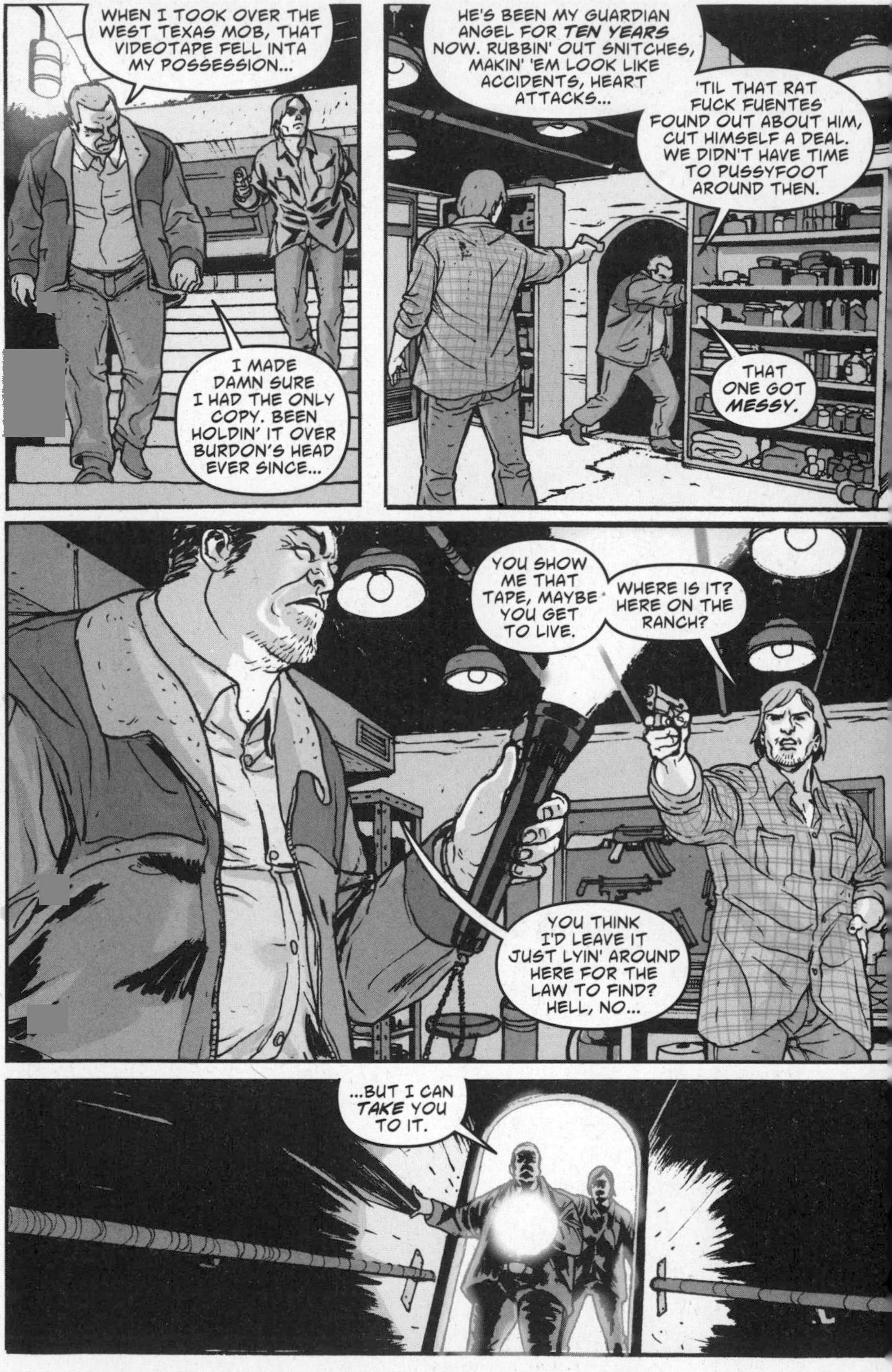
WHEN I TOOK OVER THE WEST TEXAS MOB, THAT VIDEOTAPE FELL INTA MY POSSESSION...
I MADE DAMN SURE I HAD THE ONLY COPY. BEEN HOLDIN' IT OVER BURDON'S HEAD EVER SINCE...
HE'S BEEN MY GUARDIAN ANGEL FOR TEN YEARS NOW. RUBBIN' OUT SNITCHES, MAKIN' 'EM LOOK LIKE ACCIDENTS, HEART ATTACKS...
'TIL THAT RAT FUCK FUENTES FOUND OUT ABOUT HIM, CUT HIMSELF A DEAL. WE DIDN'T HAVE TIME TO PUSSYFOOT AROUND THEN.
THAT ONE GOT MESSY.
YOU SHOW ME THAT TAPE, MAYBE YOU GET TO LIVE.
WHERE IS IT? HERE ON THE RANCH?
YOU THINK I'D LEAVE IT JUST LYIN' AROUND HERE FOR THE LAW TO FIND? HELL, NO...
...BUT I CAN TAKE YOU TO IT.

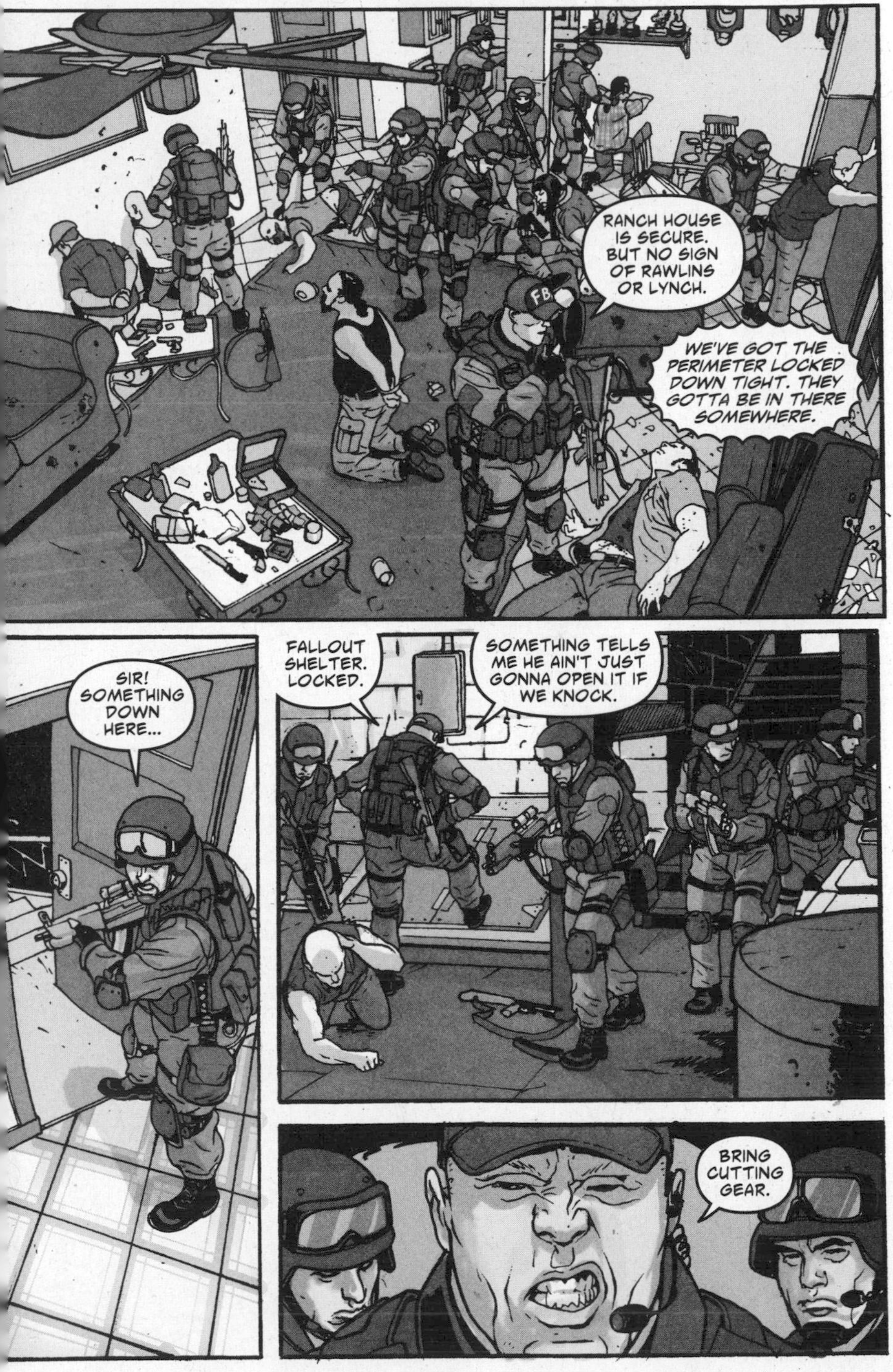
RANCH HOUSE IS SECURE. BUT NO SIGN OF RAWLINS OR LYNCH.
WE'VE GOT THE PERIMETER LOCKED DOWN TIGHT. THEY GOTTA BE IN THERE SOMEWHERE.
FBI
SIR! SOMETHING DOWN HERE...
FALLOUT SHELTER. LOCKED.
SOMETHING TELLS ME HE AIN'T JUST GONNA OPEN IT IF WE KNOCK.
BRING CUTTING GEAR.

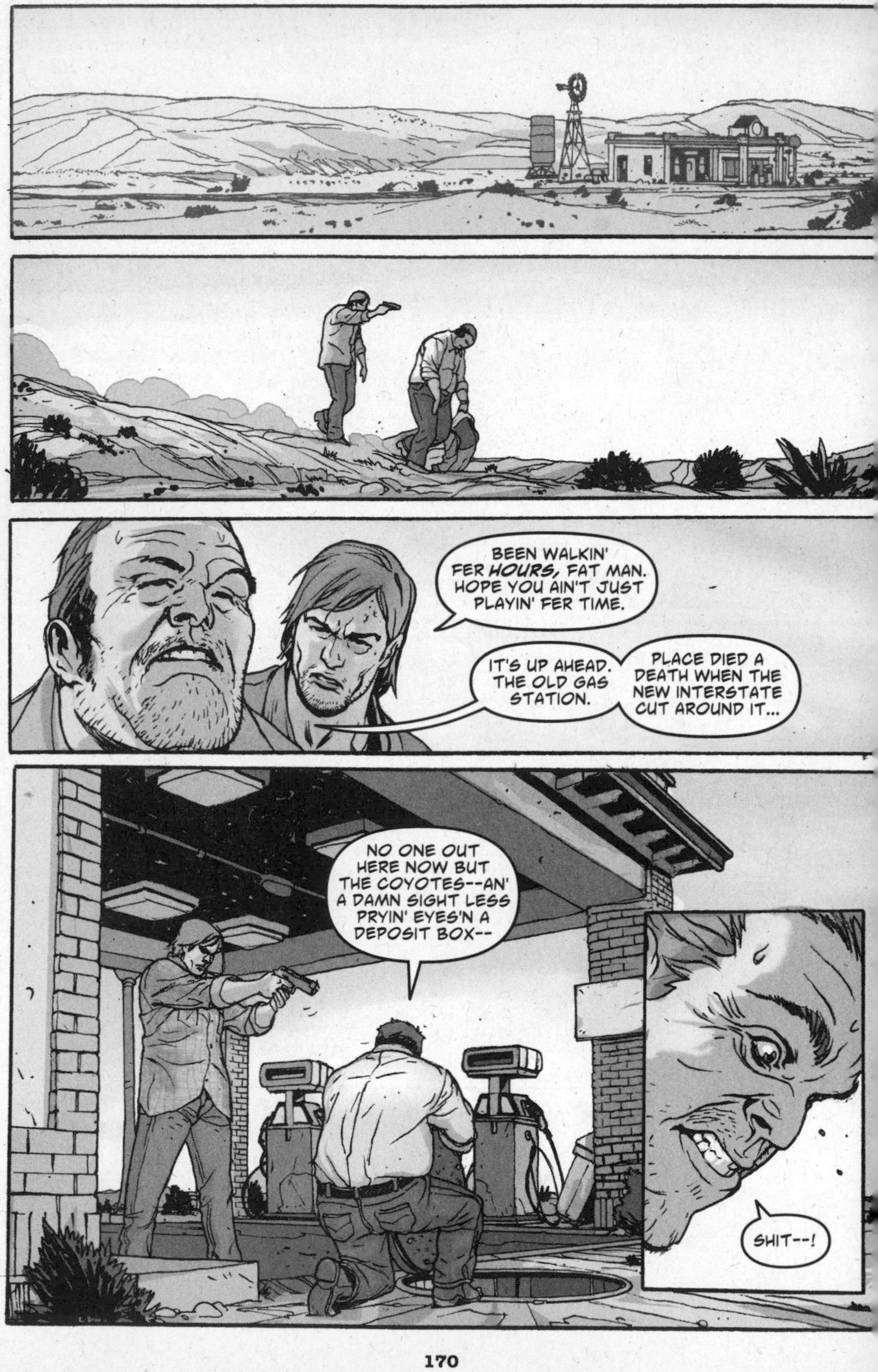
BEEN WALKIN' FER HOURS, FAT MAN. HOPE YOU AIN'T JUST PLAYIN' FER TIME.
IT'S UP AHEAD. THE OLD GAS STATION.
PLACE DIED A DEATH WHEN THE NEW INTERSTATE CUT AROUND IT...
NO ONE OUT HERE NOW BUT THE COYOTES--AN' A DAMN SIGHT LESS PRYIN' EYES'N A DEPOSIT BOX--
SHIT--!

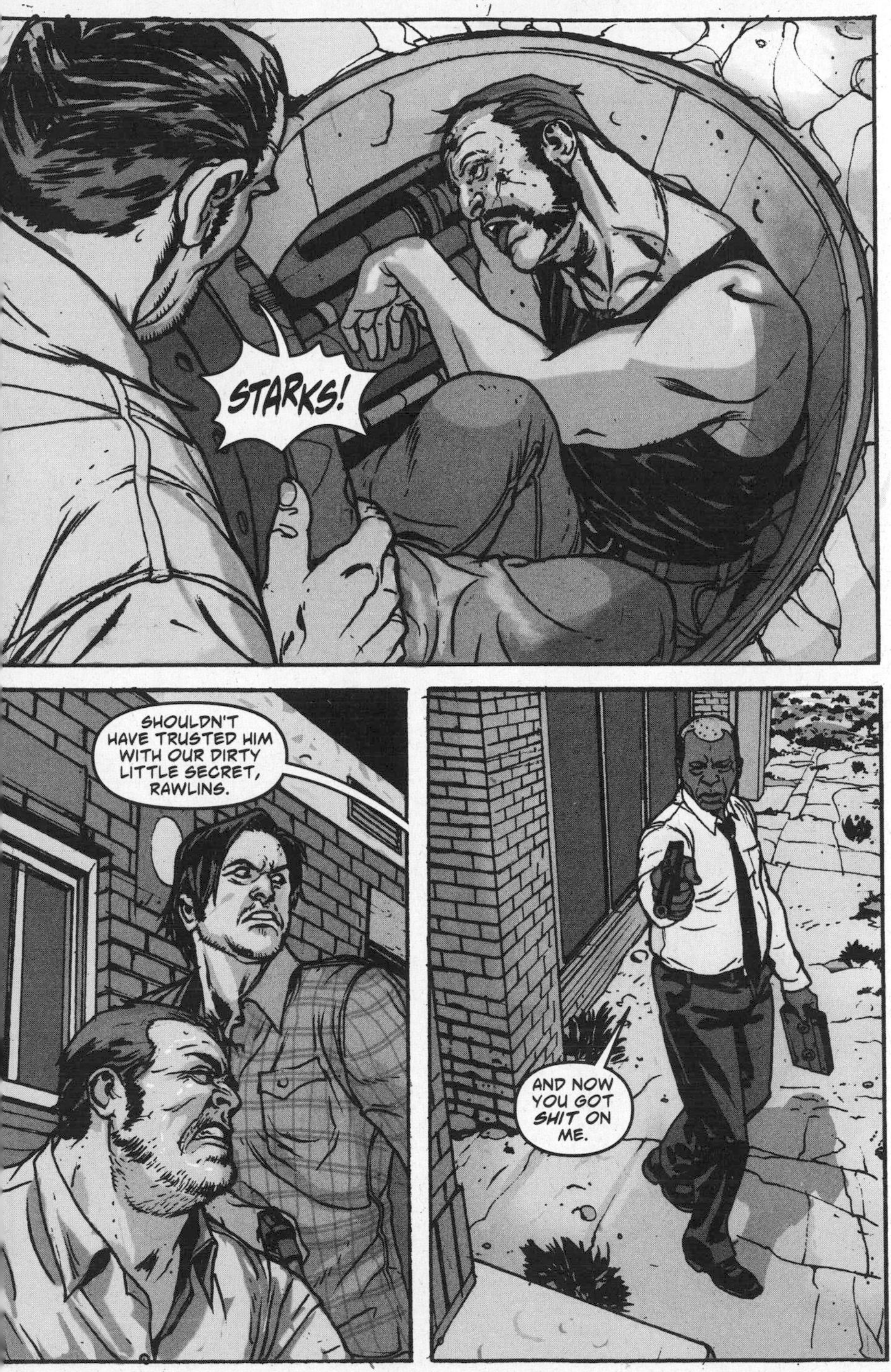
STARKS!
SHOULDN'T HAVE TRUSTED HIM WITH OUR DIRTY LITTLE SECRET, RAWLINS.
AND NOW YOU GOT SHIT ON ME.

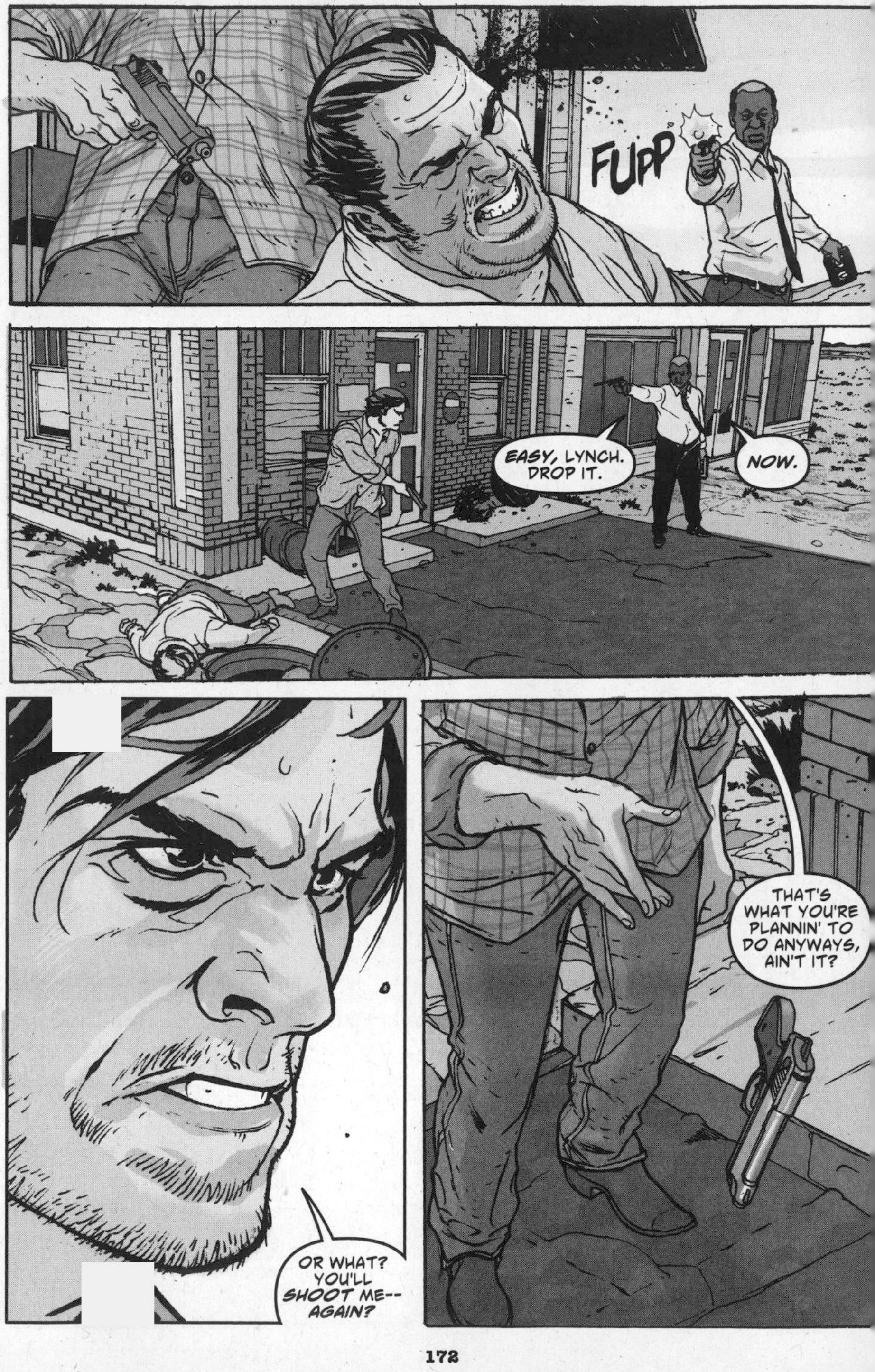
FUPP
EASY, LYNCH. DROP IT.
NOW.
OR WHAT? YOU'LL SHOOT ME-- AGAIN?
THAT'S WHAT YOU'RE PLANNIN' TO DO ANYWAYS, AIN'T IT?

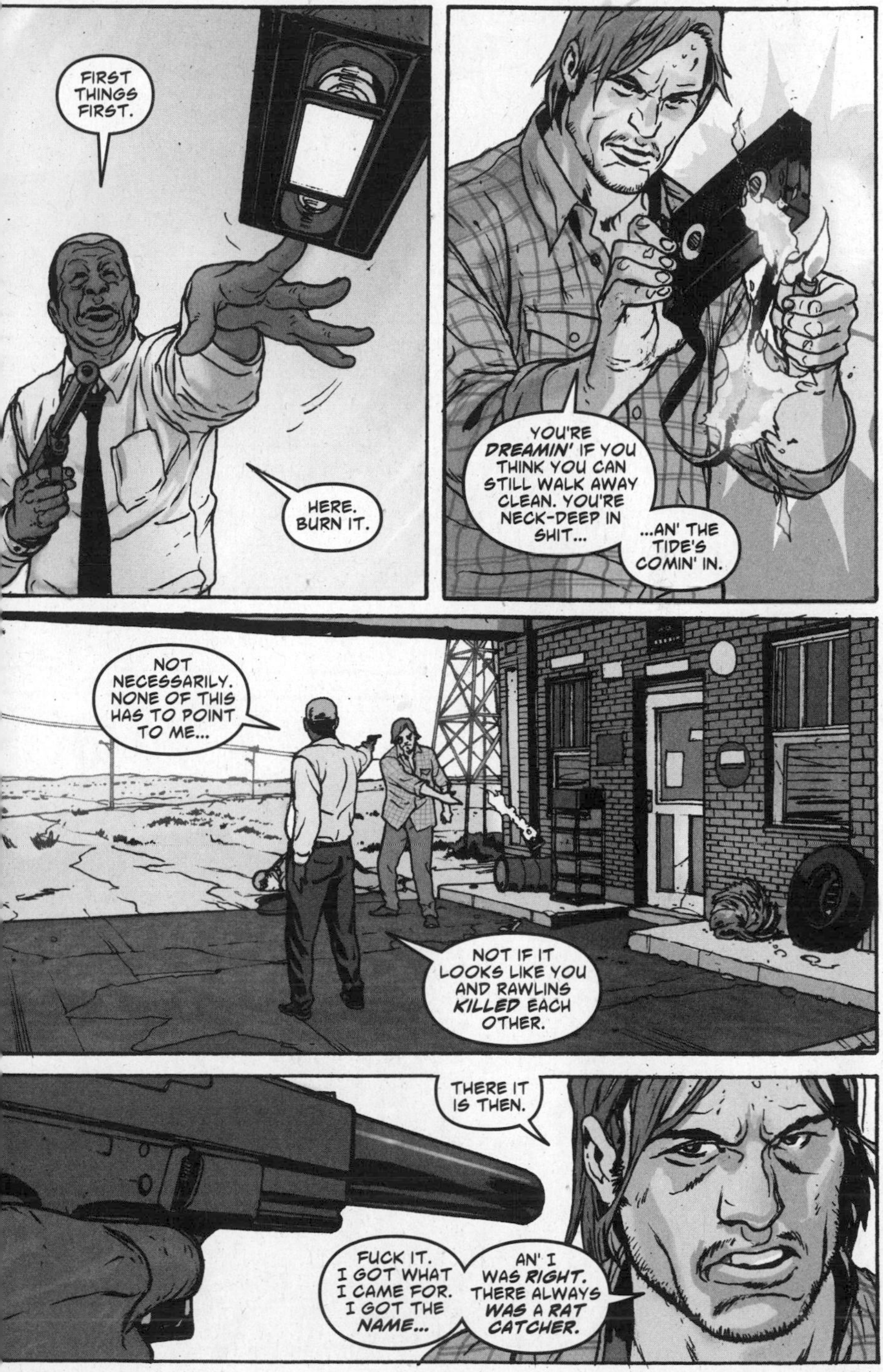
FIRST THINGS FIRST.
HERE. BURN IT.
YOU'RE *DREAMIN'* IF YOU THINK YOU CAN STILL WALK AWAY CLEAN. YOU'RE NECK-DEEP IN SHIT...
...AN' THE TIDE'S COMIN' IN.
NOT NECESSARILY. NONE OF THIS HAS TO POINT TO ME...
NOT IF IT LOOKS LIKE YOU AND RAWLINS *KILLED* EACH OTHER.
THERE IT IS THEN.
FUCK IT. I GOT WHAT I CAME FOR. I GOT THE *NAME*...
AN' I WAS *RIGHT*. THERE ALWAYS *WAS* A *RAT CATCHER*.

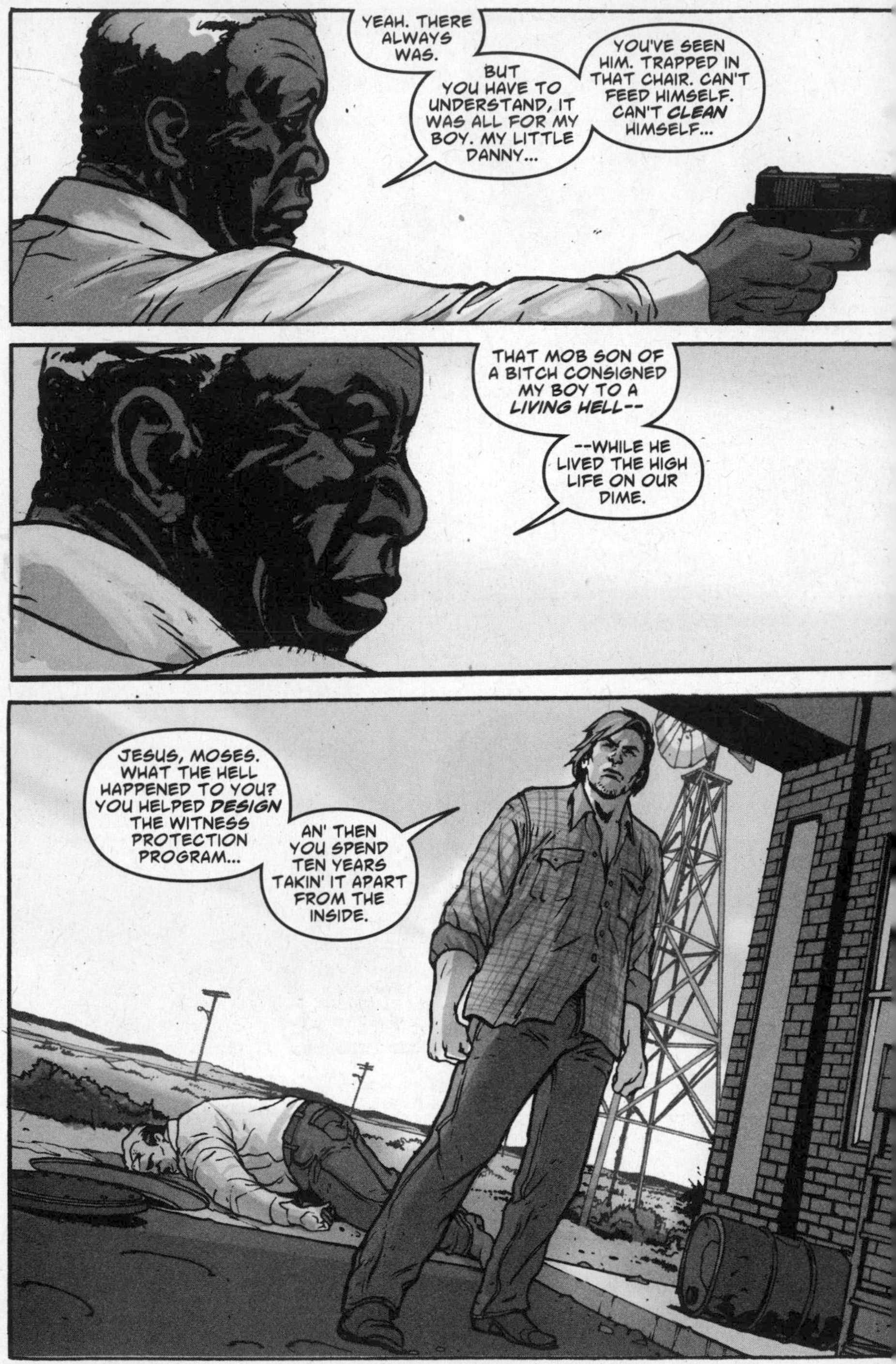
YEAH. THERE ALWAYS WAS.
BUT YOU HAVE TO UNDERSTAND, IT WAS ALL FOR MY BOY. MY LITTLE DANNY...
YOU'VE SEEN HIM. TRAPPED IN THAT CHAIR. CAN'T FEED HIMSELF. CAN'T CLEAN HIMSELF...
THAT MOB SON OF A BITCH CONSIGNED MY BOY TO A LIVING HELL--
--WHILE HE LIVED THE HIGH LIFE ON OUR DIME.
JESUS, MOSES. WHAT THE HELL HAPPENED TO YOU? YOU HELPED DESIGN THE WITNESS PROTECTION PROGRAM...
AN' THEN YOU SPEND TEN YEARS TAKIN' IT APART FROM THE INSIDE.

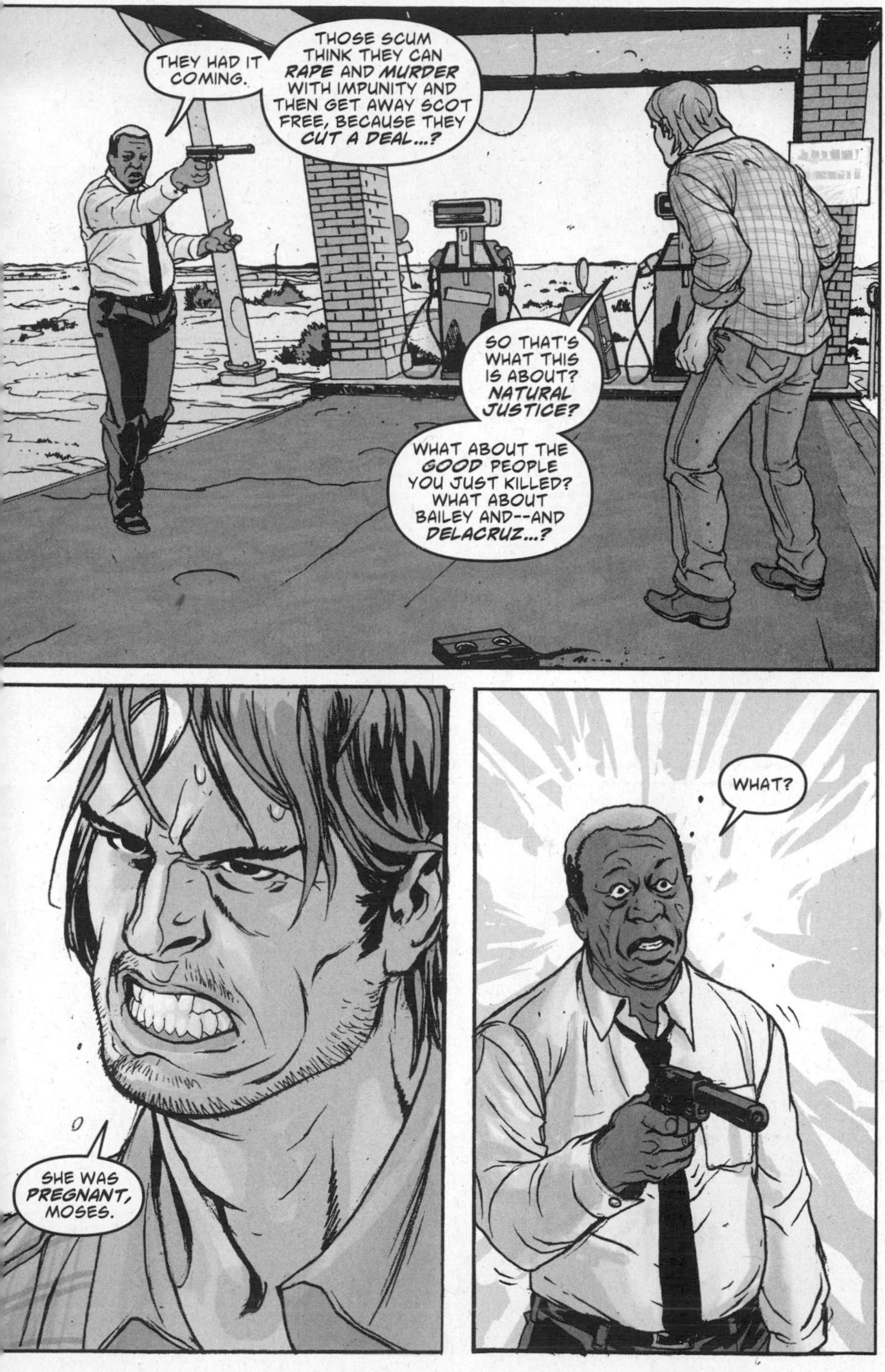
THEY HAD IT COMING.
THOSE SCUM THINK THEY CAN *RAPE* AND *MURDER* WITH IMPUNITY AND THEN GET AWAY SCOT FREE, BECAUSE THEY *CUT A DEAL...?*
SO THAT'S WHAT THIS IS ABOUT? *NATURAL JUSTICE?*
WHAT ABOUT THE *GOOD* PEOPLE YOU JUST KILLED? WHAT ABOUT BAILEY AND--AND *DELACRUZ...?*
SHE WAS *PREGNANT,* MOSES.
WHAT?

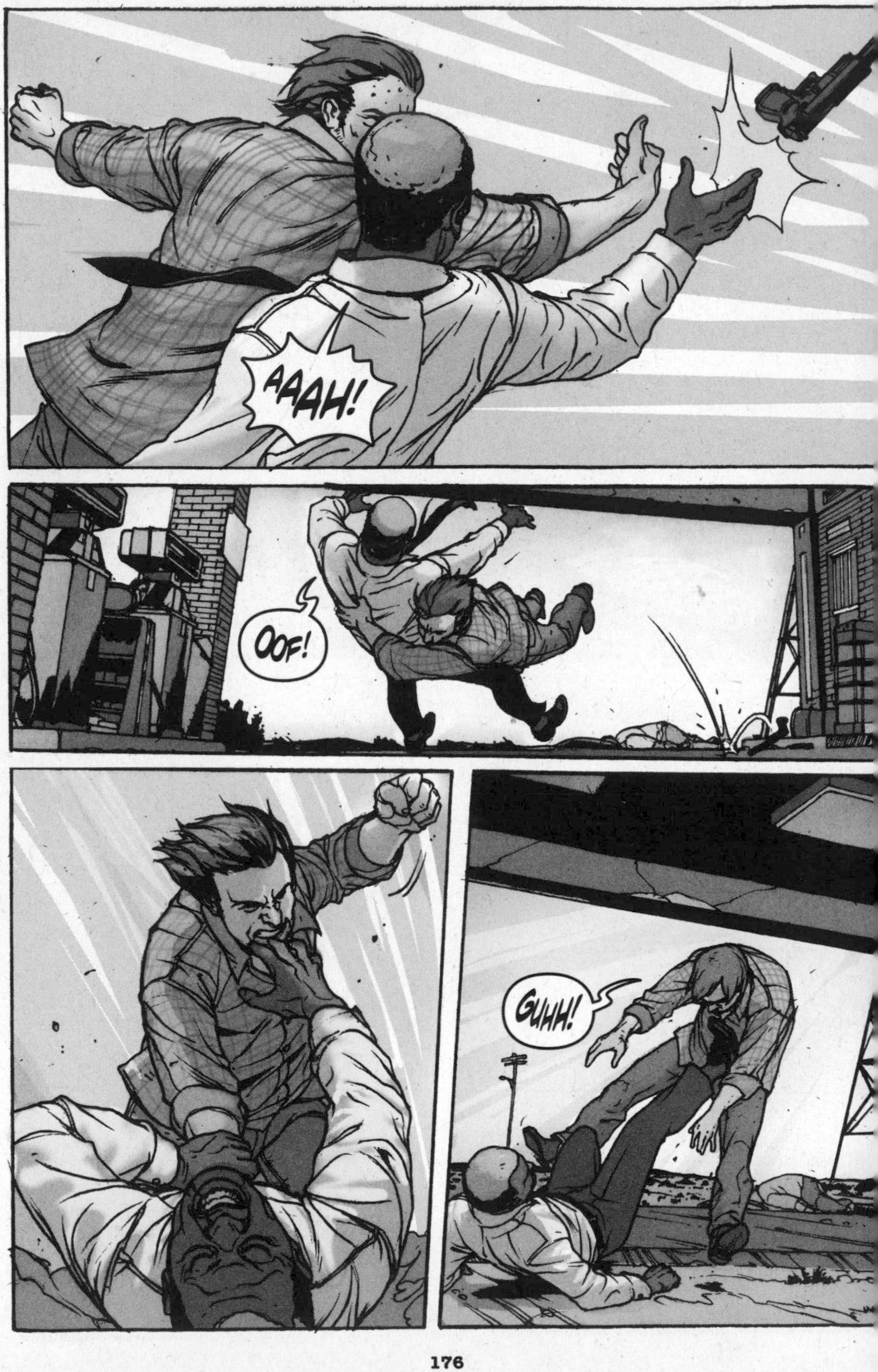
AAAH!
OOF!
GUHH!

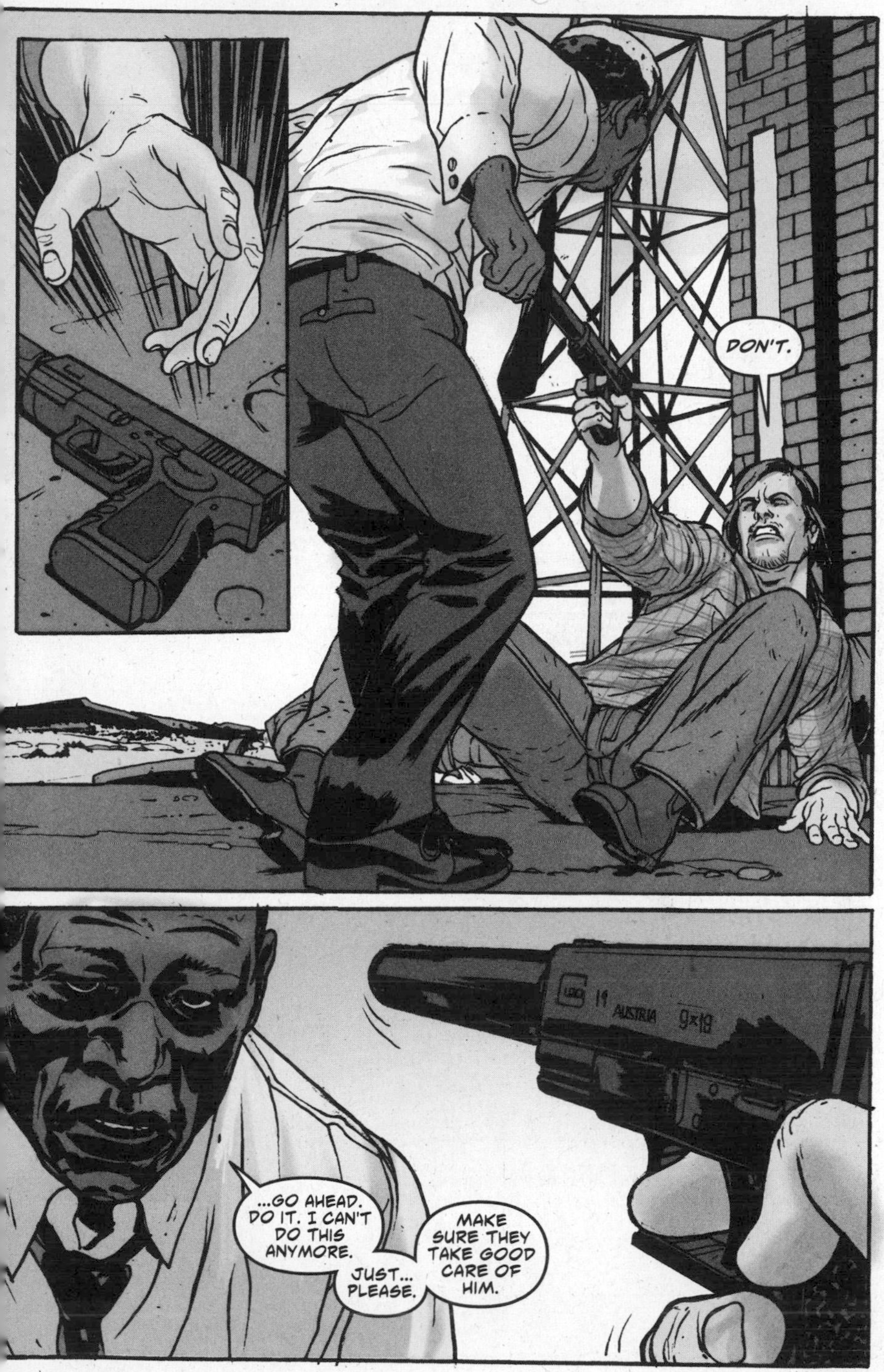
DON'T.
...GO AHEAD. DO IT. I CAN'T DO THIS ANYMORE.
JUST... PLEASE.
MAKE SURE THEY TAKE GOOD CARE OF HIM.

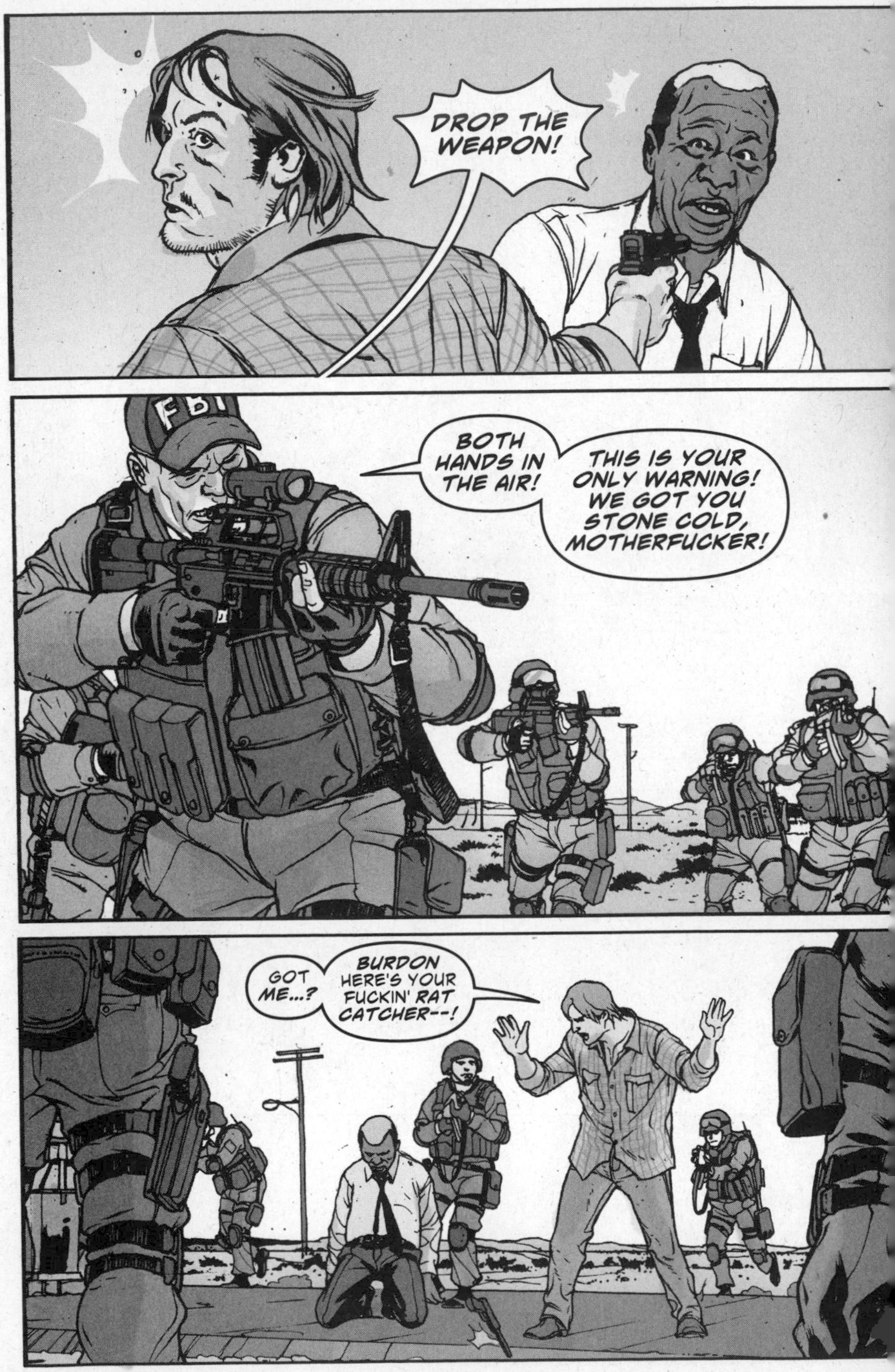
DROP THE WEAPON!
BOTH HANDS IN THE AIR!
THIS IS YOUR ONLY WARNING! WE GOT YOU STONE COLD, MOTHERFUCKER!
GOT ME...?
BURDON HERE'S YOUR FUCKIN' RAT CATCHER--!

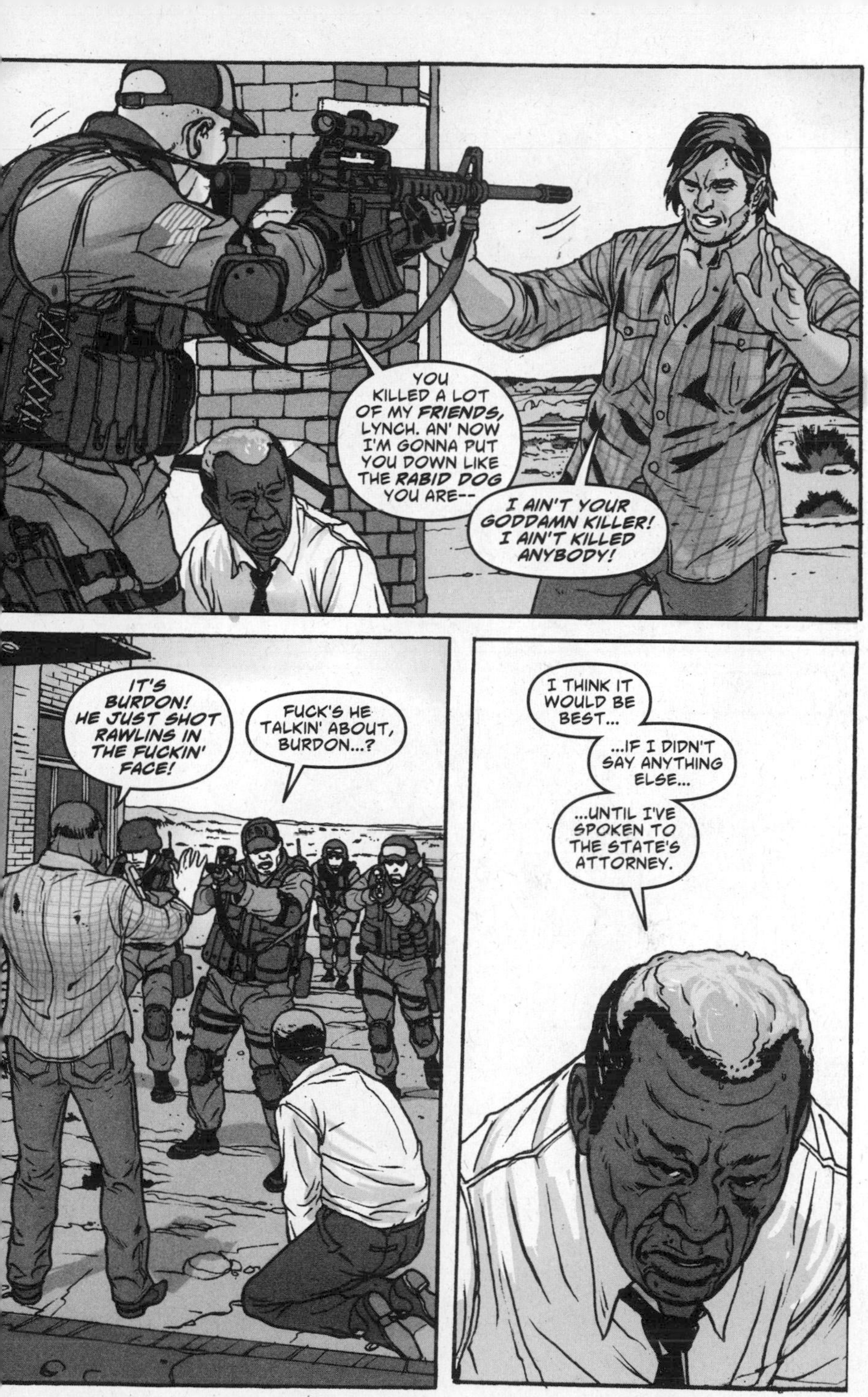
YOU KILLED A LOT OF MY *FRIENDS*, LYNCH. AN' NOW I'M GONNA PUT YOU DOWN LIKE THE *RABID DOG* YOU ARE--
I AIN'T YOUR GODDAMN KILLER! I AIN'T KILLED ANYBODY!
IT'S BURDON! HE JUST SHOT RAWLINS IN THE FUCKIN' FACE!
FUCK'S HE TALKIN' ABOUT, BURDON...?
I THINK IT WOULD BE BEST...
...IF I DIDN'T SAY ANYTHING ELSE...
...UNTIL I'VE SPOKEN TO THE STATE'S ATTORNEY.

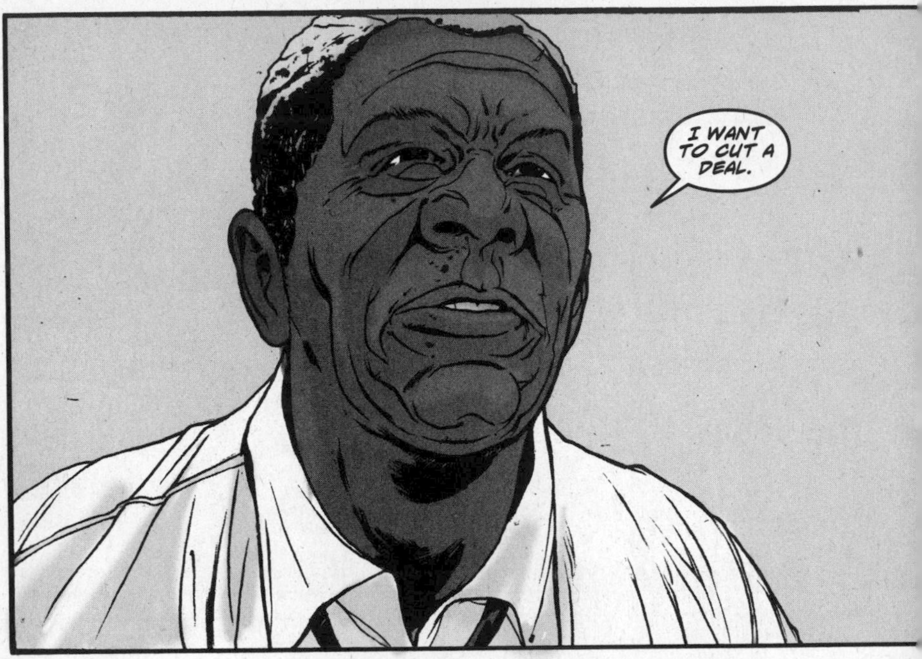
I WANT TO CUT A DEAL.

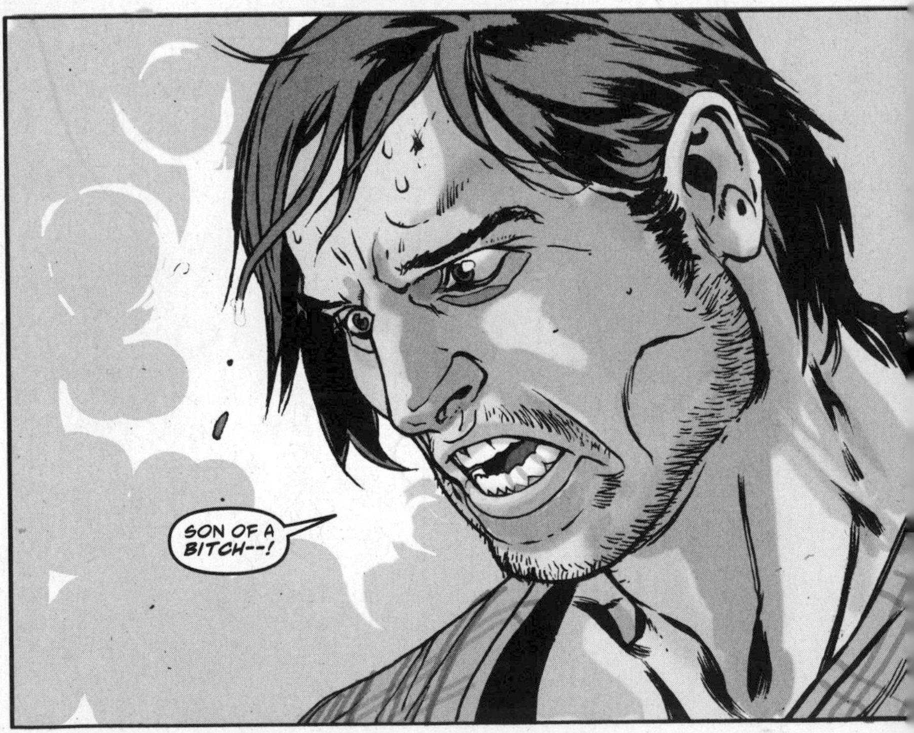
SON OF A BITCH--!

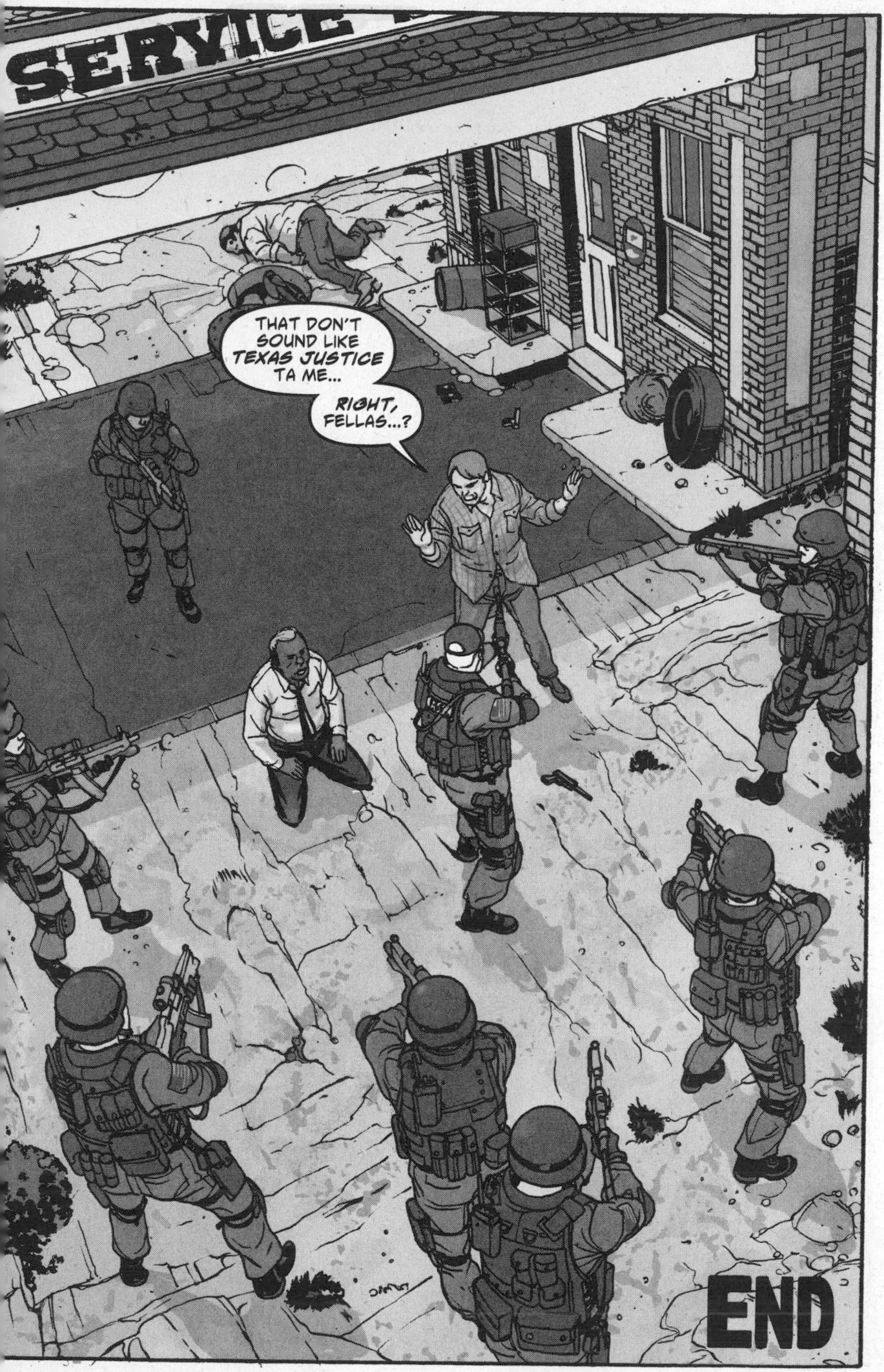
SERVICE
THAT DON'T SOUND LIKE *TEXAS JUSTICE* TA ME...
RIGHT, FELLAS...?
END

IAN
RANKIN
#1 INTERNATIONALLY BEST-SELLING AUTHOR OF EXIT MUSIC
WERTHER DELL'EDERA
DARK
ENTRIES
JOHN CONSTANTINE
GRAPHIC

DON'T MISS THESE OTHER VERTIGO CRIME BOOKS

DARK ENTRIES

Occult detective John Constantine has seen his share of strange things in his career, but nothing could prepare him for the horrors of... reality television. "Haunted Mansion" is currently the hottest show on TV, but when the macabre house actually starts attacking the contestants, Constantine is hired to be the ultimate mole. Locked inside with a cast of wannabe-celebrities, his every move being monitored by a deadly figure from his past, Constantine must figure out who (or what) is pulling the strings before he gets cancelled – *permanently*.

Written by **Ian Rankin**, the Edgar-winning author of the "Inspector Rebus" series and the #1 international-bestselling author of *Exit Music*. Art by **Werther Dell'Edera**.

FILTHY RICH

Richard "Junk" Junkin has always lived on the wrong side of trouble... A former pro football star whose career was cut short by injury (and a nasty gambling problem), Junk now spends his time dreaming of what might have been, selling cars in Jersey and lusting after the boss's unbelievably spoiled, unbelievably sexy and unbelievably rich daughter, Victoria.

So when the boss asks him to be Victoria's personal bodyguard while she tears up the New York City club scene, Junk leaps at the chance. But before long, he finds that Victoria wants a lapdog and not a chaperone, someone who's going to do all of her dirty work – *all* of it – someone who wants to get filthy rich...

Written by **Brian Azzarello** – the multiple Eisner Award-winning writer of Vertigo's long-running crime series 100 BULLETS and *The New York Times* bestseller JOKER. Art by **Victor Santos.**

BRIAN AZZARELLO
NEW YORK TIMES BEST-SELLING AUTHOR OF JOKER
VICTOR SANTOS
FILTHY
RICH
GRAPHIC

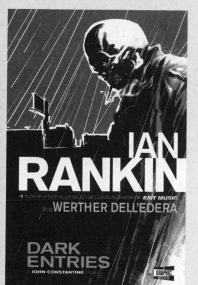

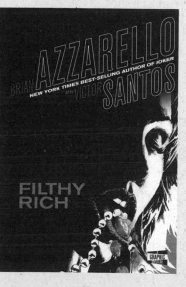

MORE FROM VERTIGO CRIME

AVAILABLE NOW

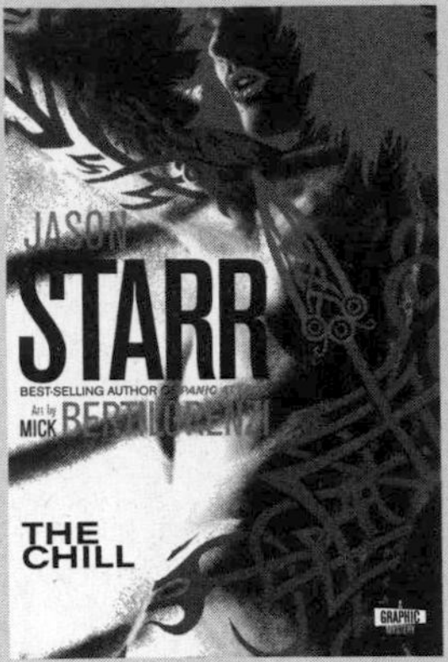
JASON
STARR
Art by
MICK
THE
CHILL

THE CHILL

Written by **JASON STARR**
(Best-selling author of *Panic Attack* and *The Follower*)

Art by **MICK BERTILORENZI**

A modern thriller steeped in Celtic mythology – a broken-down cop tracks a seductive killer who possesses the supernatural power known as "the chill." Can he stop her before her next victim dies horribly... but with a smile on his face?

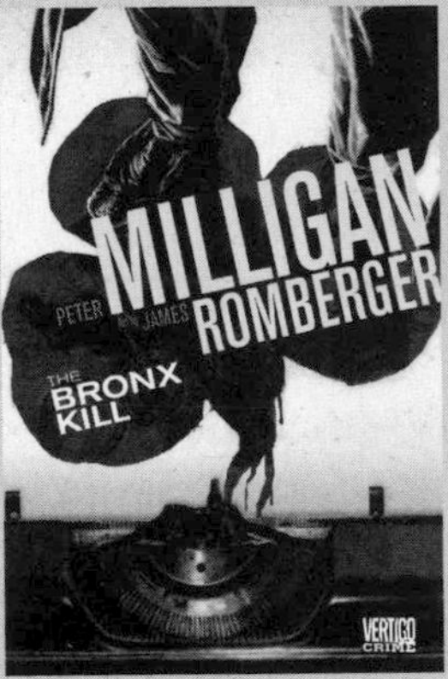
PETER
MILLIGAN
JAMES
ROMBERGER
THE
BRONX
KILL
VERTIGO
CRIME

THE BRONX KILL

Written by **PETER MILLIGAN**
(GREEK STREET)

Art by **JAMES ROMBERGER**

A struggling writer is investigating his Irish cop roots for his next novel. When he returns home from a research trip, his wife is missing and finding her will lead him to a dark secret buried deep in his family's past.

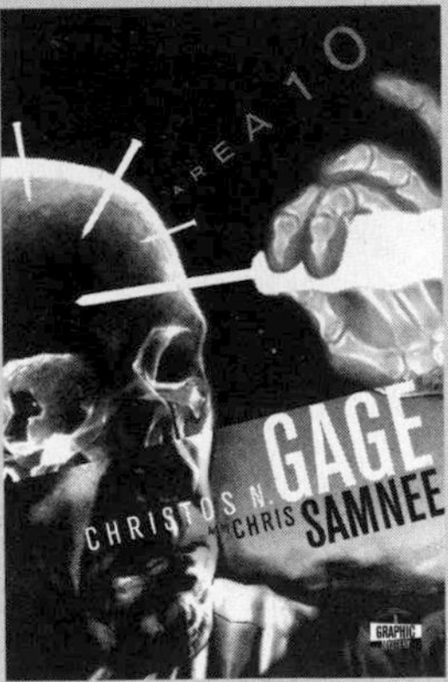
AREA 10
CHRISTOS N.
GAGE
CHRIS
SAMNEE

AREA 10

Written by **CHRISTOS N. GAGE**
(*Law & Order: SVU*)

Art by **CHRIS SAMNEE**

When a detective – tracking a serial killer who decapitates his victims – receives a bizarre head injury himself, he suspects a connection between his own fate and the killer's fascination with Trepanation – the ancient art of skull drilling.

VERTIGO CRIME